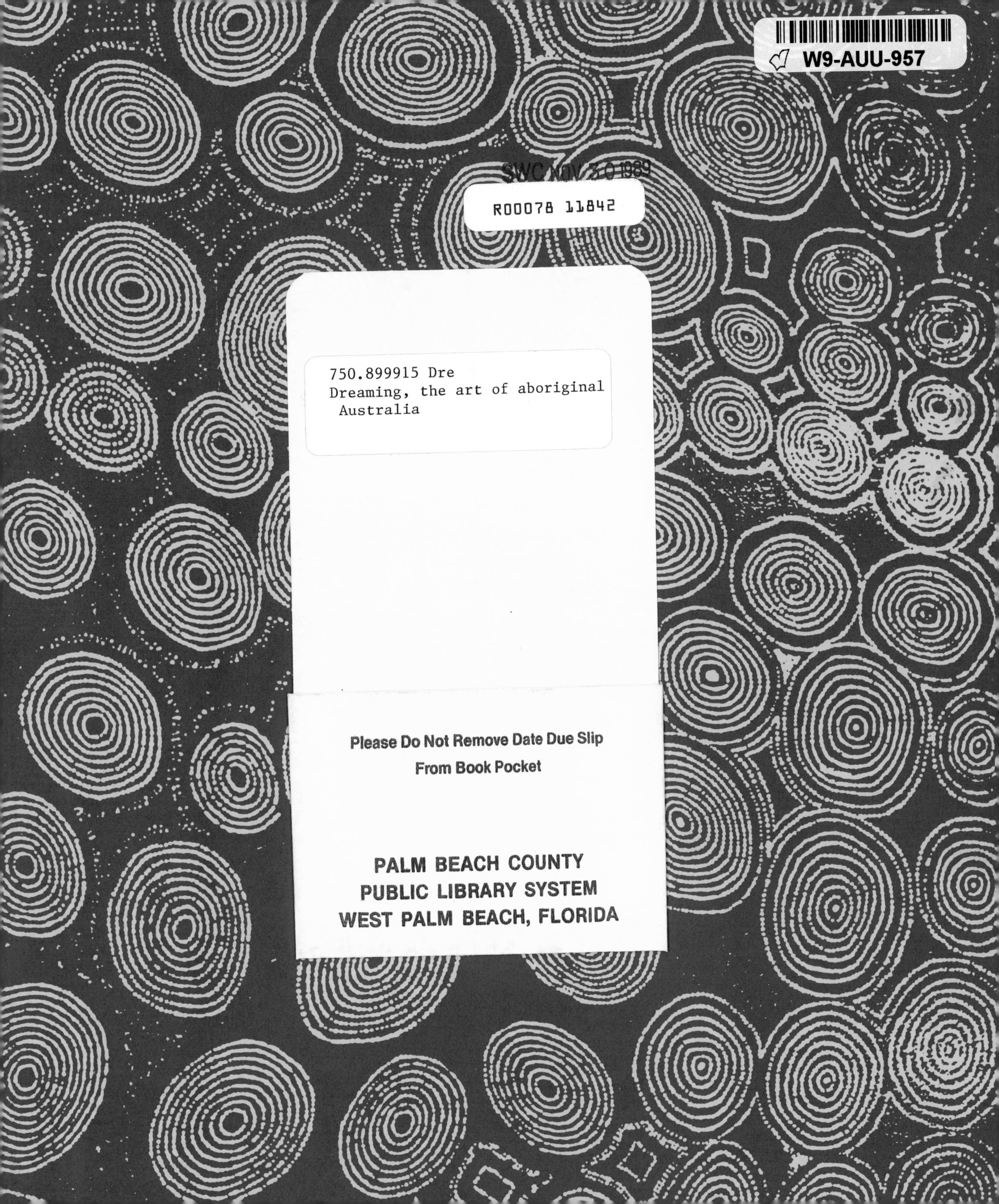

DREAMINGS:

The Art of Aboriginal Australia

DREAMINGS:

The Art of Aboriginal Australia

PETER SUTTON
CHRISTOPHER ANDERSON
PHILIP JONES
FRANÇOISE DUSSART
STEVEN HEMMING

Editor: PETER SUTTON

George Braziller Publishers
IN ASSOCIATION WITH
The Asia Society Galleries, New York

Published on the occasion of

DREAMINGS:
The Art of Aboriginal Australia

organized by The Asia Society Galleries, New York
in collaboration with the
South Australian Museum, Adelaide

The Asia Society Galleries
New York
OCTOBER 6–DECEMBER 31, 1988

The David and Alfred Smart Gallery
University of Chicago, Chicago
JANUARY 26–MARCH 19, 1989

Museum of Victoria
Melbourne
SEPTEMBER–DECEMBER 1989

South Australian Museum
Adelaide
FEBRUARY–APRIL 1990

IN MANY ABORIGINAL COMMUNITIES photographs of deceased Aboriginal people are often destroyed or suppressed until the end of the mourning period, which may last one or more years. Care has been taken to exclude from this book photographs of individuals that might fall into this category at the time of publication. No secret/sacred or otherwise restricted images or information have, to the authors' knowledge, been included in the book.

FRONT COVER:
Five Dreamings, Michael Nelson Jakamarra, assisted by Marjorie Napaljarri.

BACK COVER:
Wallaby from Thawungadha, attributed to George Ngallametta, assisted by MacNaught Ngallametta, Joe Ngallametta.

First published in the United States of
America in 1988 by
The Asia Society Galleries
and George Braziller, Inc.

Andrew Pekarik, *Director, The Asia Society Galleries*
Osa Brown, *Assistant Director, Publications Manager*

Editor: Judith Smith
Designer: Peter Oldenburg

Printed and bound by
Toppan Printing Company Ltd., Tokyo, Japan

For information address the publisher:
George Braziller, Inc.
60 Madison Avenue, New York, New York 10010

LIBRARY OF CONGRESS CATALOGUING IN PUBLICATION DATA:
Dreamings, the art of aboriginal Australia / [edited] by Peter Sutton. p. cm.
Catalogue of an exhibition held at the Asia Society, New York, Oct.–Dec. 1988; and at 4 other museums, Jan.–Dec. 1989.
Bibliography: p.
Includes index.
ISBN 0-8076-1201-4 ISBN 0-87848-068-4 (pbk)
1. Art, Australian (Aboriginal)—Exhibitions. I. Sutton, Peter, 1946– . II. Asia Society.
N7401.D73 1988 750'.899915—dc19 88-10435
CIP

First Edition

TABLE OF CONTENTS

This exhibition and book have been made possible by a major grant from the

NATIONAL ENDOWMENT FOR THE HUMANITIES,

a United States government agency.

Additional support was provided by

FRIENDS OF THE ASIA SOCIETY GALLERIES
THE ANDREW W. MELLON FOUNDATION
THE STARR FOUNDATION
WESTPAC BANKING CORPORATION

LENDERS TO THE EXHIBITION

Aboriginal Arts Board
Art Gallery of South Australia
Mrs. Douglas Carnegie O.A.M. and Sir Roderick Carnegie
Flinders University Art Museum
Tim and Vivien Johnson
Duncan Kentish
Macleay Museum
Museum of Victoria
National Museum of Australia
Eric H. Pinkerton and Josie A. Pinkerton
Gabrielle Pizzi
Private Collection
South Australian Museum

FOREWORD

THE SOUTH AUSTRALIAN MUSEUM is pleased to work in association with The Asia Society Galleries to present this outstanding exhibition and book on the art of the Aboriginal people of Australia. This is an undertaking of some significance: never before have examples of Aboriginal art been selected and assembled in this way for exhibition in the United States and Australia. The selection of the works of art and the consultations with the Aboriginal people responsible for the art were themselves undertakings of some magnitude. Those involved in this process displayed the skill and sensitivity necessary to ensure the enthusiastic support of the Aboriginal people whose works were chosen for exhibition.

While the South Australian Museum holds the world's largest collection of Aboriginal material, it has drawn on the collections of other Australian institutions and of private collectors to present this comprehensive exhibition of paintings and sculptures. Extensive conservation was required to prepare the art works for travel. The State Conservation Centre of South Australia performed this work and provided the mounting and transportation systems. The staff of the International Cultural Corporation of Australia provided much of the necessary advice and coordination.

Apart from Françoise Dussart, the authors of this book are members of the Division of Anthropology of the South Australian Museum, Adelaide. Dr. Peter Sutton, Head of the Division, is an anthropologist and linguist who has worked with Aboriginal people in many parts of Australia since 1969 and is the author of numerous publications about Aboriginal culture and languages. Dr. Christopher Anderson, an anthropologist and Curator of Social Anthropology, has extensive experience with Aboriginal people in Cape York Peninsula and Central Australia. Philip Jones, Curator of Social History, is a historian of anthropology who has carried out fieldwork among the people of the Lake Eyre basin. He is co-author with Peter Sutton of a book on Aboriginal sculptures of that region. Steven Hemming, Curator of Aboriginal History, has close links with Aboriginal communities of the Lower Murray River region and takes a special interest in the history of contact between those people and European Australians. Françoise Dussart is an anthropologist currently completing Ph.D. studies at the Australian National University. She specializes in the Warlpiri culture of Yuendumu, with a particular focus on women's religious ceremonies in that region.

An international project of this scope would have been impossible without the support and cooperation of a large number of individuals and institutions. We are especially grateful for this support. Michal Kluvanek, who photographed many of the art objects for the book, deserves our thanks for the consistent quality of his work and his constant forbearance in meeting our demands. We also wish to acknowledge the invaluable assistance of the individuals and the Australian institutions listed on page 265. Several people read all or parts of the draft manuscript of the book and made helpful comments, among them Vincent Megaw, Howard Morphy, Luke Taylor, Dick Kimber, John Kean, Christopher Pearson, Helen Jones,

Robert Foster, and Philip Clarke. Kaye Clark and Michael Maeorg, with other South Australian Museum staff, provided invaluable research assistance to the authors.

We are particularly indebted to the Aboriginal artists and their families who have worked to explain the meaning and significance of Aboriginal art. The individuals listed on page 265 have been especially helpful in this process. Without their generous cooperation, and that of other Aboriginal people too numerous to list here, this project would not have reached such a successful conclusion.

It was Andrew Pekarik, Director of The Asia Society Galleries, who approached the South Australian Museum with the idea of introducing in this particular way the art of Aboriginal Australia to American audiences. The concept of the exhibition, the selection of works, and the successful execution of the project owe much to his enthusiastic participation. The staff of The Asia Society Galleries created the form of the exhibition and was responsible for producing this book. We especially thank Osa Brown, Assistant Director of the Galleries and Publications Manager, who played a major role in coordinating the project, and Judith Smith, the editor of the book, who worked closely with the authors to shape the presentation of the material.

This exhibition and book are significant not only in the works of art they present but also in their success in bringing into a harmonious working relationship people from three different cultures. Had there been no understanding of the need for these relationships, the project could not have gone forward.

LESTER RUSSELL
Director, South Australian Museum

PREFACE

THIS EXHIBITION began with the suggestion of John Taylor, then Consul-General of Australia in New York. I was initially skeptical of the idea, as I was completely ignorant of what Australian Aboriginal art is. Very little of it has been seen in America, and it is ignored in most histories of world art. After some investigation I was shocked to find it one of the most exciting art traditions I had encountered in Asia or the Pacific. I was moved not only by the remarkable images and designs of its paintings, but also by the astonishing density and complexity of their meanings.

The spiritual systems of Aboriginal art seemed to me to rival those of better-known Asian cultures. This richness of the Aboriginal artistic heritage is all the more striking because it arises in a society whose material culture is virtually non-existent. It was as if almost all of the human creative energy of a culture over tens of thousands of years old had been invested in the development of the society's spiritual, intellectual, and social life. The paintings that seemed to me so fresh and imaginative were in fact the symbolic record of this achievement over millennia.

Despite my eagerness to have the Asia Society introduce this art to American audiences, I was frustrated by the difficulty of finding the proper curators and art objects. Thanks to Ruth Barratt I met Peter Sutton, her brother, and discovered the South Australian Museum. We would not have gone forward with this project had we not had the good fortune of receiving the close cooperation of that museum through its director, Lester Russell. For the South Australian Museum, which had never before participated in an international project of this kind, this exhibition is an act of faith and generosity, and I am deeply indebted to Lester Russell for his enthusiasm, commitment, and organizational ability.

Despite the great range and depth of the South Australian Museum's holdings, we needed significant loans from other collections to expand the comprehensiveness and aesthetic importance of the exhibition, especially in the areas of acrylic paintings and sculpture. Australian public institutions and private collectors were particularly open and cooperative. Their kindness and enthusiastic support was vital to this exhibition and demonstrates their concern and respect for the art and its makers.

An exhibition that imaginatively presents Aboriginal art within the richness and complexity of its culture requires a curator of unique authority, intelligence, and creativity. Peter Sutton has combined all of these qualities and more in a measure to which this remarkable book attests. His own deep understanding of Aboriginal culture was expanded through the thorough research and efficient teamwork of the other principal participants, Christopher Anderson, Philip Jones, Françoise Dussart, and Steven Hemming.

Any exhibition and book of this scope are a nearly miraculous concurrence of efforts, each having its effect at precisely the right moment. For help in the initial preparation for the exhibition I am indebted especially to Robert Edwards, Director of the Museum of Victoria, and Carol Henry of the International Cultural Corporation of Australia. I also want to express my thanks to Dana Stein-Dince, Registrar,

The Asia Society Galleries, who has been responsible for the complex task of getting the art safely here and on display, and to Mary Linda, Curator, who helped with the installation. Cleo Nichols, exhibition designer, and David Harvey, graphics designer, saw to it that the display was both attractive and instructive.

Osa Brown, Assistant Director, produced this book, closely coordinating and overseeing every stage from photography to press, and played a major role in the presentation of the exhibition. Without her dedication, energy, imagination, and humor, this project would have been impossible. I am very grateful to Judith Smith, who edited this text with wit, patience, and a tireless devotion to quality. Her commitment to the success of this publication and display was extraordinary and is deeply appreciated. I would like to express my gratitude to the exceptionally talented Peter Oldenburg, who created the splendid design of this book. Special thanks to Becky Mikalson for capably organizing the thousands of illustrations and papers, and to Pamela Sapienza for skillfully assisting with the book's production. I would also like to thank Mickey Endo of Toppan Printing for being so consistently helpful and Rose Wright for competently typing the complex manuscript.

Our indispensable partner in this project was the National Endowment for the Humanities. This United States government agency has played a major role in the development of museum exhibitions that introduce Americans to unfamiliar cultures, ideas, and art to enrich their lives and broaden their understanding. Through generous planning and implementation grants the NEH made it possible for us to take the risk of doing something new and important.

With humility and deep respect I also wish to personally thank the people of Aboriginal Australia, who were so hospitable and patient with me in their explanations of the art and so generous in their willingness to have us show and describe this art in America. This spirit of understanding and cooperation across distances of space and culture guided the preparation of this exhibition, and I hope that our joint effort will contribute to its growth. Our three societies have much to benefit from it.

ANDREW PEKARIK
Director, The Asia Society Galleries

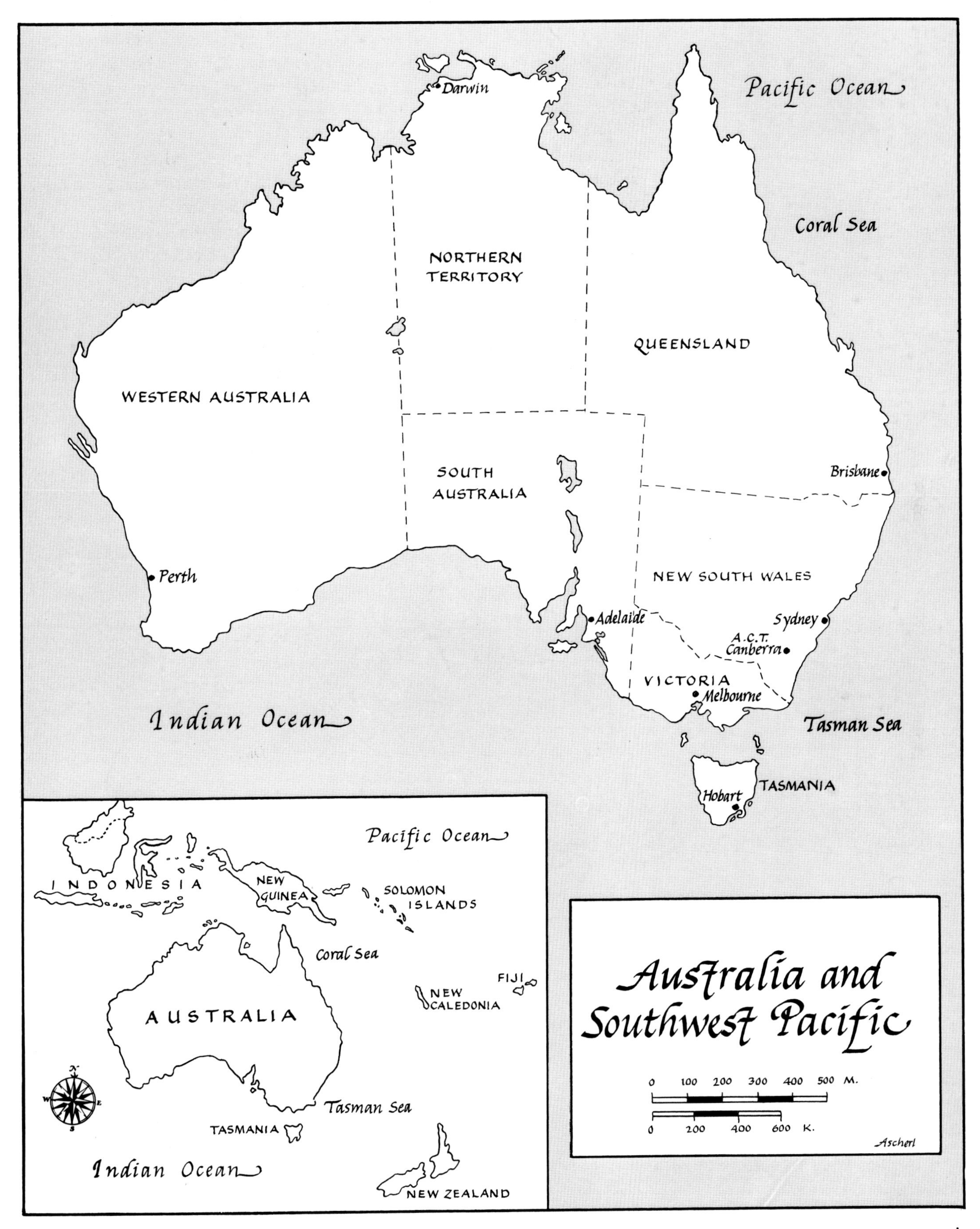
Australia and Southwest Pacific
Pacific Ocean
Coral Sea
Darwin
NORTHERN TERRITORY
QUEENSLAND
WESTERN AUSTRALIA
SOUTH AUSTRALIA
Brisbane
NEW SOUTH WALES
Perth
Adelaide
Sydney
A.C.T.
Canberra
VICTORIA
Melbourne
Indian Ocean
Tasman Sea
TASMANIA
Hobart
Pacific Ocean
INDONESIA
NEW GUINEA
SOLOMON ISLANDS
Coral Sea
FIJI
NEW CALEDONIA
AUSTRALIA
Tasman Sea
TASMANIA
Indian Ocean
NEW ZEALAND
0 100 200 300 400 500 M.
0 200 400 600 K.
Ascherl

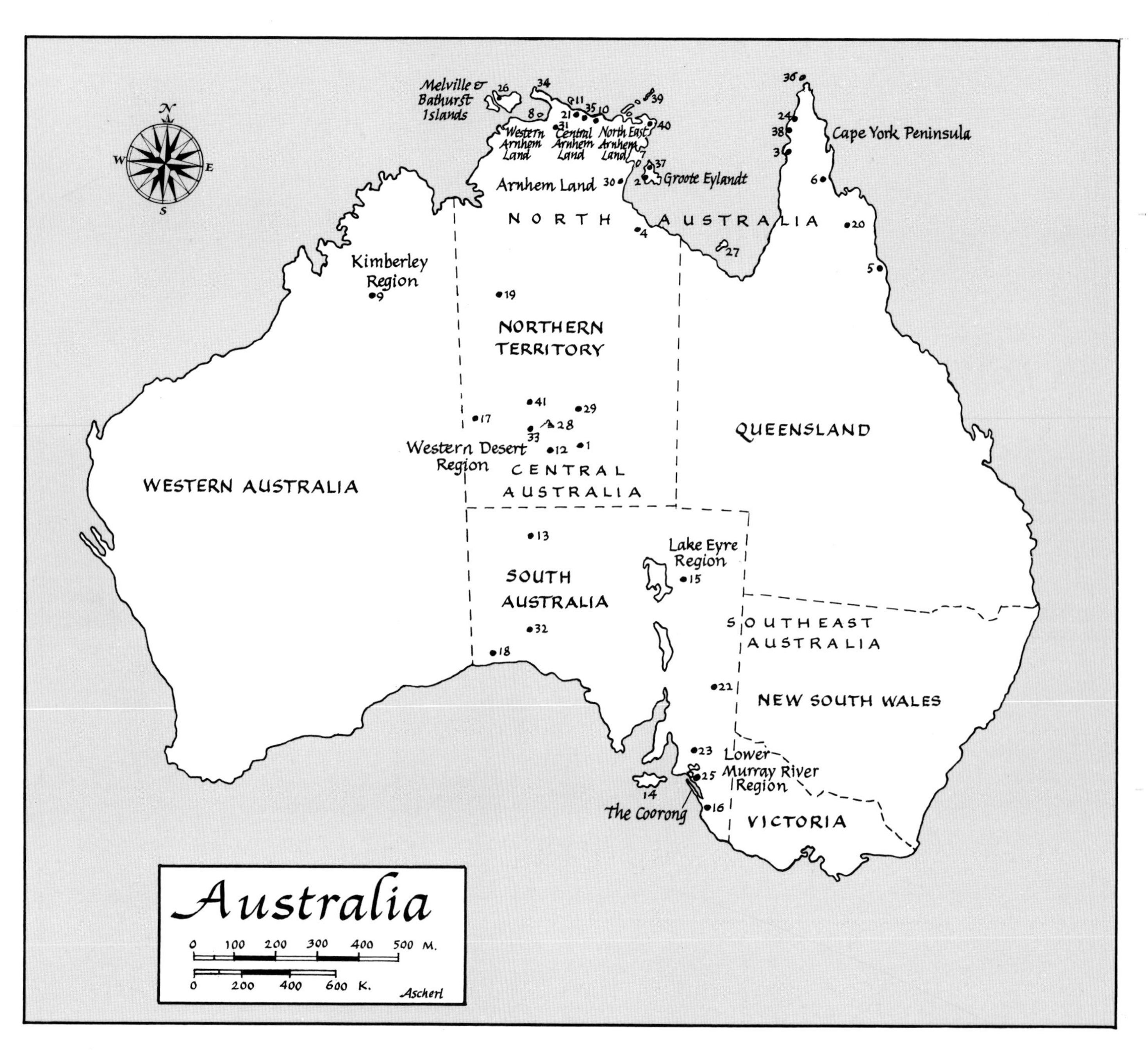

1. Alice Springs
2. Angurugu
3. Aurukun
4. Borroloola
5. Cairns
6. Coen
7. Djarrakpi
8. Field Island
9. Fitzroy Crossing
10. Garttji
11. Goulburn Island
12. Hermannsburg
13. Indulkana
14. Kangaroo Island
15. Killalpaninna
16. Kingston S. E.
17. Kintore
18. Koonalda
19. Lajamanu
20. Laura
21. Maningrida
22. Mannahill
23. Mannum
24. Mapoon
25. Meningie
26. Milikapiti (Snake Bay)
27. Mornington Island
28. Mount Allan
29. Napperby
30. Numbulwar
31. Oenpelli
32. Ooldea
33. Papunya
34. Port Essington
35. Ramingining
36. Thursday Island
37. Umbakumba
38. Weipa
39. Wessel Islands
40. Yirrkala
41. Yuendumu

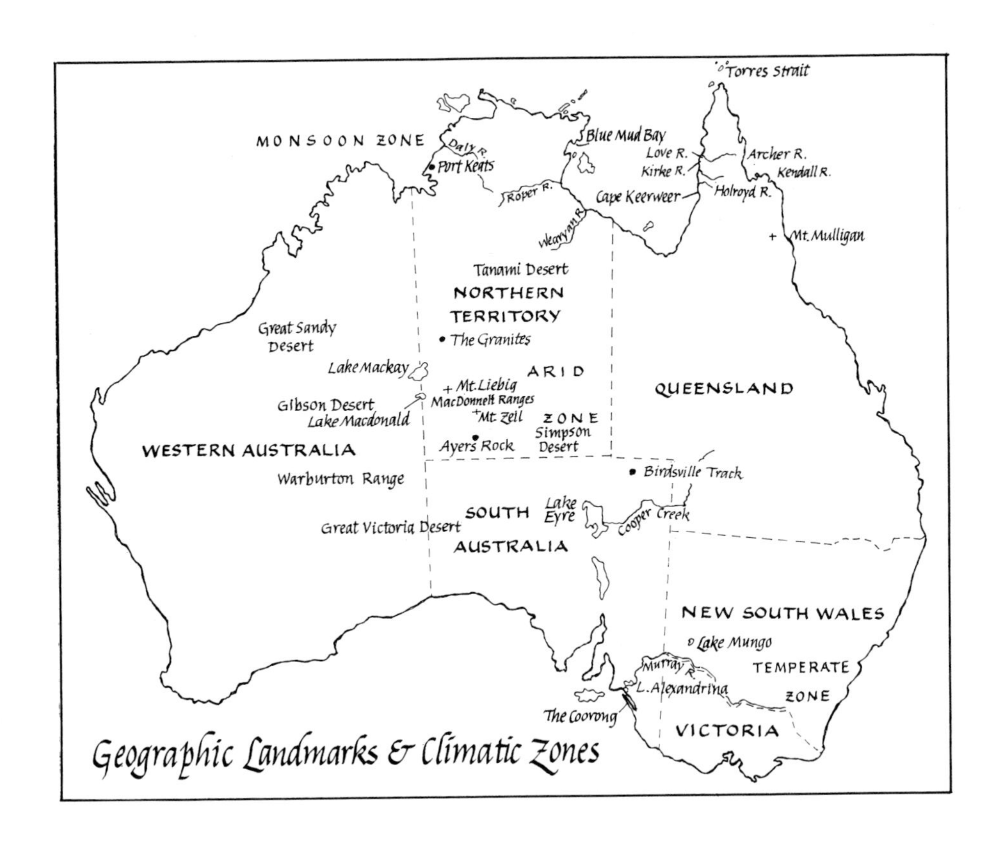

Geographic Landmarks & Climatic Zones

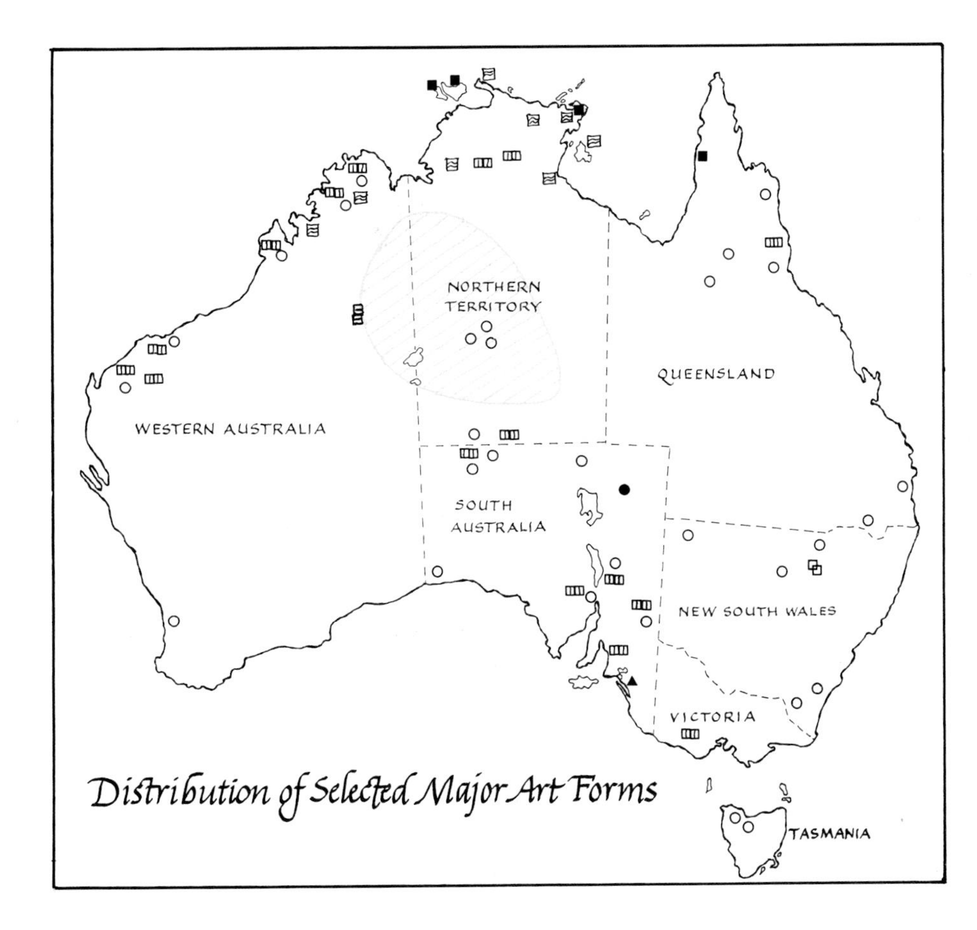

Distribution of Selected Major Art Forms

KEY
- Bark Paintings
- Rock Paintings
- Rock Engravings
- Carved Trees
- Wooden Sculptures
- Toas
- Lower Murray Shields
- Acrylic Paintings

Introduction

PETER SUTTON AND
CHRISTOPHER ANDERSON

THIS BOOK and the exhibition that it accompanies grew out of a concern to explore the significance of Aboriginal art, both to its practitioners and to a wider public, and to offer a basis for the interpretation and appreciation of the art. Accordingly, this text was planned from the outset as a unity and is not simply a collection of essays on related topics.

We have not included, either here or in the exhibition, works from every corner of Australia, nor do we give examples of every type of Aboriginal art. Excellent surveys of the field are available, and interested readers will find them listed in the references at the end of this volume.[1] We have instead chosen in this book to concentrate on acrylic paintings from Central Australia, bark paintings from Arnhem Land, sculptures from Cape York Peninsula and the Lake Eyre region, and a variety of works from the southeastern part of the continent. The exhibition coverage is largely restricted to a broad band passing from north to south down the center of Australia, excluding New South Wales, Victoria, Tasmania, and most of Western Australia. The selection thus represents each of the three main cultural and geographical zones of Aboriginal Australia—the tropical north, the desert hinterland, and the temperate southeast.

This is a historical treatment, not a survey of current work as such, although many contemporary works, especially from the Western Desert region, are included. The number of Aboriginal artists in the cities is still small, and in both quantity and quality their work, on average, does not compare with that of people from more remote areas. This also is not a selection of only the "best" works, however that term might be defined. Many equally excellent works had to be excluded, and some works that are included were chosen for purposes of comparison or to illustrate specific points, and not necessarily because of their aesthetic appeal, rarity, or historical position, or the importance of their artists. In short, this is not a Who's Who of Aboriginal art.

Most of the works are from the collection of the South Australian Museum. This is partly because it is by far the largest Aboriginal collection anywhere; it is representative of the whole of the continent and of most periods since the 1840s; and its documentation, both of the objects themselves and of their historical contexts, is unusually thorough.

This book is unique in its field in at least three ways. It contains the first extended overview of the history of Aboriginal art scholarship (Chapter V). It presents a substantial analysis of the Aboriginal aesthetic which shows how it is integrated with the distinctive worldview and social values of Aboriginal tradition (Chapters I, II, III). And it examines the cultural, economic, and political context of the production of Western Desert paintings for an Australian and world art market (Chapter IV).

In June–August 1987 the authors, accompanied by Andrew Pekarik of The Asia Society, traveled to the relevant Aboriginal communities in the regions of their particular specializations to consult with artists and other senior people about the works being considered for exhibition and publication. Where artists could be contacted, we interviewed them about their paintings or sculptures and, in a number of cases, collected important new information about the works. We were checking the accuracy and completeness of our information, but we were also seeking to involve community members in the process of the exhibition and publication.

One of our concerns was to avoid making public anything that properly belonged to a secret/sacred or non-public category under Aboriginal law. We also needed permission to cite the names of deceased artists, as the taboo on using the name of a dead person can sometimes last several years in an Aboriginal community. In one case, the artist of a bark painting had died only days before we arrived at his home community Yirrkala, and we had to withdraw the work from both the book and the exhibition because of mortuary taboos. In another case, a bark painting by a deceased Central Arnhem Land artist was withdrawn because of objections to its being seen by a wide public in the Central Arnhem Land area. In general, though, our selections were acceptable. Aboriginal artists' enthusiasm for this undertaking has been remarkable and deserves special mention. We hope that this book and exhibition befit that trust and exemplify the extraordinary qualities of Aboriginal art that inspired our efforts.

The Politics of Representation

Aborigines in Australia are a tiny minority who retain a distinct identity and range of cultures in a society dominated by Western cultural traditions. In these circumstances, scholars and museums are easily open to the accusation that they create the terms on which Aborigines are represented to others, thus serving the dominant society and its ideology.

One response to this charge is that books and exhibitions about Aboriginal art actually promote Aboriginal interests and perhaps even challenge the dominant ideology from time to time.[2] Furthermore, Aboriginal cultures, like most others, are no longer closed systems in which the only legitimation of assertions is that which comes from within the group. The cultures of the Aborigines and those of the curators, collectors, and other admirers of Aboriginal art form a set of historically entwined interests that cannot be separated from each other. The toa sculptures of Lake Eyre, for example, are highly significant for Aboriginal cultural history, but they are also significant for Lutheran mission history in colonial South Australia and for the history of the interpretation of Aboriginal art by scholars in a range of disciplines.[3] Such arguments, however, have not impressed those who believe that the control of the Aboriginal heritage and its interpretation should lie exclusively with Aborigines.

On Defining Art

The very application of the term *art* to things made by Aboriginal people has been interpreted by some critics as an act of cultural colonialism. They say that art is a concept alien to Aboriginal culture. The evidence cited for this assertion is that the usual definition of art depends on its applicability to things found in institutions such as art museums, or to things defined as such by art curators and the art market. These critics contend that Aboriginal languages have no word for art, while many other languages do. But this is problematic.

Speakers of European languages, for example, may share essential meanings for the various terms translatable into English as *art*, but they seldom agree entirely on the range of things to which such terms should be applied. One person's art may be another person's junk or kitsch. Speakers of Aboriginal languages are in this sense very similar. Each of the various languages has a term that essentially means sign, design, pattern, or meaningful mark.[4] It is used to describe paintings and other designed things made by people, but it may also describe the patterns of honeycombs, spiders' webs, the wave-marked sand of the beach, variegated butterfly wings, and a host of other manifestations of similar formal properties. These usually include a combination of repetition, variation, symmetry, and asymmetry; and, like the designs of human artifacts, they are seen as ultimately derived from the Dreaming, the power-filled ground of existence. (The concept of the Dreaming and Dreaming Beings is discussed in detail in Chapter I and elsewhere in this book.)

There are areas of overlap between these Aboriginal terms and European terms such as *art*, *l'art*, and *Kunst*. While the latter are not normally used of things created by nature, they are used of things created by sentient, intelligent beings. Dreamings are just such beings, and they create the patterns in the world that manifest their presence as signs. In North East Arnhem Land traditions, the wax hexagons of a beehive are *miny'tji*, or designs, just as the diamond shapes in a painting of Wild Honey Dreaming are *miny'tji*, and they manifest the same spiritual and intelligently ordering essence (see Figs. 11–13). But one Aboriginal group does not usually have exactly the same Dreamings as another, nor the same range of physical environments. The specific items encompassed by the Yolngu word *miny'tji* in tropical North East Arnhem Land and by the Warlpiri word *kuruwarri* in the desert at Yuendumu, in spite of the semantic closeness of the two terms, are bound to be different. What is shared, however, is a common conception of intentionally meaningful forms, or signs.

None of these signs, in the Aboriginal cultures of the precolonial past, were part of an art market in a commercial sense, but they were currency in a competitive political economy. Rights in them could be traded, bequeathed, and, at times, even stolen for their high value. Human artifacts were also subject to similar transactions.

As long as we restrict our sense of the English term *art* to that elementary level at which it connotes visible and intentional signs made by intelligent beings, we are not stretching a point when we say that Aboriginal paintings, carvings, and other works are art, not "by metamorphosis"[5] and not merely because they now are in the global art market, but because they share with similar artifacts the act of representation and a particular potential for meaning.

Aboriginal Artists

In this book we often refer to Aboriginal "artists." Few of those represented would actually fit the modern world's stereotypes of people in that category. With the exception of some urban Aborigines, most have never been trained at art schools. Many, in fact, have never been to any kind of formal school. In most cases, they learned their artistic skills from other Aboriginal people, with occasional recent help from non-Aboriginal arts advisors.

Except for urban Aborigines, few Aboriginal artists show much interest in art traditions other than their own. For example, few acrylic painters in Central Australia could name any North Australian bark painters, and vice versa. Few, also, could name any major European or Asian artists. The look of modern Aboriginal acrylic paintings has led many casual observers to conclude that the creators of these works are in touch with and aware of global movements such as Minimalism. In fact, it is probably safe to say that none of the Western Desert artists in this book have ever heard of Minimalism. They also have little inclination or opportunity to frequent the kind of museums and galleries where such art is hung. (Most of their visits to art museums or commercial galleries are for the purpose of attending the openings of their own shows, usually hundreds of miles from home.) The work of these artists comes out of their own rich artistic system.

The Cultural Background

Australian Aborigines—the original inhabitants of the continent—are one of the best known and least understood people in the world. Since the nineteenth century they have been singled out as the world's most primitive culture and the living representatives of the ancestors of mankind. Aborigines are therefore probably more familiar to the rest of the world than are the white Australians who immigrated to the continent from Britain and other European countries. In reality, Aboriginal culture, as anthropological work over the last hundred years has revealed, is a complex, subtle, and rich way of life. On our way toward describing and understanding Aboriginal art, we need to look briefly at this culture, what it was in the past and what it has become today.

Aborigines have occupied Australia for at least forty thousand years (Fig. 1). They came originally from southeast Asia, entering the continent from the north. (Present-day Australia, including Tasmania, was then one continent with what is now New Guinea.) Although Aborigines are Homo sapiens, biological isolation has meant that they are not racially closely related to any other people. Because of their relative cultural isolation, Aborigines were forced to develop their own solutions to the problems of human adaptation in the unique and harsh Australian environment. The result was a stable and efficient way of life. Probably because of its effectiveness, the society was slow to change, especially technologically. This gave to Aboriginal Australia the appearance of unchangingness. The archaeological record reveals, however, a number of innovations, among them the earliest known human cremations, some of the earliest rock art, and certainly the first boomerangs, ground axes, and grindstones in the world.[6]

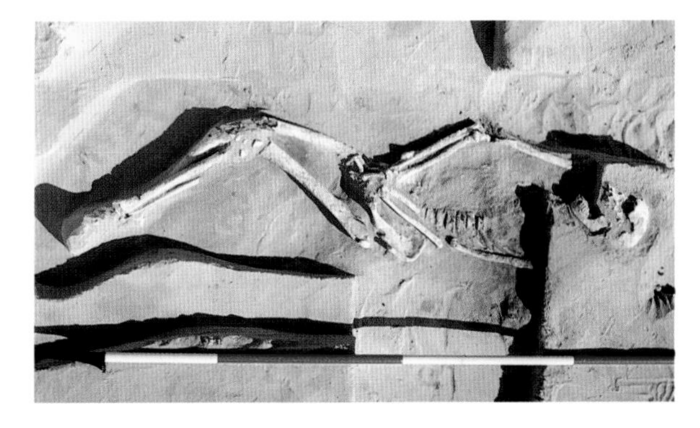

FIG. 1
Human burial with ochred bones 30,000 years old, Lake Mungo, New South Wales, 1974.

The stereotype of Aborigines passively succumbing to the dictates of their environment has also been recently questioned. We now know that they altered the landscape in significant ways, using what has been called "fire-stick farming" to control underbrush growth and to facilitate hunting. Aborigines also altered species occurrence of flora and fauna by resource management and possibly assisted in the extinction of prehistoric animals.

The notion of pristine natives with a "pure" culture was an artificial one: many Aborigines had considerable contact with Melanesians and Indonesians long before the European colonists arrived in Australia. Aboriginal groups also influenced each other. Waves of change swept the entire continent—changes in tools and implements, in social organization, and in ceremonial practices and mythological concepts. Aboriginal culture was dynamic, not static. The Aboriginal culture of the last two hundred years, the period after the arrival of the colonists, has also been dynamic. This is why it is difficult to speak of a hard and fast dichotomy between Aborigines "before" and "after" contact with the Europeans. Nevertheless, it is useful to look at Aboriginal culture at the point of first contact and as it is today.

Aboriginal Society at the Instant of Contact The population of Australia at the time of the arrival of the whites in 1788 was probably between 250,000 and 500,000.[7] The pattern of Aboriginal settlement was like that for present-day Australians, except in the tropical north, with most of the population living along the coasts and rivers. Densities varied from one person for every thirty-five square miles in the arid regions to five to ten persons for every one square mile on the eastern coast.[8] Residential groups ranged in size from ten to fifty people, with some temporary ceremonial gatherings reaching up to five hundred.

Most people tend to think of Aborigines as a unified, homogeneous group. Yet the Aborigines never used one collective term to describe themselves. No one individual Aborigine, in the precolonial past, would have known of the existence of many of the other Aboriginal peoples and regions of the vast continent of Australia, which covers nearly three million square miles—almost the area of the United States.

To the Aborigines, the differences between individual groups were important and were continually emphasized. There was no concept of a pan-Australian identity. Even the idea of Aboriginal "tribes" is problematic.[9] Smaller local groups were the basic units of Aboriginal society. These groups shared cultural traits and had economic and ceremonial dealings with other groups, but they did not form large confederacies for such purposes as warfare or conquest. In many regions an individual, by virtue of birth, belonged to a clan that was closely associated with—"owned," in a certain sense—particular areas of land. Through other kinship ties and through marriage, an individual might have acquired rights in several areas of land. These relationships, along with residence and travel for economic reasons, produced a complex pattern of land affiliation and identification with local areas. The result was that all parts of Australia, while not always wholly occupied at any one point in time, were claimed by Aboriginal individuals and groups under a customary system of land-tenure law.

The primary structures of Aboriginal society were based on kinship. Every known person was considered to be kin, either by blood ties or fictively. Terms of reference for others were almost always those of kinship—a "kind of mother," a "kind of brother," and so on. With these relationships came rights, obligations, and appropriate ways of behaving. This is not to say that Aborigines blindly followed timeless rules, but rather that kinship provided a baseline from which to operate in the society. People doubtless bent and broke rules, creating new ones over time, as with law and custom in any society.

One cultural trait normally shared by several local groups was that of language. Here again we encounter a Western stereotype of Aborigines. Aboriginal people did not speak "primitive languages" based on imitations of so-called natural sounds. Aboriginal languages were fully developed systems of communication that allowed the expression of concepts as sophisticated as those in any language. Prior to 1788, there were in Australia about two hundred distinct languages, further divided into many hundreds of dialects.[10] In some parts of the country—the Western Desert region of Central Australia, for example—people over an area of thousands of miles spoke virtually the same language; in others, such as Western Cape York Peninsula, members of a local group spoke several different languages. Multilingualism was the norm rather than the exception throughout Australia.

Diversity in Aboriginal culture was also a product of the wide range of physical environments that Aborigines occupied: from the snow areas of the high country in the southeast to the beaches and rain forests of the tropical north, from the rich lands of the major river systems to the desert regions of the center. Adaptation to these environments led to the development of different economic systems, involving a variety of tools, technology, and living and work patterns.

For all Aborigines, though, life was sustained by hunting and gathering, rather than by cultivating crops. This nomadic life provided the Aboriginal people with a healthy diet, and in some areas, such as coastal Arnhem Land, subsistence required the equivalent of only three day's work a week.[11] To varying degrees, Australian Aboriginal economies were predicated on mobility and a corresponding absence of concern with accumulation of goods and property. Material culture was kept to a minimum and was simple, ingenious, and multifunctional (Fig. 2). Movements about the country were not random or aimless wanderings in search of food. People undertook regular seasonal moves over particular areas to exploit certain resources and to participate in ceremonial gatherings with other groups. These movements were territorially restricted by Aboriginal law: no one person, before colonization, could move at will across Australia.

FIG. 2 / CAT. 78
Aboriginal Inhabitants, 1844–45.
George French Angas, South Australia.
Watercolor on paper, 49 × 32.5 cm.

Economic specialization in traditional Aboriginal communities was minimal. Most adults were able to perform any of the subsistence tasks done by others in the group. Division of labor was primarily based on gender: men hunted large game; women gathered small ground reptiles and other animals as well as vegetables. In coastal and riverine areas both men and women fished and gathered shellfish. For technological reasons, extensive food storage was not possible, which meant that most food, once obtained, had to be consumed immediately. Because of this and because of the nature of Aboriginal kinship obligations, sharing was a major and defining ethos of the culture. To be human was to share.

Government in precontact Aboriginal Australia was not located in an external body set up to implement rules independently or on a representative basis. Law and order was maintained through the infusion of religious ideology into everyday actions and through enforcement by senior men and women, with serious infringement sometimes resulting in death. Personal autonomy was high, however, and it was sustained by an appropriate ideological underpinning.

The attainment of religious knowledge began with initiation during adolescence and became a lifelong quest. Both men and women had specific religious ceremonies and held specific aspects or segments of mythic information. Some of these ceremonies were secret and restricted, others public.

Interpersonal and group politics was a major factor in Aboriginal social life and was integral to religious knowledge and its control. At several points in this book we stress the inseparability of politics from the religious, aesthetic, and other aspects of Aboriginal art. This approach is deliberately in contrast with some earlier works that have tended to treat Aboriginal art as somehow removed from transactions between people, and it arises out of an increased recognition of the role of continuous negotiation in the daily reconstitution of any living culture.[12]

Many of these "classical" features of precontact Aboriginal society are still part of Aboriginal life in some areas of Australia. It is in these areas—the Northern Territory, far northern Queensland, and parts of Western Australia and South Australia—that we speak of tradition-oriented Aborigines and the survival of the classical culture. Although they have been affected by and participate in the broader, dominating system of Australia, these Aborigines maintain beliefs, social practices, and a worldview that are oriented more toward an Aboriginal world and history than a European one. To understand Aborigines in contemporary society, however, we must consider the impact of the European colonists on Aboriginal society, and Aboriginal responses to the colonists.

Colonists and Aborigines The white settlement of Australia was part of the great colonialist expansion by European powers in the seventeenth, eighteenth, and nineteenth centuries. Dutch explorers charted the seas to the west and north of Australia in the 1600s and had contact with Aborigines on the western coast of Cape York Peninsula and Western Australia. The British "discovery" of Australia by Captain James Cook in 1770 was the result of both a search for new resources and land and a race to beat the French into the Pacific region. Although Aborigines in many parts of Australia had already had contact with other non-Aborigines, it was the contact with white European settlers that had the most lasting and significant effects on the Aboriginal people.

Beginning in 1788 with the establishment of a permanent British settlement in southeastern Australia, Europeans spread out along the coasts, up the river systems, and finally into the less hospitable center and far north. The time taken for this process was such that there were Aborigines living in Central Australia in the 1930s who until that time had never seen white people. Contact was thus not a uniform process occurring everywhere at once.

Fighting often occurred when the European settlers encountered Aborigines. Between 2,000 and 2,500 non-Aborigines were killed during the settlement era, from 1788 to the 1930s.[13] Perhaps ten times that number of Aborigines were killed during the same period. The principal reason for this conflict was not general resistance to white settlement but rather the response by Aborigines to particular actions on the part of the colonists, such as trespass on restricted sites, taking of scarce resources, or interference with women. Epidemics and lower standards of health, hygiene, and nutrition brought on by social disruption also led to massive losses in the Aboriginal population. Disease—notably smallpox, measles, venereal disease, and tuberculosis—accounted for up to two-thirds of all Aboriginal deaths and for high infertility rates.[14]

From an Aboriginal viewpoint, however, the most serious consequence of European settlement must have been the loss of their land. Land was central to Aboriginal religious life and the primary basis of economic survival. The alienation of lands by white settlers was done in ignorance of and active disregard for the complex cultural system governing Aboriginal ownership and occupation of the land. To the Europeans, land was a resource to be exploited for commercial gain. The result for the indigenous population was twofold: first, Aborigines were prevented from using their traditional lands for hunting and camping and in many cases were forcibly moved from the land; second, the ecological balance of the environment that

FIG. 3
Mission church at Killalpaninna (Pastor Johann Reuther, standing at far right), Lake Eyre region, ca. 1895.

FIG. 4
Aboriginal camp near Killalpaninna, Lake Eyre region, ca. 1895.

Aborigines had developed over thousands of years was drastically upset by the uncontrolled introduction of new plants and animals.

Although violence was a significant part of the frontier reaction to the settlers, Aboriginal culture was sufficiently strong to permit the incorporation of some elements of European society (Figs. 3–4). This process included the interpretation of white people as returned Aboriginal ancestors and the adoption of foreign words and concepts (for example, the inclusion of Bible figures such as Adam and Eve in traditional mythology). Foodstuffs such as tea, sugar, tobacco, and flour were quickly absorbed into Aboriginal economies, often replacing traditional goods. The use of steel and glass, too, increased the efficiency of traditional technology. These positive reactions to European settlement, however, were outweighed by the many negative consequences of contact.

Government Settlement Policies The most significant shifts in the distribution of the Aboriginal population occurred as a result of government policies. In the early days of contact, the colonial government encouraged missionaries and other settlers to gather together Aborigines from the surrounding areas and settle them into European-style communities. At the turn of the century, state governments began establishing their own settlements for Aborigines. Through resettlement the government sought to stem Aboriginal problems such as illness and malnutrition and to assimilate Aborigines into the European community. As an adjunct, these policies removed Aborigines from land needed for development and reduced conflict between settlers and Aborigines.

The government's policies almost always ignored Aboriginal attachment to the land and often combined disparate and sometimes antagonistic Aboriginal groups in new settlements. Settlement also undermined the basis for the traditional hunting and gathering life of the Aborigines and forced them into wage labor to survive. They became sheep and cattle stockmen, pearl shell divers, and seasonal workers in agriculture, mining, and logging. Cyclical declines in the demand for Australian commodities, along with the imposition in the 1960s of equal wages for Aborigines, reduced the demand for Aboriginal workers, causing many to become refugees in their own land, living on the margins of Australian society.

Contact with the European settlers wrought massive social and cultural changes in Aboriginal communities. The effects of these changes varied considerably across the country. In the northern and central parts of Australia the Aborigines retained many of their traditional social practices and distinctive worldviews, while in the southern urban areas these traditions were either radically altered or disappeared altogether. Of the original two hundred Aboriginal languages, only about twelve are still spoken by more than a few hundred people each, and the majority are virtually extinct.

FIG. 5
Aboriginal and Islander Dance Theatre, Sydney. Tracey Moffat, 1986.

Aboriginal Society in the 1980s In 1987 the official census reported 227,645 Aboriginal people in Australia, out of a total population of some 16,000,000. Of these, about forty-four percent live in remote and rural areas; the remainder live in the major cities or towns (Fig. 5). Migration to urban areas began to accelerate only in the 1950s as the Australian rural economy declined. The Aboriginal population in small outback towns and in Aboriginal settlements is growing at a rate almost twice that for white Australians. In both urban and rural areas, Aboriginal unemployment is high, reaching up to seventy-five percent in some places. Housing conditions, health-care standards, and educational levels are also considerably below those of other Australians.

Government policy toward the Aboriginal people has gone through several phases since the arrival of the Europeans. In the beginning, colonial governments sought to segregate the Aborigines on the assumption that they would eventually die out. By the 1930s the government recognized that the Aboriginal population was actually increasing. It responded to this change with policies designed to assimilate Aborigines, in the hope that they would become like other Australians. This approach was not seriously questioned until the 1960s, when it became clear that the policies were not solving Aboriginal problems and that most Aborigines did not wish to be assimilated. A referendum in 1967 granting the federal government overall responsibility for Aborigines and the inauguration of the Whitlam Labor government in 1972 led to radical changes in Aboriginal policy. This culminated in land-rights legislation, under which land in several states was returned to Aboriginal owners, and in the beginnings of a policy of self-management for the Aborigines.

In the outback areas, many Aborigines moved away from the large settlements into which they had been collected and began to establish smaller, more homogeneous communities at outstations on land to which they had traditional ties. In the more populated areas, Aboriginal claims to land and to compensation for its loss have met with comparatively more resistance on the part of the government and other Australians. Many non-Aborigines argue that land rights and related policies are nothing more than romantic attempts to return to the past. While land rights as defined under Australian law recognizes Aboriginal cultural heritage and offers some recompense for past treatment of the Aborigines, it has also brought about greater participation by the Aborigines in Australian life. Independent Aboriginal business enterprises and community services only appeared for the first time in many areas with the advent of legal ownership of land and the reorganization of residential communities along more traditional lines.

Despite the enormous pressures exerted on it, Aboriginal culture has retained its uniqueness and much of its strength. It is a way of life that has many continuities with its precolonial past. At the same time, much of its nature stems from Aboriginal responses to the European presence and to forces external to the Aborigines and their society. The art produced in Aboriginal Australia over the last century can perhaps best be seen in this light.

We begin, in Chapter I, by exploring the key concept of the Dreaming, its infusion of significance into every corner of the Australian landscape, and its role in forming the spiritual and political identities of individuals and groups. In Chapter II we look at obstacles that have stood in the path of a wider appreciation of what Aboriginal art has to offer and consider a number of ways in which a better informed and more sensitive eye may be brought to bear on these works. Chapter III broaches the complex topic of the relation between form, feeling, and literal meaning in Aboriginal art, exploring three subjects by way of example: the toa sculptures of the Lake Eyre region, images of the body in Arnhem Land bark paintings, and composition in Western Desert acrylic paintings. Chapter IV is a case study of two particular communities of painters in remote parts of Central Australia: Papunya and Yuendumu. The traditional religious basis of the art, its role in local political, social, and economic life, and its mediation of relationships between Aborigines and the non-Aboriginal majority in the rest of Australia and the world are each discussed. In Chapter V we cast a long look back over the history of changing perceptions of Aboriginal art, as recorded in exhibitions, catalogues, manuscripts, books, and photographs, and relate these phases to shifts in colonial and postcolonial Western thought. Chapter VI examines continuities and discontinuities between the remote past and the dynamic present of Aboriginal art. It shows that some Aboriginal traditions have survived relatively unchanged in outward form, while others have been drastically altered or even completely destroyed by the impact of colonization and culture clash. The efflorescence of contemporary Aboriginal art, and its influence on non-Aboriginal artists, concludes this discussion.

Dreamings I

PETER SUTTON

On a hot October day in 1977, some Aboriginal people were moving along the remote Kirke River in Cape York Peninsula, pointing out to me the locations and significance of the named places there. We were "mapping the country." As we rested in the shade by the lagoon called Waarang, an old man in our party, Jack Spear, had stripped and was bathing in the cool waters of his mother's clan country, speaking to its ancestral spirits and asking for their tolerance and protection.

FIG. 6
Totemic Dog sculpture, 1962. Artist unknown, Western Cape York Peninsula. Painted wood and nails, H. 43 cm.

Someone called out to a dog, using its Aboriginal name Yempunchelkanh (Heaps-up Grass). I asked Peter Peemuggina what this meant. He explained that the dog was owned by a man of Marsupial Mouse clan, and the dog's name was an oblique reference to this totemic Mouse and to the way it heaps up grass when making a nest. "Indeed," I said, "so what about your own dog?" "Oh, she is called Ngakkuyee'anh (Makes Ripples), because I am Shark."

This was systematic. Under local tradition all the dogs had names like this, based on the sacred emblems of their owners' landholding groups. (Fig. 6.) The emblematic animals, plants, and other entities were the clan totems. Noticing my intense interest, Peter Peemuggina summarized, and with great feeling, in these words from his own language: "*Epama epam*!"—literally, "nothing is nothing."

A looser translation would be to say that everything has meaning. In a traditional Aboriginal sense, the world is made of signs. One may not know more than a fraction of their meanings, and not all their meanings are of equal significance, but the presumptive principle is that there is no alien world of mere things beyond the signing activity of sentient, intelligent beings. Idle doodling, or the making of meaningless marks, is alien. Galarrwuy Yunupingu, son of Arnhem Land artist Munggurrawuy (Fig. 116), has written:

> When I was 16 years old my father taught me to sing some of the songs that talk about the land . . . One day, I went fishing with Dad. As I was walking along

> behind him I was dragging my spear on the beach which was leaving a long line behind me. He told me to stop doing that. He continued telling me that if I made a mark, or dig, with no reason at all, I've been hurting the bones of the traditional people of that land. We must only dig and make marks on the ground when we perform or gather food.[1]

The meaningfulness of Aboriginal art to Aborigines has gradually been emerging from a long period in which it has largely been ignored by non-Aborigines, apart from a few anthropologists, collectors, and art curators. These meanings have thus far remained largely irrelevant to the appreciation of Aboriginal art works as objects of intense attention, as forms with high aesthetic potential. An acknowledgment that they mean something literal to Aborigines, rather than any particular grasp of the relation between that literal meaning and aesthetic experience, has tended to constitute the basis of a kind of distant respect for the content of the works.

A central message of this book is that while the literal meanings, the visual devices, the aesthetic potential, and the social-contextual significance of Aboriginal art may each be distinguished in theory, they all interact in practice to constitute the total meanings of the works for Aborigines. Those who seek an understanding of the art need to approach it on all these fronts.

The Dreaming and Aboriginal Religion

Most Aboriginal art, at least until comparatively recently, has been enmeshed in religious performance and the social networks and territorial groupings of its practitioners. The imagery of Aboriginal art, and that of the songs, dances, and ceremonial paraphernalia, is related both to the vast bodies of Aboriginal mythic narrative and to the wider symbolisms of daily life and belief. Together these symbolisms constitute a complex code of interaction that continually remodels, and at the same time reflects, Aboriginal cosmology, sociality, and notions of the person. Reproducing the culture, in this sense, is also in Aboriginal eyes reproducing or "following up" the Dreaming.

This is no mere blind adherence to custom. Careers are built, managed, and sometimes lost in the competitive activity that in part constitutes any Aboriginal artistic system. But Aborigines do not see the Dreaming as beyond or above the fundamental principles of personal autonomy, cooperation, competition, and conflict. Dreamings behaved just as human beings do.

What Are Dreamings?

This is anthropologist W. E. H. Stanner's account of the efforts of an Aboriginal man to teach him the meaning of the concept usually referred to in English as the Dreaming, in its manifestation as a Dreaming Place:

> My father . . . said this: 'My boy, look! Your Dreaming is there; it is a big thing; you never let it go [pass it by]; all Dreamings [totem entities] come from there.' Does the white man now understand? The blackfellow, earnest, friendly, makes a last effort. 'Old man, you listen! Something is there; we do not know what; *something*.' There is a struggle to find words, and perhaps a lapse into English. 'Like engine, like power, plenty of power; it does hard-work; it *pushes*.'[2]

Dreamings are Ancestral Beings. In that sense, they both come before, and continue to inhere in, the living generations. Their spirits are passed on to their descendants. Shark Dreaming, or Honey Ant, Yam, Cough, and the hundreds of other Dreamings known across Australia are part of the spiritual identities of those Aborigines who claim them as their Ancestral Beings or totems. Groups of people who share the same Dreamings may constitute totemic corporations, sets of people bonded by a common link to the spiritual. Particular Dreamings that function in this way as signs of groups, emblems of local and corporate identity, provide much of the spiritual underpinning of traditional communal title to land. To falsely claim the Dreaming of another group is a serious infringement of Aboriginal law.

In the myths, Dreamings are born, live, and sometimes die, but they are also eternally present. The spiritual dimension or domain in which they have their existence is the Dreaming, also sometimes referred to as the Dreamtime. Because it is foundational, the Dreaming is sometimes described as the beginning of the world. This was the period when the Ancestral Beings moved about, forming the landscape and creating the plants, animals, and peoples of the known world. They also founded the religious ceremonies, marriage rules, food taboos, and other laws of human society.

In that sense, the Dreaming is the Law. But in the Dreaming, Ancestral Beings frequently broke the Law, just as people do today. The Dreaming is thus the generative principle of the present, the logically prior dimension of the now, while also being a period in which the plants and animals were still women, men, and children, before their transformation into their present forms took place.

The concept of the Dreaming, the organizing logic of so much of the symbolism of Aboriginal art, is not easily explained partly because it is unlike the foundational concepts of most other religious systems. The Dreaming is not an idealized past. The Dreaming, and Dreaming Beings, are not the products of human dreams. In most Aboriginal languages the concept referred to in English as the Dreaming is not referred to by words for dreams or the act of dreaming, even though it may be through dreams that one sometimes gets in touch with the Dreaming. The use of the English word *Dreaming* is more a matter of analogy than of translation.

The animate beings of the Dreaming are not night visions, nor are they idealized persons. They are Ancestral Beings. They exhibit all the faces of human virtue, vice, pleasure, and suffering. Images of these beings, their places of travel and habitation and their experiences, make up the greatest single source of imagery in Aboriginal art. While most are characterized as the animals and plants of Australia (Kangaroo Dreaming, Cheeky Yam Dreaming, for example) or as heroic individuals (the Two Young Women, the Apalach Men), some are less readily grasped as totemic beings by outsiders (Cough Dreaming, for example, or Dead Body, Itchiness, and Diarrhea).

In traditional Aboriginal thought, there is no central dichotomy of the spiritual and material, the sacred and secular, or the natural and supernatural. While each of the Dreaming Beings and their physical counterparts and manifestations (as animals, plants, water holes, rock formations, or people) are distinguishable, Dreamings and their visible transformations are also, at a certain level, one.

The centrality of place—particular lands and sites of significance—in this imagery enables even the religious sculptures to be regarded as "landscapes." For the tradition-minded, the art works themselves may belong on a continuum of manifestations of the Dreaming, together with the artists who made them, the natural species projected in the totemic designs, and the topographic features of the landscape. Landscape features themselves are the marks made by the Dreaming Beings, elements of a larger system of meaning (Fig. 28). The single most common subject matter of Aboriginal art is landscape-based myth.

FIG. 7
Central Australia, Michal Kluvanek, 1987.

Landscape, Totems, and Symbolism

Aboriginal images of landscape, in the religious traditions at least, are not attempts to capture appealing views of nature.[3] They are representations of instances of Dreamings. In Aboriginal terms, all landscape is someone's home. *Land*, *country*, *camp*, and *home* are encompassed by a single term in Aboriginal languages. The places represented in tradition-oriented Aboriginal art are usually the concentration points for intense religious, political, familial, and personal emotions.

Most works labeled "traditional," as well as the so-called transitional works such as Western Desert acrylic paintings on canvas and board, represent the places, events, and Dreaming characters of myths. These myths, in spite of their occasional cosmic overtones or their universal human psychological elements—such as the imagery of swallowing and disgorgement, or conflict and sexuality—are generally unintelligible to non-Aborigines.

Many Aboriginal myths are accounts of ancestors' travels from site to site, broken most frequently by incidents of hunting and gathering food, fighting enemies, and engaging in ceremonies with other characters of the

FIG. 8
Lake Albert, Lower Murray River region, 1986.

FIG. 9
Aboriginal men making bark paintings (left, Taimundu; right, Papatama), Groote Eylandt, 1922.

"founding dramas."[4] Few traditional Aboriginal myths actually consist of explanations of natural curiosities of the type made popular in collections of Aboriginal stories published for children. These are the "just-so" stories with invented titles such as "How the kookaburra got his laugh" or "How the porcupine got his quills." Aside from the "camp stories" told to children, few of the myths could be described as moral tales or fables. The key characters of the more important myths are hardly models of approved behavior. Liberal misdemeanors by mythic ancestors are frequently unjustified and go unpunished, or if punished, then to an extent that often goes beyond any conceivable justice. Explicit moral comment is rarely a feature of traditional Aboriginal narratives, or even of historical reminiscences. Listeners must make their own judgments, if any.

Apart from any wider meanings they might have, many of the myths are centrally concerned with underpinning the rights of particular human groups to specific areas of land, and they often symbolize relationships of alliance or political disjunction between territorial groups, especially in the case of traveling myths.[5] Even these myths to some extent lead a life of their own, not quite matching with current land tenure or the current state of intergroup politics.

In traditional Aboriginal thought, there is no nature without culture, just as there is no contrast either of domesticated landscape with wilderness or of interior scene with an expansive "outside" beyond four walls. In its focus on specific sites in the landscape, this type of art is centered on linked points marked by their social and religious significance in human affairs, not on their appearance alone. Their aesthetic is not a matter of "beauty," as such. (We return to this issue in Chapter III.) Site-based, mythic representations in Aboriginal art are landscapes of landscapes, or conceptual maps of designs already wrought, not views of nature. As a Cape York man once said, "The land *is* a map!"

The Ancestral Beings, or Dreamings, who carved forms out of the formless world and molded the shapes of the creeks and desert sandhills and rainforests also brought human sociality and culture. Thus, there is no geography without meaning or without history. In the harsh desert of the Lake Eyre region, the concept of the Dreaming or ancestor is spoken of in English by local Aboriginal people as "History." The Ancestral Beings themselves are the "Histories," and the sacred sites are "History Places." In tropical Cape York Peninsula the same kind of Ancestral Beings are spoken of in English as "Stories," and their sacred dwelling places are "Story Places." The land is already a narrative—an artifact of intellect—before people represent it. There is no wilderness.

> . . . most of the choir and furniture of heaven and earth are regarded by the Aborigines as a vast sign system. Anyone who, understandingly, has moved in the Australian bush with Aboriginal associates becomes aware of the fact. He moves, not in a landscape, but in a humanized realm saturated with significations. Here 'something happened'; there 'something portends.'[6]

Or, as Aboriginal people sometimes say of unexplained phenomena, "It must be *something*."

In this kind of tradition, the sculptures, paintings, dances, and songs that relate to the Dreaming are conceived as reproductions of works that have been created by conscious and spiritual beings. Any regularity in what a European might call "nature" will in most Aboriginal languages be referred to by the same term as that used for paintings, and in essentially the same way it is seen as a sign of intent toward people, as a pattern of marks made by a conscious and social being, which is a Dreaming.[7] Painted cross-hatching, dotting, or other such patterns are generally referred to by the same term as that used to describe the forms of honeycombs, reptile scales, spider webs, and similar patterned and symmetrical forms. Religious designs, and these other so-called natural designs, are all from the Dreaming. In fact, only the Dreamings were original and creative; people simply copy. When a "new" sacred song or design originates with an individual, it is said to have been "found" by them, often in a dream or some other extraordinary experience. In the older, conservative Aboriginal tradition, human artistic creativity or originality is denied and, if attempted, disapproved of.

Style, and the reasons for making art, do change. Most "traditional" art of 1987 is distinct from, although very similar to, work from the same areas made forty years ago (compare Figs. 61–62). And some neo-traditional work not only innovates with form, but it also innovates with regard to Aboriginal customary law.

FIG. 10
Wandjina Figure, 1984. Ray Meeks, New South Wales. Oil on canvas, 93 × 63 cm.

FIG. 11
Moiety and clan designs, North East Arnhem Land (after Morphy 1977, 1980).

Yirritja Moiety

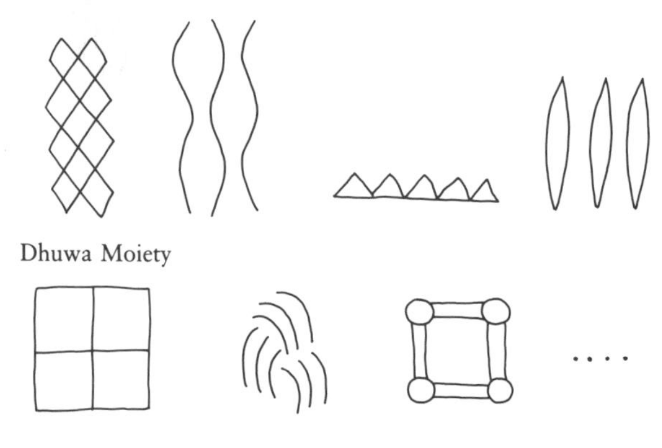

Various Yirritja Clan Designs for Similar Subjects
Clans:

Dhalwangu *Munyuku* *Gumatj 1, 2* *Gumatj 3* *Madarrpa*

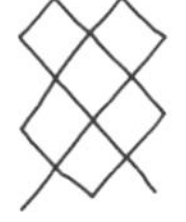

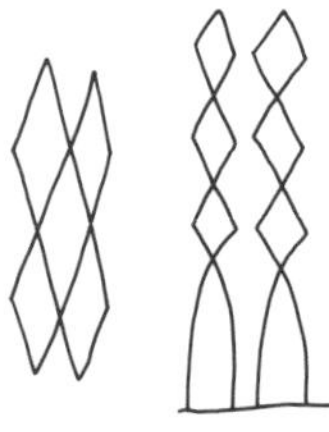

Clan Designs: With Old People, Everything Politics

Many Australian artists, including some urban and rural Aboriginal artists, have borrowed stylistic features from the Aboriginal traditions of northern and Central Australia, often amalgamating elements from several different styles in a single work.[8] It is almost commonplace, for example, for a human figure to be portrayed by these artists with an X-ray-style body (as in Western Arnhem Land, Fig. 55), a face and head form like a Wandjina (from the Kimberley, Fig. 76), and with breasts or decorative areas marked with dotted circles (as in Western Desert art, Fig. 157). The urban Aboriginal artist Ray Meeks has done a number of these eclectic works, among them the painting of the Wandjina figure shown here (Fig. 10). In the more conservative traditions of remote Australia, this kind of appropriation of designs is not only frowned on but may be considered a serious infringement of Aboriginal law. Designs are not public property. Ancestral Beings, Dreamings, gave them for certain groups to hold in sacred trust. Infringements of this copyright are in some places still met with vigorously applied sanctions. (Australian law also recognizes Aboriginal copyright, but only for whole images, not particular motifs.)

The traditional owners of Aboriginal designs may be loose regional groupings, members of cult lodges linked by Dreaming tracks, or members of patrifilial clans, and so on, depending on which part of Australia is involved. This particular system appears to be most pronounced and fine-grained in North East Arnhem Land, in which Yirrkala is located. When interviewed about certain paintings that we wanted to use in this book, Gambali, a senior member of the Aboriginal community at Yirrkala, alerted us to the possible harm that would come from the misappropriation of other people's designs. Even to "speak for" another group's clan design was to invite serious trouble, especially from "the old people" (the tradition-oriented Aborigines). "With old people," he warned, "everything politics."[9]

In North East Arnhem Land, clan designs fall into two main groups associated with the two intermarrying moieties (halves) of society (Fig. 11). Clans, which are the primary landowning units and generally small groups of people linked by descent in the male line, belong to one moiety or the other. Each of the clans has its own distinctive designs. These designs, as Howard Morphy notes, "cover the surface of the painting in areas defined by figurative representations and certain other components . . . These designs consist of repeated sequences of geometric elements elaborately infilled with cross-hatching. The designs vary according to which Ancestral Beings the design is associated with and which clan it belongs to."[10]

Morphy lists distinct variations on the diamond pattern associated with each of five clan groups (Fig. 11). These are clans connected by the journeys of a set of Ancestral Beings that includes Fire and Wild Honey. The mythic

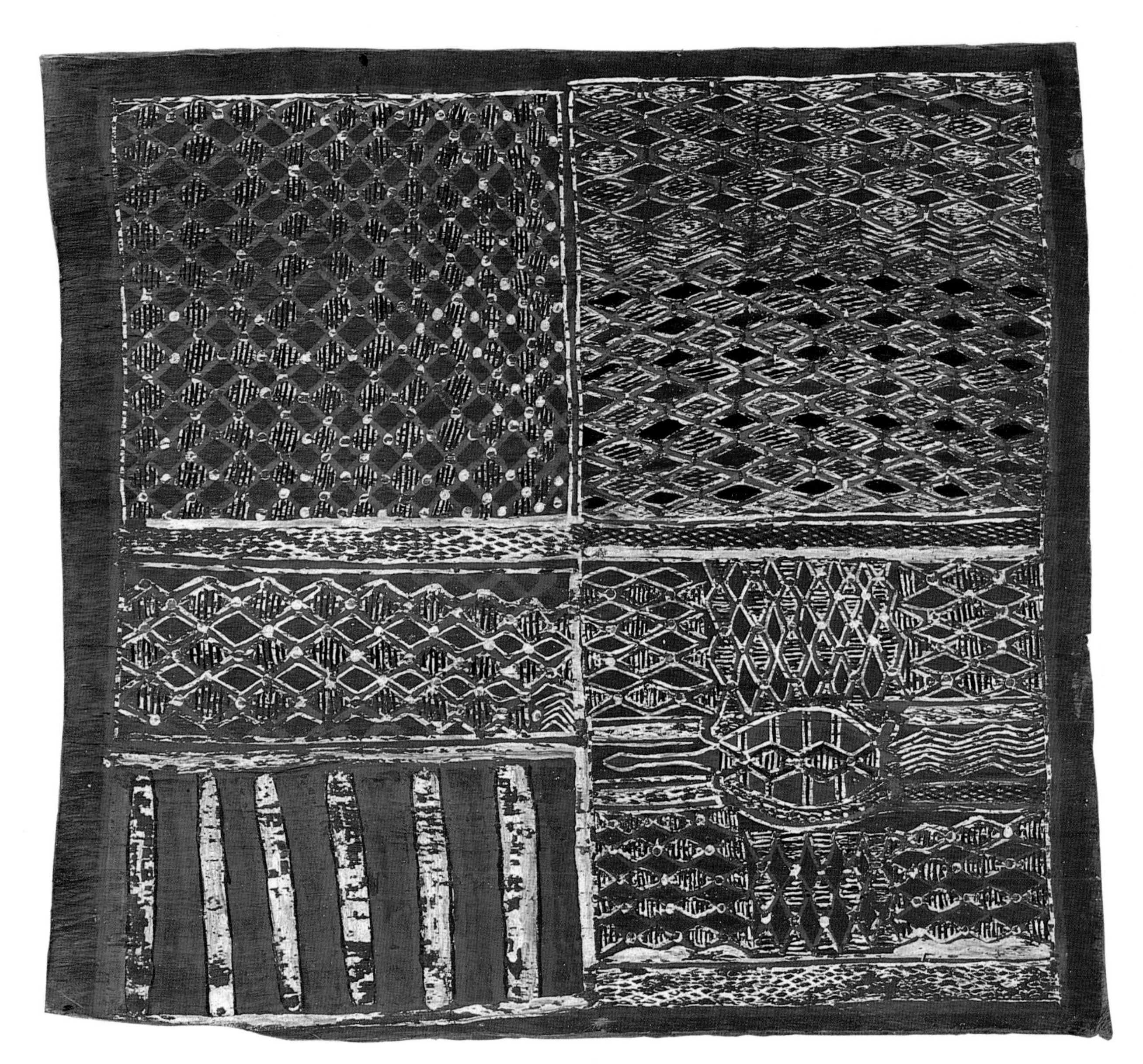

FIG. 12 / CAT. 26
Tortoise, Honey, and Spikerush, 1952. Birrikitji Gumarna, North East Arnhem Land. Ochre on bark, 57 × 62 cm.

FIG. 13
American Indian designs representing wasps' nests and wild honey (after Boas 1927).

explanations for the origins of these various designs refer to the cells of beehives (Fig. 12); the patterns of folded paperbark; and the markings of fire, including those burnt onto a Crocodile's back, forming the cellular pattern of its scales, during mythic events. In the Gumatj fire pattern "red diamonds, red and white cross-hatched diamonds, black diamonds and white diamonds are said to represent flames, sparks, charred wood and smoke respectively"[11] resulting from these events.

Morphy's major study of the artistic system of North East Arnhem Land[12] shows that there is no simple relationship between the painters as members of clans, the Dreaming sites of clan estates (owned lands), and the clan designs. The artistic system of this region encodes relations between people and land, but not in exactly the same form as other systems in the culture. While North East Arnhem Land paintings are seen explicitly as

FIG. 14
Wagilag Ceremony, ca. 1963.
Mathaman, North East Arnhem Land.
Ochre on bark, 157.5 × 62.8 cm.

assertions of clan land ownership, different individuals tend mainly to paint only certain parts of their clan lands. Smaller paintings tend to show fewer episodes of myths than larger ones. Particular ancestral designs used in a painting emphasize some parts of a clan's lands rather than others by calling attention to sites where the ancestors traveled. The paintings are thus not simply topographical maps but actually map relationships between certain mythologically significant features in the landscape. (Figs. 12, 14–15, 43–44, 81, 116, 249, and Cat. 27–28.)

Some North East Arnhem Land clans have made certain formerly secret designs available for public viewing—and for the painting market—to a greater extent than other clans, and the levels of meaning made available to viewers vary. The use of figurative elements appears to have increased considerably after the 1940s and 1950s (see Fig. 15).

While traditionally there is no distinct artist category in Aboriginal society and a relatively large proportion of adults may paint, the right to paint the most important designs is a sign of status and knowledge. Yet some of the most eminent clan members do not paint at all. Simplistic accounts of such a system are clearly worse than misleading.

The political economy of owned designs is paralleled in complexity by the religious politics of land interests, and the two spheres overlap considerably. If tradition-based Aboriginal two-dimensional art, such as bark painting and Western Desert canvas painting, may thus be categorized as a form of religious and political landscape, what of sculpture? Can statues be maps? Are Aboriginal sculptures also political as well as religious statements, and are they objects of strategic as well as aesthetic importance? In general, yes. These domains are distinguishable, but often organically inseparable, in Aboriginal cultures.

Sculpture as Narrative: The Aurukun Case

In Western Cape York Peninsula a tradition of carved wooden figures, now recognized as unique in the history of Aboriginal art, has effloresced since about 1950.[13] Carved wooden ceremonial objects, and some ceremonial beeswax figurines, were collected there in the 1920s and 1930s by the anthropologist Ursula McConnel,[14] but these were largely secret or semi-secret objects and, apart from two wax figurines, simple in form.

In about 1950 some one hundred ceremonial items from Aurukun Mission were donated to the anthropology museum of the University of Queensland by Rev. J. B. McCarthy. Many of these items were carved figures of animals and people. In 1954, 1955, and 1958 the Aurukun missionary William MacKenzie sent nearly forty ceremonial sculptures to the museum, along with excellent documentation, which showed that they were related to the mythic and ceremonial life of the groups that had been gradually settling at Aurukun since the early 1900s. In 1962 Frederick McCarthy of the Australian Institute of Aboriginal Studies visited Aurukun at the invitation of MacKenzie to film performances of these ceremonies, most of which involved the use of complex sculptural forms (Figs. 16–17). There he made a large collection of the sculptures, now in the National Museum of Australia. Seven of them are published here (Figs. 18–24).[15] The tradition of carved wooden figures has continued in a modified form. Although the ochred figures are used only in ceremonies and have never been made for sale, some small unpainted figures of totemic animals were being made for the craft market in 1987.[16]

FIG. 15 / CAT. 31
Possum Story from Djarrakpi, ca. 1967. Narritjin Maymurru, North East Arnhem Land. Ochre on masonite, 89 × 40 cm.

FIG. 16 (FACING PAGE)
Jackson Woolla dancing with the Crippled Boy of Thaa'puunt (Fig. 23), Um Thoch, Western Cape York Peninsula, 1962.

FIG. 17
Peret Arkwookerum and others dancing with the Wallaby from Thawungadha (Fig. 24), Um Thoch, Western Cape York Peninsula, 1962.

FIG. 18 / CAT. 97
Saarra, the Seagull Hero, 1962. Artist unknown, Western Cape York Peninsula. Wood, ochre, charcoal, nails, burlap, and leather, 132.5 × 46 cm.

FIG. 19 / CAT. 98
Bonefish Man from Archer River, 1962. Arthur Pambegan, Jr., Western Cape York Peninsula. Wood, nails, bark, cockatoo feathers, bush string, ochre, and black pigment, 72 × 56 cm.

18

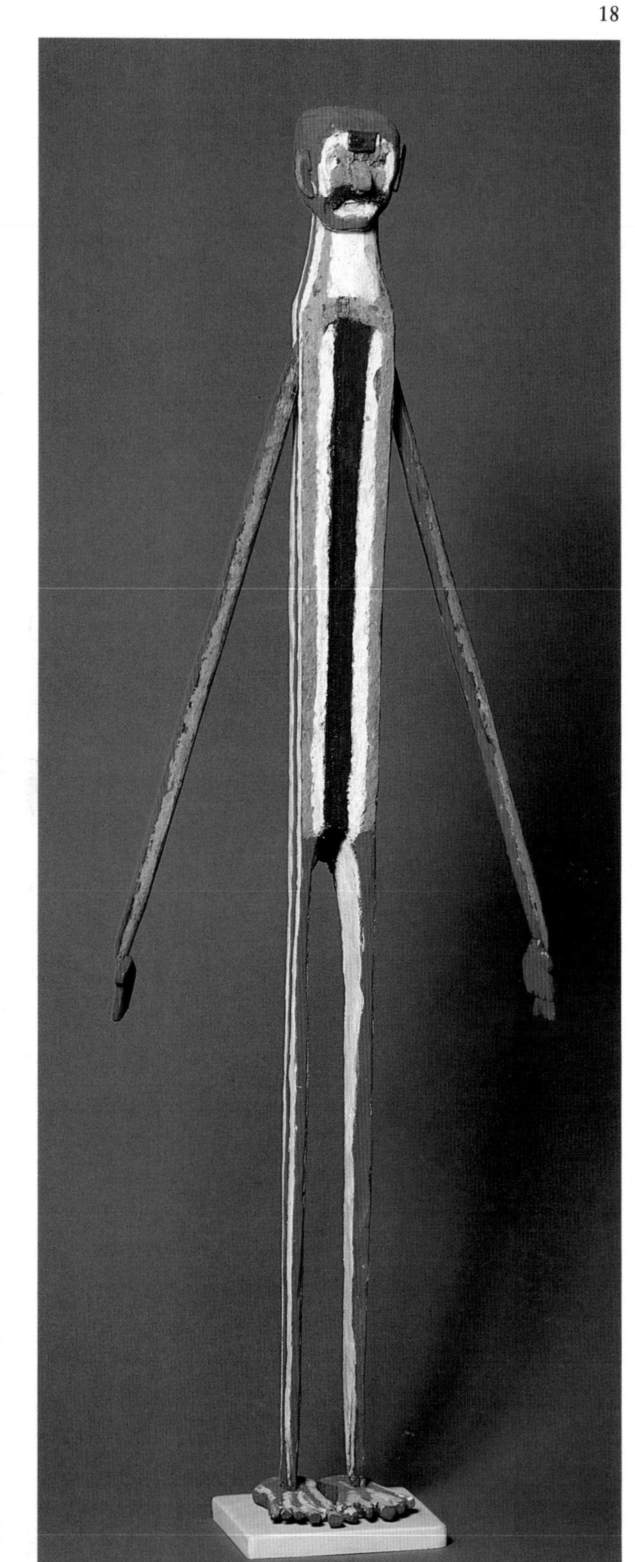

FIG. 20
Echidna from Thaamakan, 1962. Artist unknown, Western Cape York Peninsula. Wood and ochre, 17 × 43.5 cm.

FACING PAGE

FIG. 21 / CAT. 99, 100
The Younger and Older Apalach Brothers, 1962. Attributed to Uki Pamulkan and Don Tybingoompa, Western Cape York Peninsula. Left: Wood, nails, and ochre, 84.5 × 19.5 cm; right: wood, nails, ochre, horsehair (?), and xanthorrhea (?) resin or beeswax, 118.5 × 40 cm.

FIG. 22 / CAT. 101
Shark from Cape Keerweer, 1962. Lesley Walmbeng, Western Cape York Peninsula. Wood, ochre, and plastic buttons (?), 30 × 61.5 cm.

FIG. 23 / CAT. 102.
Crippled Boy of Thaa'puunt, 1962. Jackson Woolla, Western Cape York Peninsula. Wood, ochre, nails, glass beads, bone, horsehair, and resin or beeswax, 74.5 × 21.5 cm.

FIG. 24 / CAT. 103
Wallaby from Thawungadha, 1962. Attributed to George Ngallametta, assisted by MacNaught Ngallametta and Joe Ngallametta, Western Cape York Peninsula. Wood, ochre, nails, and resin, 68 × 11 cm.

19

20

23

21

22

24

FIG. 25
The Two Young Women of Cape Keerweer, 1987. Angus Namponan, Peter Peemuggina, and Nelson Wolmby, Western Cape York Peninsula. Wood, nails, ochre, and eucalyptus bark, left, 70 × 42 cm; right, 73 × 35 cm.

The Two Young Women of Cape Keerweer In 1987 two extraordinary wooden figures were made by Angus Namponan, assisted by Peter Peemuggina and Nelson Wolmby, for the performance of a ceremony to release from the Aurukun jail the spirit of a young Aboriginal man who had died after attempting to hang himself in his cell (Figs. 25–26). The back-

FIG. 26
Ceremony to release the spirit, Aurukun Jail, Western Cape York Peninsula, 1987.

ground of these two figures—the *Two Young Women of Cape Keerweer*—gives insight into the religious, territorial, political, and aesthetic systems of the peoples of Western Cape York Peninsula and also shows that such systems cannot be treated in an art-world vacuum away from the facts of post-colonial Aboriginal life, even in a remote enclave.

The story behind the Two Young Women is this:

> A baby was very sick. It was being looked after by two sisters. These young women were Quails. One stood on the high sandhill at Pulthalpampang, near Aayk, on the south side of the Kirke River estuary. She sang her mourning-style totemic song, her Wuungk. The sister on the north side of the estuary, at Poenp, sang her own Wuungk back, in another language—Wik-Ayangenych. They each admired the other's lovely songs (Fig. 27 shows women dressed for Wuungk).[17] But the baby died of its sickness, there at Pulthalpampang. And its relatives failed to cry for that baby. The Pelicans, Spoonbills, Ibis, White Cranes, Yellow Cranes, Blue Cranes, Black Cormorants, Kite Hawks, Magpie Geese—they were people then—they did not cry. So the two young women decided to cross the Kirke estuary (Man-Yelk). They moved to its center, and there sank beneath the water into a deep cave (Fig. 28). There they turned into Sharks, and from there that cloudy water turned into clear water (*ngak apalach*), and their relatives, all the Bird people, turned to "wild" flying birds then.
>
> When that mother Shark comes in near to shore and is speared, people take the young sharks from her belly, then sing to make her come alive again. They sing once. Then they sing again: she starts to move. Then they sing the third time: she rolls over, belly down, and swims away.
>
> This is why, when people of the Kirke River area dance Apalach (Clear Water), they dance Shark, and wear the spotted paint which is seen, in the sculptures illustrated here, on the Two Young Women (Fig. 25), the Apalach Brothers (Fig. 21), and the Freshwater Shark (Fig. 22). The spots are the dappled sparkles of Clear Water.

FIG. 27
Two young women in mortuary dress, Aurukun, Western Cape York Peninsula, 1933.

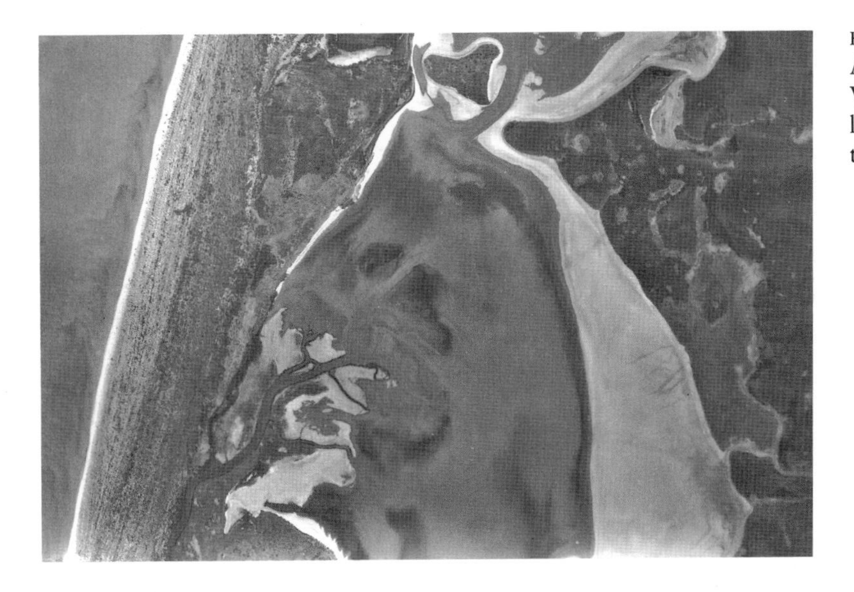

FIG. 28
Aerial view of Cape Keerweer area, Western Cape York Peninsula. The larger dark patch in the estuary is where the Two Young Women sank down.

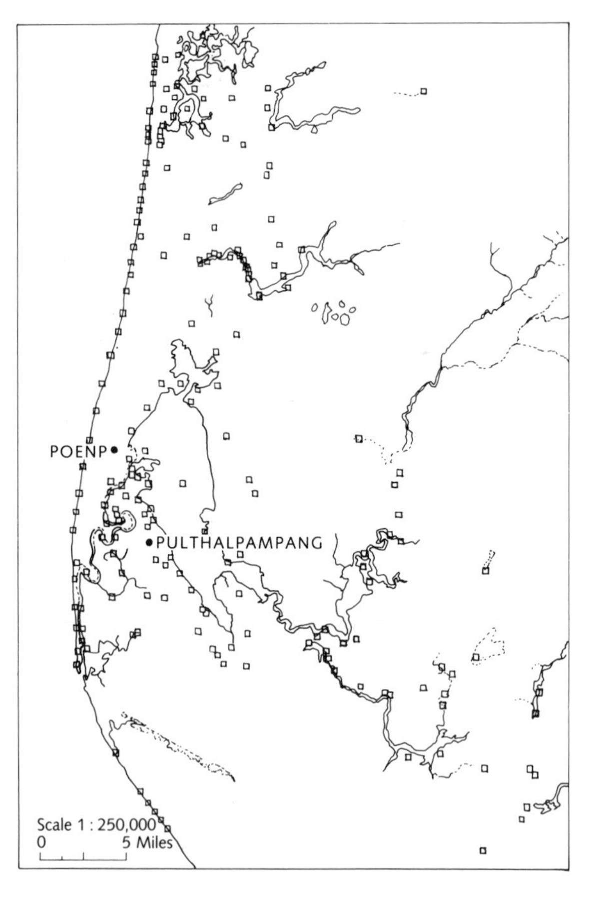

FIG. 29
Named sites (indicated by squares) in the Cape Keerweer area, Western Cape York Peninsula. For Poenp and Pulthalpampang, see Figs. 30–31.

FIG. 30
Johnny Ampeybegan, Jack Spear, and Paul Peemuggina (left to right) standing on the Shark totemic center at Poenp, Western Cape York Peninsula, 1976.

FIG. 31
The sandhill at Pulthalpampang where the Quail Woman sang her mourning song (with Marjorie and Bruce Yunkaporta and family), Western Cape York Peninsula, 1976.

This story can make little sense to an outsider unless certain local facts are known. The sites from which the two sisters arise (Pulthalpampang and Poenp) are in different clan estates, on opposite sides of one river. Members of the clan groups that own these sites and their respective estates are, if in the same generation, classified as siblings, even though they may possess different languages.[18] They collaborate in reenacting their common founding drama in Shark totemic ceremonies. Poenp is in fact the hill of shellgrit swept up by Shark's tail (Figs. 29–30). Pulthalpampang is what is left of the mountain Wonhthalp, which Quail moved inland to Coen in anger at the lack of grief shown by relatives when her baby died (Figs. 29, 31).

The two sisters, driven together by tragedy, sink beneath the water at a point on the boundary between the estates of their respective clans, a signal that no dispute should arise between the clans. The story may be interpreted as a hedge against any potential decay in an old alliance, a warning against coldheartedness among middlingly close kin, and a wild card leaving options open for linkages outside the immediate region—Coen is a long way away.[19]

The sculptures produced for the ceremony at the Aurukun jail symbolized the traditional alliances around the lower Kirke River, from whose clans the parents of the dead boy came. The figures are also strong aesthetically. They convey the vitality of youth and motherhood, which is particularly emphasized in the breasts. The angled, handless arms frame slim torsos topped by heads with generous thatches of hair, which are suggestive of the "big-hair" style locally found so attractive among women. But the figures are also covered with white dots. These are much more than mere decoration. The dotting style *is* Apalach: it connotes the shimmering variegation of light on clear water, which itself connotes the most affluent season of the traditional calendar. This is the time when the monsoon floods start to drop, the sediments settle, and the waters become clear and sparkling. Apalach (Clear Water) is itself the titular symbol for an alliance even wider than the Kirke River itself, that of a regional ceremonial group from whose hundreds of members the principal performers were drawn for the jail ritual. The *Two Young Women* thus also represent this regional group. The "sparkling"

of their dotted paint is a clear example of the strong social element in the Aboriginal aesthetic.[20]

The Aesthetic Locus of Aboriginal Art

The anthropologist Jacques Maquet suggests that each culture has a particular aesthetic locus, a center from which the aesthetic drive and criteria for artistic excellence radiate. While there may be continuity across all the things made in a society, the subject matter of the aesthetic locus is privileged. For sixteenth-century Japan, Maquet suggests that the center of this locus is the tea ceremony, from which criteria for quality in landscape gardening, architecture, interior decoration, ceramics, laquerwork, and textile design radiated. For thirteenth-century Europe, he suggests the "Christian cult" (buildings, statues, liturgical garments, ceremonial objects) as the aesthetic locus. For mid-twentieth-century North America, Western Europe, and Japan, "industrial design has become an important part of the aesthetic loci of the cultures of these areas."[21]

The key locus of the Aboriginal aesthetic, in the classical tradition, is ceremony (Fig. 32). This is an essentially social aesthetic, not one of alienation or of social rebellion or of largely private experience. It is very far from modernism. A prime example of how this aesthetic works in Aboriginal art is the case of the circle and the circle-path design. (See Figs. 33–44.)

FIG. 32
Initiation Ceremony, 1948. Kulpidja Bara, Groote Eylandt. Ochre and manganese on bark, 65 × 43.5 cm.

> The circle as a spatial form . . . permits an intimacy of face-to-face relations that no other formation can. . . . Thus, the circle reduces to a minimum the social as well as the physical separation of those who make it up: for a time it makes inappropriate, indeed obliterates, all other social categories; it concentrates a unified totality around a centre. In these ways it makes possible a unison towards a dominating object.[22]

In this passage Stanner connects the physical arrangements of ceremonies at Port Keats to the symbolism of an apparently static, geometric form: the circle. It is the circle that, in Western Desert art at least, has the widest number of connotations and thus the greatest semantic density.[23] Similar, though perhaps less far-reaching, analyses could be explored for the circle-path combination, the fork motif, and other key Aboriginal designs (see Chapter III). But these are old, "traditional" forms.

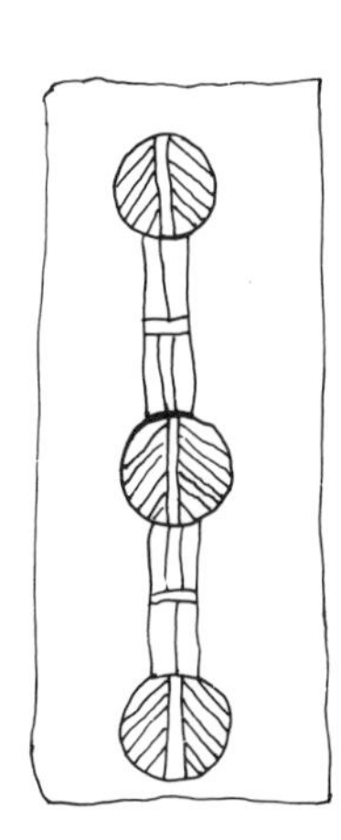

FIG. 33
Sketch by C.P. Mountford of site-path design from Ancestral Journey from Blue Mud Bay to Central Hill, 1948. Minimini Mamarika, Groote Eylandt. Ochre on bark.

What of more recent, urban Aboriginal art? That which is promoted and labeled as such is still very social in its approach, since much of it is

FIG. 34
Rock-engraving motifs, Yunta Springs, South Australia (after Nobbs 1984).

FIG. 35 / CAT. 91
Plain Ringed by Sandhill, ca. 1904. Artist unknown, Lake Eyre region. Wood, reeds, vegetable fiber string, and gypsum, 22 cm.

FIG. 36
Untitled, 1986. Lippsie Whiskey, Central Australia. Linocut, ink on paper, 30 × 30 cm.

FIG. 37
Tingarri at Lake McDonald, 1979. Uta Uta Jangala, Yinyilingki, Central Australia. Acrylic on canvas, 187 × 154.5 cm.

41

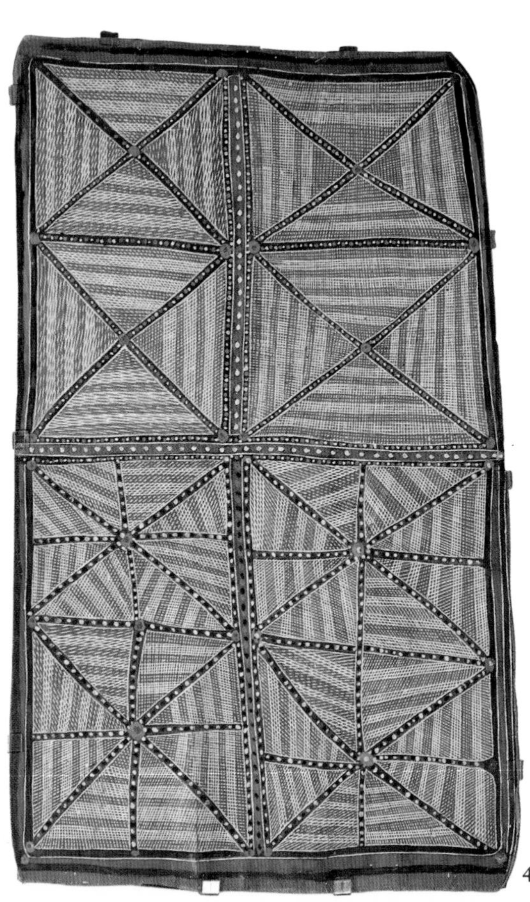

42

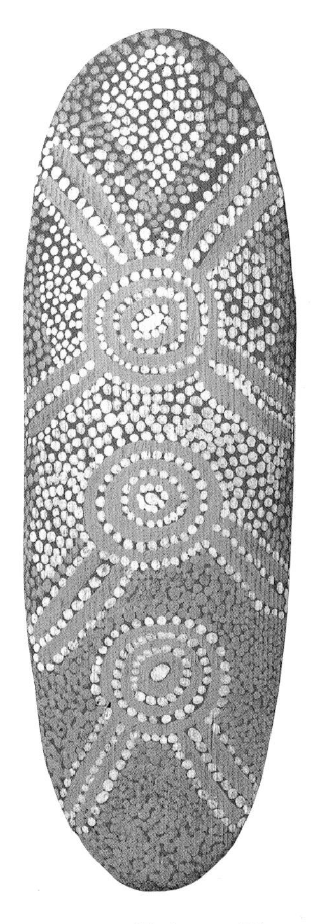

FIG. 38 / CAT. 71
Hare Wallaby Dreaming, 1976. George Jangala, Brown's Bore, Central Australia. Acrylic on beanwood shield, 76 × 25 cm.

FIG. 39
Yam Dreaming, ca. 1974. Billy Stockman Japaljarri, Papunya, Central Australia. Acrylic on board, 122 × 91.4 cm.

FIG. 40
Untitled, ca. 1970s. Artist unknown, Port Keats, Northern Territory. Ochre on bark, 111 × 45 cm.

43

44

FIG. 41
Spirit of the Artist's Dead Wife, 1954. Jacky Navy, Melville Island. Ochre on bark, 33.5 × 65 cm.

FIG. 42
Mardayin Ceremonial Design, ca. 1969. Yirawala, Western Arnhem Land. Ochre and charcoal on bark, 80 × 45 cm.

FIG. 43
Nyapililngu, 1978. Narritjin Maymurru, North East Arnhem Land. Ochre on bark, 108 × 63 cm.

FIG. 44
Spring Waters at Rapaingu, Joined by Ancestral Tracks, 1947. Gungoilma, North East Arnhem Land. Ochre on bark, 74 × 49 cm.

FIG. 45
Take the Pressure Down, 1987. Mitch Dunnet, Adelaide. Acrylic on canvas, 119 × 68 cm.

about establishing, displaying, and arguing for "Aboriginality." A good deal of it is the art of identity assertion and of protest, not of ceremony, and it is therefore no less social in intent than an Arnhem Land clan design. Ray Meeks, the Sydney Aboriginal artist, writes:

> Aboriginal people have always had a vast, rich culture, and I am part of this. There are many things which are too numerous to mention about the treatment of Aboriginals. But through my art I have identity and strength. It would be true to say that I am hunting for lost pieces of myself, but through my culture I have many answers.[24]

In 1987, the same year that Namponan and others made the *Two Young Women from Cape Keerweer*, Mitch Dunnet, an inmate of Adelaide Gaol, painted *Take the Pressure Down* (Fig. 45 and Fig. 46 by Aboriginal photographer Polly Sumner). This was the year in which an Australian government Royal Commission was set up to inquire into the unusually large number of Aboriginal deaths in police custody—many of which involved suicide by hanging. Each of these two very different works reflects an Aboriginal response to the tragic loss of life. One response was mediated by a traditional performance based on ceremonial group solidarity, the other by the entry of a painting in an urban Aboriginal art exhibition for which television news coverage was sought and obtained. Both responses constituted a firm element of assertion of Aboriginal identity to a wider world.

The artists who made the figures of the *Two Young Women* and the people who performed dances in front of the figures may have much in common with the urban jail artist who painted the hanged Aboriginal youth, but they may also be seen as located on different points in a timeworn historical process. The Cape Keerweer people lived essentially beyond the impact of white Australian culture until the 1920s. Many of them came to settle for most of the year at Aurukun Mission as late as the 1940s. Even then, the nearest major centers of non-Aboriginal population were far away at Cairns, Thursday Island, and Port Moresby. Until recently the dominant civic culture to which they have been mainly exposed—if not the underlying political and administrative framework in which they are encapsulated—has been essentially their own Aboriginal culture.

FIG. 46
Mitch Dunnet, Adelaide Jail. Polly Sumner, 1987.

Urban Aborigines from southern and eastern Australia have been exposed for a much longer time to non-Aboriginal society and culture and have experienced much more profound cultural changes, yet they have not lost their sense of Aboriginal identity. More than a century of different experience separates urban Aboriginal life from that of people in some remote areas. In that period, Aboriginal material culture has gone from being a little-known facet of an exotic south seas group's obscure way of life to being seen, and to some extent known, around the world.

Responding to Aboriginal Art II

PETER SUTTON

The grace of Raphael's language continued to acquire energy and his idealization was enriched by a full vitality from the time he began to work in the Stanze and reached the apex in the Stanza di Eliodoro. But it was only in the cartoons for the tapestries that the idealized beauty and harmoniously vigorous elements that constitute his Renaissance Classicism become colored with a severe and magnificent dignity. Raphael is a great artist; not even at this point does he copy his forms from antique art.[1]

THIS PASSAGE of art-historical criticism, chosen virtually at random from a book on the Italian Renaissance painter Raphael, was obviously written by someone who is well acquainted not only with the works of a particular artist but also with the central vocabulary of a whole cultural tradition. In the order in which they appear here, we have that tradition's concepts of *grace*, *energy*, *idealization*, *enrichment*, *vitality*, *progress to an apex*, *idealized beauty*, *harmony*, *vigor*, *dignity*, the *great artist*, and, finally, the *original work*.

These are not necessarily the key ideas of Raphael and the cultural context in which he worked, nor are they necessarily those of artists and art historians generally in our own times. Almost all these ideas have been subjected to powerful critiques in recent decades. But they do encapsulate a particular tradition of thinking and feeling about art objects, one that has enjoyed great prestige in the European cultural world for over two hundred years. It is important to understand that most of these ideas would be all but meaningless to most of the Aboriginal artists whose works are represented in this book. Aboriginal artists have their own aesthetic and metaphysical values that they apply to visual representations, but they are generally not like these.

It is not surprising, then, that European colonists responded to the paintings and constructions of the Aborigines in the way they did. Whatever those works may have been, they were not to be regarded as objects of complex aesthetic, narrative, or religious meaning, nor as the progressive achievements of specially talented individuals. They may have been meaningful to the "natives,"[2] but native cultures were of small diplomatic, strategic, or economic account, and they were also considered to be too simple, repetitious, and custom-bound to be of any great intellectual interest. As noted in Chapter V, in the case of African and Oceanic cultures this situation only began to change significantly in the early twentieth century.

In this chapter we examine the obstacles that have stood in the way of an appreciation of Aboriginal art. We then discuss what kinds of knowledge can contribute to a richer response to the art. We approach this last task by showing how a knowledge of the symbolism of bark paintings, and of stylistic variation between bark painters, can add to one's sensibility to the qualities of individual paintings.

The Obstacles

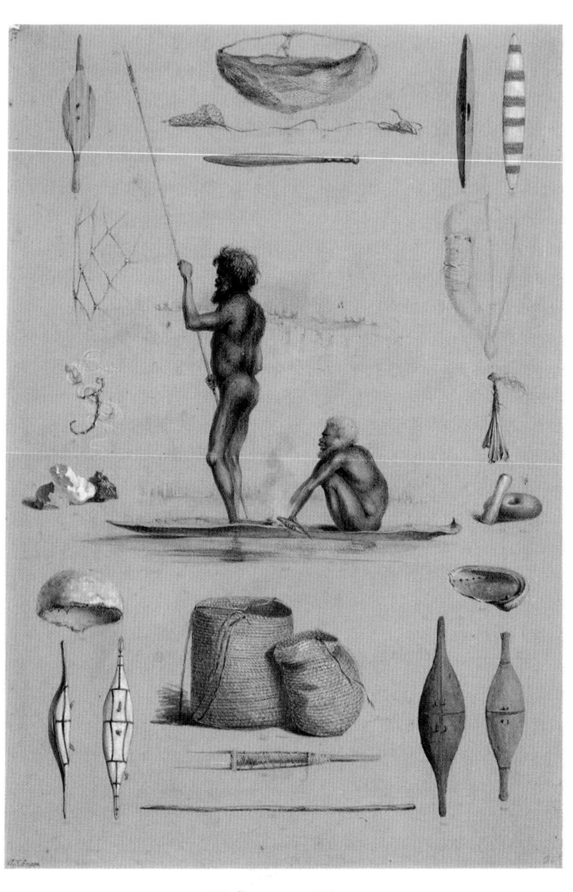

FIG. 47 / CAT. 77
Aboriginal Inhabitants, Implements, and Domestic Economy, 1844. George French Angas, South Australia. Watercolor on paper, 49 × 34 cm.

Whether it was because of their rarity, the abstruseness of their cultures of origin, or the low esteem in which their makers were held, Australian Aboriginal works in the past failed to capture the attention of the European and North American art world. It is important to remember that the most spectacular Aboriginal traditional art tended to be that reserved for sacred ceremonies and that colonists were generally not permitted ready access to such events. It is also possible that Aboriginal art was simply not easily read by the colonial European eye. The general absence of highly finished, regular, and repetitive ornamental designs in the first Aboriginal works known to the West contrasted with Oceanic ornament generally, and with the Polynesian in particular (Fig. 47). By the mid-nineteenth century European authorities on decorative art were citing Oceanic art, notably that of New Zealand's Maoris, as fine examples of design,[3] but not that of Aborigines. Even today, as seen in the fabric-printing industry, it is the ornamental, schematic, two-dimensional, and repetitive elements—not the sculptural, iconographic, or metaphysical facets—of Aboriginal art that have been most readily borrowed and understood by Europeans and others.[4]

Even though Aboriginal art works have become more accessible to outsiders through books, films, museums, and the art market since the 1940s, the recognition of these works as something of cultural value and interest has encountered two major obstacles. One has been the general unintelligibility of Aboriginal worldviews, symbolic systems, and visual conventions to those from radically different cultures. The other has been the unwillingness of most non-Aborigines to work to overcome this problem. Since the late nineteenth century two sets of events have occurred that have begun to change this.

First, particularly since the critical years 1904–11, modernism has broken down the dominance of decaying academic art conventions. The Western tradition, in particular, has refreshed itself by the absorption of what were once regarded as exotic visual forms, most importantly those from African, Oceanic, and American Indian sources.[5] The modern temper, still very much with us in the so-called post-modern era, remains one characterized by introspection, anxiety, relativism, eclecticism, and a sense of lost meanings.[6] Disturbed by transience, yet prepared to create transient art, suspicious of beauty but committed to feeling, and wary of the mechanistic and utilitarian tendencies inherited from the Age of Science, the modern temperament is still open to new—or very old—exotic kinds of art as sources of stimulation (see Chapter V).

Certain European-Australian artists now turn to Aboriginal art—especially that which lies largely within the classical tradition of precolonial Australia—for this kind of stimulation, as much because of the meaningfulness of the art as because of its visual properties. This is not, then, simply an extension of early twentieth-century primitivism, which rested primarily on a hunger for new and vital imagery and cared little for the meanings attributed to the works by the artists. (Picasso once said, in effect, "Everything I need to know about Africa is in those objects."[7]) But that wave of early primitivism has broken down the barriers of prejudice against non-illusionist art, so that the form of Aboriginal art now seldom constitutes an absolute barrier to its acceptance.

The second major change that has brought recognition for Aboriginal art in the non-Aboriginal world is the move away from indifference to Aborigines and toward some real interest in analyzing and explaining Aboriginal culture.[8] To a significant extent this has been contingent on a recognition by non-Aboriginal Australians of the need to carve out and accept their own distinctive Australian identity. If Australians are to have a deeper understanding of their own landscape, they can no longer ignore the ancient landscape-centered culture of the Aborigines.[9]

Especially since the 1920s, a growing number of non-Aboriginal people have been willing to put in years of effort to acquire an understanding of particular Aboriginal art traditions. The survey works of the anthropologists Daniel S. Davidson and Frederick McCarthy in the 1930s and the groundbreaking study of Nancy Munn in the 1950s in Central Australia were followed in 1964 by Ronald Berndt's edited volume of papers that illuminated the significance of works in the first major traveling exhibition of Aboriginal art to tour Australia (1960–61). A number of new studies of Aboriginal art have been published in the 1980s,[10] and the frequency of Aboriginal art exhibitions has increased exponentially. With the general improvement in official and popular attitudes toward Aborigines has come greater recognition and promotion of Aboriginal art. The number of devotees among the non-Aboriginal population of Australia and elsewhere is growing, but for many the art of Aborigines remains remote, obscure, or unappealing.

Visual Conventions What are the particular obstacles to the enjoyment of a response to Aboriginal art by non-Aborigines?

One is the Aboriginal use of visual conventions that differ from those of the traditional academic or commercial art systems of many other cultures. This is not really a problem for people who are in touch with, and have some understanding of, contemporary art in the world's metropolitan centers, but many do not. The especially difficult conventions include the use of nonfigurative symbols with multiple meanings; a more heavily conceptual than illusionistic approach to representation; inconsistencies between the orientations of parts of a figure or of separate figures against a single ground; a use of symmetry and repetition that may seem to belong more to a decorative than to a fine-art category; and the use of extremely simple and roughly executed images, often in unfamiliar media.

We return to most of these in Chapter III, in the discussion of Aboriginal representations of the body and the particular visual conventions of bark and acrylic paintings. Here, though, it is appropriate to deal with the problem of simplicity. While most bark and acrylic paintings are more visually complex than most rock art, the visual simplicity of much Aboriginal art, together with its occasional resemblance to child art, has always been an obstacle to its acceptance by those from other cultures (Figs. 48–49).

FIG. 48
Rock art, Yankee Hat 1, New South Wales.

The anthropologist Franz Boas devoted an entire book to the subject of "primitive art."[11] He began by arguing convincingly that the notion of a distinct primitive mentality (in the sense of a less intelligent form of humanity) was both scientifically unsustainable and morally destructive, a view that is now almost universally accepted. Nevertheless, Boas continued to use the term *primitive art*. One of the defining characteristics of such art, he said, was its tendency to symbolize things by a representation of what the artist saw as their essentials. "Children's drawings are essentially of the character here described. They are . . . compositions of what to the child's mind appears essential, perhaps also as feasible." Boas referred to this distinction as one of "abbreviated" versus "realistic" suggestion of form, the abbreviated method being the one that selected and represented the most characteristic traits of something.[12]

These contrasts can be fitted into a simple "primitive versus civilized art" distinction only with the greatest of difficulty, however. Stick figures may occur in both Western child art and Aboriginal rock paintings (Fig. 48), but one may ask: Is an anatomically detailed Aboriginal X-ray painting "abbreviated" simply because it selectively represents important internal features rather than the appearance of skin and fur? And is a Parisian Impressionist's racehorse, perhaps "abbreviated" to a smudge on the canvas, to be considered simple or primitive because it is as unelaborated as one drawn by a child? The formal simplicity of the Impressionist's smudge rests on the intellectual complexity of late nineteenth-century European art theory.

The formal simplicity of much Aboriginal art similarly belies its embodiment of complex social, mythic, and ceremonial meanings. It often rests on

FIG. 49 / CAT. 1
The Sea-dogs, 1954. Big Tom, Melville Island. Ochre on bark, 31 × 80.5 cm.

that preference for cryptography and obliqueness demanded by a restricted economy of religious knowledge, the basis of so much power in traditional Aboriginal society.[13] But while the Impressionist painter sought to achieve something like a *copy of* a visual impression, the Aboriginal artist generally seeks to create reductive *signs for* the things represented. In other words, the Impressionist's approach is predominantly perceptual, while the Aboriginal artist's approach is generally more conceptual.[14]

Aboriginal art is thus the very opposite of irrational or prerational activity. Picasso is said to have liked African art partly because "he found it 'raisonnable'—that is, a result of the *reasoning* process—hence conceptual. . . . Picasso's overall criticism of the received art of his youth was that artists had forgotten how to be simple . . . It was clear that what he meant by [simplicity] was not just the absence of elaborate effects but an economy that implied the distillation of complexities."[15]

Media The European colonists of Australia often disparaged the arts of the Aborigines on the grounds that they were "crude" or "rude," not only because of the slight degree of finesse with which they were so often executed but because of their media. Another obstacle to a positive response to Aboriginal art, then, has been the use of unfamiliar and natural media, such as roughly chopped sheets of eucalyptus bark or the walls of rock shelters.

FIG. 50
Dedication paintings on aluminum dinghy, North East Arnhem Land, 1968.

FIG. 51
The Two Traveling Women at the Site of the Putja Water Hole, 1985. Turkey Tolsen Jupurrurla, Central Australia. Acrylic on canvas sneakers.

Where Aboriginal artists have used smoother and more regular media, canvases, artists' boards, plywood, or even neatly finished sheets of bark, this problem may have been less noticeable, but their art has then encountered another obstacle: the prejudice of those who regard such innovations as "inauthentic."

A more subtle cultural barrier rests on differences between attitudes to the material life of the art objects themselves. Most portable Aboriginal art, in the classical tradition at least, was made for short-term purposes; after it was used, it was left to decay in the elements or was intentionally destroyed, often as part of a ceremony. In fact, things made by people were seldom kept for long periods, by the standards of most other cultures.[16] The transience of the medium was not felt to be inconsistent with the sacred quality often attributed to the object itself.

In Aboriginal eyes, it was the design that mattered most, not the object that it decorated.[17] An image of a sacred water hole, a clan hatching style, or a depiction of a certain Dreaming was usually transposable between media. The same design might be painted, for example, on a boy's body during initiation, on the walls of a wet-season shelter, on a painting made for sale, on a bark or log coffin, on an aluminum dinghy (Fig. 50), or on a pair of sneakers (Fig. 51). The design—not the object itself—is what has continuity.

An understanding of the media used in Aboriginal art, and of the technologies behind their preparation, can be important to appreciating style.

Textural qualities in bark painting, for example, reflect the interplay of decorative devices with the particular physical characteristics of ochres, available paintbrush materials, and the surfaces of bark.[18] It is also necessary to consider the absolute shape and size of the media used.

In Central Australia, painting was in the past performed on large, irregular surfaces such as rock walls and slabs or on ground areas made of pulverized termite mounds. It was also performed on the far more symmetrical and limited forms of the human body and of mainly ovate artifacts such as shields, wooden dishes, sacred boards and stones, and ceremonial posts. Very few of these media were rectangular in shape.[19] The Western Desert acrylic painters have now added to these older media the rectangular canvases and artists' boards that arrive ready-made or are prepared in the community craft shop. Right-angled corners and straight sides have suddenly exerted new pressures on ancient design practices.[20]

Bark painting, at least in several parts of North Australia, was established well before the arrival of Europeans and the cash market. Records of early observers report that Aboriginal people painted the insides of their bark shelters.[21] In a number of early bark paintings there is evidence of faded or removed imagery being overpainted (Fig. 52), as in rock shelters. Even very early barks are roughly rectangular, although the older ones do have more ragged edges (compare Figs. 53, 55–57 with Figs. 58, 92). The architecture of bark shelters (Fig. 59) and the need to maximize the size of a sheet of bark taken from a tree for such a purpose leads naturally to a preference for long rectangular forms.[22]

FIG. 52
Freshwater Crocodile, period 1921–28.
Artist unknown, Western Arnhem Land.
Ochre on bark, 152 × 49 cm.

In preparing barks used for painting, two shallow rings some distance apart are cut around the trunk of a eucalyptus tree. This is usually done around the time of the wet season, as the running sap makes it easier to pry off the bark. The bark sheet is then singed to remove loose bark and help flatten it. It may also be weighed down with stones or sand to make it flat. It is scraped clean and a ground of pigment is laid on the inner surface (Fig. 60). The outlines of main designs, including borders within which details will be added, are then drawn. This is followed by the addition of more motif details and, finally, repetitive and decorative elements such as cross-hatching and dotting. The pigments used—mainly red and yellow ochres, kaolin, and charcoal—are natural solids which are ground or crushed and mixed with water and a fixative. The major fixative used now is the wood glue Aquadhere (orchid juice is still sometimes used). Brushes are made from sticks, pandanus (screw pine) fibers, human hair, and other materials; occasionally a commercial brush is used, especially for laying the ground on the bark's inner surface. Many bark painters, particularly since the 1950s, attach supporting rods to the top and bottom ends of the bark.[23]

An interesting feature of the highly rectangular bark paintings of Western Arnhem Land[24] is their use of compression. This is in contrast to the treatment of subjects in Western Arnhem Land rock painting in which figures

53

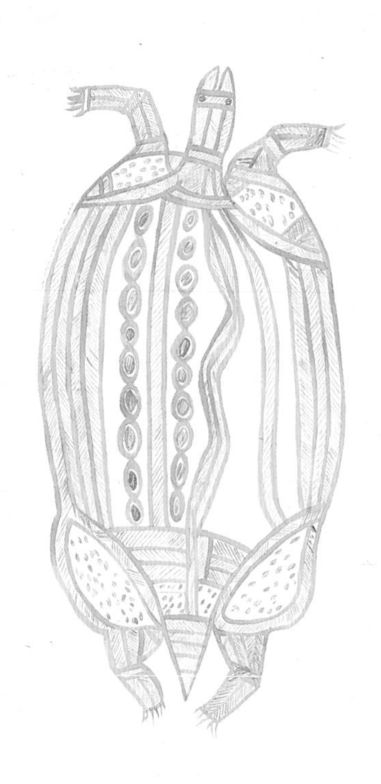

54

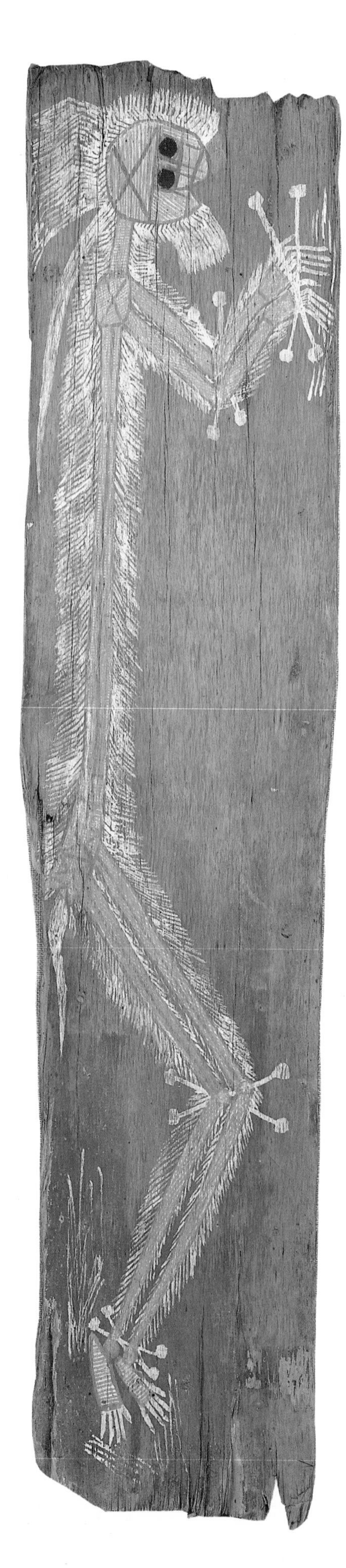

FIG. 53 / CAT. 8
Saltwater Turtle, ca. 1884. Artist unknown, Western Arnhem Land. Ochre on bark, 83 × 63.5 cm.

FIG. 54
Sketch of bark painting (Fig. 53), 1888. G. T. Pank, Jr., Adelaide. Watercolor on paper, 102 × 67.5 cm.

FIG. 55 / CAT. 9
Spirit Called Auuenau, 1912. Artist unknown, Western Arnhem Land. Ochre on bark, 149 × 33 cm.

FIG. 56 / CAT. 10
A Spirit Being, 1914. Artist unknown, Western Arnhem Land. Ochre on bark, 117 × 48 cm.

FIG. 57 / CAT. 32
Canoe and Figures, 1922. Attributed to Taimundu, Groote Eylandt. Ochre on bark, 22.5 × 15 cm.

FIG. 58 / CAT. 21
Female Lightning Figure, ca. 1974. Bilinyarra Nabegeyo, Western Arnhem Land. Ochre on bark, 55 × 34 cm.

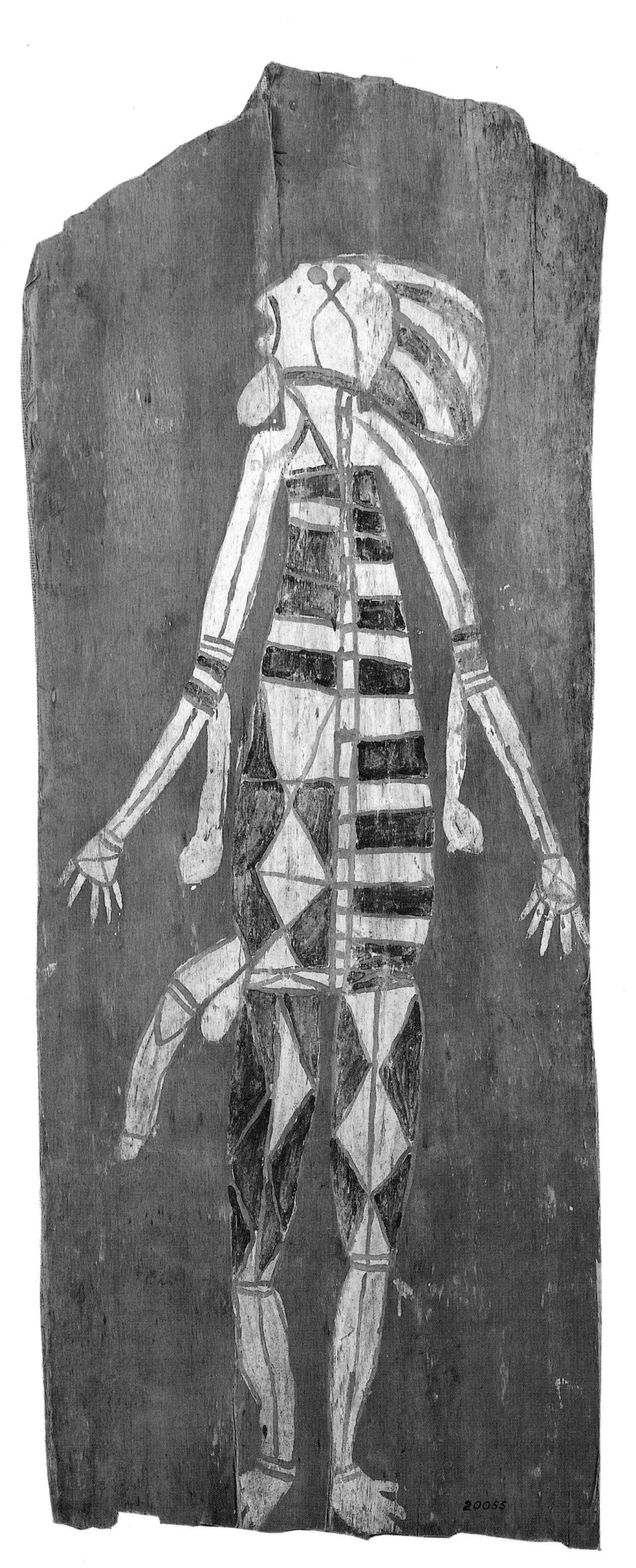

56

57

58

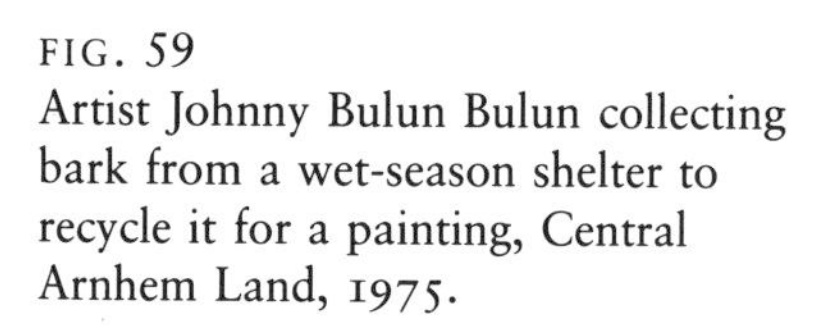

FIG. 59
Artist Johnny Bulun Bulun collecting bark from a wet-season shelter to recycle it for a painting, Central Arnhem Land, 1975.

FIG. 60
Bilinyarra Nabegeyo preparing inner surface of bark for painting, Kalawadjbarra, Western Arnhem Land, 1987.

FACING PAGE

FIG. 61
Kapalawurlgwurlgu, 1986. Sambo Mundiliwuy, Western Arnhem Land. Ochre on bark, 79 × 41 cm.

FIG. 62
Ancestral Being, 1948. Artist unknown, Western Arnhem Land. Ochre on bark, 44.5 × 24.2 cm.

FIG. 63
Depictions of kangaroos from rock-art sites, western New South Wales (after McCarthy 1976).

FIG. 64
Serpent Swallowing Wawilak Sisters, and Wallaby, ca. 1968. Yirawala, Western Arnhem Land. Ochre on bark, 55 × 90 cm.

FIG. 65
Serpent and Woman, rock art, Kimberley region.

FIG. 66
Rainbow Snake, rock art, Central Arnhem Land (after Brandl 1973).

FIG. 67
Borlung, the Rainbow Snake, based on a 1969 bark painting by Mandarrk, Central Arnhem Land (after Brandl 1973).

tend to be relatively elongated or open. People are shown in elongated and squatting positions (splayed, limbs bent, crossed, or intertwined) in both media, but there is a tendency for the human figures on bark to be compressed rather than extended (Figs. 58, 61–62, 77). Kangaroos in rock art are depicted with their tails reasonably well extended, in the standard hopping mode (as in other parts of Australia, Fig. 63), while in bark paintings they are frequently shown with their tails drawn tightly to the body or even turned into anatomically impossible and very striking attitudes (Fig. 64). Reptiles, in rock art and even on engraved trees,[25] tend to be shown at full stretch. Snakes, for example, may appear in rock art as long meandering lines (Figs. 65–66). In bark paintings they more often are coiled or bent back

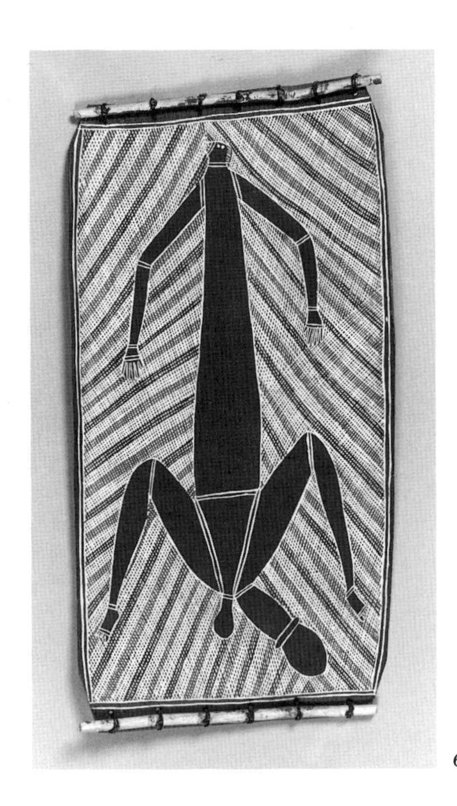

61

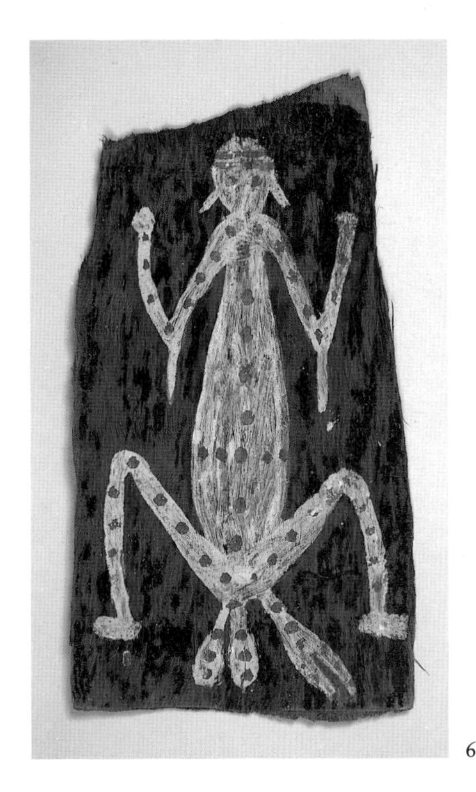

62

63

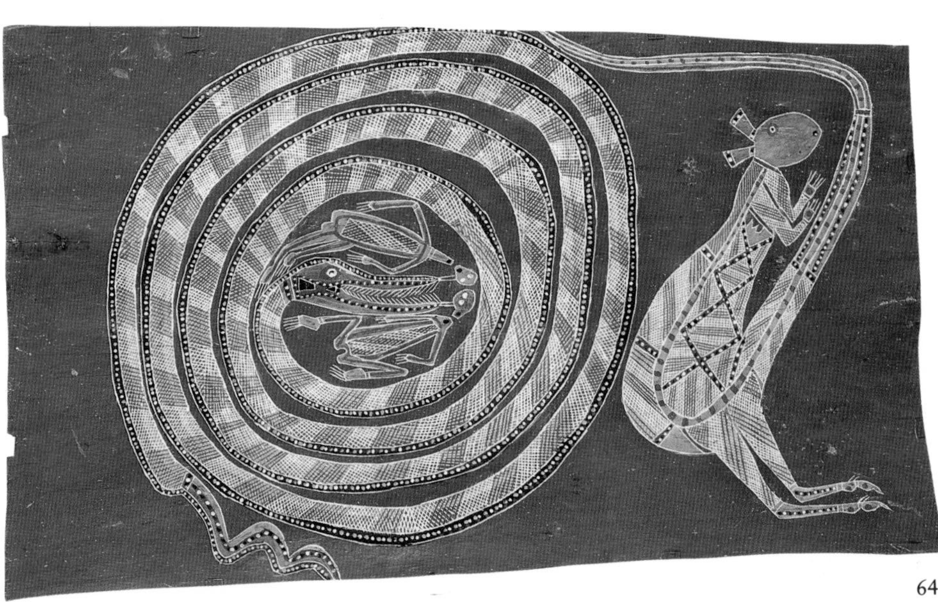

64

65

66

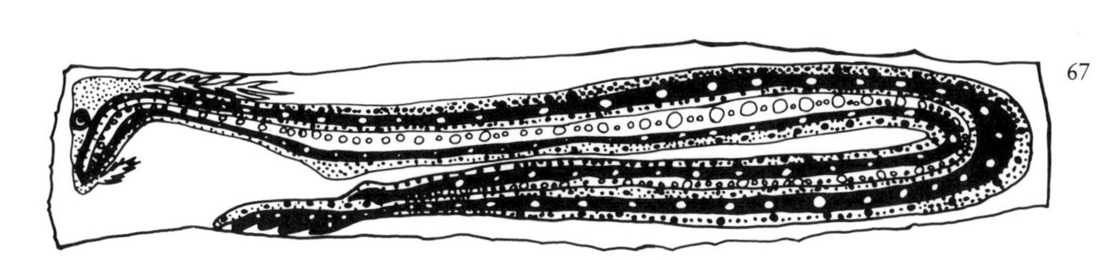

67

FIG. 68
Female Rainbow Snake, Alligator Rivers region (after Brandl 1973).

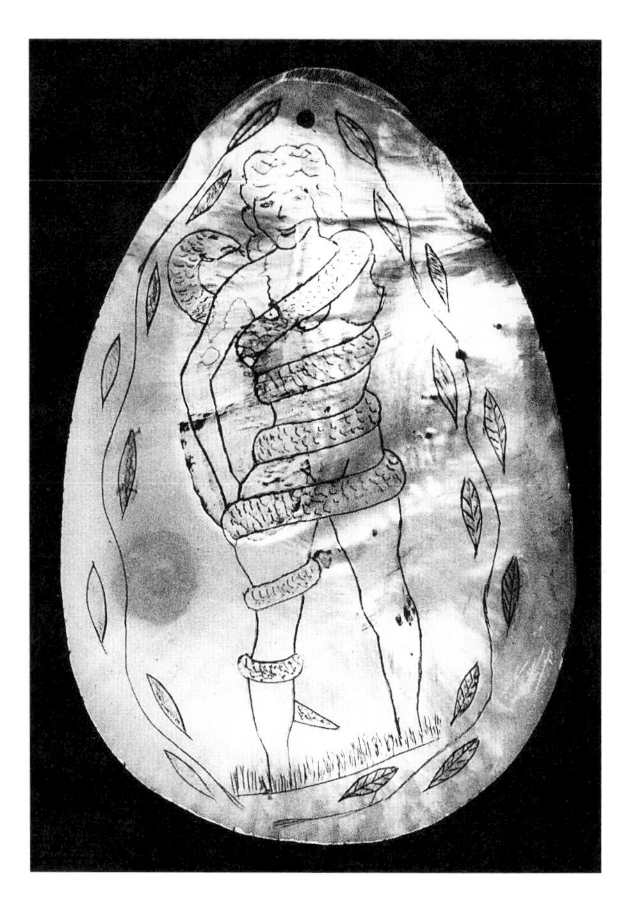

FIG. 69
Woman Entwined by a Snake, ca. 1978. Lickie Nollier, Western Australia. Incised pearl shell, L. 15.5 cm.

FIG. 70
Children's Python at Tilpakan, ca. 1980. Turkey Tolsen Jupurrurla, Papunya, Central Australia. Acrylic on board, 51 × 40 cm.

FIG. 71
Mother, Daughter, and Snake, 1948.
Artist unknown, Western Arnhem Land.
Ochre on bark, 47.5 × 82.5 cm.

on themselves (Figs. 64, 67).[26] This permits a large-scale representation of the entire creature on a bark's limited rectangular field. In the Dreaming stories of Western Arnhem Land and in other parts of Australia, the Serpent is frequently found eating and later disgorging human or other beings.[27] Correspondingly, in Aboriginal art the snake motif frequently encompasses—either by encircling or by engorging—human figures, often those of women (Figs. 68–69; also see Fig. 70). The snake as a key symbol of sexual danger is also typified by Fig. 71. The myth behind this painting is as follows:

> The Snake Man Yirrbardbard found a hollow log which he wanted for a drone tube to play in ceremonies, but it was too unwieldy so he left it behind. He then visited a woman who was promised to him as a wife, but she refused him, as he had a barbed penis. In an act of revenge, he transformed himself into a serpent and crawled into the hollow log. The woman and her mother saw snake tracks entering the log and tried to get the snake out, poking it with a stick. Yirrbardbard then bit the daughter on the hand, and she died. The painting depicts the phase of the story in which the women try to capture the snake, at a site near a rocky hill at Wurrakak in whose caves Yirrbardbard used to live.[28]

In snake pictures such as these we see a collaboration of materials, methods, and mythic psychology to produce a startlingly memorable and energetic range of related images. Symbolisms of this type tend to communicate well across cultures because, among their many possible levels of meaning, they render visible something that is emotionally recognizable to most of us.[29] Symbolisms of engorgement and genital sexuality communicate to us on an elementary, visceral level. But the artist's compression of such images, while it consists of a reduction, usually does not *simplify* them, even though it may move them closer to the "abbreviation" of child art and further from the "realism" of the anatomy of kangaroos, or closer to the geometry of the

spiral and further from the relative disorder of the uncoiled snake. In such cases of reduction, loss is gain: intensity is added to the work's morphology of feeling, like the coiling of a spring.

Subject Matter It is sometimes the case that the subject matter of an Aboriginal work is familiar but considered inappropriate for general public viewing by conventional standards of taste in some other culture. This, then, can be the obstacle of moral disapproval, or at least distaste.

Erotic subjects are common in many art traditions, but a significant portion of what scholars would normally include in this category in Aboriginal art emphasizes a very genital kind of sexuality that many outsiders would mistakenly associate with graffiti (Figs. 72–74). By definition, graffiti are customarily considered illegitimate, oppressive, or at least dissentient. They reflect protest, hate, or the defiance of moral taboos; they are largely the products of "non-artists"; and erotic graffiti are supposed to degrade rather than to elevate, the very opposite of a traditionalist's view of what art is about. But it is difficult to maintain this typically Western distinction between graffiti and art.[30] Aboriginal erotic images derive from an entirely different tradition and are most likely to have been performed as acts of sexual magic or as expositions of mythic themes, not as "dirty pictures." In fact, some of the standard motifs of Western graffiti are generally absent from Aboriginal material culture.[31]

A more serious obstacle to their wider appreciation is the extreme particularism of Aboriginal art works. This is not to say that a painting of a woman or a lagoon, for example, may not be recognizable as such across cultures. But the Aboriginal work will generally refer to a *particular* mythical woman or a *specific* lagoon, each of which is connected in a significant way with the artist. Idealized, imaginary, or merely anonymous subjects may typically dominate in other traditions, but not in the Aboriginal.[32]

On the other hand, images of totemic species are not portraits of particular birds, snakes, or tubers, but representations of their spiritual essence: the painting of a totemic kangaroo is not a "kangaroo," for example, but "Kangaroo" or "Kangaroo Dreaming" (albeit one who traveled only to certain sites in Kangaroo country).

Worldview and Belief Another obstacle to the non-Aboriginal response to Aboriginal works can be described as a basic ontological gap, a difference of underlying worldviews. Traditional Aboriginal thought is not progressivist. Things will always be the same. The proper life is one lived under what Stanner describes as a "mood of assent," an assent to the terms of an existence in which there is felt to be "a necessary connection between life and suffering."[33] This is neither pessimism nor fatalism. The Law is the same forever, and the Dreaming is outside of birth and death; but in one's spiritual dimension one also *is* the Dreaming, so it is not remote. But the

Dreaming, unlike some other pantheons, is not made up of personifications of moral, spiritual, or aesthetic qualities. Dreamings are never idealizations. They are not worshiped or prayed to, and there is no overt form of sacrifice. Correspondingly, the images of Aboriginal art are not personifications, idealizations, or idols. Nor are paintings and sculptures of Dreamings allegorical.

In much of the world's art and thought, mythical persons have served as emblems of moral states, natural phenomena, and bodies of knowledge and feeling. Many of these mythical beings are idealizations. Northern Europe had its gods of Fertility, Peace, Plenty, Battle, Thunder, and Death. Mediaeval and Renaissance Christian art had its personifications of Faith, Hope, and Charity, of the Seven Deadly Sins, the Seven Virtues, and even the Seven Liberal Arts.[34] Many find it tempting, therefore, to apply this model to Aboriginal art.

FACING PAGE

FIG. 72 / CAT. 6
Copulating Couple, ca. 1877. Artist unknown, Western Arnhem Land. Ochre on bark, 50 × 13 cm.

73

FIG. 73
Copulating Couple, rock art, Western Arnhem Land.

74

FIG. 74
Love-making, 1981. Trevor Nickolls, Sydney. Oil on canvas. Destroyed by the artist in 1985.

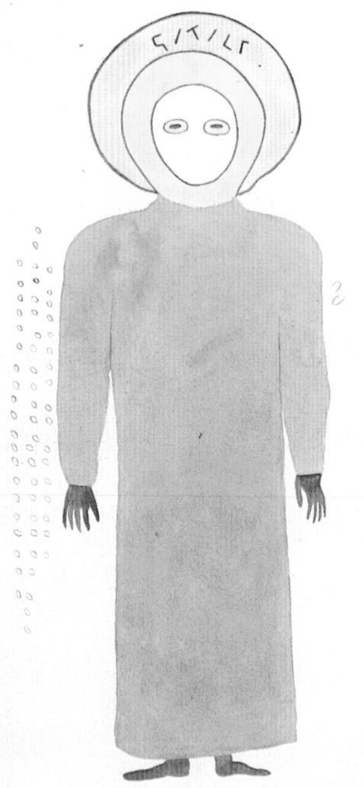

FIG. 75
Clothed Figure, ca. 1888. G. T. Pank, Jr., after George Grey. Watercolor on paper, 102 × 67.5 cm.

FIG. 76
Wandjina Man with Long Neck, 1953. Karuwara, Derby, Western Australia. Crayon on paper, 54.2 × 35.5 cm.

One might be struck, for example, by a superficial similarity between the mythic meaning of the Nordic god Thor and the representations of Wandjina in the Kimberley region (Figs. 75–76), the Lightning Brothers of Delamere in the Northern Territory, Nagorgo of the Katherine region, Namarrkon of Western Arnhem Land (Figs. 58, 77, 92, 119), and the rain-making spirits Wuluwaid and Bunbulama of North East Arnhem Land.[35] They all have to do with thunder and lightning, and all noticeably have elongated forms protruding from their heads or headgear, or halo-like arcs around their heads. But they come from different casts of mythic characters and play entirely different roles in very remote religious and social systems.

Aboriginal people, at least those of a conservative religious persuasion, do not think of their Dreaming Stories as myths, in the sense of traditional stories that are literally fanciful but that survive because they have some kind of moral, aesthetic, or sentimental value. They consider them to be accounts of important facts about the world. They are true history.

In some other traditions, mythic characters are often openly conceived as inventions representing some quality, political group, or state of being. In Aboriginal thought, mythic figures are not so much representatives as they are manifestations. They are not considered to be the artifices of human storytellers. Similarly, the landscape features formed out of the acts, or even the body parts or exuviae, of the mythic beings are not seen in Aboriginal tradition to be literary metaphors or symbols of Dreamings. They are their transformations.[36] Thus, just as images of places are landscapes of landscapes (see Chapter I), so images of people are portraits of portraits. Mythic people, and artists, are manifestations of Dreamings.[37] Aboriginal religious art, to take this analysis one step further, is itself often regarded by its makers more as manifestation than as mere representation. A painted design or sculpted form may therefore be considered not merely a human being's depiction of an ancestral Crocodile (or Kangaroo or Woman), but an instance of that Dreaming's manifestation in the world. This is why pictures and carved figures can make people sick, give them strength, or cause accidents to happen—or so many Aboriginal people believe.

Here lies yet another obstacle to the wider appreciation of Aboriginal art: the barrier of belief. While Aboriginal people may believe in the reality of the Dreamings, the spirits, and the monsters represented in their art, most others do not.

What, then, would make a difference to our responses to Aboriginal art? Knowing more facts about Aboriginal culture can help, especially if works are to be understood in their social, political, and economic contexts and if their literal level of meaning is to make sense. But this sort of knowledge, while hardly common as yet, can be much overrated: it does not guarantee a rich grasp of the art. The meaning of a symbol such as a circle or a depiction of a snake is not simply the object it represents; it is also what the object itself stands for. The circle may represent a water hole, but the water hole is also a powerful symbol of life, a home destination, and frequently the focus of mythically significant events.[38] The snake may be a water python, but because of that it may also be a symbol of life-giving water, an engorging mother, and a penis.

Simply knowing which objects in the world are denoted by which symbols certainly adds to the surface intelligibility of a painting, sculpture, or sand design. It also enables one to see how a myth and its pictorial representation are structurally related. Frequently, though, this is the only level at which any explanation of Aboriginal art objects is offered in exhibitions and publications. Aboriginal artists themselves usually do not go very far beyond this representational aspect when talking about their work. This is partly because of religious restrictions on divulging knowledge and partly because a verbally detailed, explicit, and analytical style of education is foreign to Aboriginal tradition. Sacred understanding largely comes from seeing, and particularly from seeing performances and the execution of designs, together with listening to the often cryptic glosses offered by elders at such events.

FIG. 77 / CAT. 20
Lightning Figure, 1986. John Mowandjul, Western Arnhem Land. Ochre and charcoal on bark, 65.5 × 39.5 cm.

Iconic Meaning in Bark Paintings

In this section we dwell in some detail on the story elements represented in particular works of Aboriginal art, but we also look at the relation between those representations and their less literal, more purely visual significance. Our discussion focuses on examples of North Australian paintings, moving from west to east along the coast, beginning at Melville Island.

FIG. 78 / CAT. 5
The Death of Purrukuparli, 1954.
Marruwani, Melville Island.
Ochre on bark, 89 × 24 cm.

FIG. 78a
1. Whirlpool
2. Purrukuparli
3. Purrukuparli's footprints
4. Purrukuparli's arms, holding his dead son
5. Tjinini's body
6. Thaparra, the Moon, asking for Tjinini's body
7. The Moon in the sky
8. Plain throwing stick
9. Forked throwing stick
10. Thaparra's fireplace
11. Thaparra's firestick
12. Thaparra's campfire
13. Purrukuparli's cockatoo-feather head ornament
14. Purrukuparli's firesticks
15. Purrukuparli's water hole
16. Purrukuparli's campfire
17. Purrukuparli's cane armlets
18. Purrukuparli's goose-feather balls

The Death of Purrukuparli (Fig. 78) In 1954 the ethnologist and collector C. P. Mountford visited Milikapiti on Melville Island and while there commissioned Tiwi artist Marruwani to paint a group of bark paintings. One of Marruwani's paintings concerned the Death of Purrukuparli, today the best-remembered traditional story at Milikapiti.

In the version of the story recorded by Mountford,[39] Purrukuparli lived with his wife Pima and baby son Tjinini on Melville Island, at a place called Impanari. Purrukuparli was strongly attached to his son. When Pima was away food-gathering during the day, she would leave Tjinini in the shade of a tree and go to meet her lover Thaparra. One hot day, Pima returned late to find that the shade had moved with the passage of time and that her baby had died of exposure to the intense heat. Purrukuparli, enraged and grief-stricken, beat his wife. He then engaged Thaparra in a fight, and both were badly wounded with throwing sticks. Thaparra asked for the body of Tjinini, promising to bring it back to life in three days. Purrukuparli refused, picked up his son's body, which was wrapped in paperbark, and walked backwards with it into the sea, never to return. His footprints still remain visible on the ground. At the spot where he drowned, there appeared a whirlpool, which has continued to be a sign of danger to any visitors there. When Thaparra saw what had happened, he transformed himself into the Moon, who dies for three days each month and whose face bears the scars of his fight with Purrukuparli. All these main elements in the story are represented by motifs in the painting (Fig. 78a).

This work is partly figurative, but not at all illusionistic in approach. The dominant element is a muscular and balanced construction in the upper half, outlined in yellow and white. Unlike the other motifs, which are simpler and marked off in either yellow and red or yellow and white, it contains a complex of semantic elements (the whirlpool, Purrukuparli, Purrukuparli's footprints, the body of the child). Our attention is drawn to this section for three reasons: it is the most massive in form; it contains the most references; and it is the one heaviest with emotion. These interlacing meanings gain from each other, and they demonstrate the poverty of a purely visual or a purely myth-oriented approach to significance in this kind of art.

Mimi Spirits (Fig. 79) This painting by the famous Western Arnhem Land painter Yirawala features three main figures: two women and their husband, all of whom are ancestral Mimi spirits. The women are shown dancing after having given birth. The stirruplike appendages hanging from the hips (and one elbow) of the figures are bags in which the Mimis carry the children. The central female figure has a "power bag" protruding from one shoulder, and the man on her right has feathers protruding from his knees and ankles as he sings with the women. These figures are said to be "close to the source of all life—and death."[40]

Yirawala's painting exemplifies those qualities now considered characteristic of Aboriginal art: in the words of Daniel Thomas, "extreme delicacy,

FIG. 79 / CAT. 18
Mimi Spirits, ca. 1970. Yirawala, Western Arnhem Land. Ochre on bark, 90 × 48 cm.

FIG. 79a

1. Female Mimi spirits
2. Male Mimi spirit
3. Power bag
4. Bags for carrying babies
5. Feathers

refinement, and gentleness."[41] Mimi spirits are supposed to be very thin—they live in the cracks of rocks. Here, even their hair is shown as a series of fine parallel lines, a common feature of art in Western Arnhem Land. The feathers at the man's joints are a comb of hairlines, only a little finer than his toes and fingers. The heads of all the figures are small, tapering, and lit by gaping mouths in profile. A white background—more usual in the Kimberley region, but common in Yirawala's work—gives the whole image a certain airiness. The cross-hatching on the torsos and thighs, a sign of a particularly sacred element, is straight, fine, and symmetrical.[42] The women have tiny breasts shown in profile beneath each arm. The man's gender is marked by an absence of breasts. (Fig. 79a.)

It was these gracile qualities, perhaps more than any other factor, that in the 1960s and 1970s brought Yirawala recognition as the most famous Aboriginal artist since Albert Namatjira (Figs. 245, 247).

FIG. 80 / CAT. 25
Sacred Places at Milmindjarr', 1982.
David Malangi, Central Arnhem Land.
Ochre on bark, 107 × 79 cm.

Sacred Places at Milmindjarr' (Fig. 80) Purchased in 1982 by the South Australian Museum, this work arrived from Ramingining, Central Arnhem Land, with little documentation. In July 1987 we interviewed the artist David Malangi about the painting. It is a partial representation of the mythic geography of his own clan country in the area of Ramingining. The symmetry of the Malangi bark painting is no mere decorative device; it has religious, political, and social connotations. The story concerns the travels of the founding ancestral figures known over much of Arnhem Land as the Djan'kawu Sisters. As they traveled from place to place, paddling their canoe and walking overland, they created the clans (landowning groups) and their languages, naming natural phenomena and creating spring waters by plunging their digging sticks into the ground. In Manharrngu clan country they created the well Milmindjarr' and had a ceremony there. They were looking for fish, and caught a small Catfish, which is represented in the painting. They gave birth to the peoples of the area. The tide swells, rising up the river's course, which is entered by fish. Later, the tide will turn, and water and fish will be borne out into the sea.[43]

Elements from only a few episodes of this story are shown in the painting (Fig. 80a). When we asked Malangi about the significance of motif 7, his reply was, "I know. You don't know." The line of secrecy is constantly being drawn in such contexts.

Non-Aboriginal people respond in at least two very different ways to this style of painting: some see it as suitably refined, others as verging on slickness. It is true that in comparison with other Aboriginal art styles, the Malangi painting is executed with more finesse and employs stronger contrasts in color. The same can be said of bark paintings from North East Arnhem Land, especially those done since the 1960s.

FIG. 80a

1. Seawater and tidal stream. The coast opposite Milingimbi is at the bottom, and the tides rise up the river in the center of the painting. The river is all Dhaamala.
2. Garangala Island, David Malangi's country, south of Murrunggwa
3. Milmindjarr', the well
4. The "waterlily" called *ragi* (spikerush, *Eleocharis dulcis*)
5. Spikerush corms, with skin removed
6. Black and white leaves of the spikerush
7. David Malangi's Dreaming
8. White, yellow, and red ochre in regular alternation
9. Catfish Dreaming (Djikkarla)
10. Liver of Catfish
11. "Paint to make him pretty" (Malangi)
12. (Meanings secret)
13. "Little rivers"

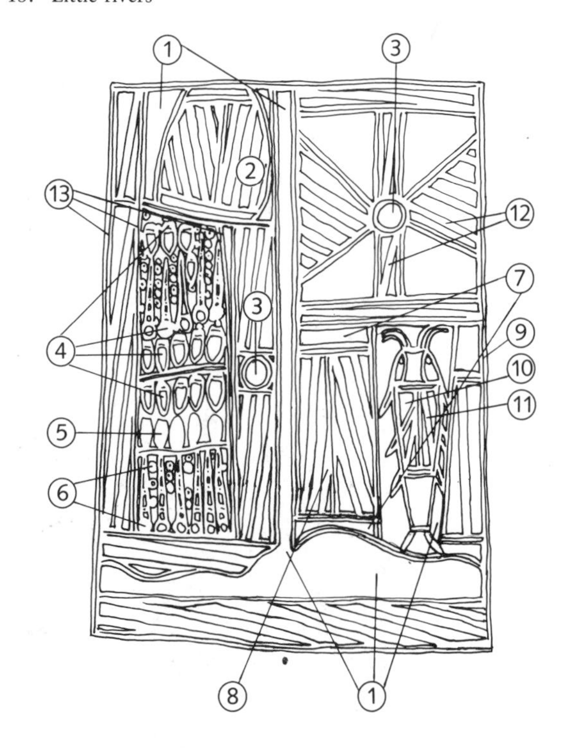

FIG. 81 / CAT. 29
Squid and Turtle Dreamings, 1972.
Liwukang Bukurlatjpi, North East Arnhem Land. Ochre on bark, 92 × 52 cm.

FIG. 81a

1. Male Squid
2. Female Squid
3. Night
4. Sunset
5. Sunrise
6. Midday
7. Female Turtle

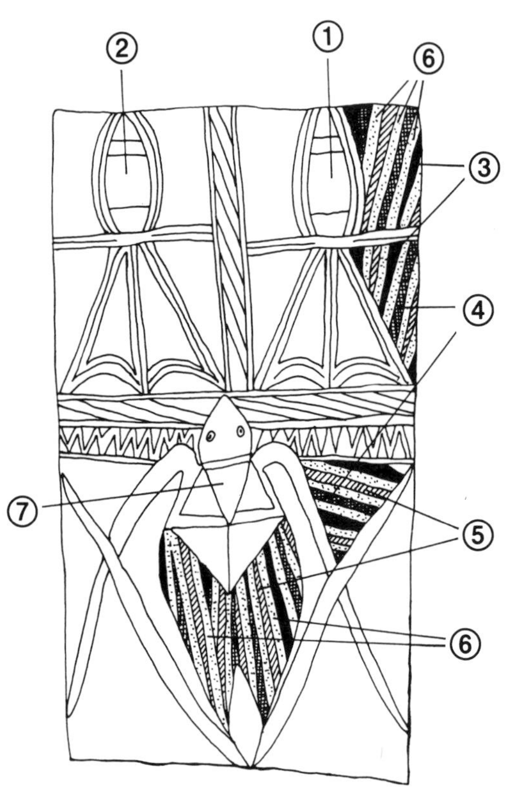

Squid and Turtle Dreamings (Fig. 81) Liwukang Bukurlatjpi (Fig. 82), usually known as Liwukang, painted this work at Galiwinku, North East Arnhem Land, in 1972. It concerns the landscape history of the Wessell Islands area. On the left is the female Squid, who created all the families and places along the Wessell Islands chain. She is still present there in the form of a rock formation at the island of Djidinja, where the black mark of the Squid's ink can be seen flowing from land to sea. The black paint on the Squid represents this ink. The male Squid, on the right, allocated the places created by the female Squid to estates owned by different Aboriginal clans, the same clans that exist today. Going south along the chain, he handed named sacred places over to each of about eleven clans.[44]

FIG. 82
Liwukang Bukurlatjpi, Yirrkala, North East Arnhem Land, 1987.

This Squid is locally known as a healer. In the early 1970s, during a meeting of members of the Australian Institute of Aboriginal Studies in Canberra, an Aboriginal man from Cape York Peninsula, believing that he had been a victim of sorcery, hallucinated while at the home of the Institute's Principal, Peter Ucko. Another visiting member, a senior Aboriginal man from Arnhem Land with strong Wessell Islands connections, asked the Principal for squid. Miraculously, a tin of squid was produced from the larder, and the Arnhem Land man applied the squid, with the suction rings on his fingers, to the Cape York visitor's torso, singing appropriate songs. The hallucinations eventually subsided, some time after the event.[45]

The bands of cross-hatching next to the male Squid and on the Turtle's carapace contain the color sequence black, red, yellow, and white. These represent night, sunset, sunrise, and still water at midday, respectively. The Squid, as Liwukang explained during our consultations at Yirrkala in 1987, transformed itself into Turtle. This Turtle is associated with the relationship between weather and the relative safety of sea travel. Once a year she travels underwater north along the Wessell Islands chain. When she comes up to the water's surface, she exhales air which turns into clouds, and these clouds are a sign that the sea is smooth, the weather is calm, and the fishing is plentiful. (Fig. 81a.)

Some non-Aboriginal people find this style appealingly intricate, an attractive feat of skill. Others find it too regular and symmetrical, not sufficiently sensuous, overloaded with contrasts of intensity, and spatially overcrowded. The cross-hatching is especially important to the Arnhem Landers' response to this kind of work. A key visual element in their aesthetic is that of shimmering brilliance—the kind of effect achieved through cross-hatching and one indicative of ancestral power (see the discussion of the aesthetic system of the Yolngu in Chapter III).

The Kestrels (Fig. 83) Manggangina Wurramara, known in English as Big Macka, painted this work in 1948 at Umbakumba, Groote Eylandt, for Mountford, who was collecting artifacts there.[46] The Kestrel is shown at Yibilyubilyumanja with his chicks, who were hatched there. He was at first a man, camping at the sacred place Aringkari on Bickerton Island. Then he

FIG. 83 / CAT. 33
The Kestrels, 1948. Manggangina Wurramara, Groote Eylandt. Ochre and manganese on bark, 68.5 × 33 cm.

met the serpent Alja (Rainbow) at Mungwujirra, and Angwala the Crab (Fig. 95). After a further camp, which left permanent stains on the cliffs at Uralili Bay, he and his family were transformed into birds. The nest where their chicks were hatched is now a water hole in the middle of a large depression. Similar and further camps left other natural features, until Yinikarrka (Kestrel) and his wife and one chick came to rest, each in one of three caves on the eastern coast of Groote Eylandt. A previously unpublished sketch map by Mountford (Fig. 84) records some of the geographical elements in this story.[47]

Non-Aboriginal people usually respond more positively to this earlier Groote Eylandt style, with its black backgrounds and isolated figures, than to more recent barks from the same island. The oldest bark paintings from Groote Eylandt, mainly collected in the period between 1922 and the 1930s, have isolated figures, but their plain grounds are mostly either unpainted bark or red-ochred open areas. In Groote Eylandt paintings of the middle period, the 1940s and 1950s, black backgrounds appear to dominate. Especially since the 1960s, Groote Eylandt artists have tended to fill the picture field with motifs and with dashed or hatched lines in the ochre color range. The earlier styles, exemplified here in Figs. 57, 95, and Cat. 35, are especially appealing to non-Aborigines because of the sensation of floating, weightless motion conveyed by figures that generally show only formal indications of motion, if any at all.

Black Bream (Fig. 85) This apparently simple painting on the lid of a biscuit box from Port Melbourne has no known painter. It was one of fifteen similar paintings bought from Mounted Constable Stott by the South Australian Museum in 1910. (For another example of a work from the Stott collection, see Fig. 86.) It was probably painted in 1909, an early date for any Aboriginal portable art. In 1987 John Bradley of the Aboriginal Sacred Sites Authority in Darwin interviewed knowledgeable Borroloola (Northern Territory) people and provided the following details about the subject of the painting.[48]

The fish was identified as Black Bream, known in the local language Yanyuwa as *a-Mayin* or *a-Marrinda*. It also carries the further title *a-Wuyurrangka*, which is its power name (ceremonial name). Black Bream is a major Ancestral Being for members of the Wuyaliya semimoiety and particularly for members of the patriline associated with South West Island. At the northwestern tip of this island, at a site called Rruwarrabarrarala, is a large rock that represents this ancestral Bream. In the Borroloola region the Black Bream is a feature of a major ceremony known as Wambuyangu, which is secret (restricted mainly to initiates) and which is the equivalent of the Yabudurruwa of the Roper-Bamyili area.[49]

With these details in mind, it should be impossible to view this painting as simply a picture of a fish, even though one cannot be absolutely certain that the interpretation is the same one the painter would have given to the work in 1909. Our knowledge of even these few attributed meanings beyond the marks before us usually colors our perceptions.[50]

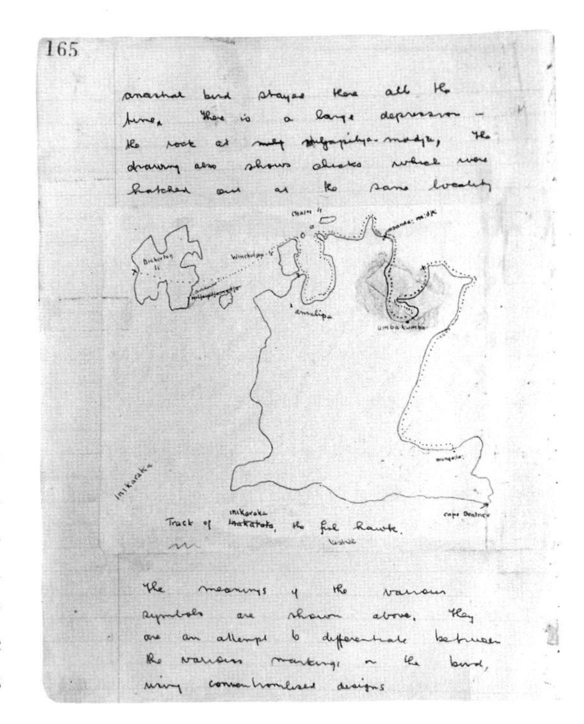

FIG. 84
Sketch map of sites in the Kestrels Story, 1948. C. P. Mountford, Groote Eylandt, 13 × 16 cm.

Styles in Bark Painting

To return to our theme: Does it help one's appreciation of Aboriginal art to know the basis of the different regional styles of the art work? Here we offer some reasons why this knowledge is useful, using bark paintings as an example. Styles in bark painting vary not only geographically but also from group to group, from person to person, and from period to period within each geographical area. Being able to identify where an image belongs enriches our grasp of the image itself. This is partly because such knowledge places that image into a set of tensions, contradictions, and reverberations with and direct reminders of others that are like it, and yet unlike it.

A musical note has little meaning in and of itself. It gains its meaning in large part by entering into relations of consonance, dissonance, and mathematical relatedness with other notes.[51] The intensity with which an image speaks to us is not merely a result of the sheer volume, brightness, or regularity of its own contents. It arises from variations in related volumes, brightnesses, and regularities and irregularities, and from the tensions that exist between these related forms. Such tensions may be between lines in a hatched area; between segments of hatching or human figures on a single ground; between a series of works by a single maker or a group over time or between those of a set of communities or regions. Knowledge of variation in art is more than a consciousness of propositions about historical or stylistic

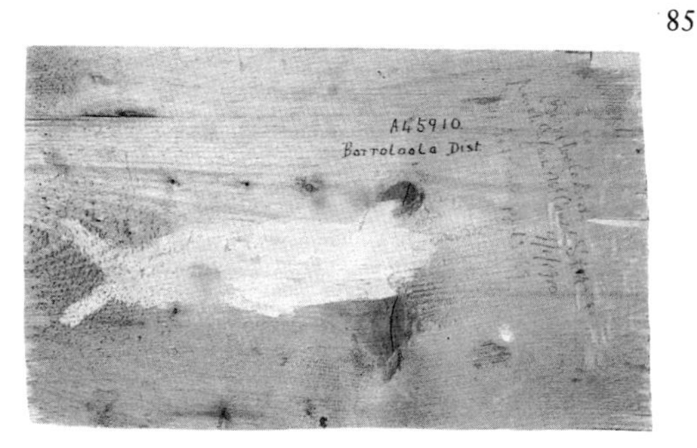

85

FIG. 85 / CAT. 37
Black Bream, ca. 1909. Artist unknown, Borroloola, Northern Territory. Ochre on wood, 23 × 38.5 cm.

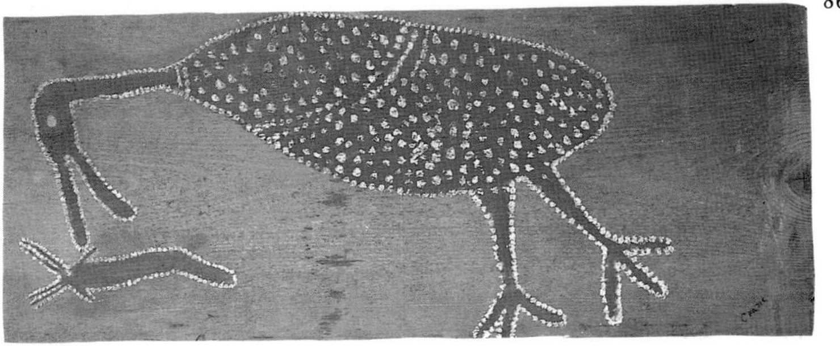

86

FIG. 86 / CAT. 36
Crane and Freshwater Shrimp, ca. 1909. Artist unknown, Borroloola, Northern Territory. Ochre on wood, 24 × 60 cm.

facts; such knowledge informs and affects our aesthetic response to each new image.[52]

The main stylistic regions for bark painting are usually identified as (proceeding west to east) the Kimberley, Port Keats,[53] Melville and Bathurst Islands, Western Arnhem Land, Central Arnhem Land, North East Arnhem Land, Groote Eylandt, and Mornington Island. In the late 1980s the boom in Aboriginal art production led to Aboriginal paintings on bark being produced in places as far afield as Aurukun and Mount Mulligan (Cape York Peninsula), southern Queensland, and even the Lower Murray River. The Cape York barks are usually in the style of Mornington Island, and southern and urban barks tend to copy Arnhem Land styles. A precise study of what constitutes these regional styles and of how they relate to each other has yet to appear.

If regional styles have usually had cavalier treatment in the literature on Aboriginal art, writers have been even more reluctant to say what it is about an individual Aboriginal artist's work that distinguishes it from that of others (even though it is clear that these authors have preferences based on such differences).[54] To explore this problem of visual quality in Aboriginal art, we now return to the subject of the Aboriginal aesthetic and to the relationship between the particular visual character of Aboriginal paintings and our responses to them.

The Morphology of Feeling III

PETER SUTTON

IN THIS chapter we explore the basis of the morphological meaning of Aboriginal art—that is, its visual logic and the way forms come together to create the look of the art. The look becomes more richly readable the more one is familiar with how it is composed and what range of variations it entails. Thus we are concerned here mainly with the role of form and composition in creating visual effects and aesthetic responses, but we necessarily also touch on the relationship between the morphological meaning and the literal or referential meaning the art offers. (This second aspect of meaning is dealt with in more detail in Chapters II and IV.) By way of example, we focus on the toa sculptures of the Lake Eyre region, images of the body in Arnhem Land bark paintings, and composition in Western Desert acrylic paintings.

Aboriginal Aesthetics

> The celebrants of Murinbata rites arrange themselves in spatial patterns. These have a geometric idiom—arcs, circles or ovals, points and straight and curved lines. Each rite exhibits a somewhat different combination of the same elements. The compositions give an austere beauty to the inactive phases and an excited vitalism to the active phases. In both they are impressive essays in dynamic symmetry and asymmetry.[1]

These remarks about the ceremonies of Port Keats Aborigines in the period 1934–58 by W. E. H. Stanner come to the heart of the matter: ceremony is the key locus of Aboriginal classic art; the renewed recombination of a limited number of elements lies behind the austere economy and the consistency of the art; and a tension between symmetry and asymmetry is a central force in its aesthetic (Figs. 87–88).

This aesthetic, so clearly expressed in the idiom of sacred performance and visual art, permeates Aboriginal daily life. Again, Stanner wrote:

FIG. 87
Sites in Murinbata Country, 1959.
Pandak, Port Keats, Northern Territory.
Ochre on masonite, 89 × 156 cm.

> I have no direct testimony by the aborigines to cite as evidence that they wittingly imitate environmental things in their ritual use of geometric shapes, but the indirect evidence of intellectual and aesthetic influence is not unimpressive. (a) They are acute observers of their natural scene and little in it escapes notice, particularly the presence of shapely visual form or pattern. Anything that is symmetrically patterned attracts notice, and the same is true of marked asymmetry. (b) The word *dirmu* [*dirrmu*][2] is applied to a wide range of phenomena: to (i) bodily decorations in dances and mimes, (ii) ancient cave-paintings, and (iii) the spiral, concentric and radial whorls of shells, the segmentation of honeycomb, the divisions of spider-webs, the crystals of rock-minerals, the colour-markings of birds, the skin-patterns of reptiles. (c) The usages of the word *dirmu* make it clear that it denotes visual form or pattern, and that it implies (i) the consequences of intent or purpose and (ii) the handiwork of beings, or the outcome of events, significant for man. The conception of non-intentional form or pattern seems foreign to the mentality. (d) The elements of *dirmu* are geometric shapes and it is to the totality of outward form or appearance resulting from a complex of such elements that the word *nginipun* [shape] is applied. . . . My hypothesis is that the geometric forms enter the general system of symbolism as *conventional signs*. Their significance, which is always one of a completed and final action, is a kind of command for an exemplifying action by living men as the appropriate response.[3]

Apart from passages that resemble this in their generality, even though few can match Stanner's depth and eloquence, the literature on Aboriginal art offers amazingly little on Aboriginal aesthetic systems. The only substantial essay in this field is by Howard Morphy,[4] who gives an account of the aesthetic system of bark painters in North East Arnhem Land, where the people are known as the Yolngu (Figs. 12, 15, 81, 116, and Cat. 27–28). His points can be summarized as follows:

Yolngu talk about the qualities of paintings in ways that overlap with the ways Europeans do, but their emphasis is very different.

Yolngu are unlikely to say of a painting that it is beautiful or well balanced, for example. Aesthetic values are spoken of, but not as a reason for painting pictures.

Yolngu do not discuss aesthetic quality along an axis of Beauty versus Ugliness, or of Harmony versus Dissonance. The key axis of their qualitative visual response is one of power—Ancestral Power, Dreaming Power.[5]

Some people are recognized by their local peers as better painters than others. The basis of this recognition is skill.[6]

Creativity is not openly valued—in fact, it is explicitly denied a role in painting. Clan designs were created by clan ancestors, the Dreamings, not by people. People reproduce them.

Yolngu designs are said to contain spiritual power. They are traditionally produced as elements of ceremonies in which clan members reassert their claims to the land figured in the designs and get in touch with spiritual power.

According to Morphy, the main objectives of a Yolngu artist are to produce a correct design; to produce an ancestrally powerful design; and to produce a painting that enhances the object on which it is painted. (One should add here that Yolngu artists frequently paint in order to obtain money, to fulfill ritual obligations and opportunities, and to further their careers in the cultural and political dynamic of local Yolngu and wider Australian society. The three motivations listed by Morphy assume that a decision to paint has already been taken on various grounds such as these.) The third objective—enhancement of the object—is mainly achieved by transforming the original dull and rough outline design into a clearly defined, delicately executed, and bright or shimmering state through the use of cross-hatching (for example, Fig. 81). We would add that it is not the sheer intensity of brightness or tone that appears to count, so much as the variations in intensity produced by formal consonance, dissonance, and relatedness across the hatched sections. As in the case of the dotted sections of Western Desert acrylics, the rhythmic structure produced by sections of cross-hatching offers complex tensions and their resolution.[7] "It is the quality of *brilliance* that is associated in Yolngu art with ancestral power and with beauty."[8] The brilliance, the Yolngu say, makes the gut (the seat of the emotions) go happy. Brilliance is a percept based on variation.

The narrative content of such an Aboriginal painting interacts with its visual devices to produce a combined effect, so it is not easy to distinguish responses one might have to the metaphoric symbols of a work from one's responses to the visual effects of devices such as cross-hatching, outlining and size of figures, range of color values, or relations between figures and their contexts. Both kinds of response can be evaluated along a single axis of Power, in Aboriginal thought, just as both can be evaluated along a single axis of structural logic (balance, symmetry, contrapuntal harmony, perspective) in the mind and eye of any viewer.

FIG. 88
Totemic Site: Dreaming of Birds, Flying Foxes, and the Bat Relating to Kunmanngur, the Rainbow Snake, 1959. Kianoo Tjeemairee, Port Keats, Northern Territory. Ochre on bark, 50.8 × 32.4 cm.

FIG. 89
Toas signifying paired mythic features or two sites. Left to right: two tree stumps; two hills (mother and daughter); two sandhill spurs; unknown; a tree fork; and two notched well ladders, ca. 1904. Artists unknown, Lake Eyre region. Wood, gypsum, and ochre, H. from 2.3 to 5.3 cm.

But to know about someone else's aesthetic apparatus is not to share it. Aesthetic responses by members of different cultures may have much in common, but they are still very strongly molded by the culture one has grown up in. Many of us understandably resist the idea that aesthetic appreciation is something other than a basically private and intuitive experience. Yet a good deal of recent anthropological literature has demonstrated that most emotions are cultural constructions and can take quite different forms in different societies.[9]

Form and Feeling: The Toas of Lake Eyre

Sexually colored responses to images, for example, rest on a universal human basis, but they manifest themselves in a multitude of forms, depending on the culture. Yet it is the universal basis that makes it relatively easy for us to connect with the erotic art of another culture. Much Aboriginal art is intentionally erotic at some level or other.[10] The toas of Lake Eyre contain a good deal of implicit and explicit sexual symbolism and provide a suitable case study in this instance.

Toas are small carved, molded, and painted constructions of wood, gypsum, and ochre, often topped by embedded pieces of vegetation, feathers, bone, hair, or pieces of small artifacts (Fig. 238). Ostensibly "way-markers" left in abandoned Aboriginal camps, toas are also complex signs for the mythic geography and deeper mythic significance of the sites they refer to. (See Chapter VI for a further discussion of toas.) The toas' extraordinary visual appeal to a wide audience has ensured them a special place in Aboriginal art history, even if their representation as art has been a subject of vigorous debate.[11] Their unpredictability, their compact, dense imagery, and their grace of form are striking. One of the toas' commonest forms is that of the long wooden stem topped by a knob, often finished with with a spray of fiber. This basic combination is a phallic motif common in Aboriginal ceremonial sculptures such as the posts and headdresses of cult performances associated with reproduction and sexuality.[12]

The Aboriginal aesthetic—in the classical cultures, at least—is intensely social, as we have seen. Aboriginal phallicism, and Aboriginal vulva-or womb-centered imagery, is usually concerned as much with social and political reproduction as with sexual reproduction or personal sensuous pleasure.[13] In a traditional Aboriginal context, sexual affairs can almost never be kept secret, and they have community-wide implications: they can easily unbalance sets of balanced interests, unless the right family members approve. An emphasis on symmetry in this aesthetic tradition matches the profound strains of balanced dualism, reciprocity, and equality that underlie the intellectual framework of so many Aboriginal social institutions and their cultural emblems, especially those associated with marriage.

Symmetry and duality literally spring from the tops of many of the toas (Fig. 89). There is a series of two-pronged forks of various shapes and a series of double knobs or crossbars, some with different colored extremities.[14] Many of these forms suggest paired features of the human body such as the joining of limbs to trunk, and many refer literally to the dualisms of breasts, buttocks, testicles, eyes, and ears. These particular toas exemplify an Aboriginal emphasis on clear dualities in design, as well as a typically strong tendency toward symmetry about a vertical axis that is longer than the horizontal.

Some of the toas are circular in shape, and others bear painted circles or rounded shapes.[15] The circle, an almost universal motif in Aboriginal art, reflects the intimacy and egalitarian spatial symbolism of the arrangement of people around a single campfire—an image possessing logical, social, and aesthetic reverberations that are intermingled in this form, as we saw in Chapter I. The nonfigurative character of the circle makes it available for a vast number of referential meanings.[16] But most of those meanings are variations about a core shape or structure that suggests roundness, inclusion, enclosure, centrality, and unhierarchic order. This is a case where a single, recurring form helps constitute the distinctive look of a particular tradition (Figs. 35–44, 90–91). We return to the use of circles later in this chapter, where we look at composition in Western Desert acrylics.

FIG. 90 / CAT. 64
Two Men Dreaming at Kulunjarranya, 1984. Tommy Lowry Japaljarri, Kintore, Central Australia. Acrylic on canvas, 121.5 × 183 cm.

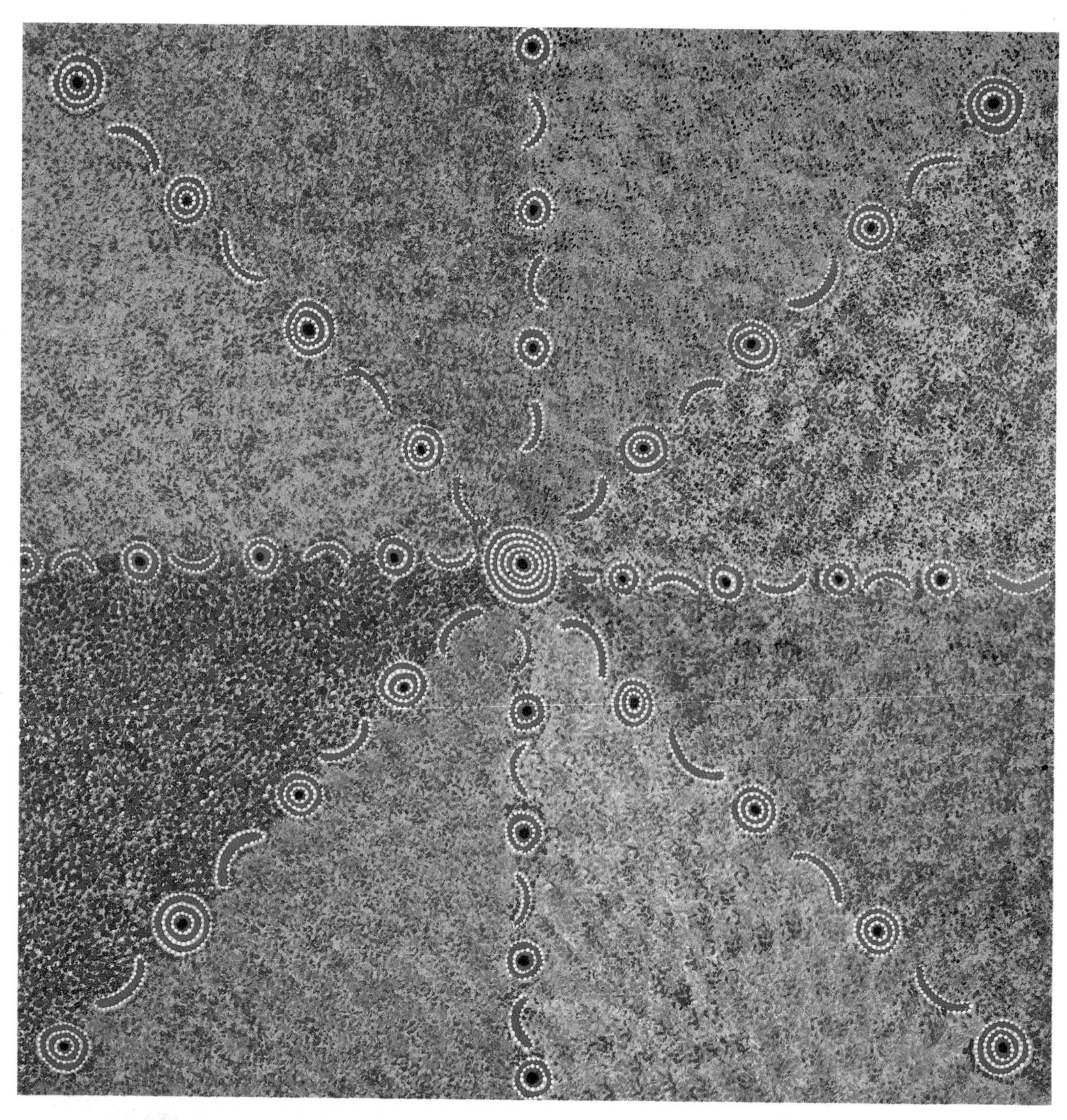

FIG. 91 / CAT. 65
Witchetty Grub Dreaming at Mt. Zeil, 1986. Theo Brown Jakamarra, Mbunghara, Central Australia. Acrylic on canvas, 122.5 × 122.5 cm.

Images of the Body: Arnhem Land Bark Paintings

The basic rule of orientation for all species in Arnhem Land art is to show the subject as if it were lying at rest and seen from above, from a point perpendicular to the midpoint of the body.[17] Species are typically depicted in Arnhem Land art (and in much two-dimensional Aboriginal art) in the following manner:

Mammals and *fish* are shown in profile. Mammals usually have all limbs shown (Fig. 93). Certain types of flattish bottom-feeders—notably, catfish, rays, and sharks—are shown dorsally (Fig. 80). Fruit bats are shown ventrally (Fig. 94).

Birds are shown in profile, wings folded (Figs. 15, 57, 83, 200).

Turtles, *tortoises*, *frogs*, and *crabs* are mostly shown dorsally and splayed (Figs. 12, 53, 95).

Reptiles are shown dorsally and splayed, if they have limbs (Figs. 52, 57, 120), with snakes normally depicted in either a meandering or a coiled position (Figs. 64, 71).

Echidnas are shown dorsally or in profile.

Woody-stemmed plants are generally shown in profile, but tubers or ground vines are depicted in plan view (the equivalent of dorsally and splayed for reptiles or for human hands and feet, Figs. 96–97).

Exceptions to these patterns do occur. A kangaroo, for example, may be shown vertically and splayed, especially if the narrative for the painting concerns a dead kangaroo that is being butchered (Fig. 98).

Because of the human body's physical structure, a frontal representation of it in a relaxed state, as if it were lying down, is bound to result in an image

FIG. 92 / CAT. 22
Female Lightning Figure, 1982. Djawida, Western Arnhem Land. Ochre on bark, 64 × 156.5 cm.

of considerable symmetry (Fig. 99). That is, taking the long axis as the dividing line, everything on one side of the middle line is roughly a mirror image of what is on the other side. This is virtually a guarantee of visual balance in the painted figure. It also offers the kind of completeness of representation that is often said to be a key characteristic of "primitive art" and child art. In other words, a conceptual approach not only aims for depiction of distinctive essentials but for completeness of representation. An illusionist approach may be more photo-realistic but necessarily shows less of what one knows is there.

The so-called imperfection and savageness of this kind of art, which Ruskin in the nineteenth century thought of as the basis of the very real vitality of both tribal art and child art,[18] is not the result of random acts or of

FIG. 93 / CAT. 12
Kangaroo with Young, period 1921–28.
Artist unknown, Western Arnhem Land.
Ochre on bark, 35 × 78 cm.

disordering. If anything, it is a result of *reordering*, or extreme subtraction of those elements that might lead to disorder, so that what at first appears to our senses as myriad visual impressions becomes a reasoned map of what we know, or think, is there.

In Aboriginal art, and in bark paintings in particular, frontal depictions of the human body are just such a reordering. In fact, "frontality" is too simple a description for this treatment of the subject: on closer examination of Figs. 97, 99, and 100, we see that the torso is shown from the chest side but that the feet and hands are shown as if viewed from above when soles and palms are flat on the ground. Men's genitals are shown in profile, often

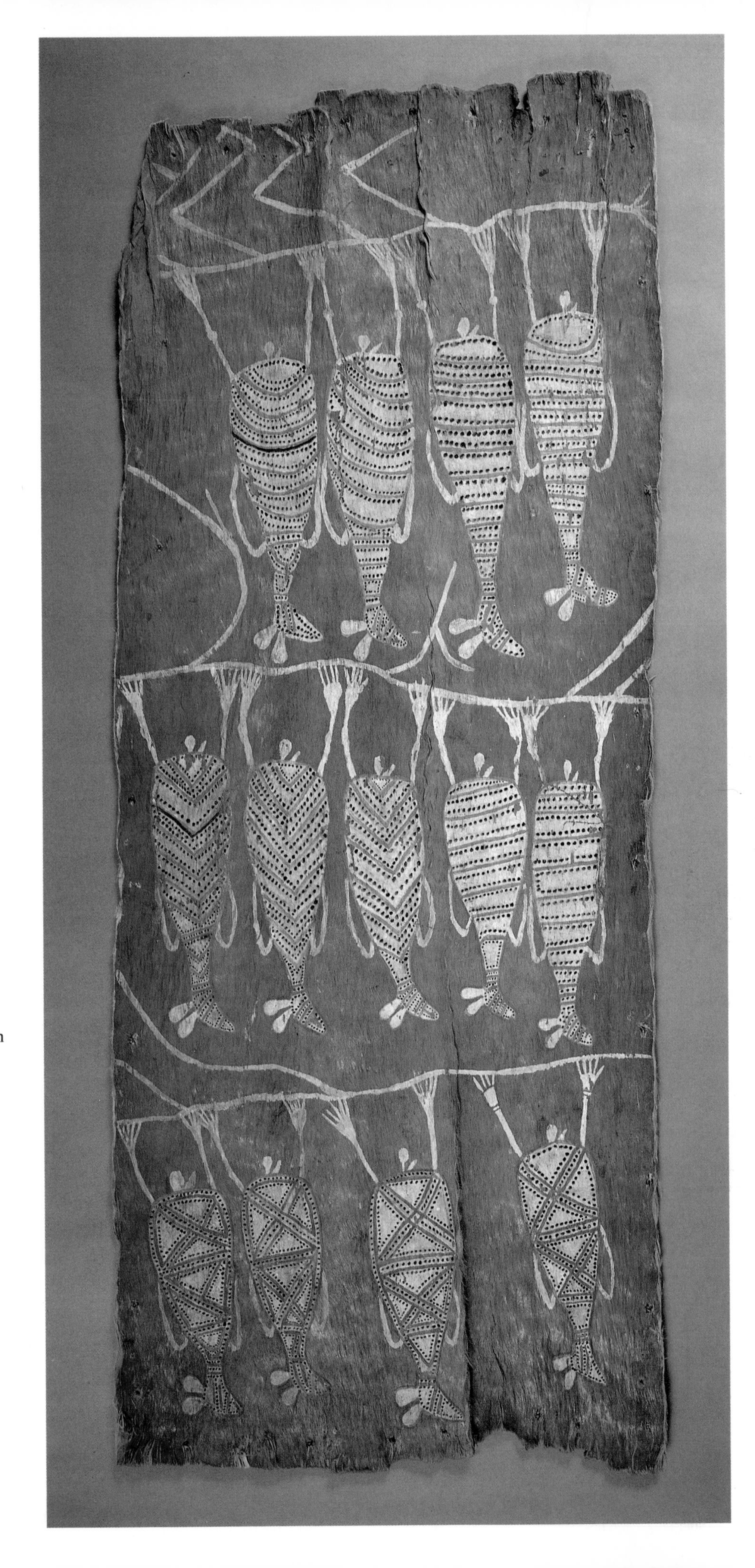

FIG. 94 / CAT. 11
Fruit Bats, period 1921–28. Artist unknown, Western Arnhem Land. Ochre on bark, 91 × 41 cm.

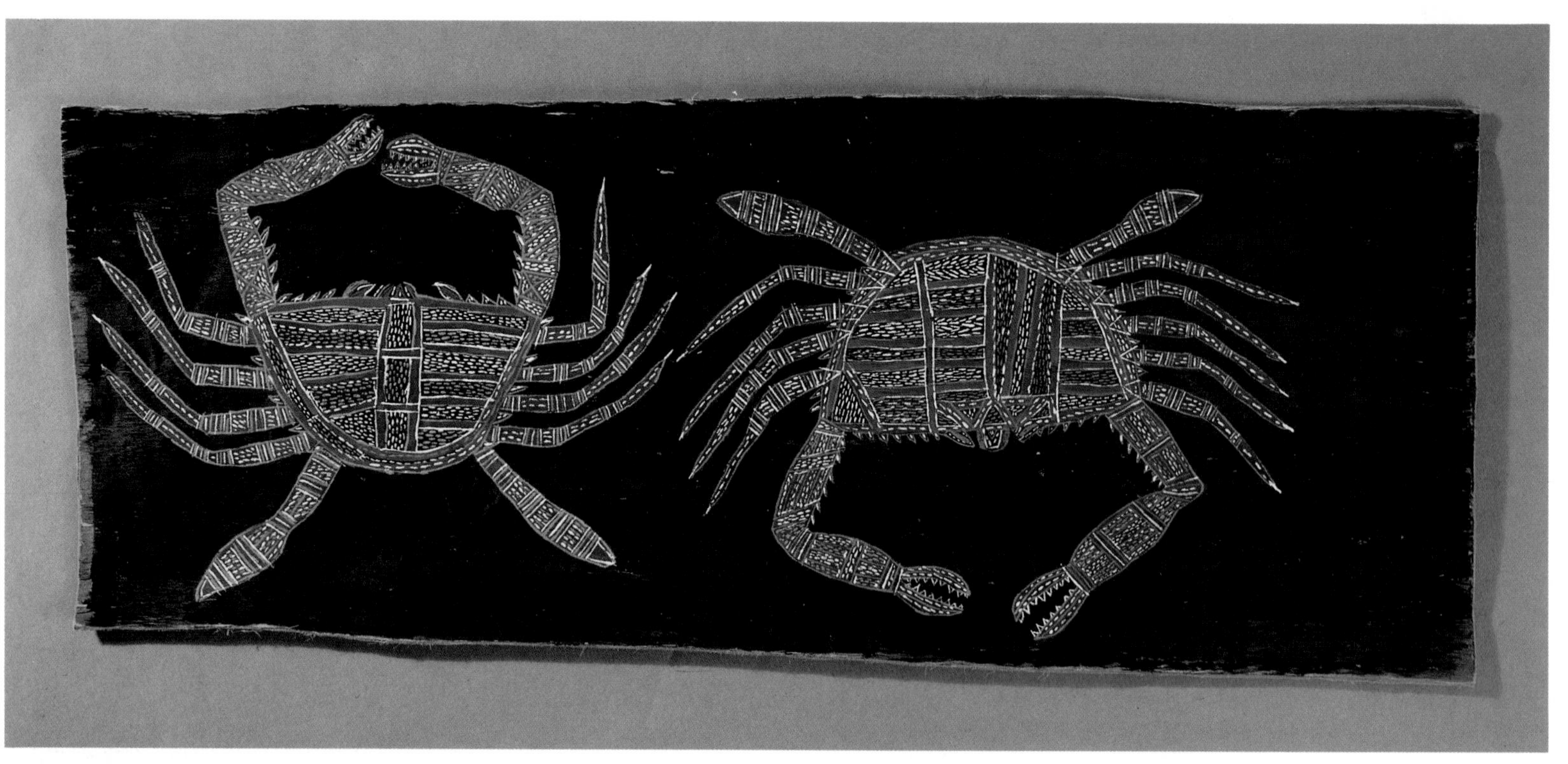

FIG. 95 / CAT. 34
Two Crabs, 1948. Dakilarra Wurramara, Groote Eylandt. Ochre and manganese on bark, 36.5 × 93 cm.

FIG. 96
Untitled, 1970s. Artist unknown, style of Central Arnhem Land. Ochre on bark, 76 × 49 cm.

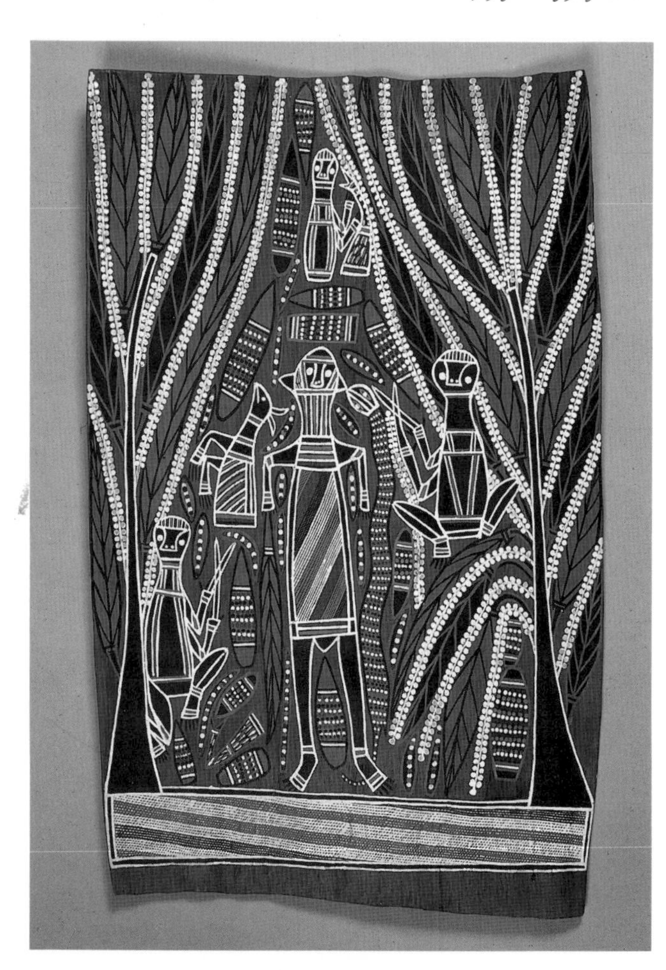

FIG. 97
Gurrmirringu Story, ca. 1982. David Malangi, Central Arnhem Land. Ochre and charcoal on bark, 95 × 59.5 cm.

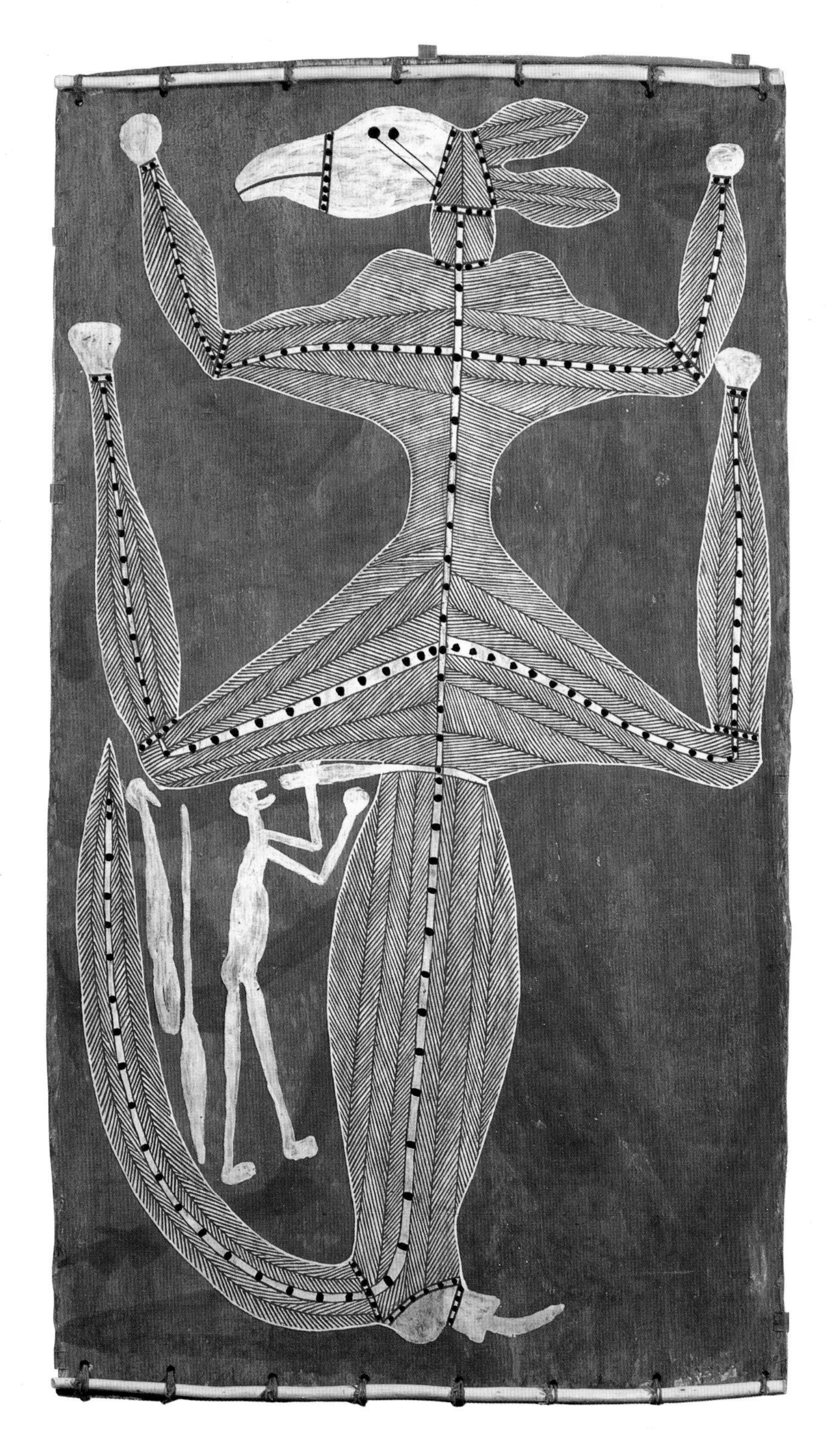

FIG. 98
Mimi Hunter Dissecting Dead Kangaroo, 1980. Didjbarrka Dirdi, Western Arnhem Land. Ochre on bark, 124 × 70 cm.

FIG. 99 / CAT. 17
Lumarluma, ca. 1970. Yirawala, Western Arnhem Land. Ochre on bark, 104 × 54 cm.

attached like a purse to one hip (a common representation in Western Arnhem Land, Fig. 56), or descending symmetrically and pointedly from the pelvis (Central and North East Arnhem Land, Fig. 96), or often not at all (North East Arnhem Land, Groote Eylandt, Figs. 32, 57). (Also see Figs. 61–62, and Cat. 27.) Women's breasts are shown in profile, attached to a frontally viewed torso, either with one breast on each side (Figs. 58, 79, 92, 102) or with both

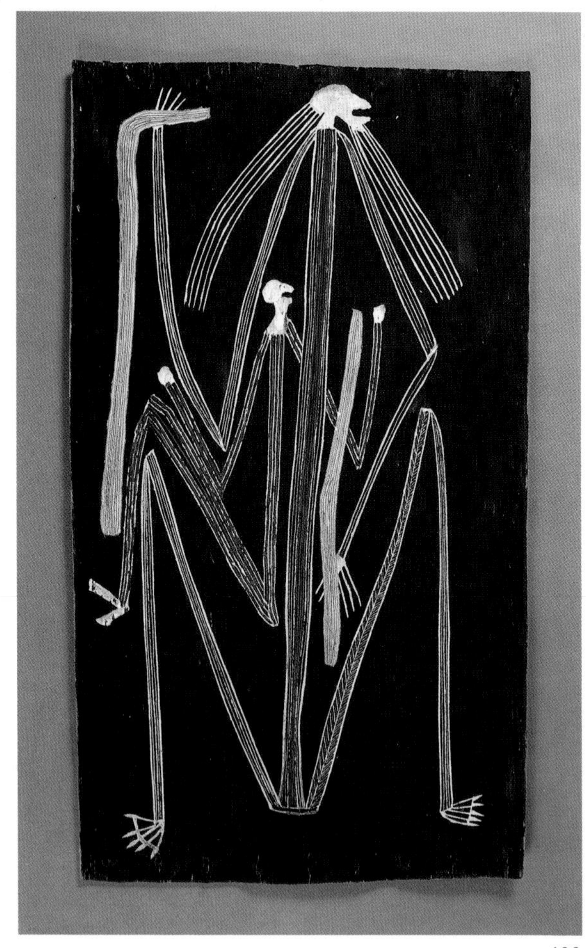

100

FIG. 100
Mimi Spirits, ca. 1969. Bob Balirrbalirr Dirdi. Ochre on bark, 82.5 × 48 cm.

FIG. 101
The Woman Akurin-dipa Collecting Yams (detail), 1948. Artist unknown, Western Arnhem Land. Ochre on bark, 71 × 17 cm.

FIG. 102
Mimi Figures, ca. 1965. Artist unknown, Western Arnhem Land. Ochre on bark, 72 × 32 cm.

FIG. 103 / CAT. 19
Spirit Figure, 1972. Attributed to Dick Nangulay, Western Arnhem Land. Ochre on bark, 37 × 57 cm.

FIG. 104 / CAT. 16
Crocodile Hunting Story, ca. 1979. Mick Gubargu, Western Arnhem Land. Ochre and charcoal on bark, 270 × 92 cm.

FIG. 105
Running women, rock art, near Oenpelli, Western Arnhem Land (after Mountford 1956).

on one side (Fig. 101); they are rarely shown frontally. The head is most often depicted frontally, but it may appear in profile (Fig. 103). Even when in profile, the eyes may both be shown on one side of the face (Figs. 55–56).[19]

These differences of orientation within a single figure will seem incoherent if one declines to view things conceptually. Similarly, the explicit representation of genitals may seem excessive unless one accepts the conceptual principle that gender can be shown significantly by emphasizing those elements most distinctive of gender. It is also important to keep in mind that this art tradition arose at a time when Aboriginal people lived largely without clothing and without the suppression of sex as a topic of daily discourse (except between well-defined kin). Appreciating the genital emphasis in Aboriginal art is not, then, simply a matter of having the right conceptualist eye but also of knowing the broader cultural context.

Energy and Action Do Aboriginal artists see these so-called frontal forms as images of dead, static, lifeless beings? Briefly, no. To the Aboriginal eye, a frontal, splayed, symmetrical image of a Lightning Dreaming figure (Figs. 92, 107, 119) or a dorsal figure of a Crocodile (Fig. 104) connotes the energy and activeness appropriate to that being. Energy, in Aboriginal art, is not to be equated simply with depictions of movement. The running Mimi figures of a Western Arnhem Land rock shelter, which were popularized by C. P. Mountford from the 1940s on and have become for many people a key symbol of what Aboriginal art is like, are not in fact very common (Fig. 105). Human figures in profile, and especially figures running, are relatively rare in Aboriginal rock art and bark paintings.[20] Images of aggressive, erotic, or disintegrative energy are, on the other hand, very common.

101

102

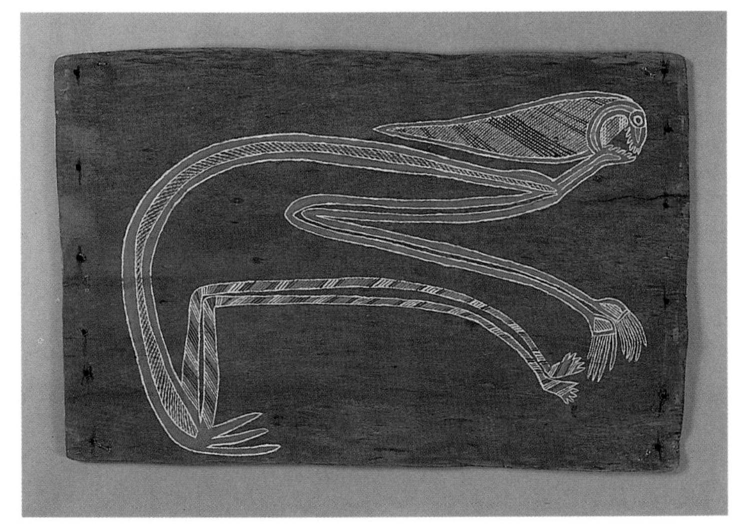

103

105

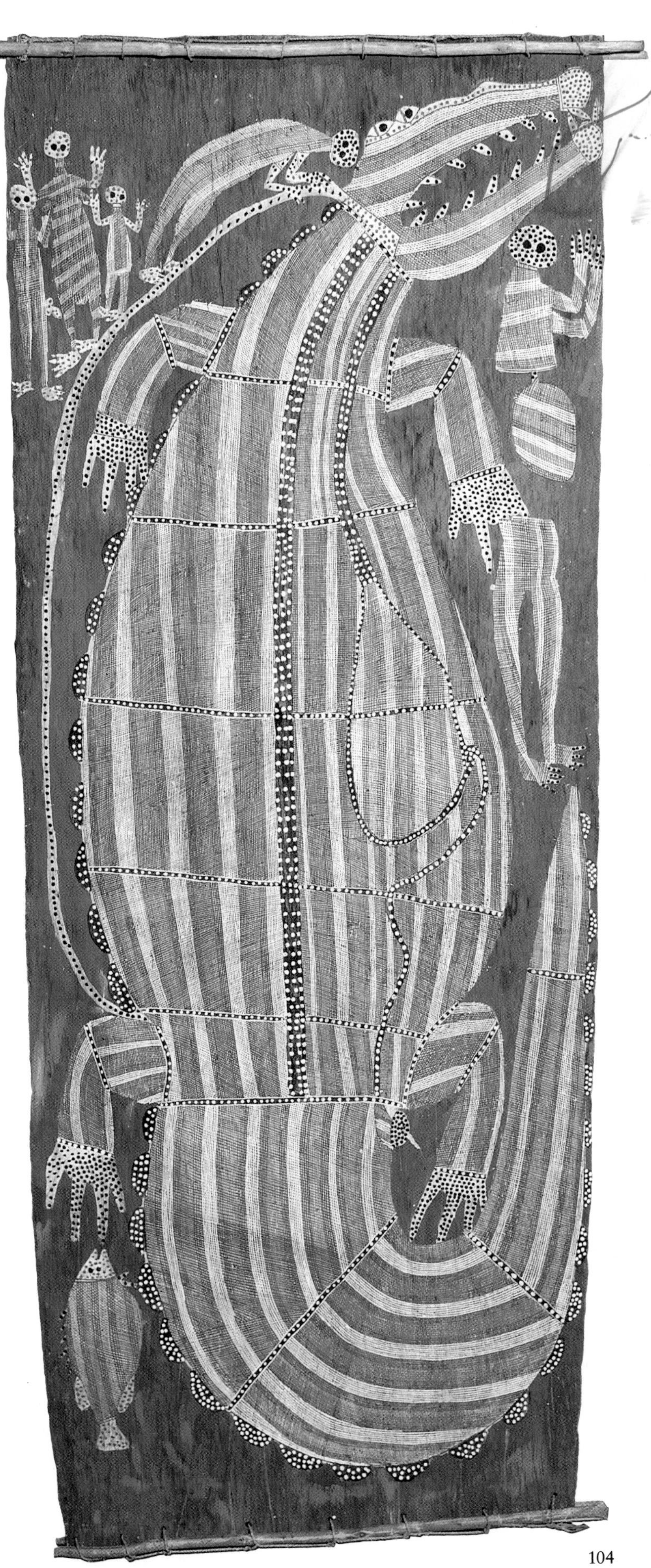

104

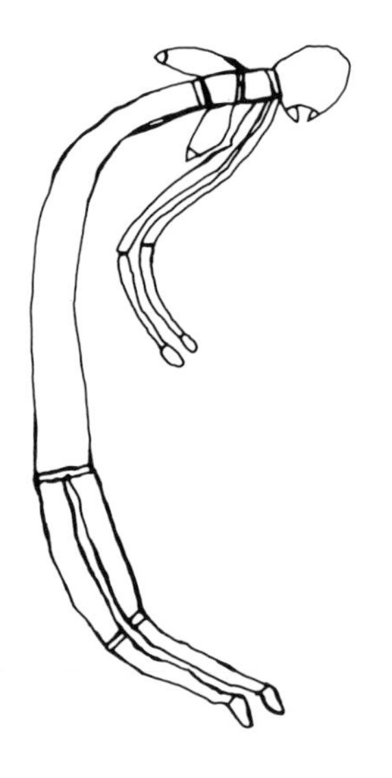

FIG. 106
Female figure, rock art, Alligator Rivers region (after Brandl 1973).

Enmity, Drive, and Heat Sorcery and sexual magic have figured among the primary motivations of Aboriginal rock art, at least in the twentieth century. (Totemic religious motives, a need to place one's personal mark, and other motives were equally significant.) The vitality of a design in this tradition lies not in the illusionistic representation of motion but in the available readings of the connotations of the image and those of its nonfigurative marks, such as cross-hatching and dotting, which communicate energy.

Age and outward appearance are not considered significant inhibitors of sexual attractiveness in Aboriginal traditional psychology, which regards sexual magic and bush aphrodisiacs as truly potent. In a similar sense, frontality in art does not detract from impressions of attractive vigor and dangerous power. To a modernist this should be no surprise: to use Jean Dubuffet as our example, his huge women combine stillness, energy, and sexuality in frontal poses that closely resemble those of Aboriginal art.

Not all figures in bark paintings and the rock art of the same regions are shown in the symmetrical, frontal stance. The twisted torso, so famous in European art history as an example of the triumph of energy over the static styles of the ancient world, may be rare, but the turned legs or the sinuous body do occur in Aboriginal art (Fig. 106). These floating figures remind us of the repeated motif of the Nereid in the European tradition. The holding of a bowed line stretched in an arc over the head of the figure is another motif of highly variable iconographic meaning but remarkably consistent form in both Arnhem Land art and the art of the Mediterranean from early to modern times.[21] The Lightning figures of Arnhem Land, with their held arcs and encircled bodies (Fig. 107), like the similar figures of the halo-topped Wandjina of the Kimberley in Western Australia (Figs. 75–76) and the rock engravings from Cape York Peninsula dating back to more than thirteen thousand years (Fig. 108), represent variants of a pattern that is characteristic of Aboriginal art in Australia, probably over many thousands of years.

FIG. 107
Lightning Figure, 1930s? Artist unknown, Western Arnhem Land. Ochre on bark, 71.5 × 37.5 cm.

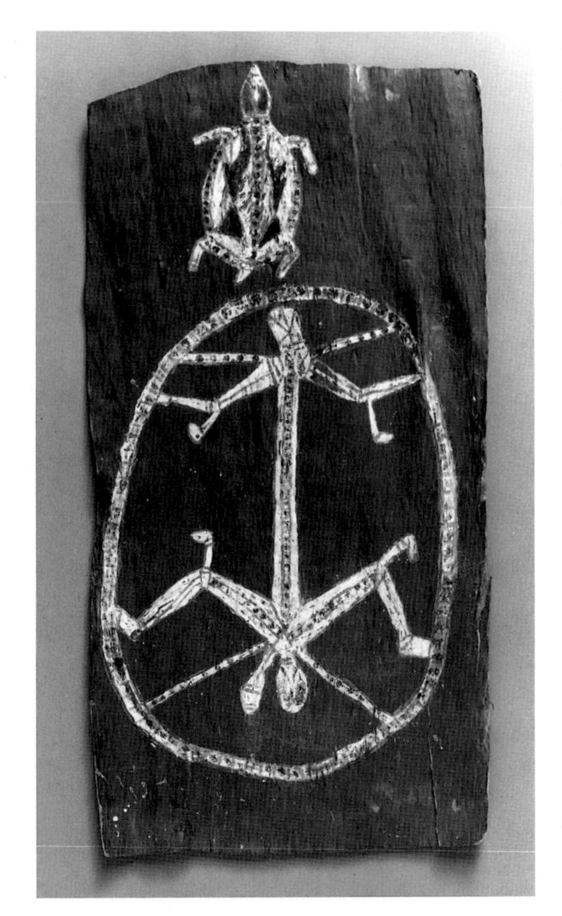

FIG. 108
Rock engravings, Laura region, Cape York Peninsula (after Rosenfeld et al. 1981).

The body in Aboriginal art, in all its varying forms, usually retains its integrity. This is not the case with paintings of enmity and destruction. The sorcery paintings (or in some cases those interpreted as such by Aborigines working with anthropologists) that occur across northern Australia in rock shelters or on bark generally show at least one of four negative states in the body: inversion, distortion, dismemberment, and undesired penetration. These are states of involuntary, rather than voluntary, action.

Inversion (Fig. 109) is a pure negation of the appropriate relation between a standing figure and the ground. Distortion (Fig. 110) is the sorcerer's willing of excess, in some cases of the swelling of infection, and a transgression of the order of natural proportion. Dismemberment (Figs. 97–98, 104, 111) is the disarticulation of that which is essentially conceived not as a seamless whole but as an articulated set of parts. Europe has a long tradition of drawing and quartering, genital amputation, and other such violations of the body's integrity, as way of politicizing the physical destruction of one's enemies. This extends even to self-destruction: when the Queen told Rumpelstilzchen his name, he was furious, and screamed, "The devil told you that! The devil! The devil!" Foaming with rage, he tore himself to pieces (Fig. 112). The Dadaist Manifesto of 1918 proclaimed its own "primitive relation to the reality of the environment" by announcing that it "has ceased to take an aesthetic attitude toward life, and this it accomplishes by tearing all the slogans of ethics, culture and inwardness, which are merely cloaks for weak muscles, into their components."[22]

FIG. 109
Inverted sorcery figure, rock art, Laura region, Cape York Peninsula (after Trezise 1971).

FIG. 110
Human figure, rock art, Pilbara region, Western Australia (after Wright 1977).

FIG. 111
Probable sorcery figure, rock art, Alligator Rivers region (after Brandl 1973).

FIG. 112
Rumpelstilzchen tearing himself apart, 1970. David Hockney. Etching.

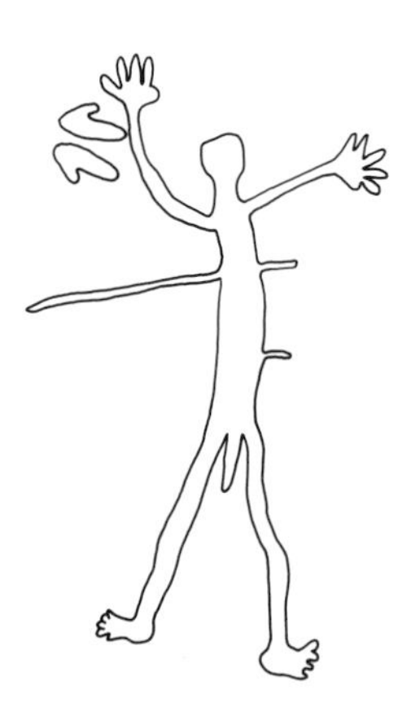

FIG. 113
Man pierced by a spear, rock art, Laura region, Cape York Peninsula (after Rosenfeld et al. 1981).

FIG. 114
Mimi Figure, 1964. Yirawala, Western Arnhem Land. Ochre on bark, 77 × 18 cm.

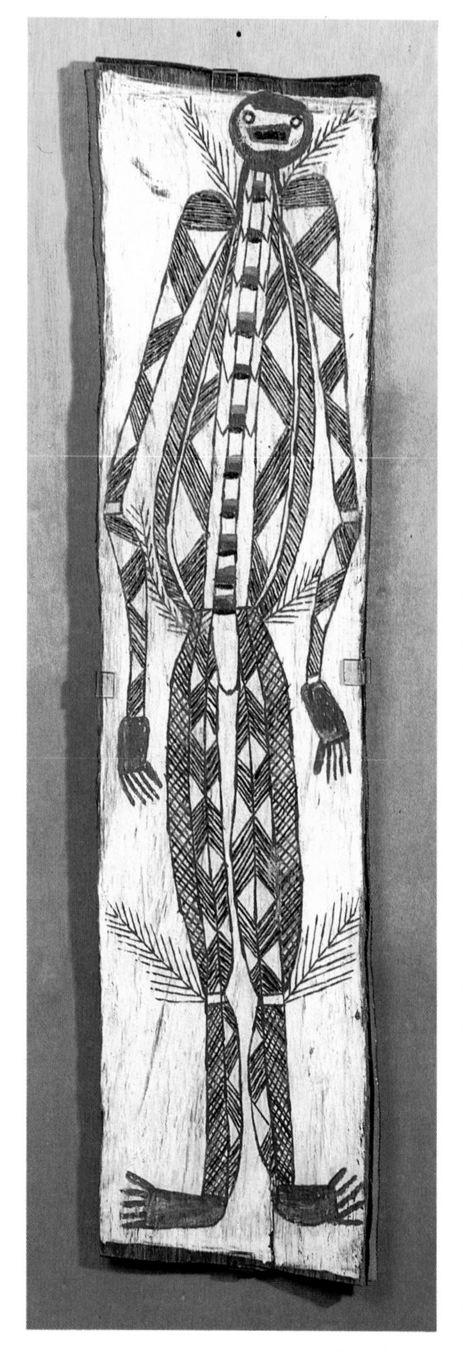

Unwanted penetration by barb, penis, bone, or spear (Figs. 113–114) is the invasion of another's personal envelope, as well as a stark image of violent injury. Sexual politics thus also emerges strongly in those Arnhem Land bark paintings that show women pregnant, pierced by many barbs, vaginas open and bristling, and men with oversized penises stuck with spines and apparently writhing in agony (Fig. 115). While women are often painted in the most fully excited and open state for penetration, men are rarely shown with explicit erections.[23] As noted earlier, phallic imagery in Aboriginal art is usually oblique and appears in the form of ceremonial poles, headdresses, signposts, and, as illustrated in Fig. 116, even a rocket. This holds true even where the men or women who make the objects may identify them explicitly as being phalluses (Fig. 117).[24] Similarly indirect references to sexual imagery are the cup-and-ring design of Queensland rock engravings (Fig. 118), interpreted by some anthropologists as being detached vulvae, and the pointed oval motif that recurs in much North East Arnhem Land art and is usually identified by the artist as a water hole, a sand-sculptured ceremonial ground, or a coffin but also interpretable as a vulva.[25] Static as they may appear, such forms are, among other things, images of drive and heat.

The Body as Assemblage Across the top end of the Northern Territory, the bodies of humans and animals are frequently depicted in Aboriginal art with the joints marked. Other internal bone structures, the ribs, especially, are also often marked. This marking is usually done with a simple

FIG. 115
Seducer, ca. 1949. Midjau-midjau, Western Arnhem Land. Ochre on bark (after Berndt and Berndt 1951), 66 × 38 cm.

FIG. 116 / CAT. 30
Space Tracking Station, 1967. Munggurrawuy Yunupingu, North East Arnhem Land. Ochre on masonite, 92 × 60 cm.

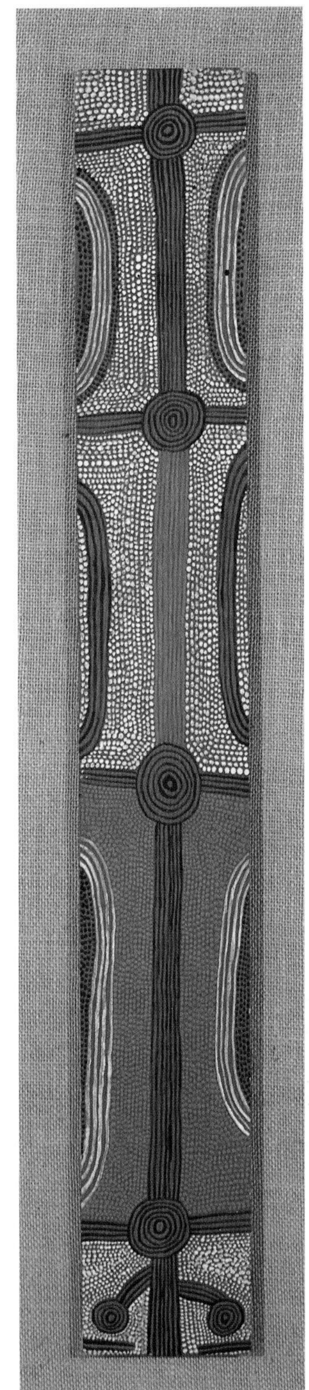

FIG. 117
Man Lying at Yumari, 1973. Uta Uta Jangala, Central Australia. Acrylic on board, 91.3 × 12.5 cm.

FIG. 118
Rock engravings, Black's Palace, Queensland.

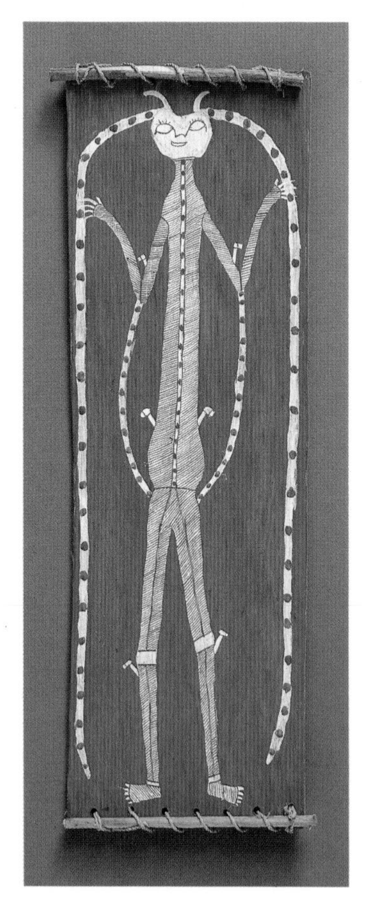

FIG. 119
Lightning Figure, 1986. Timothy Nadjowh, Western Arnhem Land. Ochre on bark, 55.5 × 18.5 cm.

crossbar at the wrists, elbows, shoulders, pelvis, knees, and ankles, and sometimes at the joints of the jaws, vertebrae, and knuckles. Barbs, bones, axes, and other forms protrude from the joints in many Western Arnhem Land figures (Figs. 55, 92, 107, 114, 119). Even the small bag hanging from the elbow of one of the figures in Yirawala's *Mimi Spirits* (Fig. 79) shares this design feature with the more malevolent examples of points and axes. This emphasis on the joints is one aspect—often the only aspect—visible of the traditional X-ray approach to the depiction of the body. In Arnhem Land, mainly in the west, it is common to show internal organs as well (Figs. 53–54, 80, 104). This is a hunter's view of the flesh. The body is an assemblage.

The body is also analogous to ceremonial knowledge: it has an outside, more or less readily available to perception, and an inside, which becomes grasped only with revelation. Anthropologist Luke Taylor has made a detailed study of this aspect of bark paintings in Western Arnhem Land.[26] X-ray paintings that show naturalistically portrayed internal organs are not merely concerned with food cuts (liver, heart, lungs, and so forth) but also communicate knowledge about the Ancestral Beings. Landscape features were formed out of the organs of Ancestral Beings, and sacred objects may be identified as bones or internal organs of Ancestral Beings, such as Kangaroo or Lumarluma (Fig. 99). The less naturalistic types of infill—those that are geometric rather than figurative and organic—found on Western Arnhem Land paintings of bodies have associations with particularly sacred matters (Figs. 93–94, 99, 120, and Cat. 13–14; compare Fig. 42).

Same Subject, Different Form The Sun Woman of Tiwi mythology appears both as a human figure (Fig. 121) and as a highly symmetrical, time-

FIG. 120 / CAT. 15
Ceremonial Crocodile, ca. 1970. Yirawala, Western Arnhem Land. Ochre and charcoal on bark, 45 × 101 cm.

FIG. 121 / CAT. 2
Sun Woman in her Hut, 1954. Tjamalampuwa, Melville Island. Ochre on bark, 58 × 47 cm.

FIG. 122 / CAT. 3
Sun Woman at Wurriyupi, 1954. Big Tom, Melville Island. Ochre on bark, 95 × 40 cm.

lapse vision of the sun and its rays (Fig. 122). These two works, from the same culture and year but by different artists, are good examples of how much we can see in an apparently simple work once we understand the particular Aboriginal approach to the problem of orientation of figures in space.

In Fig. 121, the Sun Woman is seated in her hut. Her body is shown splayed, arms and legs at full stretch away from her torso. If she is in fact seated, it is in a strained position. Her hut is represented by a black ring encircling her. The vertical supports for the hut—or perhaps they are for the bough-shade over the top of the hut, which is represented by the outer ring—are shown in profile, but exploded centrifugally, so each radiates from a center point. Thus at least three kinds of view are combined in one image: a fully splayed, ventral image of a body said to be seated, a cutaway perpendicular view of both hut and bough-shade, and a radial series of horizontal profiles of hut supports.

In Fig. 122, we see the same character as a burst of rays from a series of circular sun images. In the previous example we saw how different spatial orientations may be combined happily in one image. Here, different times of the day are combined in the moment of a single painting: the black circle at the bottom is the Sun at dawn; the next circle is the Sun at midday, then at mid-afternoon and at sunset.[27] Both paintings of the Sun Woman may be described as figurative, but they show her in her two manifestations: a human form and the form of a celestial object. These are two roughly equivalent facets, rather than two levels of interpretation, of the same thing.

Another example of different approaches to the same object are the paintings of Catfish Dreaming by the Central Arnhem Land artists Malangi

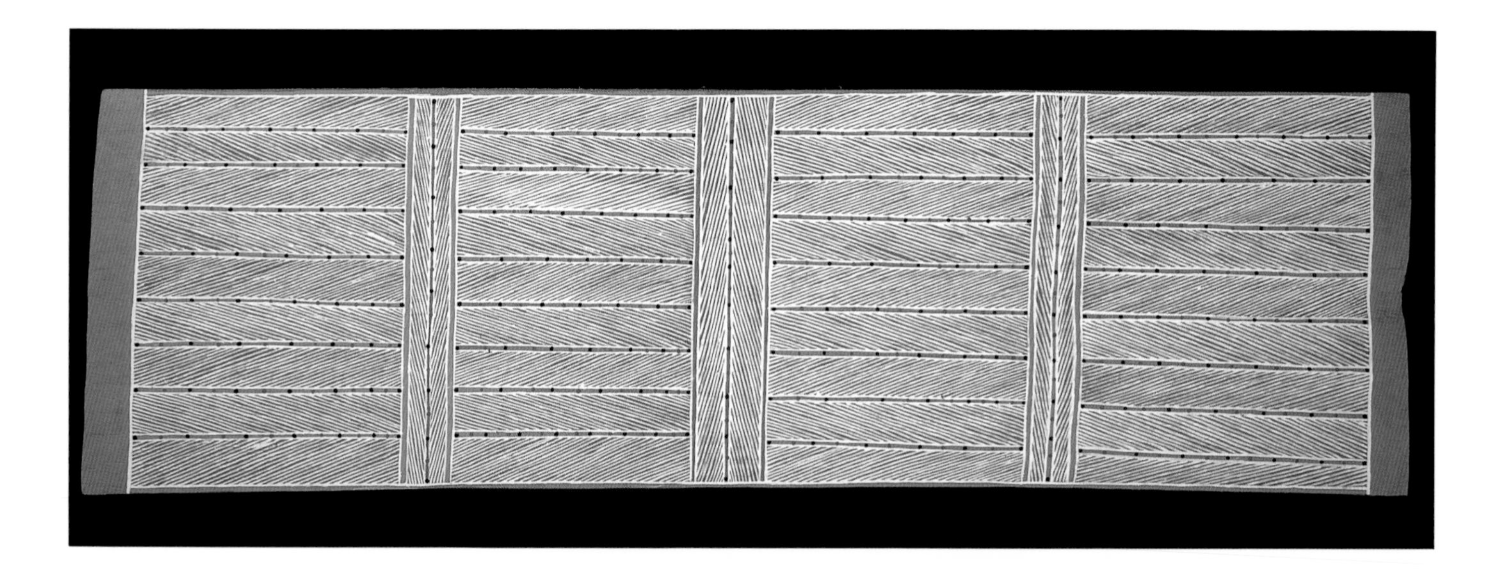

FIG. 123 / CAT. 23
Catfish Dreaming, 1987. Jimmy Wululu, Central Arnhem Land. Ochre on bark, 41 × 139.5 cm.

and Wululu (Figs. 80 and 123). Malangi has chosen to represent the Catfish as a whole, viewed dorsally (in the way bottom-feeders are usually treated in bark paintings) and surrounded by black, which signifies water. Wululu's Catfish design appears abstract by comparison, but in fact it, too, is representational: the hatched lines (compare Figs. 124–125, and Cat. 73) are the fine, parallel rib-bones of Catfish Dreaming.[28] Here, then, we have two representational but nonetheless very different views of Catfish as a fish, one based on a perceptual approach and the other, a conceptual, geometrically rectified approach. (Other images of Catfish in bark paintings are shown in Figs. 126–127.)

But what of the Crocodile Woman of Big Tom's Melville Island painting (Fig. 128)? Mountford's notes do not say it "depicts" a crocodile, but simply that the central black disk is the island Mundinyu, where the Crocodile Woman had her spiritual home. The other disks are water-bearing holes in the cliffs there; the radiating bands are ochres there; the parallel lines, gutters in the cliffs where the Crocodile Woman urinated; and the chevrons, ferns. The site and the mythic elements in this painting, however obliquely depicted or symmetrically rearranged, do refer to Crocodile Woman, but without using either her shape or any of her body parts. (Only a bodily excrescence marks her presence.) By contrast, the Crocodiles in the paintings by Gubargu (Fig. 104) and Yirawala (Fig. 120), even though they portray major charac-

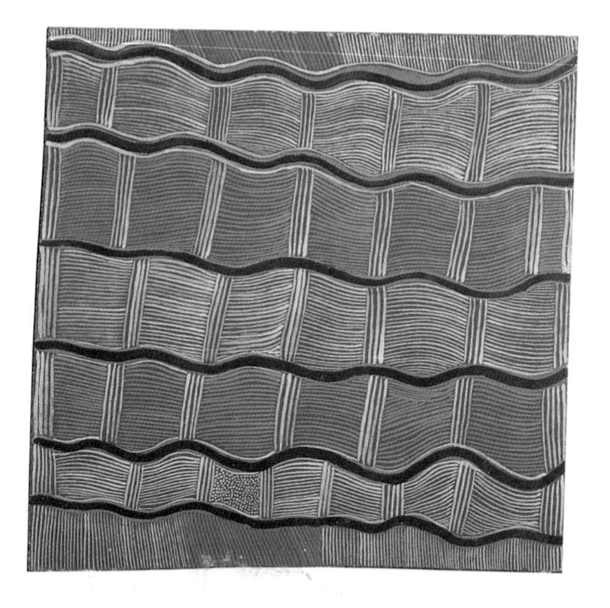

FIG. 124
Wind Dreaming, ca. 1978. Mick Namarari Japaljarri, Papunya, Central Australia. Acrylic on board, 54 × 55 cm.

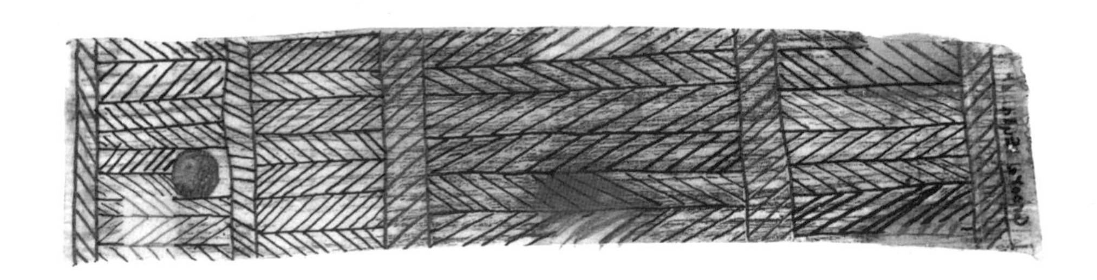

FIG. 125
Engraved design on smoking pipe, 1948. Artist unknown, Groote Eylandt (traced by C.P. Mountford).

ters in site-specific myths, are presented free of any overt figurative reference to place.

Through examples such as these we can see the usefulness of taking a particular form—in this case, that of a certain kind of body—and examining the ways it is represented in Aboriginal art. We have seen that particular techniques of representation, while perhaps seeming to be rather arbitrary, convey cultural attitudes and beliefs peculiar to or typical of Aboriginal society. Morphology and feeling are thus seldom separable. We now turn to a very different approach, in which we look not at individual themes or motifs but at the question of total composition as a manifestation of style and of worldview.

FIG. 126
Cormorant Transformed into Hollow-log Coffin, 1978. George Anaragayura. Ochre on bark, 58 × 86 cm.

FIG. 127 / CAT. 24
Catfish and Whitefish Dreaming, 1954. Artist unknown, Central Arnhem Land. Ochre on bark, 24 × 103.5 cm.

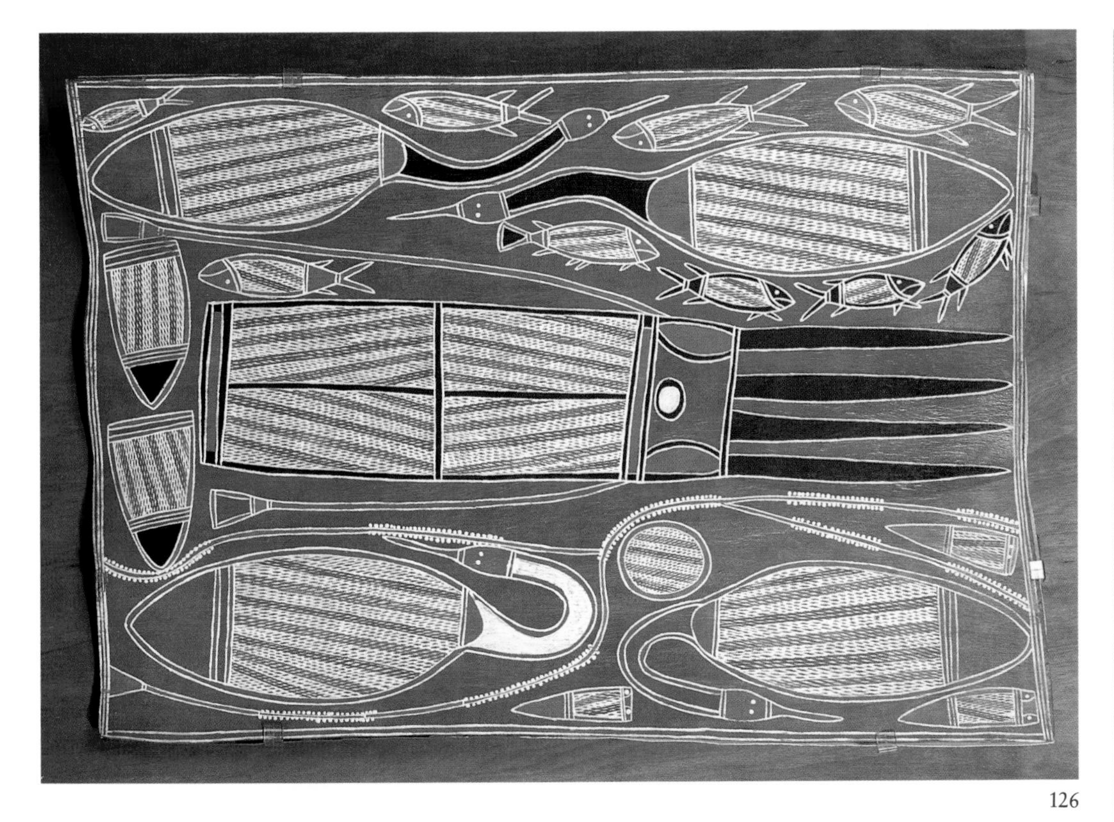

126

127

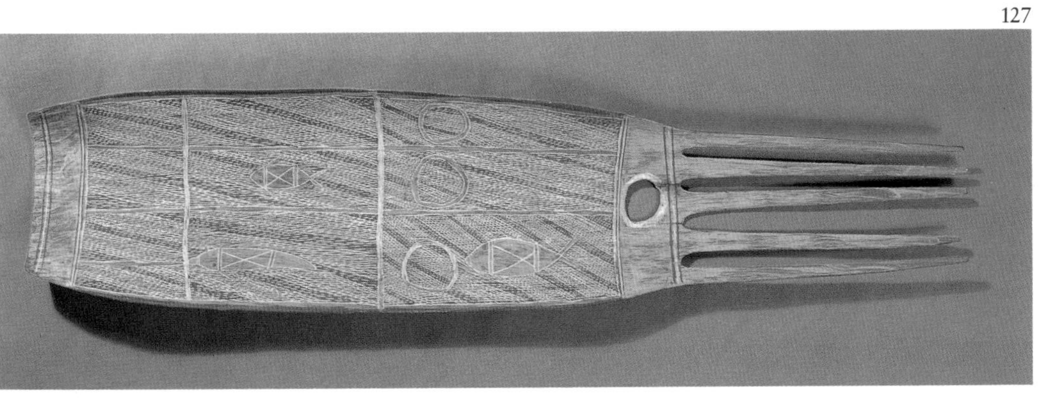

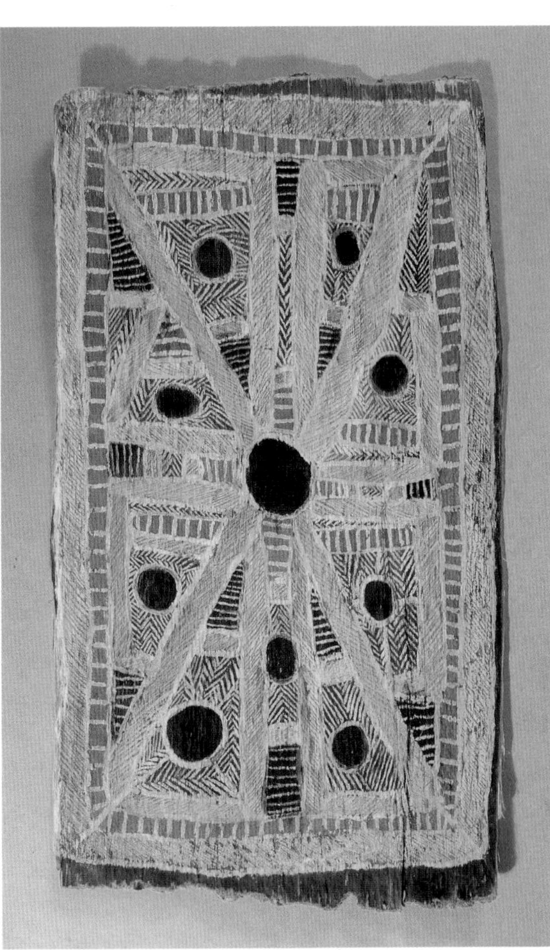

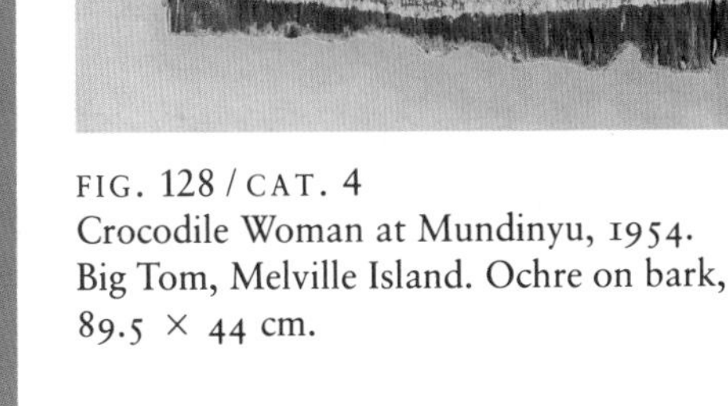

FIG. 128 / CAT. 4
Crocodile Woman at Mundinyu, 1954. Big Tom, Melville Island. Ochre on bark, 89.5 × 44 cm.

Composition in Western Desert Acrylics

For those who are unfamiliar with their literal meanings, Western Desert acrylic paintings command more immediate attention for their compositions than for their depictions of things. Their style is less obviously iconic and less figurative than that of most bark paintings.[29] With the acrylics, the focus of attention is much more often their *arrangement* of motifs on a ground or against areas of dotted background.

Compositional arrangements in contemporary Western Desert painting rest, as we saw in Chapter I, on an ancient past. As maps of political geography— only one of their many roles—these works are conservative statements about relationships between people and land, relationships sanctioned by the Dreaming. They present, and reinforce, not merely order but a particular order. It is therefore appropriate that they be schematized, rather like a subway map or a circuit diagram, compressing the unruly facts of geography into a semblance of the balance, unity, and reciprocity desired of human relations. Many of the maps of water holes drawn by Aborigines (or based on their guidance) and collected by ethnographers connect them more often than not into fictive straight lines, rectangular grids, or smooth arcs (Figs. 129–131, 134). Western Desert painting's tendency toward rectilinearity and symmetry derives from classical Aboriginal religious and intellectual systems, but this tendency has also been a major factor in making the art intelligible to viewers of other cultures and has thus underpinned its exposure to a wide audience in museums and in the art market.[30] Other important factors in this exposure have been its use of a spare and predominantly

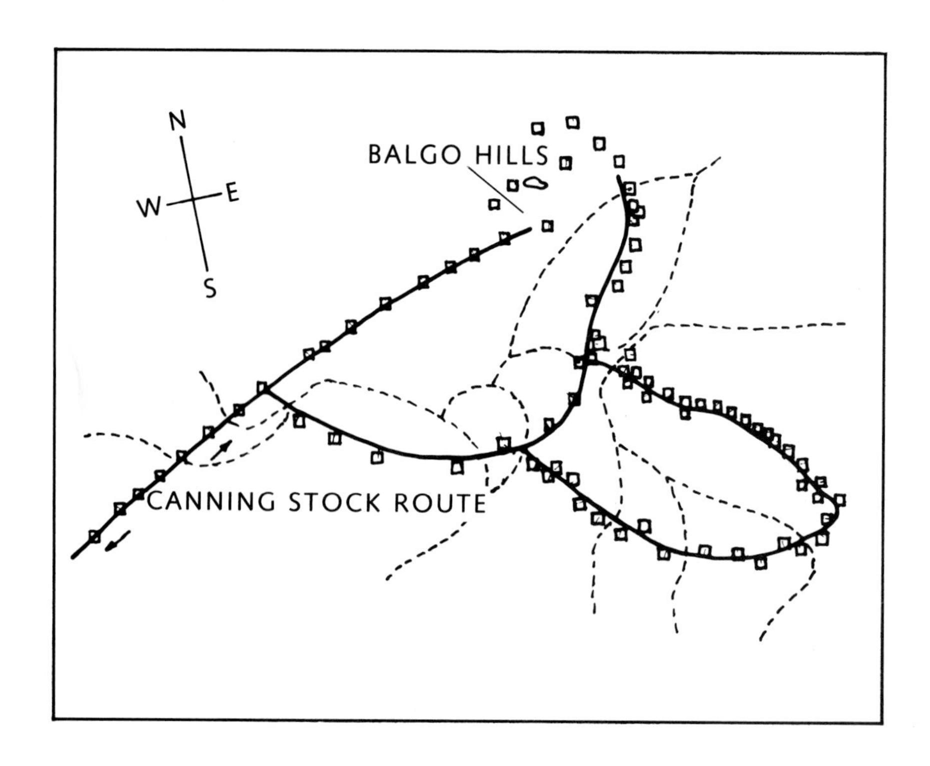

FIG. 129
Aboriginal map of Dreaming tracks, Balgo region, Western Australia (after Berndt 1972). Squares mark named sites.

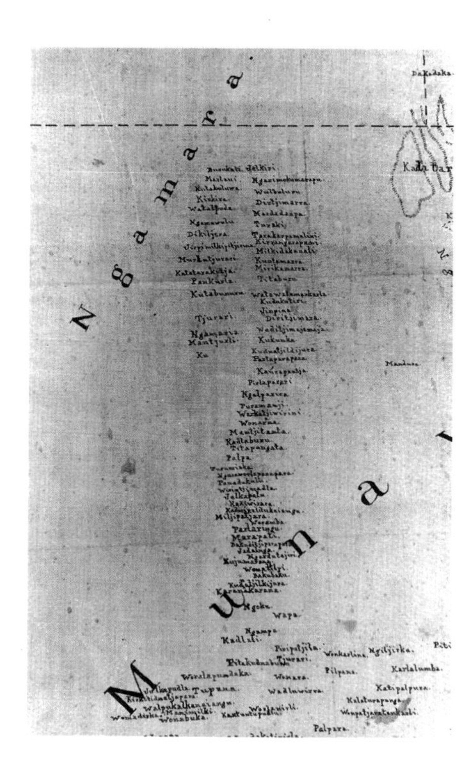

FIG. 130
Detail of Reuther/Hillier Aboriginal place-names map, Lake Eyre region, 1904.

nonfigurative style for which many urban art followers had been prepared by Minimalist painting of the 1960s and 1970s and its employment of canvas and acrylic paint, media used by "real artists."

What does the "totality of outward form" of these acrylic paintings consist of? It is more than a simple sum of the motifs and dotted backgrounds that each image contains. And yet it is these individual motifs, not the whole images, that have thus far been stressed in explanatory readings of desert painting. Writers on the art of the Western Desert and associated regions have often isolated recurring motifs and offered lists of their denotative meanings.[31] We discuss these meanings in detail in Chapter IV. Here we are more concerned with the way viewers of Western Desert acrylics respond to the paintings as pictures, and how those pictures are constructed.

A schematic diagram of the things signified by individual motifs in an acrylic painting, together with an account of the myth or myths depicted, may offer an interpretation of the whole painting.[32] (See Figs. 138a, 141a, 152a, 153a for examples of schemata.) Yet the total look of such a painting, not so much its cumulative literal interpretation, is the most critical part of what puts it in demand in the art world.[33] Writers on desert acrylics may have been at pains to offer meanings for motifs, but they have been reluctant to discuss composition. It is curious, for example, that the literature rarely comments on the relative placement of motifs and backgrounds and their framing within the confines of differently shaped canvases or boards, the visual relations between figurative and nonfigurative elements in a picture, the compound effect of juxtaposed areas of dotting, and the impact of the particular range and interrelationship of colors in the picture field.[34]

It is precisely the combination of the art's look with its status as an iconic religious form of landscape art that makes it so peculiarly attractive to the non-Aboriginal art world and to the public in general. As Eric Michaels suggests, it is the fact that the art is meaningful, not what it specifically means, that underlies much of its desirability outside Aboriginal society.[35] The other main basis for that desirability, however, is that the style is widely readable. Its readability rests in large part on the highly accessible visual logic it employs. Its morphology offers universally graspable regularities.

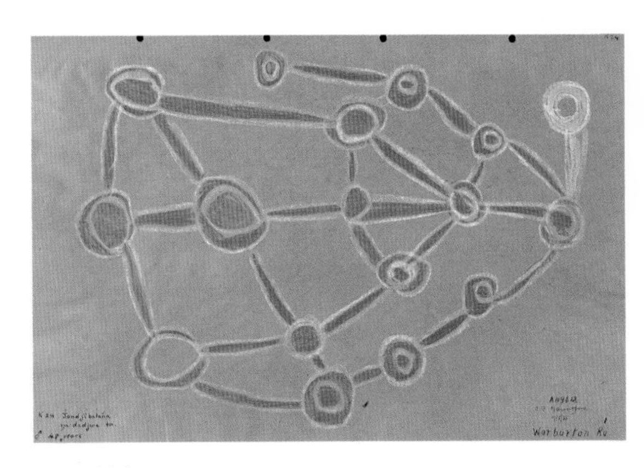

FIG. 131
Untitled, 1935. Jandjibalana, Central Australia. Crayon on paper, 35.5 × 54 cm.

Regularities of Composition: Roundels and Paths To discuss the morphological meaning of the composition of Western Desert acrylics, we need to know what kinds of compositions occur. Our examination of a sample of some three hundred of these paintings, ranging in date from about 1971 to 1987 and mainly deriving from Papunya, Yuendumu, and Kintore[36] allows some broad generalizations about their composition:

1. The majority consist basically of symmetrical arrangements. These are the patterns of the motifs, which are the elements usually laid down first by the painters before infilling and details are added. Symmetry and the use

of geometric forms increases as one moves further south and west into the Pintupi, Luritja, and Pitjantjatjara areas, from the more northern and eastern Warlpiri, Anmatyerre, and Arrernte (Aranda) areas.[37]

2. Symmetry in the work of painters originally based at Papunya increases in frequency and precision over time from the early 1970s to 1987. The size of the paintings, and consequently the average number of motifs they contain, also increases over time. Motifs retain a relatively constant size.

3. The majority of compositions, especially the more symmetrical ones, contain arrangements of circles. The circles most often occur in sets of two or more, concentrically placed. A circle or a concentrically arranged set of circles is referred to here as a *roundel.*

4. If there is only one roundel, it is at, or close to, the midpoint of the long axis of the picture field. In a square field it is at the center. It may be encircled by a figurative snake.[38]

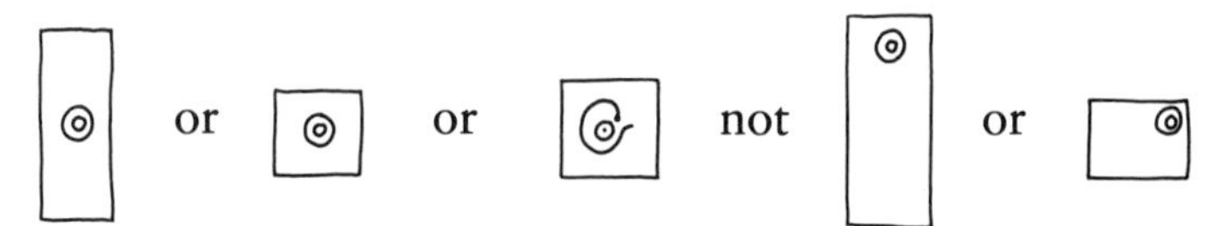

5. If the picture contains two or three roundels, they are usually in series on the center line of the long axis and distributed evenly about the midpoint of the short axis.[39]

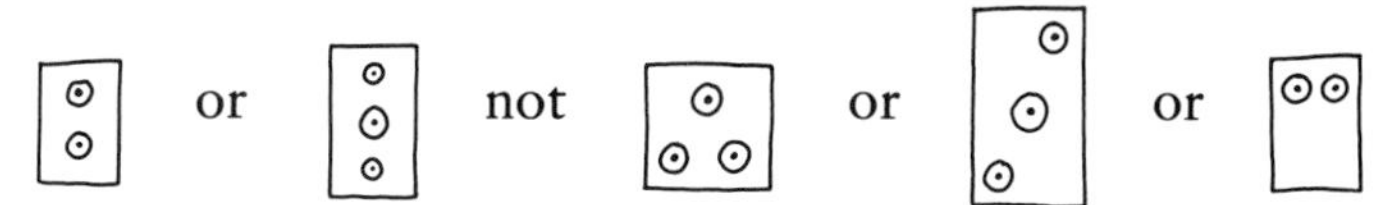

6. If there are four roundels, they are usually arranged either as described in 5 above or at the four points of a rectangle, real or imaginary. The latter may be referred to as a *foursquare arrangement.* The four points are on depicted or imaginary lines connecting the center of the picture field with either the four angles of the rectangle or the four points midway along each side of the rectangle.

or (a) or (b) not or

Arrangement (a) may be called a foursquare diagonal, and (b), a foursquare rectilinear.

7. If there is a fifth roundel, it will usually be at the center, and often larger than the others.

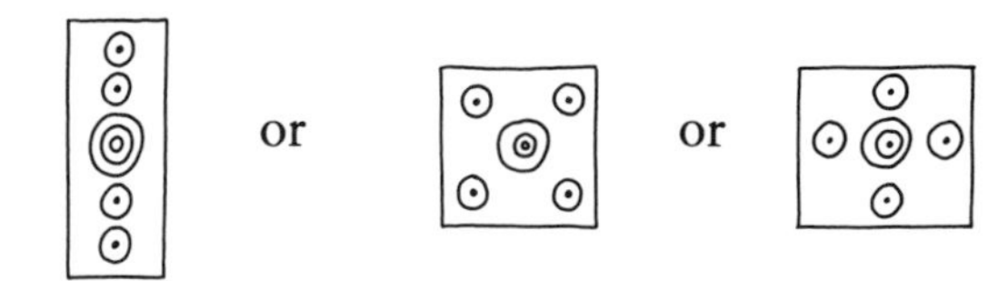

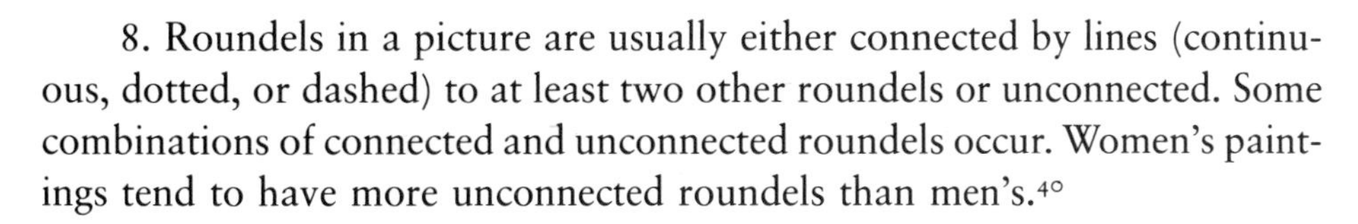

8. Roundels in a picture are usually either connected by lines (continuous, dotted, or dashed) to at least two other roundels or unconnected. Some combinations of connected and unconnected roundels occur. Women's paintings tend to have more unconnected roundels than men's.[40]

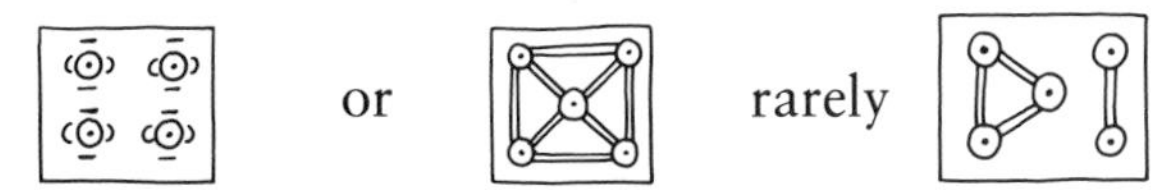

9. If roundels are unconnected they are more likely to be accompanied by other motifs, or *satellites*. Satellite motifs are usually arranged symmetrically and opposed about their roundels. With or without satellites, unconnected roundels may often be separated by arcs or bars.

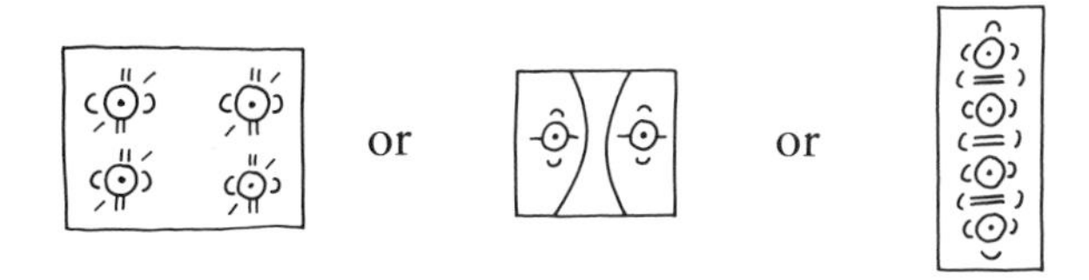

10. Motifs that occur as satellites (crescents, parallel bars, ovals, and so forth) also occur independent of roundels, usually as complementary infilling placed more or less equidistantly between roundels or other dominant focal motifs.

11. Connected roundels usually have few or no satellites.

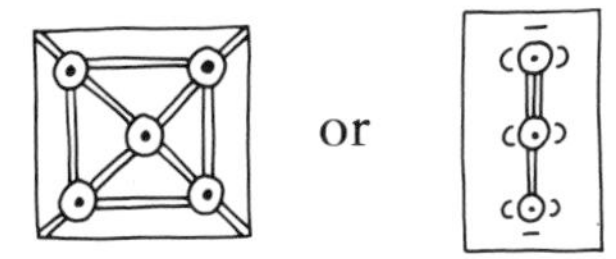

12. If a roundel has a connector leading from one of its sides, the opposite side will tend to have a parallel connector, unless the roundel is, for example, at a corner of a rectangular arrangement.[41]

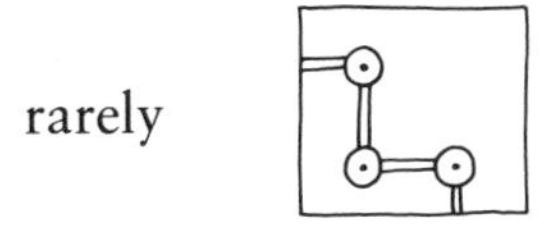

13. Connectors may leave a roundel and run to meet the edge of the picture field.

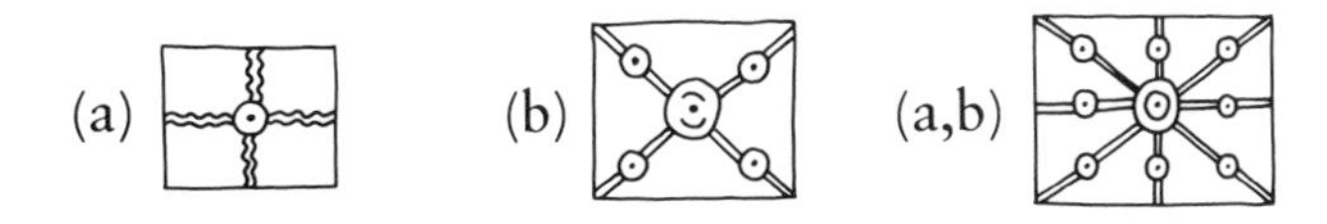

Type (a) are rectilinear radials, and type (b), diagonal radials.

14. Some radial patterns are neither rectilinear nor diagonal and are multidirectional. These may be called generalized radials. They usually consist of plant stems or animal or human tracks.

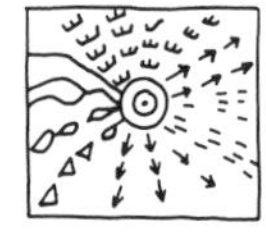

or

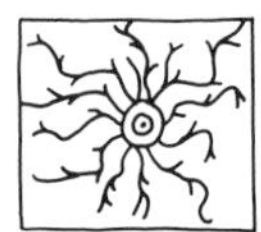

15. Where roundels occur in more than one line they tend to be in parallel lines and in approximately equal numbers in the columns and rows generated by this arrangement. The more roundels there are, however, the less likely it is that the columns and rows will be regular in numbers of roundels. (The terms "columns" and "rows" are used arbitrarily, as most acrylics of this type have no particular up/down orientation, but may be rotated to any angle for viewing.)

16. The most common number above five is six roundels, arranged in three columns and three rows. Higher numbers are often contained in patterns where there are three columns and a variable number of rows.

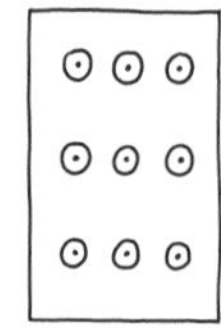
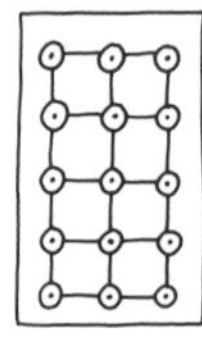
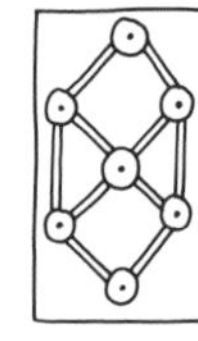
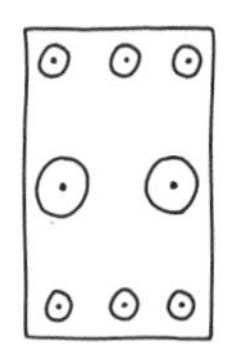

17. Where there are no roundels, and patterns are formed by areas of dotting, for example, the work still tends to be symmetrical and about a dominant long axis. If there is no roundel and no dominant long axis, the work is often a case of encirclement by a snake or consists of parallel lines of dotting. It may, however, be just a misty shroud of dottings.

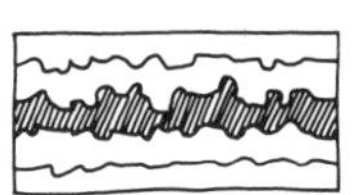

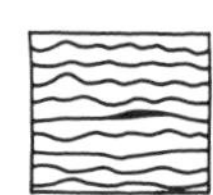
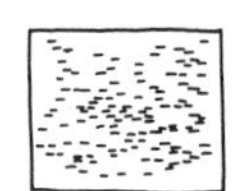

The Site-path Framework The symmetrical arrangements outlined above can mostly be interpreted as systematic reductions of or balanced extracts from the hypothetical grid or template set out here in Fig. 132. The anthropologist Daniel S. Davidson referred to the fact that Aboriginal art produces an infinite number of designs from a limited number of elements.[42] What we are suggesting here is that much Western Desert art produces a finite design by subtraction—even quotation—from a potentially infinite grid of connected places/Dreamings/people, in which real spatial relationships are literally rectified and represented by connected roundels in what Nancy Munn calls a site-path framework.[43] This framework, as shown

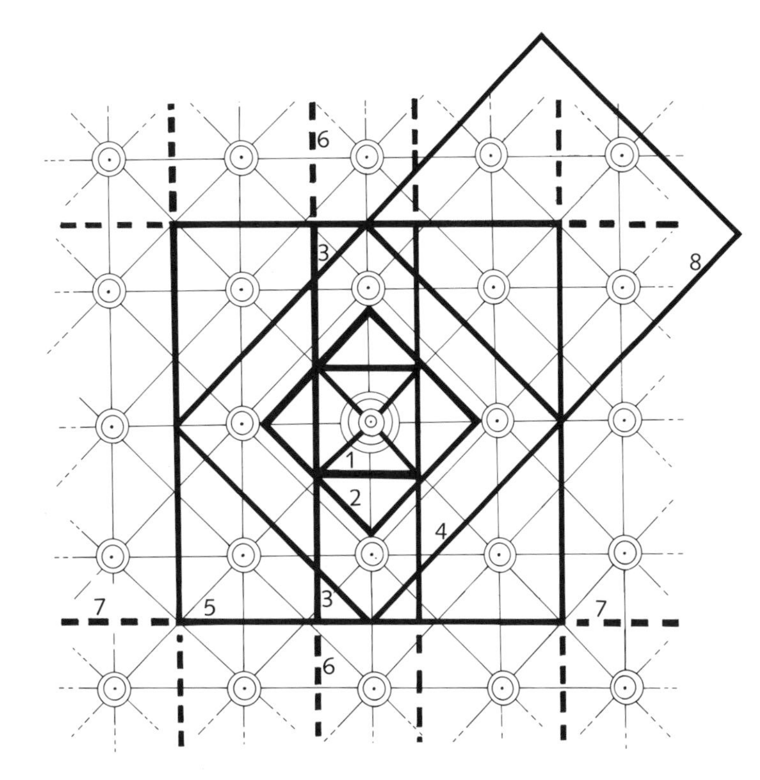

FIG. 132
The site-path framework.

For examples of works that contain structures of the type illustrated here, see the following:

1. Figs. 34, 35, 70, 121, 128, 149, 150, 155, 170, 176
2. Figs. 80, 91, 138, 144, 248
3. Figs. 33, 38, 40, 151, 171, 249
4. Figs. 15, 36, 43, and Cat. 44
5. Fig. 44
6. Figs. 117, 122, 143, 152, 153, 172, 218, and Cat. 58
7. Figs. 37, 133, 134, 148, 159, 160, 178, 179
8. Fig. 39

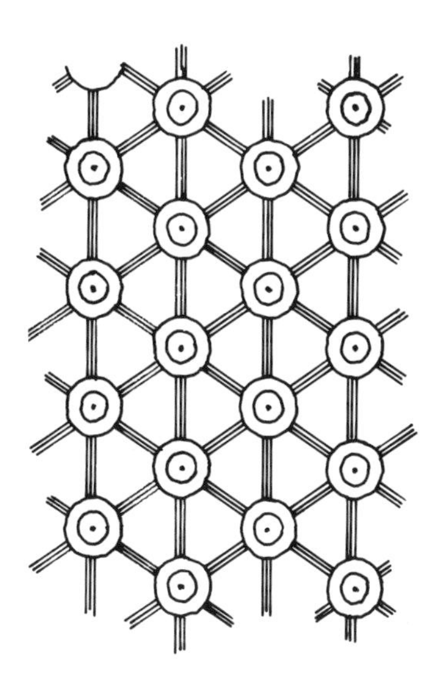

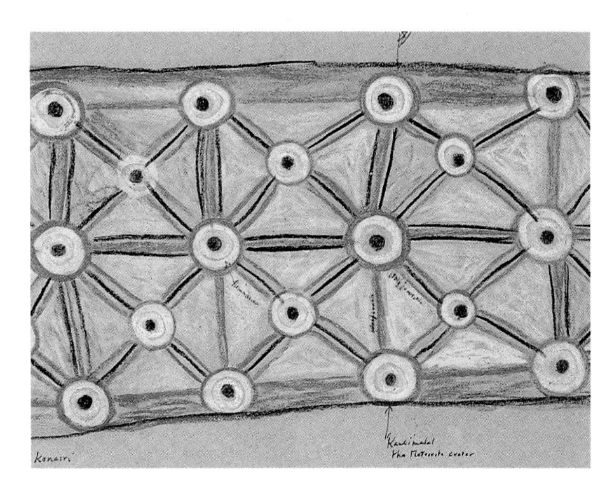

FIG. 133
Drawing of a cave painting, Central Australia (after Worsnop 1897).

FIG. 134
Waters along Stuart Creek and Meteorite Crater (detail), 1953. Bomber, East Kimberley region. Crayon on paper, 35.5 × 54.2 cm.

here, is manifested graphically as a set of circle-path arrangements. The grid may be found in a relatively full form on ancient stone objects, in a drawing of a Central Australian cave painting (Fig. 133), in a 1953 crayon drawing by an artist of the East Kimberley region (Fig. 134), and in a number of the larger desert acrylics (Fig. 37), for example.

Such an arrangement of motifs in the larger template (Fig. 132) works against the notion that particular centers in the landscape might be privileged above all others, and it reflects a culture in which there are no fully bounded groups and the underlying pattern is one of overlapping egocentric social networks.[44] The European-Australian artist Imants Tillers refers to Western Desert works as "a fragment cut from the same cloth."[45]

The most common sectors extracted in Western Desert art, and for certain sacred designs in coastal northern Australia, are outlined by the darker rectangles superimposed on Fig. 132. The addition of new sectors to any such selection is compatibly geometric and brings the likely addition of considerable complication, as each roundel has multiple potential pathways connecting it to other points. In this, the grid is a model of desert political geography (see Chapter IV). Subtractions from it reflect not only the time and space limitations of making selections for specific narrative purposes but also echo the technique of graded exposure. Although it may not be apparent from the particular selection of Western Desert art found in this book, the great majority of works produced in that style are strongly symmetrical and tend to approximate or at least to contain structures of the type shown in Fig. 132. The works illustrated in this book that exemplify these "ideal types" (including some from regions other than the Western Desert) are listed in the legend to the figure.

In classical Aboriginal society, those who control the religious knowledge have much of the power. Religious authorities in Aboriginal society are always letting others know that what they are revealing is only part of a larger whole. This may be the cultural rationale for the fact that a single, central roundel, a foursquare diagonal radial, a foursquare rectilinear radial, a line of 3 or 5 roundels, 3 rows of 3 columns of roundels, or 130 roundels variously connected and arranged in a rectangular formation can all be derived from a single deep structure by some simple derivational rules. A rectangular painting surface provides a readymade, if not quite determining, envelope for such derivations. While similar designs on oval objects have tended to be less rectilinear in approach (that is, they have fewer roundels, or just one, at each end of the design's long axis), resulting in designs of polygonal outline, the emergence of so many rectangular designs in recent years must be related to the influence of the new painting media.

Regional Styles Asymmetrical paintings occur that do contain roundels, and these tend to be in the Yuendumu style (for example, Figs. 140, 157, 159–160, 164–165). This style is distinguished by very sinuous rather than direct connectors, less predictable and less consistent color and motif content, a brighter and more riotous use of color than in Papunya style, and a greater variety of forms. The painting field is frequently divided into two roughly equivalent rectangular areas, at least one of which is usually symmetrical in its basic organization.[46] In spite of their frequent asymmetry, Yuendumu paintings still tend to have a dominant arrangement of forms along the long axis, although not always near its center line. In their tendency to combine asymmetry and symmetry in one composition, Yuendumu paintings demonstrate a greater range of style than those of other regions of the Western Desert.

Papunya acrylics by Pintupi artists, crayon drawings by Pintupi and Pitjantjatjara people of the 1930s (Fig. 131 and compare Fig. 134), and 1980s

Indulkana linocuts by Pitjantjatjara artists (Fig. 36), who are culturally more similar to the Pintupi than to the other groups represented at Papunya and Yuendumu, fall very largely within the formal patterns described above in the discussion of regularities of composition. Geoff Bardon, who worked at Papunya in the beginning period of the acrylic painting movement, noted that "the Pintupis usually have severe abstract designs that are total simplifications of complex stories and ideas" and asserted that "the bush Pintupi are universally haptic with flat one-dimensional patterns and they are least affected by European culture."[47] (Fig. 148.) He contrasted them with the Luritja and Warlpiri, followed by the Anmatyerre/Arrernte artists, who in that order showed increased use of perspective, the suggestion of three-dimensionality, and an emphasis on "visual" approaches. These may also be identically ranked in an ascending order of degree of European contact. Bardon's view is that Aboriginal art before white contact was all "haptic," or based on the logic of touch, rather than "visual."

Ironically, Michaels, who worked at Yuendumu but not Papunya, saw the greater degree of formal symmetry and emphasis on geometric arrangements in Papunya style as a product of European influence via Bardon and the other Papunya art advisors and their reflection of the tastes of the outside art world and consumers. Yuendumu art, as exemplified by the painted school doors (Fig. 140), is described by Michaels as enjoying a "boldness and energy of application," which arises to a great extent from the fact that the painters were left to execute the works without European advice.[48]

Both interpretations may be mistaken, however. Painters at the Yuendumu and Papunya settlements have, as is well known, made their style more precise and neater over time, as their skills in the new media developed and the influence of the market began to exert itself. But the assumption that they may have started from a uniform stylistic background and developed differences of style only recently is probably false. The work of Luke Taylor has shown that the "core structures" of designs on restricted objects vary stylistically from the Yuendumu area south via Papunya to Ayers Rock, and then west to Kikingura.[49] In the Yuendumu area and north of it, meandering parallel lines accompanied by roundels, tracks, and other adjuncts are most common. Moving south, the core structure becomes one of linked ovals, and then, in the Ayers Rock region, linked diamonds. West of there, around Kikingura, the linked diamonds are modified by internal bisecting lines. These designs are essentially the same ones that are so characteristic of the regional styles in acrylics and linocut prints.[50]

In this chapter we have tried to bring to consciousness some of the underlying regularities that make Aboriginal art look the way it does and some of the logic that underlies the balance and counterpoint that so many find so aesthetically pleasing. This has not been a mere exercise in structural grammar-making, however.

The aesthetic attraction of the works we have discussed is combined, in this approach, with the aesthetic attraction of descriptive and explanatory adequacy in the act of analysis. Both kinds of experience are constitutive of meanings that rest on an amalgam of emotional and rational responses. Reason is not against art. A look at any rectangular site-path acrylic by an artist from Papunya should demonstrate this. Regularity, as Oscar Wilde said, offers the eye rest, but where it does so under conditions in which the merely predictable is almost constantly avoided, it leads to reward rather than boredom.

The heavy emphasis of this chapter on visual problems has been necessary to redress the imbalance of existing scholarship in this field, which in the past has focused very largely on the sociological foundations of Aboriginal art or on its iconography. Yet these foundations are at least as interesting as the art's visual qualities, and the need to grasp them is just as vital. Once again we avoid any attempt at a detailed Australia-wide survey in the interest of providing a rich context for at least one of the major art forms represented in this book. We move, then, to our case study in the social production of an art form—that of the acrylic painters of the Western Desert.

Dreamings in Acrylic: Western Desert Art IV

CHRISTOPHER ANDERSON AND FRANÇOISE DUSSART

THE TRADITIONAL art of the vast desert country of Central Australia has always been complex and impressive. The harshness of the desert landscape and the apparent paucity of Aboriginal material culture, however, led most observers to assume that art was an impossibility in such a setting (Fig. 135). This perception was to change radically in the early 1970s, when chance and circumstance gave rise to an explosion of artistic expression in the small, poverty-stricken settlements of Aborigines on the fringes of their desert homelands. The development of this new art form—the Western Des-

FIG. 135
Pintupi family at Ngortino, Central Australia, 1963.

ert acrylic paintings—reveals not only a complex social system and a rich, meaningful worldview but a continuing interaction between the values and aesthetic systems of tradition-oriented Aborigines and other Australians.

Acrylic painting by Central Australian Aborigines is one of the most exciting developments in modern Australian art. The materials—canvas and acrylic paints—are European in origin. The content and the execution of the paintings, however, lie firmly within the framework of desert Aboriginal culture. The topics are generally mythological ones to which the painter has a particular relationship, and the set of polysemous symbols used is the same as that found in the older art forms of rock engraving, ground design, and ceremonial body painting. In contrast to almost all other types of Aboriginal art, which are usually relegated to the realms of "primitive art" or craft,[1] acrylic paintings have come to be considered part of modern Australian art. The acceptance of this new art form is partly a function of the radical changes in white Australian policies and attitudes toward the Aboriginal people since the mid-1970s. Accompanying this development is a growing appreciation by non-Aborigines of the depth and meaning of an Aboriginal worldview. To some extent, though, the acceptance of desert acrylics is due to the art's remarkable similarities to modern Western abstract painting.[2]

Surprisingly little has been written about the art.[3] Much of the literature either has appeared in obscure sources or consists of general, and sometimes superficial, descriptions of the acrylic movement. Most studies have sought to explain the meaning of the art on only one level—the mythic narrative. Our approach, by contrast, takes the production of the art and its historical and cultural context as the starting point for understanding the work. Almost all previous studies of Aboriginal acrylic painting have dwelt exclusively on Papunya, the settlement in Central Australia where the movement began in the early 1970s. In addition to describing and analyzing the art of painters originally resident at Papunya, we have taken a broader perspective and drawn extensively on ethnographic case material from Yuendumu, an Aboriginal settlement to the north of Papunya where acrylics are also produced.[4]

Landscape and Aboriginal Religion in Central Australia

The Central Australian landscape is overwhelming in its vastness, yet it is full of subtle and surprising diversity. To the uninitiated traveler, it appears as a featureless wasteland, but in fact it contains a wide range of flora and fauna that in most years provided an adequate diet for its Aboriginal inhabitants. Vast plains of spinifex grass and mulga trees are slashed by low sandstone and quartzite hills. In some parts of the country huge red sand dunes roll like waves over hundreds of miles of desert. And thrusting their way west, dominating the landscape for miles around, are the purple and red mountains of the MacDonnell Ranges. Tall ghost gum trees fringe the sandy beds of creeks, dry except during the brief rainy season. The rains turn dry salt flats into huge temporary lakes. For most of the year, though, water is found only in sheltered rock holes, soaks, and springs.

In Central Australia, as in other parts of the continent, the links between Aboriginal people and the landscape are fundamental and profound. The religious system of the Aborigines is based on the inseparability of territory, people, and mythical ancestors. This relationship is at the core of ritual art. The most typical features of the desert—sandhills, mountains, rock holes, creeks, plant and animal life—and the red, yellow, black, and white colors of its elements are represented in the complex graphic forms of the traditional art of the Western Desert. These forms, from which the acrylic paintings take their inspiration, include sand stories, rock paintings and engravings, ceremonial object and body paintings, and ground designs. They employ a basic set of symbols, such as dots, concentric circles, and curved and straight lines—all having multiple meanings depending upon the context. Particular configurations represent segments of myths or Dreamings. These stories and their depictions always refer to sites where mythic activity is believed to have occurred and where the ancestral power still remains. The modern acrylic paintings are similar in form and content to the body, rock, and ground paintings and, in effect, offer sacred designs for secular, public viewing.

Details of the creation myth vary among the different Aboriginal groups in this region. One common element is the belief that the world was originally flat and formless and that the mythic heroes emerged from the ground to shape and organize the earth as it is today. The concept of the Dreaming refers to the ancestral past, to the Ancestral Beings and their actions, to a given Ancestral Being's itinerary of travel across the landscape, and to dreams themselves in which sequences of the ancestral past are revealed. But the Dreaming is also the sacred dimension of the present, the driving force that Aborigines believe underlies the here and now.[5]

The mythic heroes or figures from the past era of the Dreaming were 'human' but sometimes appeared in the form of animals or other elements of the natural environment such as flora, fire, or water. Some remained at their place of emergence, and others traveled. They created the landscape by imprinting themselves, leaving traces of their powers, as they acted and interacted with each other. They were transformed into natural features on the ground and in the sky. The Dreaming Beings also left behind the form of social order. They lived like Aboriginal people, they foraged, they ate, they fought, they held ceremonies, they transgressed law and taboo, and they performed extraordinary feats. The sites where these particular events took place are considered sacred. Today Aboriginal people see a direct continuity between the ancestral past, their landscape, and themselves. They see the landscape as alive with the power of the ancestors and, at the same time, humanized in its essential oneness with the living.

Aboriginal Culture of the Western Desert

Many parts of pre-European Aboriginal Australia, particularly the eastern and northern coastal areas, were characterized by great diversity in environment, language, and economic, social, and cultural systems. The situation was different in the heart of Australia, where similarities of Aboriginal lifestyles existed over almost a million square miles of desert and semidesert lands. Within this area is a major cultural block—the Western Desert region—stretching from the MacDonnell Ranges near Alice Springs, down to the Musgrave Ranges in northern South Australia, and up to the Fitzroy basin in northern Western Australia, including parts of the Simpson, Tanami, Gibson, and Great Sandy deserts. It is in this region that acrylic paintings are produced.

Among the main Aboriginal groups in the Western Desert region are the Warlpiri in the north, the Walmadjarri in the northwest, the Kukatja and Pintupi in the center and the west, the Pitjantjatjara and Luritja in the south, and the Arandic groups in the east. Linguistically, it is an area of great homogeneity, with people able to understand each other over thousands of miles.[6] Given the similar environments found throughout the Western Desert region, it is not surprising that Aboriginal groups living there display similarities in material culture and social and economic organization.[7] More significant from the point of view of art is Aboriginal religion. Religious paraphernalia and religious life were more elaborate in Central Australia than in most other parts of Australia. This was one of the reasons for the intense interest in this area among European scholars and others in the early part of the twentieth century. The stark contrast between the apparently meager material culture and lifestyle of Central Australian Aborigines and their rich, complex religious tradition was part of this attraction.

Religion in the desert is distinguished from that of other parts of Aboriginal Australia by what Berndt calls its "segmentary religious complex," which is "marked by a compartmentalization of mythic tracks which correlate with particular local descent groups, each responsible for a section of the total body of religious knowledge."[8] These mythic tracks cover vast distances, linking dozens of sites and unifying many groups and individuals through shared identity and ritual responsibility. Central Australian Aboriginal religion is also characterized by complex women's ritual ceremonies and men's circumcision and subincision ceremonies, and by religious paraphernalia such as the *tjurunga* stones and sacred women's boards, whose designs are like title deeds to land. The emphasis on secrecy in religious matters reaches its zenith in Central Australia. Levels of knowledge are determined by age, gender, and position in society; until recent times, transgression of laws relating to rights and privileges of religious knowledge sometimes resulted in death.

The classical Central Australian art forms that gave rise to the modern acrylic paintings were found in most areas of the Western Desert.[9] Acrylic painting draws on several of these art forms and combines a number of their design elements. Ground paintings, done among some desert groups as part of their religious ceremonies, are perhaps the most similar in form to the acrylics. With these, an area sometimes measuring many square yards is flattened and smoothed out. Sand, clays, ochres, and other materials, including a combination of sticks, bird down, hair, plant fiber, and blood, are then used to create elaborate designs, incorporating concentric circles, furrowed lines, and raised sculpted forms. The designs are prepared for special ceremonies restricted to initiated men, although women in some Aboriginal groups also do their own ground designs (Fig. 136). The designs are destroyed during or immediately after the ceremony. Less spectacular, but no less important in terms of the influence of traditional graphic forms on acrylic painting, are the sand stories. Central Australian people often express concepts such as location, distance, and event through hand marks and designs made in the sand.[10] Similar iconographic elements appear in designs representing mythic ancestors that are painted and engraved on rock surfaces (Fig. 219), in body decoration, an important part of both secret and public ceremonies (Fig. 137), and on objects such as spears, boomerangs, shields and women's food carriers, (Figs. 38, 218, and Cat. 67, 69–70) painted for ceremonial use.[11]

Social Organization and Rights in Design

The Central Australian landscape is crisscrossed by mythic tracks representing the travels of hundreds of different Ancestral Beings. The sites associated with these travels relate to one or several Dreamings that pass through or are resident there. The sites and the Dreamings are linked with individuals and groups, and more than one group usually has rights in any given site. People acquire their rights and knowledge about their territory and Dreamings from a variety of sources, such as inheritance and place of conception, birth, and residence.

Inheritance is central in the granting of ceremonial and territorial rights and responsibilities. A daughter and a son inherit one type of rights through their father, which in Warlpiri and in other Central Australian languages classifies them as *kirda*. Inheritance from the mother's line classifies them as

FIG. 136
Anmatyerre women's ground design of Ngarlu Dreaming, Yuendumu, 1985.

FIG. 137
Warlpiri women dancing with painting at Yuendumu, 1984.

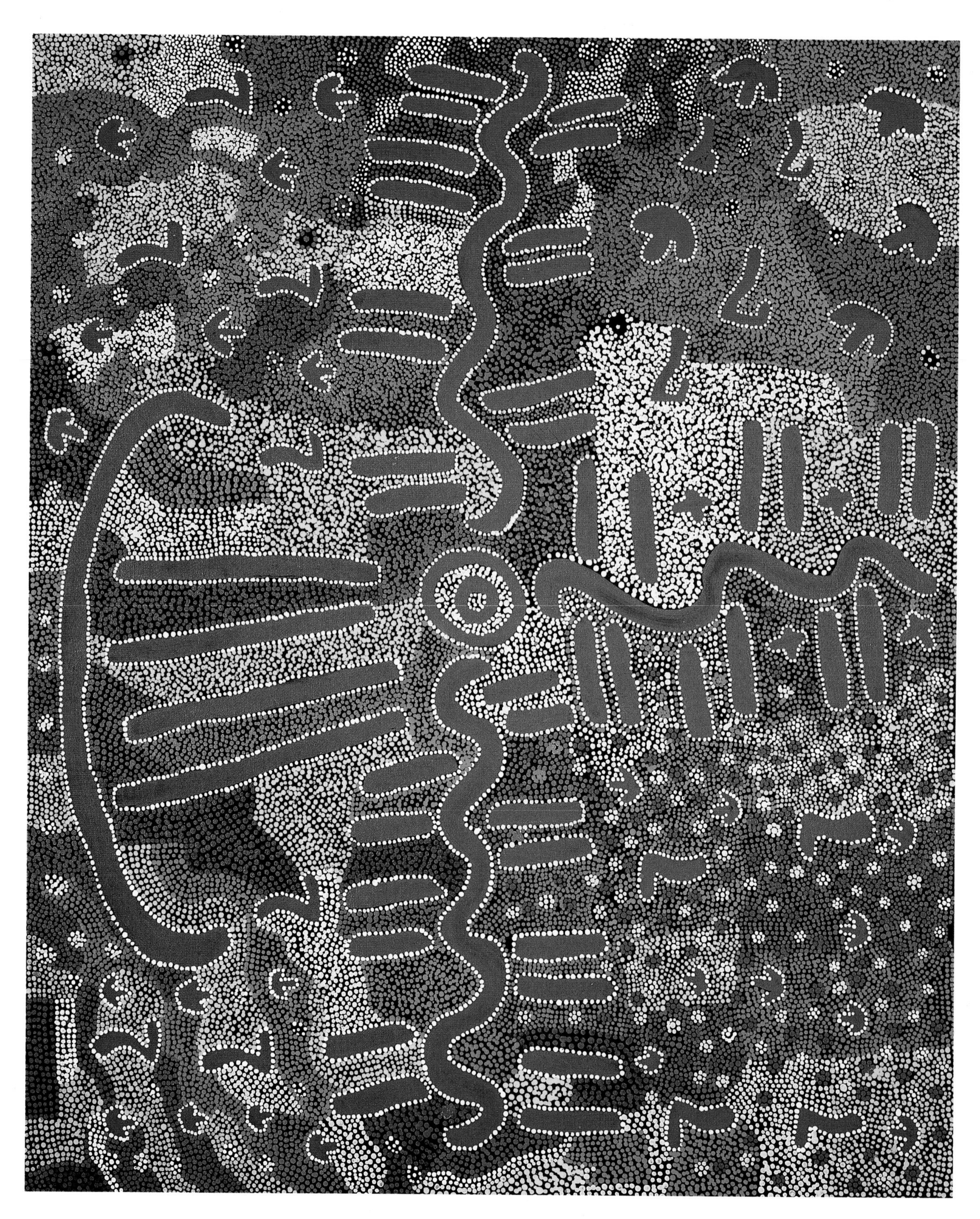

kurdungurlu. Thus for any given site and Dreaming there is a set of *kirda* and a set of *kurdungurlu*. If a woman is *kirda* for her father's country, for example, the children of her mother's brother will be *kurdungurlu* for that same area.

Kirda "own" given countries and have primary economic and spiritual rights in them. *Kurdungurlu* are guardians for the countries owned by the *kirda*. They ensure that the *kirda* fulfill their social and ritual obligations with respect to their Dreamings and associated sites and that access to economic resources in the country is maintained. Through participation in ceremonies people learn about their Dreaming Stories and associated ritual designs, songs, and dances. They are taught how designs and ceremonies should properly represent and reenact the mythical actions of the ancestors. *Kirda* and *kurdungurlu* interact closely in a ceremony through complementary roles: when *kirda* have their bodies painted for ritual purposes, the *kurdungurlu* assist by grinding the ochres, doing the actual painting, and giving advice on the appropriate symbols. In ceremonies for other sites and Dreamings, the roles are reversed.

Painted visual representations of ceremonial events can be executed on different media: the body, ceremonial artifacts and paraphernalia, and the ground. Three main categories of visual representations are used for ceremonies. Only the second and third are found in contemporary acrylic paintings. The first category is composed of designs that are used for secret ceremonies involving initiation and various religious cults and can be seen only by adult men (until recently, on penalty of death). Second are those designs that can be seen by all but are understood only by older men and women. Finally, there are public designs that can be seen and described by all. Through one's lifetime, one accumulates a repertoire of graphic forms to depict the actions of mythical beings. Yuendumu artist Judy Nampijinpa Granites, for example, inherited a segment of the travels of a Rain Dreaming from her father and father's father, and she learned about the ritual designs from her father and her father's sisters. Her painting, *Water Dreaming at Mikanji* (Figs. 138, 138a), depicts mythic actions enacted in men's and women's public ceremonies. It thus belongs to the set of graphic forms that may be seen by all and read, or explained, by the individuals who are connected with this specific Rain Dreaming associated with a particular site on the itinerary of the Rain ancestor's travels.

The History of Acrylic Painting in Central Australia

Aboriginal people express themselves through art in whatever media are available. The adoption of foreign media is not new to Central Australian artists. On their expeditions to Central Australia beginning in the 1930s, the anthropologists N. B. Tindale and C. P. Mountford took along brown paper and crayons and offered them to Aborigines in the bush and in the settlements they visited. They asked the Aborigines to draw whatever they wished,

FIG. 138 / CAT. 40
Water Dreaming at Mikanji, 1986. Judy Nampijinpa Granites, Yuendumu, Central Australia. Acrylic on canvas, 92 × 111 cm.

FIG. 138a
1. Path of the water
2. Emu tracks
3. Water bird tracks
4. Mikanji
5. Boomerangs
6. Small clouds
7. Falling rain
8. Large cloud
9. Lightning

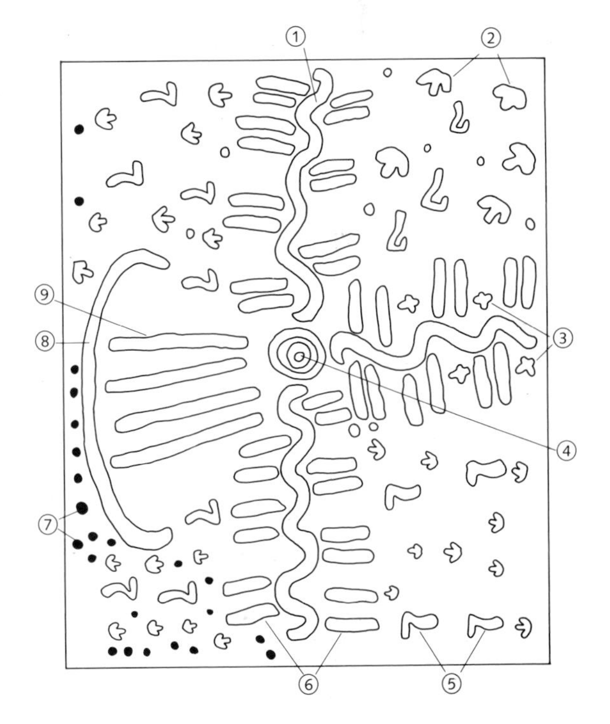

but also to describe objects of daily life and to make maps of their country. The results were impressive: several thousand drawings, many of them subtle and complex depictions of landscape and mythological events (Figs. 131, 134).[12] The similarities of these drawings to modern acrylic paintings are striking. They demonstrate not only the continuity of graphic forms over time but also the readiness of Aborigines, given the right impetus, to adopt a foreign medium for artistic expression.

Another case of Central Australian Aboriginal exposure to European artistic styles and media is that of the Hermannsburg school of watercolorists. Hermannsburg, founded in 1877 as a Lutheran church mission west of Alice Springs and today mainly made up of Aranda-speaking people from the immediate region, had a long history of involvement with the European craft market. In the early days of the settlement, Aborigines made artifacts for sale to the mission staff, and for a time the community maintained a cottage industry that produced camel-hair artists' brushes. The most important development at Hermannsburg, though, was the introduction in the 1930s of the European tradition of landscape watercolor painting by several white artists teaching at the mission. Although the Hermannsburg watercolors differed from both the crayon drawings and the modern acrylics in their use of perspective, Aboriginal painters at Hermannsburg, like the later acrylic artists, depicted sites in the landscape that were important to them.[13] In fact, some of the watercolor paintings portray significant sites as do the modern acrylics—for example, Mt. Zeil in Theo Brown Jakamarra's *Witchetty Grub Dreaming at Mt. Zeil* (Fig. 91). Australia's best known Aboriginal artist, Albert Namatjira (Figs. 245–47), was the first to paint with watercolors at Hermannsburg. The subject of one of his earliest works was Pupanyi, the Dreaming site after which Papunya, the first center for acrylic painting, was named.

The close, if indirect, relationship between Hermannsburg and the Papunya acrylic painters is not commonly known. The settlement of Papunya, a hundred miles to the northwest, has several historic links with Hermannsburg. Lutheran missionaries assisted in the establishment of Papunya in the late 1950s and in bringing in desert Aborigines, particularly the Pintupi during the mid-1960s. Some of the Aboriginal people who settled at Papunya had earlier lived in Hermannsburg, so there were kinship and other social links between the two settlements. Papunya residents were certainly aware of the success of the painters at Hermannsburg and the money that they were able to earn from the sale of their paintings. In addition, an Aranda Hermannsburg resident, Obed Raggett, worked as an assistant art teacher at Papunya in 1971 when acrylic paintings were first produced there.[14] Several of the Hermannsburg watercolorists, such as Wenton Rubuntja, are now accomplished acrylic painters, and some acrylic painters, such as Kaapa Mbitjana Jampijinpa, have done landscape watercolors. Clifford Possum Japaljarri describes later in this chapter how he began painting when one of Namatjira's sons gave him watercolors to paint artifacts for sale.

Papunya residents, like those of Hermannsburg, had made artifacts for the tourist market for many years. The acrylic artist Billy Stockman Japaljarri, for instance, sold his painted boomerangs to American servicemen during the Second World War along the Alice Springs to Darwin highway.[15] But it was the arrival at Papunya in 1971 of a young white schoolteacher, Geoff Bardon, that provided the catalyst for an explosion of artistic expression.

Papunya was set up in 1959 to bring together Warlpiri, Luritja, Anmatyerre, and Pintupi Aborigines from the eastern fringes of the Western Desert. It was administered by the Commonwealth and Northern Territory governments, which provided health, education, and housing facilities along with limited employment. The official Australian policy toward Aborigines at the time was that of assimilation to European ways. Aboriginal children at Papunya attended school, and the adults, most of whom did not speak English and lacked employable skills, were given such jobs as gardeners and street cleaners. Their income was supplemented by social-security payments.

It was into this setting that Bardon, a former art student from Sydney, arrived in 1971 to teach art to Aboriginal children in the Papunya school. Bardon developed a relationship with several important older Aboriginal men in the settlement, who as a result became interested in the media of the Western art he was teaching. In 1971 a school project to paint a mural was taken over by the older men, who completed it in traditional rock-painting style. (The subject of the painting was Honey Ant Dreaming, the Dreaming for the site after which Papunya had been named.) Following this project, the men began to paint on any materials available to them, including plywood and linoleum. Instead of imposing European notions of perspective or suggesting that the paintings reflect the physical environment of the settlement, Bardon encouraged the men to use the existing system of desert culture symbols to depict their Dreamings and links with the country. The result was staggering: between July 1971 and August 1972, 620 paintings were delivered to the Stuart Art Centre in Alice Springs, and many more paintings were produced but not sold.[16] Among the most prolific and important Papunya artists active in this period were Kaapa Mbitjana Jampijinpa (Fig. 174), Billy Stockman Japaljarri, Long Jack Phillipus Jakamarra, Old Mick Jakamarra, and Uta Uta Jangala (Fig. 169).

By mid-1971 the painting movement at Papunya was well established. Prices charged for the paintings were low, averaging about A$25 to $30 a painting, and dealers in Alice Springs were selling some of the works. In August 1971 Kaapa Mbitjana Jampijinpa shared first prize in the Alice Springs Caltex Art Award. That recognition, along with the sale of paintings, resulted in a dramatic increase in artistic activity at Papunya.[17] Bardon, finding that he could not continue to supervise the artists and keep up with his teaching duties, left Papunya at the end of 1971. In the following year Papunya painters won a second Caltex Art Award and, with the support of Robert Edwards (then of the Aboriginal Arts Board) and Dick Kimber (another local schoolteacher), established Papunya Tula Artists Pty Ltd.[18] Another prize in 1972 led to national media attention. Since that time, exhibitions of Papunya acrylic paintings have been held in cities throughout the world, including Frankfurt, Paris, London, and Los Angeles. Papunya Tula has had six successive art advisers and coordinators (Peter Fannin, Janet Wilson, Dick Kimber, John Kean, Andrew Crocker, and Daphne Williams), all of whom have played significant roles in the development of Papunya art. The company sells its paintings in its Alice Springs gallery, opened in 1985, and through agents in the major Australian cities. Prices for the works of well-known painters ranged from A$2,000 to $15,000 in 1987.

Since the late 1970s and the enactment of land-rights legislation, Aborigines from the remoter areas of Australia have been leaving the centralized settlements to set up smaller, more homogenous communities in their traditional homelands. The Pintupi left the Papunya settlement permanently in the period between 1972 and 1980 and moved west, establishing new residential communities at Yayayi, New Bore, Mt. Liebig, and Kintore in Central Australia and at Kiwirrkura in Western Australia.[19] Most of the Pintupi acrylic painters now work from these communities. Anmatyerre and Warlpiri people have also moved out of Papunya and set up outstations to the north and east of the settlement. The more relaxed and homogeneous setting of these new communities and the need to generate income to cover the costs of living in independent residential communities are two factors that have stimulated the production of acrylic paintings.

The following biographical statement by Anmatyerre artist Clifford Possum Japaljarri, recorded by John Kean in Alice Springs in 1984, summarizes much of the history of the acrylic painting movement. He begins by talking of his first works—wood carvings—done when he was at Napperby Station, east of Yuendumu:

> I been go back work Napperby. We been get a holiday. I pick'em out idea. I start from tree like this one [points to Red River gum]. I cut'em with axe and tommyhawk. I start make'em saddle first, from wood. After that I start wood carvin' . . . goanna, snake. I do it from mulga [tree] and bean tree. Like grandfather been make'em *kurdiji* and *parraja* [wooden shield and food carrier].

FIG. 139
Lightning and Thunder Dreaming at Puyurru, ca. 1976. George Jampijinpa Robertson, Yuendumu, Central Australia. Acrylic on board, 30.5 × 55.5 cm.

After that I start painting. Them watercolors. I seen'em [saw] Namatjira, living in Glen Helen Gorge [near Hermannsburg]. I got it from Namatjira's son. He give me watercolor. I start painting boomerang and then *yukurrukurru* [small boards held during ceremonial dancing]. I . . . use'em [painted] them kangaroo, them euro [wallaby], them *jampi*, them *watiya* [grass and trees]. I been get'em good money. For tourist people, you know.

Then after that one, I been go back to Bullocky Crossing, this side [east] of Papunya . . . Papunya been start now [was set up], might be a couple of building house. Schoolteacher and all been start there, teachin' all the kid long [who live at] Papunya. I go back to Mt. Allan [east of Yuendumu] again. No, sorry. They give me married long Emily [I was married to Emily first]. Then I been work [at] Mt. Allan for two years, then come back Papunya.

Schoolteacher mob give me job, school'em [teaching] all that school kid mob [wood carving]. After that Geoff Bardon been there! After that, he been start for this painting. Get them hardboard. Small one. We been do'em inside [Bardon's] house first. That was me and Tim Leura [Japaljarri] and Kaapa [Jampijinpa]. We three been workin' there. And other mob been get job and we been get pay and sell'em board. I sell'em big one, about that long [illustrates]. Two men from America. We been get job, all them Luritja side [group]. Right, after that, all them Pintupi mob been get job. We been do'em all them art board.

After that, I went back. I went back Narwietooma [pastoral station east of Papunya]. I was workin' [as] head stockman now. In holiday time I been start painting again at Papunya. [He came to Papunya during his work vacation and painted there].

Right, after that, Geoff Bardon been go away. Peter Fannin [art adviser], he start'em canvas. [Fannin, who arrived at Papunya in 1973, was the first to give canvases to the painters].[20]

FIG. 140
Yam and Bush Tomato Dreaming on Yuendumu school door, 1983. Cookie Japaljarri Stewart, Yuendumu, Central Australia. Acrylic on metal door, 200.6 × 102 cm.

Many of the Warlpiri-speaking Papunya painters have had close relations with Yuendumu, a Warlpiri settlement 75 miles north of Papunya. Yuendumu residents, who were aware of the acrylic painting movement at Papunya, had painted with acrylics on available surfaces, including rocks and plywood, in the early 1970s; by 1976 they had produced small acrylics on canvas board, with the assistance of local non-Aborigines (Fig. 139). In 1978 Western Desert symbols appeared as part of designs painted on buildings at Yuendumu. Acrylic painting at Yuendumu did not begin in earnest until the early 1980s, however, when Warlpiri women, in an attempt to earn cash income, started to use acrylic paints on artifacts and small canvas boards. They were assisted and encouraged in this by non-Aboriginal women—an anthropologist, a linguist, and several teachers—who were working at Yuendumu. While the idea of painting and the impetus to paint belonged to the Warlpiri women, the white advisers played a critical role, especially in obtaining materials and selling the works. After six months of a flourishing women's painting movement, Warlpiri men at Yuendumu began to work in acrylics. At the request of the school principal, several senior men painted their mythic-ritual designs on the doors of the community school (Fig. 140).[21] Following this, and partly because they were envious of the women's success in buying a four-wheel-drive truck with funds from the sale

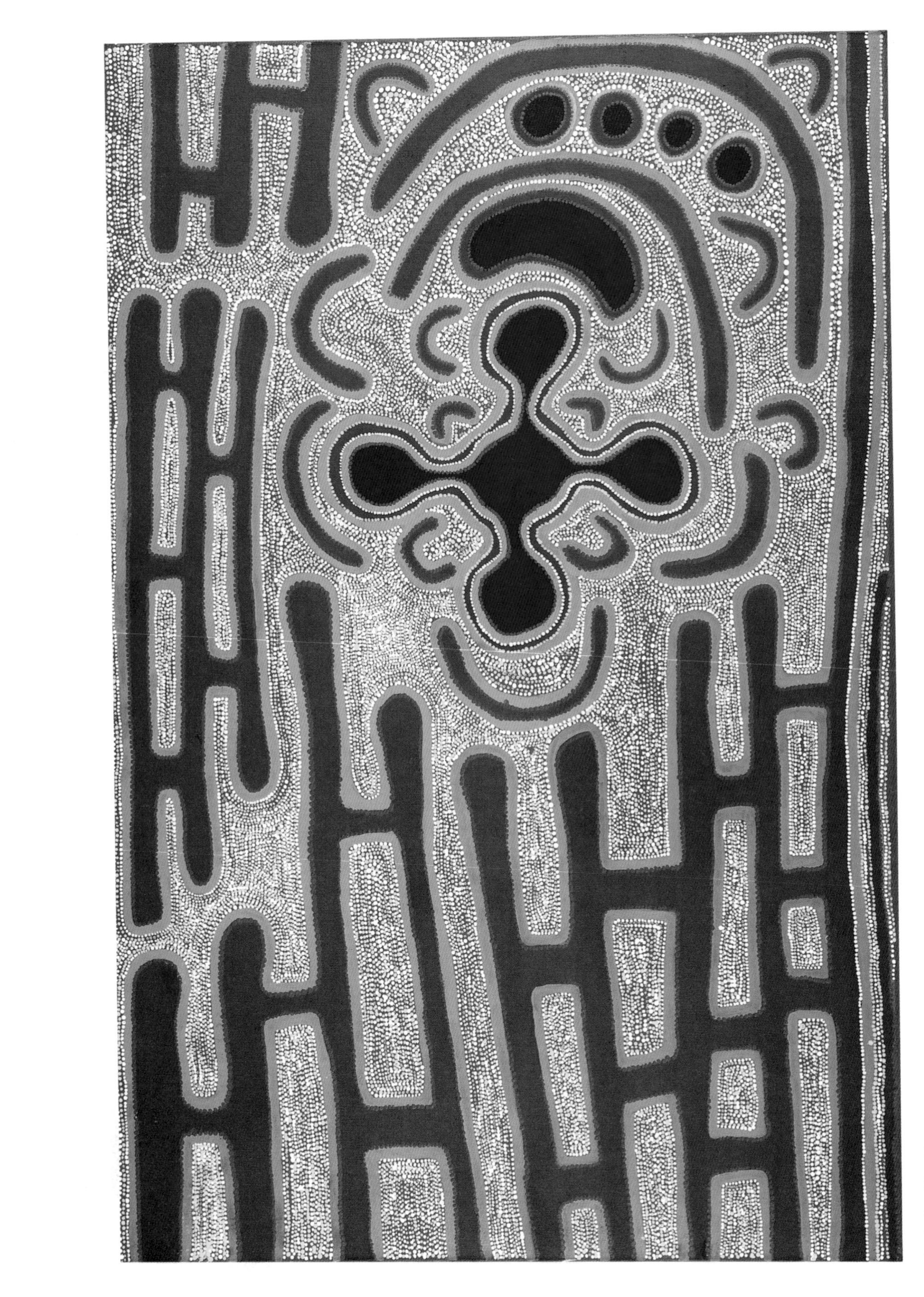

FIG. 141 / CAT. 66
Jila Japingka, 1987.
Peter Skipper, Fitzroy Crossing, Western Australia. Acrylic on canvas, 181.5 × 120.5 cm.

of paintings, the men began painting on large canvases.[22] In 1985 Yuendumu painters established the Warlukurlangu Aboriginal Artists Association,[23] which employs an art coordinator and handles the purchase of artist materials, the sales of paintings, and the distribution among the artists of money earned from sales.

Aborigines in several other communities—including Mt. Allan and Lajamanu in Central Australia and Balgo and Fitzroy Crossing in Western Australia—have also begun to paint with acrylics. (See, for example, Figs. 141, 141a.)

Painters and Painting Techniques

The Western notion of the artist did not exist in tradition-oriented Aboriginal society, as each individual was expected to learn about specific sets of designs and to reproduce them. This is not to say that some people are not more skilled than others. In body painting, for example, certain differences of skill are recognized in the differentiation of painting materials (ochres, clay, and charcoal) and symbols in the design, the placement of elements proportional to the body part on which they are painted, and the neatness and accuracy with which the painting is executed. Even though tradition may require that a *kirda* be painted by another *kirda* or a *kurdungurlu* for a given Dreaming, a person who has a reputation as a skillful painter may be asked to do the painting.

The same situation exists with acrylic paintings. In 1984, when the women at Yuendumu were painting to earn enough money to buy a truck, the most skilled painters were sometimes pressured to do acrylic paintings. Data on the painting activity at Yuendumu show that while many people began painting, only a few continued to paint. Out of a population of about 900, 222 people painted during the period between July 1985 and July 1987. Of these, seventy-two percent did five or fewer paintings, and thirty-five percent only one. Eight percent of the painters were responsible for thirty-six percent of all acrylic paintings produced in the period.[24] From this, it appears that specialization in acrylic painting emerged soon after the development of the painting movement at Yuendumu. (The issue of specialization is discussed later in this chapter.)

Yuendumu painters tend to paint Dreaming designs for which they are *kirda*, although they occasionally will paint Dreamings for which they are *kurdungurlu*. The rules for ritual assistance between *kirda* and *kurdungurlu* are less strictly observed in the execution of acrylic paintings than in other Central Australian Aboriginal art forms. Nevertheless, *kurdungurlu* will sometimes supervise the production of paintings to ensure that the Dreaming and mythic events are properly depicted, in the same way that they stage-manage ceremonies.

Michael Nelson Jakamarra, a Warlpiri painter living at Papunya, comments:

FIG. 141a
1. Mawunumpa
2. Pajpara
3. Long sandhills
4. Miljitawurru (Rain coming from the south)
5. Clouds
6. Sandhills
7. Pirril Pirril (Rain coming from the west)
8. Jila Japingka
9. Kayilipal Kayilipal (Rain coming from the north)
10. Pirntiwanampa (Rain coming from the east)

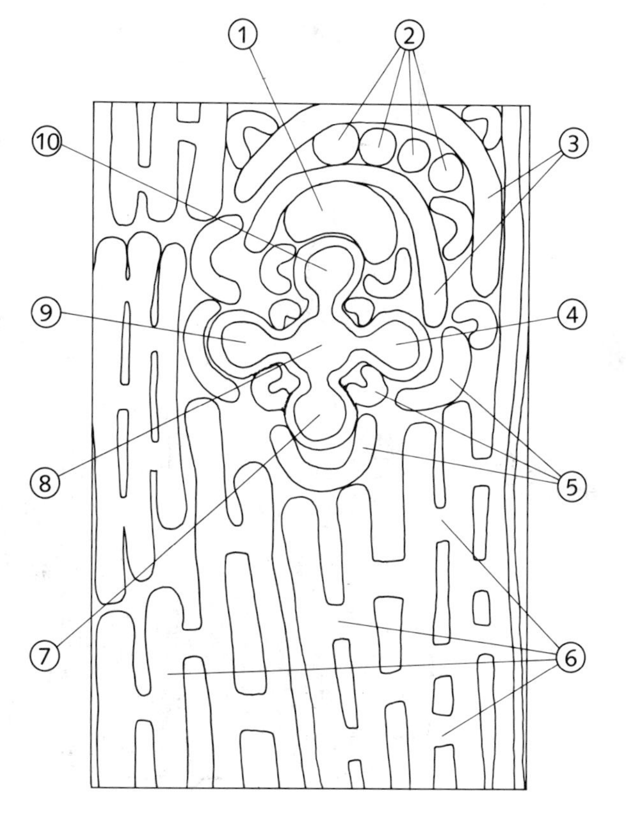

You gotta canvas, paint, and brush ready. Well, first you gotta ask your father and *kurdungurlu*. [They'll say] 'You do that Dreamin' there, which is belonging to your grandfather and father.' They'll give you a clue, they'll show you a drawing on the ground first. You've got it in your brain now. You know it because you've seen your father [in a ceremony], with that painting on his body and one on the ground. You'll see it, then you'll know it.

Right, you'll start and you'll do a painting, and if you make a mistake, well you've gotta ask again. You've gotta ask your father or *kurdungurlu*. [They'll say] 'Alright, you gotta rub that out a little bit. You've gotta do it this way.' You've got to show it to that old man and ask him if that painting's alright. [He'll say] 'Yes, carry on, you gotta finish'em off.' All the detail for the painting, you gotta ask that old man, they've gotta tell you about that story and Dreaming, which is which. You've got it in your brain.[25]

Two or three people often work on one painting. The *kirda* who is the most knowledgeable about the Dreaming event chosen for the painting sketches out or paints the main elements, or gives instruction to a more skillful painter (usually while singing the songs associated with the subject of

FIG. 142
Paddy Jupurrurla Nelson (left) and Maggie Napanangka, Yuendumu, Central Australia, 1987.

the painting). Other *kirda* or *kurdungurlu* may help paint the dots, but this is done under the control of the *kirda* who initiated the choice of the Dreaming event. Sometimes, *kirda* for a Dreaming may choose to execute a painting by themselves.

At both Papunya and Yuendumu it is more common, however, for relatives or other camp residents to assist with the painting, even if these people have no knowledge of or rights over the ritual designs. Both men's and women's paintings are often cooperative endeavors. Even in the early days of painting, Yuendumu women, although working on individual canvases, would paint together and help each other with the dotting, commenting on the mythic and aesthetic qualities of each other's work. Many paintings are mixed-gender productions—for example, brother-and-sister or husband-and-wife teams (Figs. 142–43). In *Five Dreamings* (Fig. 143), Michael Nelson Jakamarra painted the main symbols and his wife, Marjorie Napaljarri, helped with the background. Because dotting is such an arduous process, the non-*kirda* parties will often assist with this part of the painting, and the different styles of dotting are sometimes apparent (Fig. 144). People

FIG. 143 / CAT. 43
Five Dreamings, 1984. Michael Nelson Jakamarra, assisted by Marjorie Napaljarri, Papunya, Central Australia. Acrylic on canvas, 122 × 182 cm.

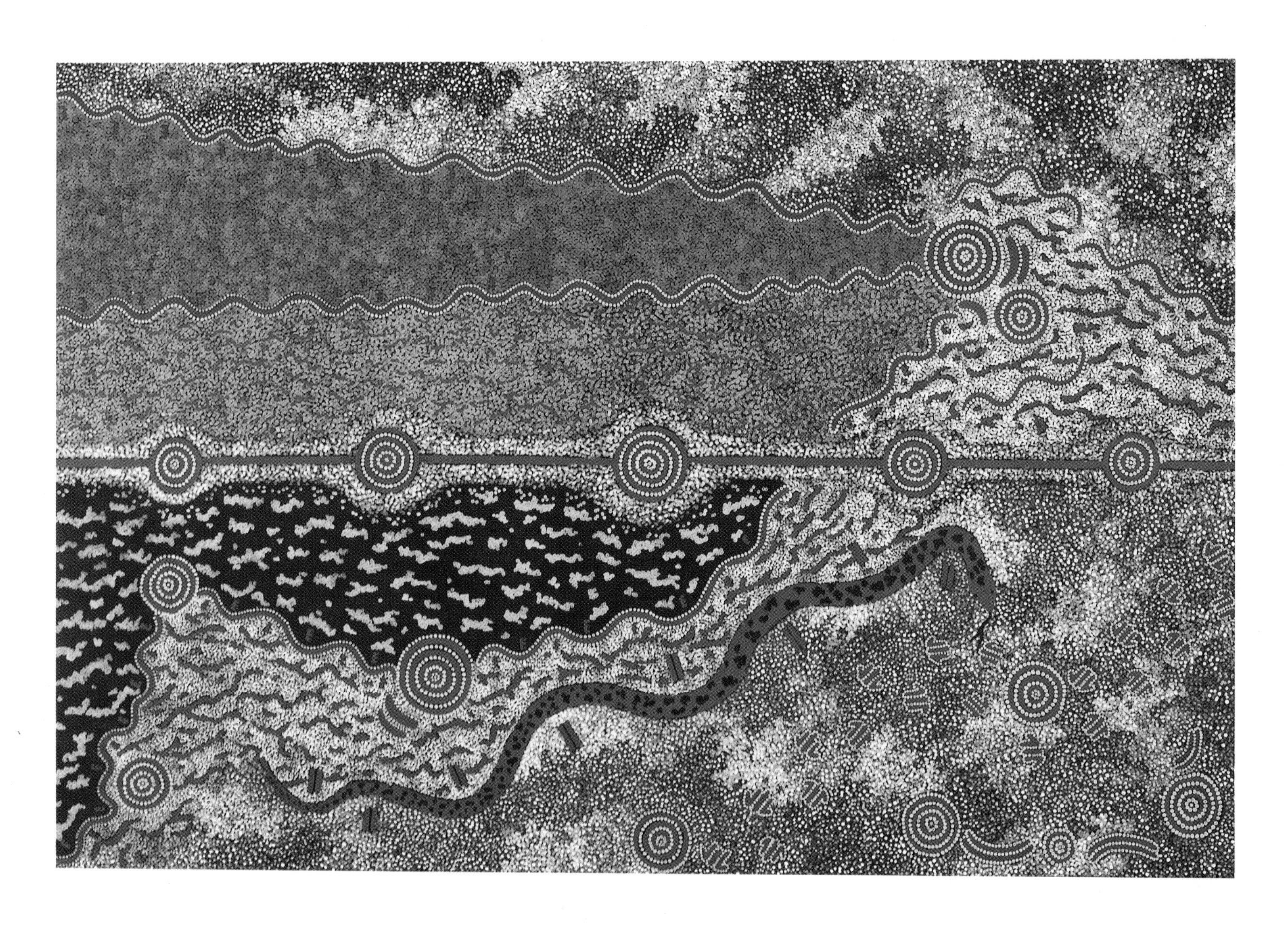

FIG. 144 / CAT. 39
Burrowing Skink Dreaming at Parikirlangu, 1986.
Darby Jampijinpa, Yuendumu, Central Australia. Acrylic on canvas,
145.3 × 94.2 cm.

who initiate the choice of the Dreaming event to be depicted will always present themselves as the painter even if they have been assisted by other people and, occasionally, even if they have done none of the actual painting themselves. *Kurdungurlu* are sometimes listed as joint painters when they have not participated in the painting, an indication of the continuing importance of the *kirda-kurdungurlu* relationship in the acrylic context.

Who is listed as the artist for a particular work generally depends on the knowledge of the art adviser keeping such records and the willingness of the owner of the Dreaming to have other people cited as co-painters. In our view, many paintings are listed as having been done by a single artist when, in fact, several people were involved.[26] An example of this is the large painting *Yumari* (Fig. 179), for which Uta Uta Jangala is listed as the only artist. In fact, Uta Uta blocked out the main elements and directed eleven other men in the execution of the rest of the painting (Fig. 145).[27]

To Aborigines, the most important factors in the painting process are the choice of the Dreaming event to be depicted and the relationship between the given country or site, the Dreaming, and the initiator/painter who claims rights in a painting that uses his or her ritual designs. The right to paint a particular Dreaming event and its graphic forms (and even to tell the story of

FIG. 145
Uta Uta Jangala (left) directing the painting of Yumari (Fig. 179), assisted by (left to right) Anatjari Jampijinpa, Dinny Jampijinpa, John Jakamarra, Kania Japangardi, Charlie Japangardi, and Yala Yala Jungarrayi Gibson (back to camera), Papunya, Central Australia, 1981.

FIG. 146
Maggie Napangardi painting Initiated Women Dreaming at West Camp, Yuendumu, Central Australia, 1987.

a painting) belongs to the *kirda*. But the *kurdungurlu* and other assistants must be compensated for their involvement, as is the case in a ritual context. They generally will ask for, and sometimes receive, part of the proceeds from the sale of the painting.

Acrylic Production and Art Coordinators

Art advisers play a significant role in the actual production of paintings as well as in the documentation and marketing of completed works. In the case of Papunya, the non-Aboriginal staff members of Papunya Tula, based in Alice Springs, deliver stretched canvases and paints to the artists' camps. At Yuendumu, a resident art coordinator has the painting materials brought in, stretches and primes the canvases, and then paints them with background colors (usually of the artist's choice). The canvases and paints are then distributed as needed. Painting is normally done in the painter's home camp (Fig. 146). The main symbols are put on with ordinary painter's brushes. Small bush sticks, matchsticks, or surgical cotton sticks (with the cotton removed) are used for dotting (Fig. 147). Paint is mixed and stored in cut-off soft drink cans. Papunya artist Michael Nelson Jakamarra summarizes what happens after a painting is completed:

> If Daphne [Williams, Papunya Tula art coordinator] comes around when your painting's finished, she will ask you the stories about that painting. So you gotta tell'em straight story [the correct one]. She writes it down, then writes down the check. Then there you are.[28]

In both communities the art advisers collect the completed paintings to be sold and gather documentation, including information on the Dreaming Stories depicted in the works. An initial payment is made to the artists upon completion of the painting; final payment is made upon sale of the painting. Paintings are sold either to people who visit the community or, more often, on consignment at exhibitions. Artists sometimes take paintings into Alice Springs to sell. This practice is discouraged by the artists' organizations and their advisers because it tends to undercut the pricing levels established by them and prevents them from being reimbursed for the cost of materials.

Acrylic Paintings and Levels of Interpretation

> I grab out that idea. I can see'em. I must have a picture in here [pointing to his head]. And it comes out just like that. The idea. We don't practice you know. We just work with the idea. We put one color first. We just get four or might be six tins (cans). We make'em six differen' color. Alright, I start out now on this

one first, in the center, like a story [that is, the main Dreaming design is put onto the painting]. Right, after that we gotta put'em 'nother different color, finish'em right out. Tell that story for European. Alright, after that I gotta think about for 'nother story now, and after I finish'em, 'nother story. All the way like that.[29]

In this statement the Papunya artist Paddy Carroll Jungarrayi presents a producer's view of the creation of acrylic paintings. Although, as he notes, the paintings are done for non-Aborigines, the reading of the paintings by the viewer involves interpretation on several different levels. Such interpretation rests on knowledge of the iconography or symbolic representation of images, the role of color in that process, the narrative content of what is being depicted, and the position of the painting within a cultural and social framework.

Iconography To recognize most elements in Western Desert acrylic painting the viewer must know the site and the Dreaming depicted in the painting. The meanings of the symbols vary, depending on the context and the viewer's level of ritual knowledge. Nevertheless, there are some standard design elements.[30] Concentric circles usually represent campsites or rock holes, and straight lines between circles illustrate the routes traveled between camps or places. Wavy lines across a painting usually symbolize water or rain (Fig. 148); small U-shaped figures represent people sitting, and straight lines next to them, weapons or domestic implements (Fig. 156). Some objects are shown in a less stylized manner—for example, the hair spindle (Fig. 149)—while others are obscured or hidden, as in Fig. 150, where a ritual headdress is hinted at. Tracks, whether human or animal, are often depicted in plan view as they appear on the ground (Fig. 138); lizards and snakes are frequently shown as seen from above (Figs. 70, 143). Significant plant species are generally shown in a stylized but figurative manner (Fig. 151). There appears, at least at Yuendumu, to be a relationship between the increase in number of paintings sold and the use of figurative elements in paintings, which relates to Aboriginal attempts to make their works more accessible to non-Aborigines.

In the early days of the acrylic movement, Papunya painters sometimes depicted mythic events involving Dreaming heroes by showing them as humanlike figures. Many of the paintings of this period can no longer be exhibited because they depict secret elements (for example in the ceremonial body decoration of figures). The illustration of figures in paintings ceased about 1974, probably because the painters and other Aboriginal viewers believed that such paintings were too explicit. Since that time, some senior painters, such as Clifford Possum Japaljarri (Figs. 152, 152a) and Tim Leura Japaljarri (Figs. 153, 153a) have occasionally shown human figures as skeletons.

Dotted primary motifs and backgrounds have become the hallmark of the acrylic movement. The dotting derives from the daubing of "dots" of white down fluff onto the still-wet coatings of ochre and blood applied to objects to be used in ceremonies. (Painted dots of ochre are also used for

FIG. 147
Uta Uta Jangala painting Yumari (Fig. 179), Papunya, Central Australia, 1981.

FIG. 148 / CAT. 57
Kangaroo and Shield People Dreaming at Lake Mackay, 1980. Timmy Japangardi, Papunya, Central Australia. Acrylic on canvas, 186 × 155 cm.

FIG. 149 / CAT. 51
Man's Love Story, 1981. Clifford Possum Japaljarri, Papunya, Central Australia. Acrylic on canvas, 52 × 41.5 cm.

FIG. 150 / CAT. 54
Kulijarra, 1981. Tim Woods Jampijinpa, Papunya, Central Australia. Acrylic on canvas, 80.3 × 99.2 cm.

ritual purposes).[31] Warlpiri women say that they obtained the dotting process from men; it was not generally done in women's art prior to the development of acrylic painting. The dotting is usually applied as background to the main elements, in different colors and in different patterns, often imparting a mosaic quality to the paintings. Sometimes paintings are wholly made up of dots (Figs. 154–55). According to Warlpiri painters, there are three main ways of doing the dots for a painting, and they describe these in terms of how people walk about in the bush. The first, *yirrarni kanardi*, refers to walking straight:

The second, *wirlki wirlki yirrarni*, refers to clusters of boomerangs with right angles at one end:

Finally, there is *rdaku kari rdaku kari*, "to go from hole to hole," as when hunting goannas:

Acrylic painters will often combine in a single work several graphic forms that were formerly used in only one particular context. In Molly Nampijinpa Langdon's painting (Fig. 156), for example, the central motif is

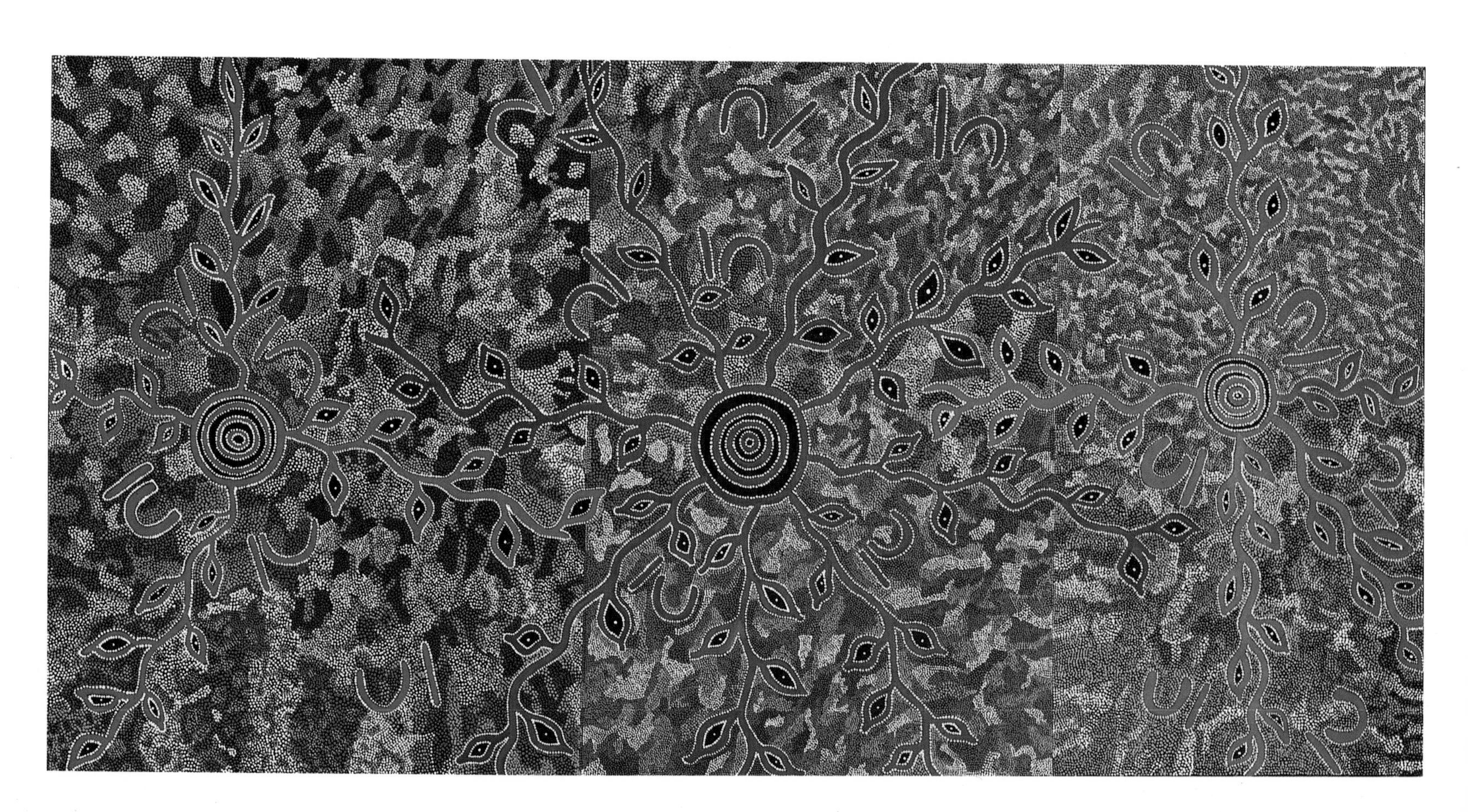

FIG. 151/CAT. 46
Bush Cabbage Dreaming at Ngarlu, 1986. Cookie Stewart Japaljarri, Alma Nungarrayi Granites, and Robin Japanangka Granites, Yuendumu, Central Australia. Acrylic on canvas, 120.5 × 237.5 cm.

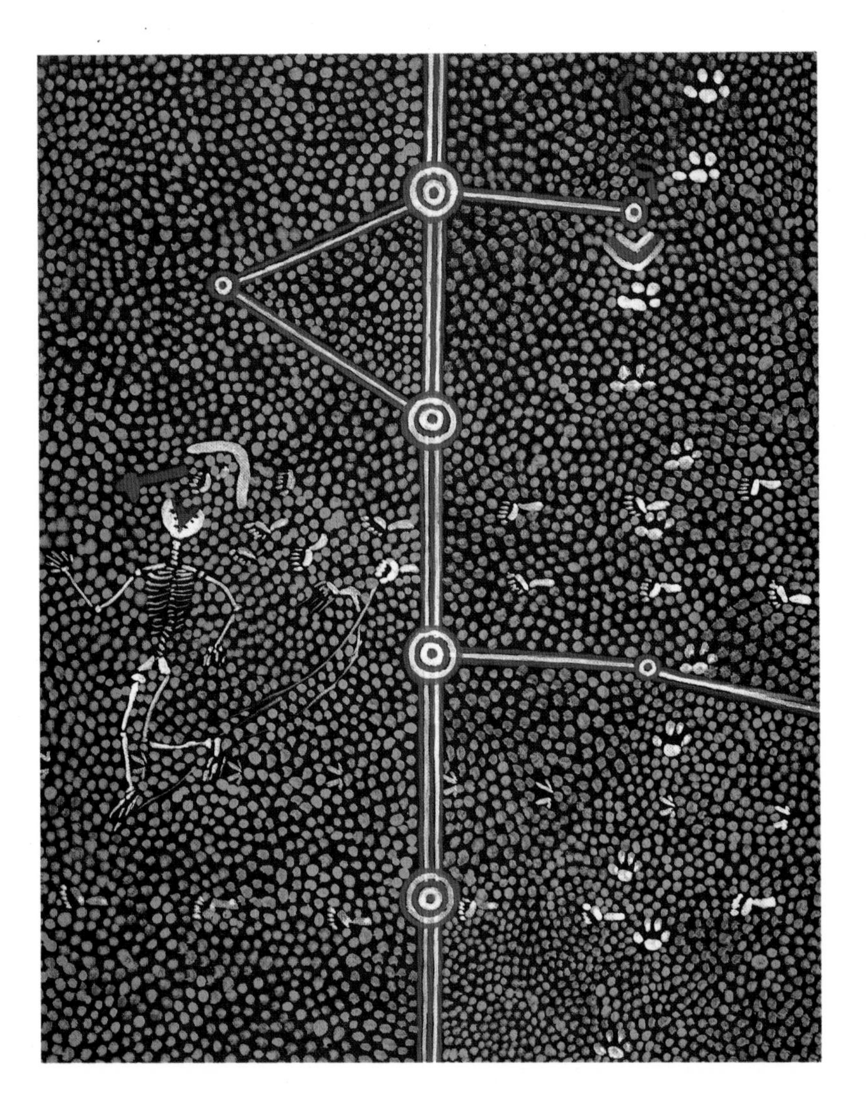

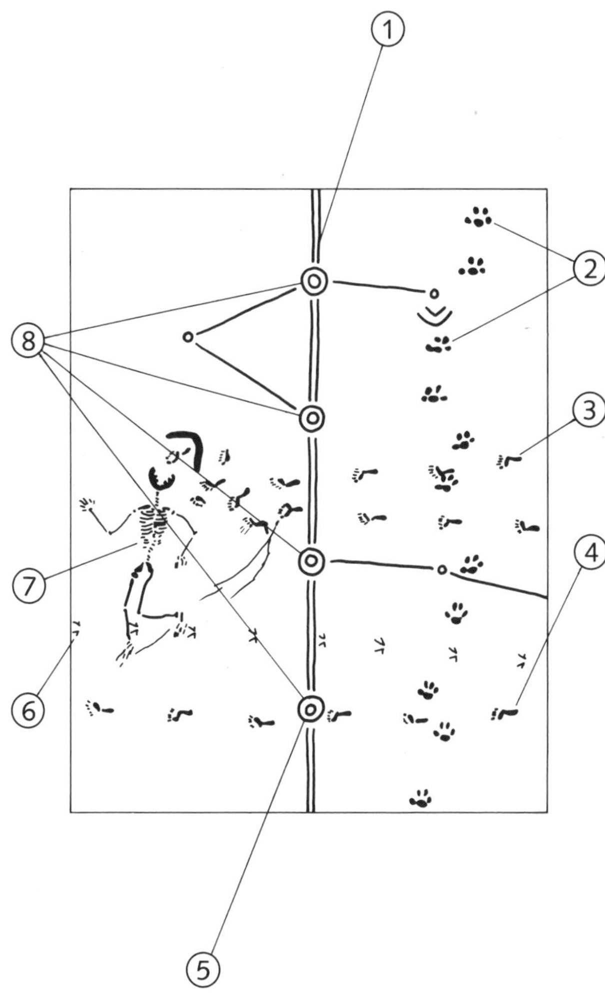

FIG. 152 / CAT. 50
Five Dreamings, 1976. Clifford Possum Japaljarri, Mbunghara, Central Australia. Acrylic on board, 50 × 40 cm.

FIG. 152a
1. Honey Ant Dreaming track
2. Dingo/Man tracks
3. Two Men coming from Aralukaja
4. Ancestral Nungarrayi woman's tracks
5. Yuendumu
6. Hare Wallaby Dreaming track
7. Man killed after fight and chase
8. Honey Ant Dreaming sites

an interpretation of a body painting for the Fire Dreaming associated with the site of Ngarna, south of Yuendumu. What in body painting is a solid line becomes on the canvas a dotted one. Other elements in the painting, such as the U-shaped forms, could have been used on a wooden ritual artifact or in a sand story. Thus on the surface of the canvas, and using acrylic paint, the painter has expressed her knowledge about the myth depicted by employing its various graphic representations that are normally rendered on different surfaces.

Color The range of colors used in acrylic paintings varies according to four main factors. First, some colors are associated with specific Dreaming figures and myth segments. In Budgerigar Dreaming the bird eats a black and yellow seed; this seed is represented with charcoal and yellow ochre in body paintings and on ritual paraphernalia. Colors are also associated with particular sites and ceremonies. It is commonly held among the Warlpiri at Yuendumu that the four basic color elements used for ritual purposes originated from an elemental fire. Table I lists the four colors and the substances

FIG. 153 / CAT. 52
Possum Spirit Dreaming, 1980. Tim Leura Japaljarri, assisted by Clifford Possum Japaljarri, Papunya, Central Australia. Acrylic on canvas, 213 × 701 cm.

FIG. 153a
1. Dreaming journey lines
2. Resting places in the Spirit journey
3. Windbreaks for the Corroboree Men
4. Old Man's Dreaming
5. Yam Dreaming
6. Running Water
7. Campsites
8. Death Spirit Figure
9. Sun and Moon Dreaming

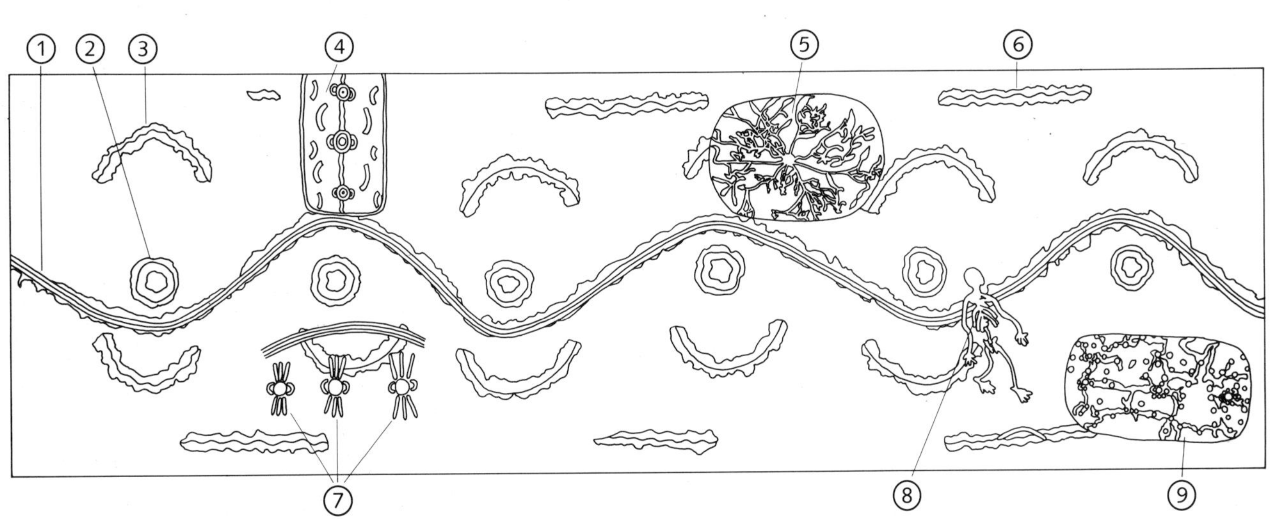
1
2
3
4
5
6
7
8
9

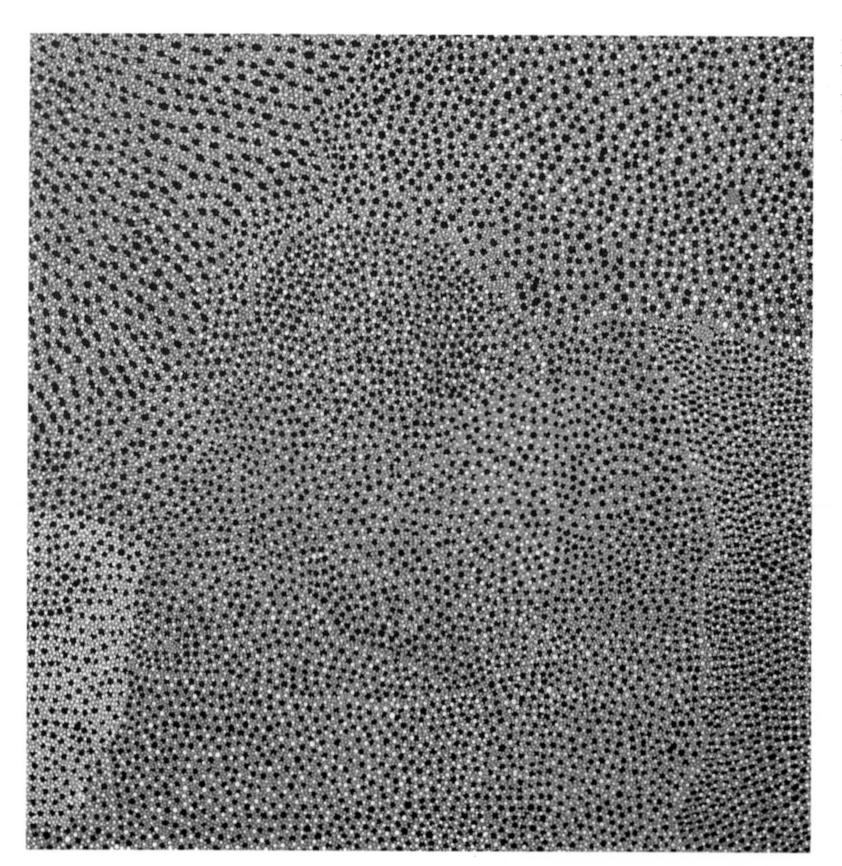

FIG. 154 / CAT. 56
Wallaby Dreaming, 1982. Mick Namarari Japaljarri, Kintore, Central Australia. Acrylic on canvas, 101.7 × 102.4 cm.

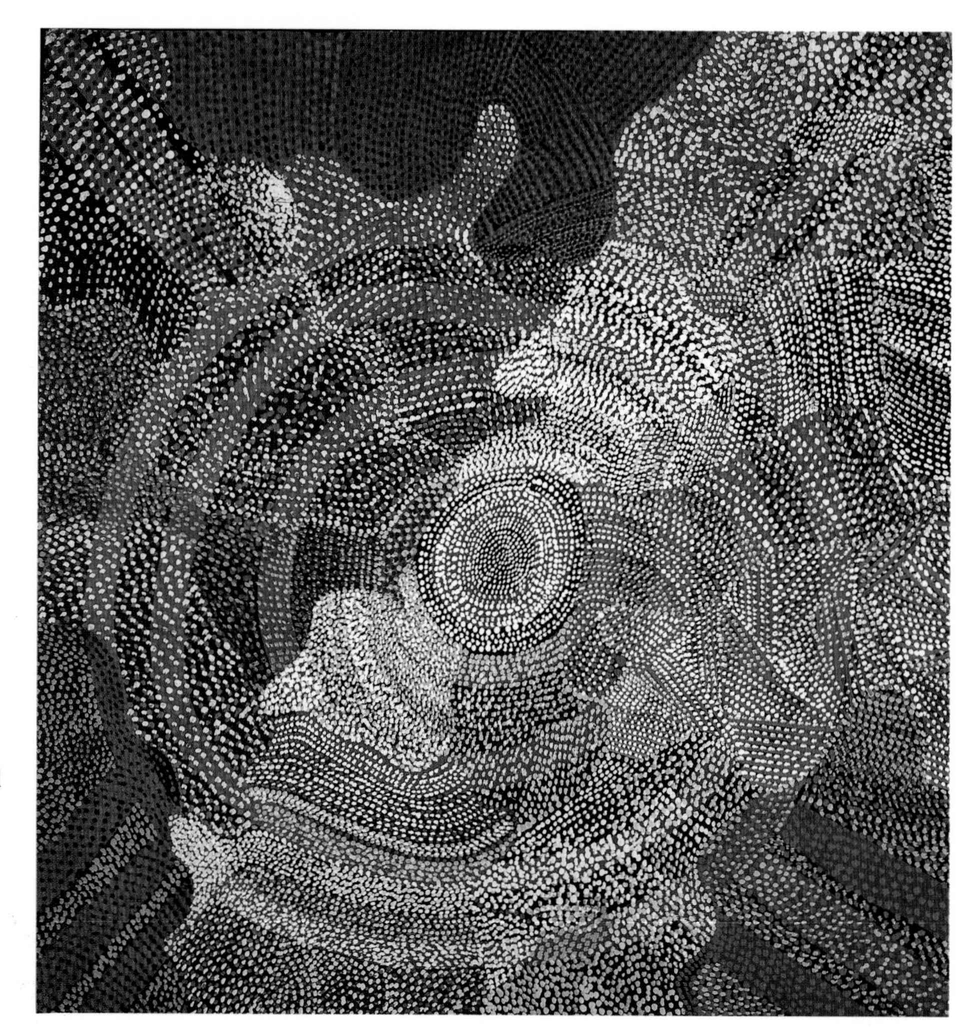

FIG. 155 / CAT. 55
Bushfire Dreaming, ca. 1976. Johnny Warangula Jupurrurla, Papunya, Central Australia. Acrylic on hardboard, 61.5 × 63 cm.

from which they are derived. Aboriginal people do not simply make use of the colors found in their environment; the colors form part of the graphic system and encode a particular Aboriginal view of their relations with the environment. Their classification of colors is part of an active perception rather than merely a reflection of nature. Although colors may be referred to by their primary terms, there are distinctions made within categories of colors, for example, between a shiny white and a plain white, and special terms are used for certain types of iridescent, shiny red ochre from a particular site.

TABLE I Warlpiri Colors

COLOR	ELEMENT
yellow *karntawarrakarntawarra*	yellow ochre and site from which it comes (*karntawarrakarntawarra*)
red *yalyuyalyu*	red ochre (*yurlpa*) used for initiation ceremonies; special red orche (*karrku*) and site from which it comes (Karrku)
white *kardirri*	pipe clay (*ngujunguju*) and chalk (*karlji*) used for the mourning ceremony
black *maru*	charcoal (*pirilyi*)

FIG. 156
Fire Dreaming at Ngarna, 1984. Molly Nampijinpa Langdon, Yuendumu, Central Australia. Acrylic on canvas, 60.5 × 45.7 cm.

People refer to a color element in relation to how it will be used and to the quality of the color needed. They say that one cannot use *karlji*, or chalk, for body painting because it is reserved for mourning purposes and also because it is not as shiny as some pipe clays. Similarly, *karrku*, a red ochre, is rarely used for body painting during circumcision ceremonies as it is very shiny and therefore considered too sacred.

Each Dreaming or Dreaming segment and its related subsection group is associated with a specific set of colors and color sources. Thus, among the Warlpiri at Yuendumu, black and white (charcoal and pipe clay) belong to Emu Dreaming and to the jampijinpa/nampijinpa, jangala/nangala subsection groups; yellow is associated with Snake Dreaming and the jakamarra/nakamarra, jupurrurla/napurrurla subsections. Acrylic painters generally follow these color associations, although less systematically than in other art forms such as body and ground painting. In George Jampijinpa Robertson's *Lightning and Thunder Dreaming at Puyurru* (Fig. 139), the change from white to yellow in the color of the lines flowing from the central roundel symbolizes a change in the type of country over which the Dreaming figure traveled and in the subsection affiliation of the Dreaming at a particular site.

A second, and perhaps equally important, factor in color choice is the range of acrylic paints available to the artist. In most cases, paints are supplied by art advisers and other non-Aborigines working in the communities, although artists sometimes buy their own paints. At Papunya, in the early days of painting, artists used whatever colors happened to be available. The move to restrict the choice to those colors that were considered more traditional was in part the decision of Aboriginal leaders,[32] but it also came about because some advisers deliberately introduced certain colors and limited the supply of others based on their own views and interests. Consequently, Papunya painters were often only given white, black, red, and yellow paints, which they then mixed to obtain other colors. Nowadays, Pintupi and other painters of the Papunya movement[33] generally paint with this restricted palette of four colors and their combinations. Clifford Possum Japaljarri comments:

> All them dot, yellow and red, everything. [First, we] put circle, circle and Dreaming [to represent] body painting or might be ground paint. And after that one, you put'em differn'-differn' color. That's my idea . . . Not them white men color. No, them native color, them red one, them white one, black one. I start [with] *yurlpa*, *karrku*, *ngujunguju*, *karntawarra*. From four paint: red one and a yellow, black one, white one, from four paint . . . I mix'em 'nother four more, I mix'em from white 'nother four more.[34]

Most Papunya artists maintain that the use of basic colors is more traditional. It also reflects, however, their attempt to respond to what they think non-Aborigines expect to see in an Aboriginal painting. In the case of Yuendumu, colors vary according to the aesthetic tastes of the artists and the preferences and views of the non-Aborigines who buy and supply the paints. Some paintings, such as Paddy Jupurrurla Nelson's *Wild Yam Dreaming at*

Yajarlu (Fig. 157), are executed in more traditional colors; others tend to be brighter and more diverse in color—for example, *Burrowing Skink Dreaming at Parrikirlangu* by Darby Jampijinpa (Fig. 144). There appears to be no direct relationship between age, gender, or Dreaming groups and the use of particular colors. Another factor affecting color choice, in addition to the painter's own aesthetic preferences, is the degree of skill a painter has in mixing acrylic paints to obtain different colors. Generally speaking, creativity and experimentation with colors occurs more in acrylic paintings than in ceremonial-related painting, where variation is mainly found in the placement and size of symbols in overall pictorial designs.

FIG. 157 / CAT. 42
Wild Yam Dreaming at Yajarlu, 1986.
Paddy Jupurrurla Nelson, Yuendumu, Central Australia. Acrylic on canvas, 77 × 85.5 cm.

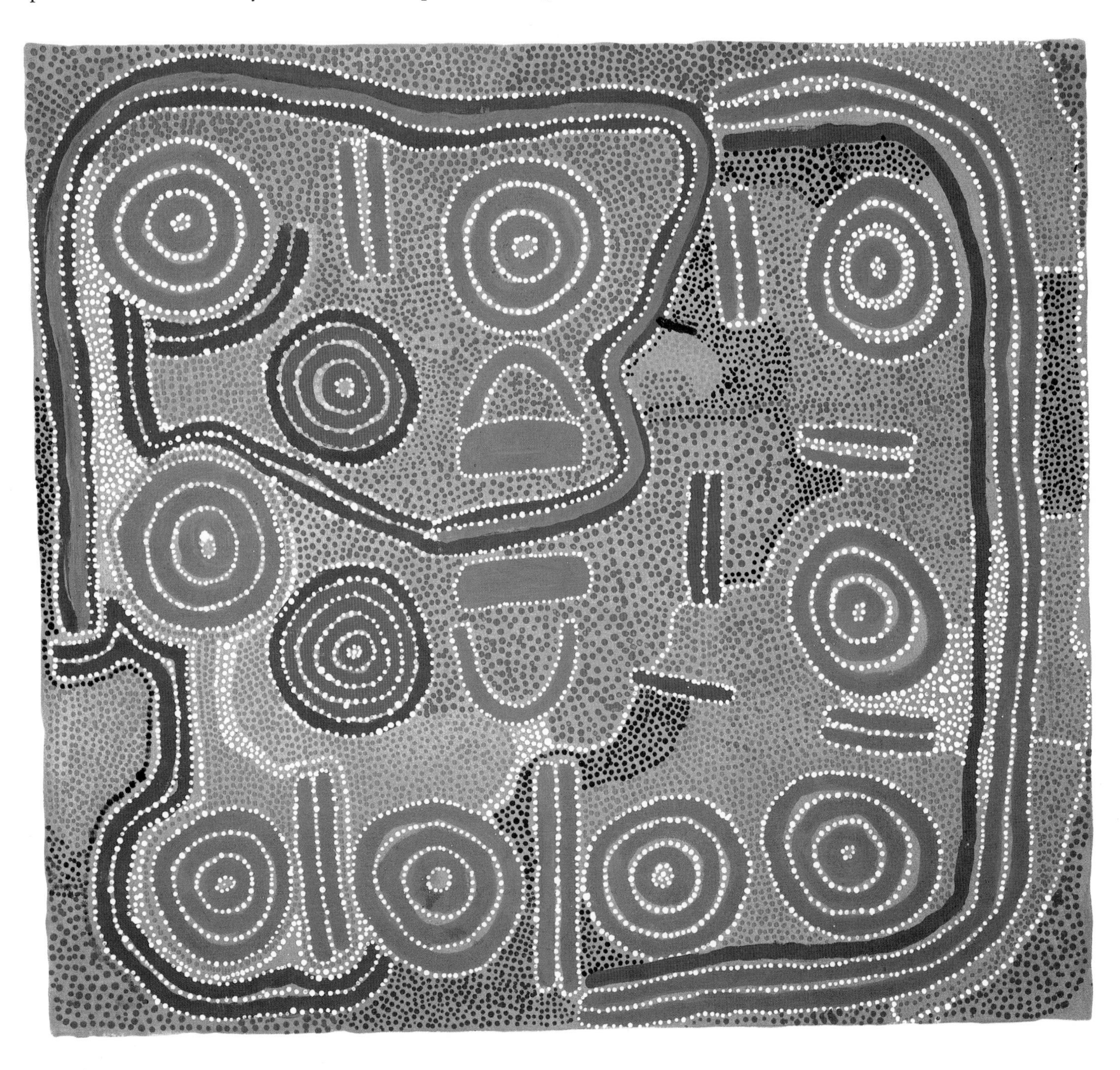

Color differences between Papunya and Yuendumu paintings are probably more a function of the nature of acrylic paint than any other factor. The difference appears to be one of brightness and hue rather than color itself. Acrylic paint generally offers, in the hands of most artists, an extreme dichotomy of dark or bright, whatever the color. In contrast, the sources of traditional colors—ochres and clays—vary greatly, providing many different shades (Fig. 158). Some commentators on acrylic painting have mistakenly suggested that because Yuendumu paintings are often done with bright, even garish, colors they are somehow less traditional than the generally darker paintings of, for example, Pintupi artists. Both darkness and brightness are important concepts in the Western Desert aesthetic. The apparent differences are a function of the medium of acrylic painting and not of tradition.

The Graphic Narrative: Content and Levels of Meaning Desert acrylic paintings generally depict mythic events or segments of Dreamings associated with particular sites. Some paintings also portray actual events in the recent past that are considered part of the Dreaming. An analysis of the Dreaming subjects in 1108 paintings from Yuendumu reveals a strong correlation between the content of people's everyday lives and the significant elements of their religion (Table II).

TABLE II Dreaming Content of Paintings: Yuendumu 1986–87

Plants and plant foods 32.3%	Water 8.0%
Reptiles 14.3%	Birds 4.7%
Mammals and marsupials 12.6%	Fire 4.3%
People 11.5%	Miscellaneous 3.7%
Ants and insects 8.6%	

Source: Warlukurlangu Association records

When asked about their paintings, artists usually respond that the painting "means" or is "my country," that is, it is a depiction of the painter's territory. When queried further about the Dreaming Story, the artist will often identify the main ancestor depicted and perhaps the primary site at which the ancestor undertook the actions portrayed in the painting. At this point, the artist may also point out iconographic elements. It is possible for an outsider, especially if working in the local language, to gain further insight into the narrative of events described in the painting, but even then access to the different levels of meaning may be restricted.

This pattern is typified in the painting by Darby Jampijinpa (Fig. 144). The painting is of Parrikirlangu, an area over which Jampijinpa has certain ownership rights, and the Dreaming is Liwirringki (Burrowing Skink). The public version of the story is that it describes men hunting for Liwirringki by the use of controlled fires and burning. The fire is represented by the long straight lines; the fire sticks used for the burning are the adjacent short lines. The concentric circle at the center and the circles at the end of the lines represent the camps where the men cooked the meat of the animals they killed. There are, however, at least two other levels of meaning to the story, the first of which the artist describes:

> These are old people, old men who lived there. This Dreaming really belongs to older men with white hair like me. It is really their Dreaming. They are really the Dreaming. There was a Burrowing Skink. The west side [of the site and the left side of the painting] belongs to jampijinpa/jangala [subsections] and the east side belongs to jakamarra/jupurrurla. The old ancestors, the old men in the Dreamtime, stayed there on both sides. We were all one mob, my patrimoiety. We all share the same Dreaming, Burrowing Skink Dreaming.
>
> Young men were camped at Yajarlu with the old men. The women were camped to the south. The old men, *kurdungurlu*, were looking after the young men and went to dig yams to feed them. Once they were fed, the young men went hunting for Burrowing Skink and for kangaroo to give as ritual offerings. They came back to the soakage at Yajarlu and put the meat in a pile.[35]

The next level is secret, but the artist gave us permission to describe it in general terms as a representation of the young men undergoing a set of secret ceremonies at the site, in which they are being shown sacred objects and given certain knowledge. Jampijinpa referred to the painting in English as "proper dear one"—"dear," in this sense, meaning religiously important, powerful, and potentially dangerous. The fact that the public version of the story hints at this secret level of meaning exemplifies the principle in Aboriginal society that secrecy is not an absolute but a continuum: people are entitled, according to their status, to possess (that is, to discuss) different levels of knowledge about the same thing.

In Jampijinpa's painting, the old men in the story are both subject and object: Liwirringki is both an old man at Yajarlu and the animal being hunted and eaten. The old men who are owners of the Dreaming today are

FIG. 158
Sand and Ochre, 1987. Nikolaus Lang, Adelaide, South Australia. Colored sand and ochres on brown paper, 500 × 600 cm.

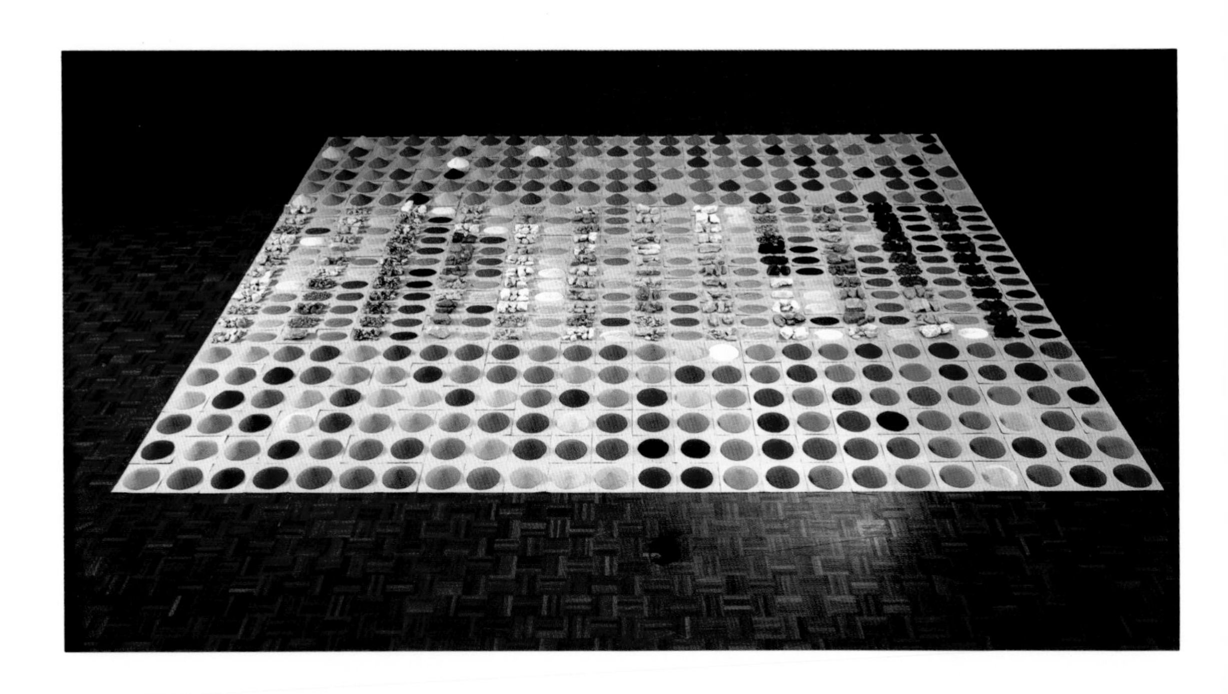

FIG. 159 / CAT. 45
Sugarleaf Dreaming at Ngarlu, 1986. Lucy Napaljarri, Hilda Napaljarri, and Ruth Napaljarri, Yuendumu, Central Australia. Acrylic on canvas, 173 × 187.5 cm.

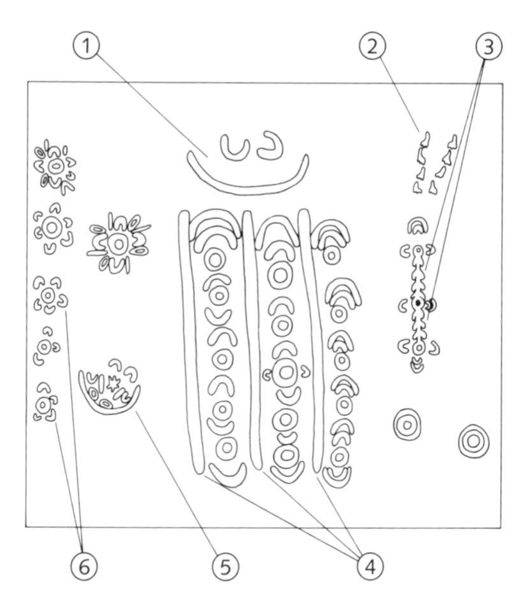

FIG. 159a
1. Napangardi's camp
2. Jungarrayi's footprints
3. Women dancing
4. Ceremonial poles
5. Windbreak (birthplace of two Jampijinpa boys)
6. Women gathering Yanyirlingi

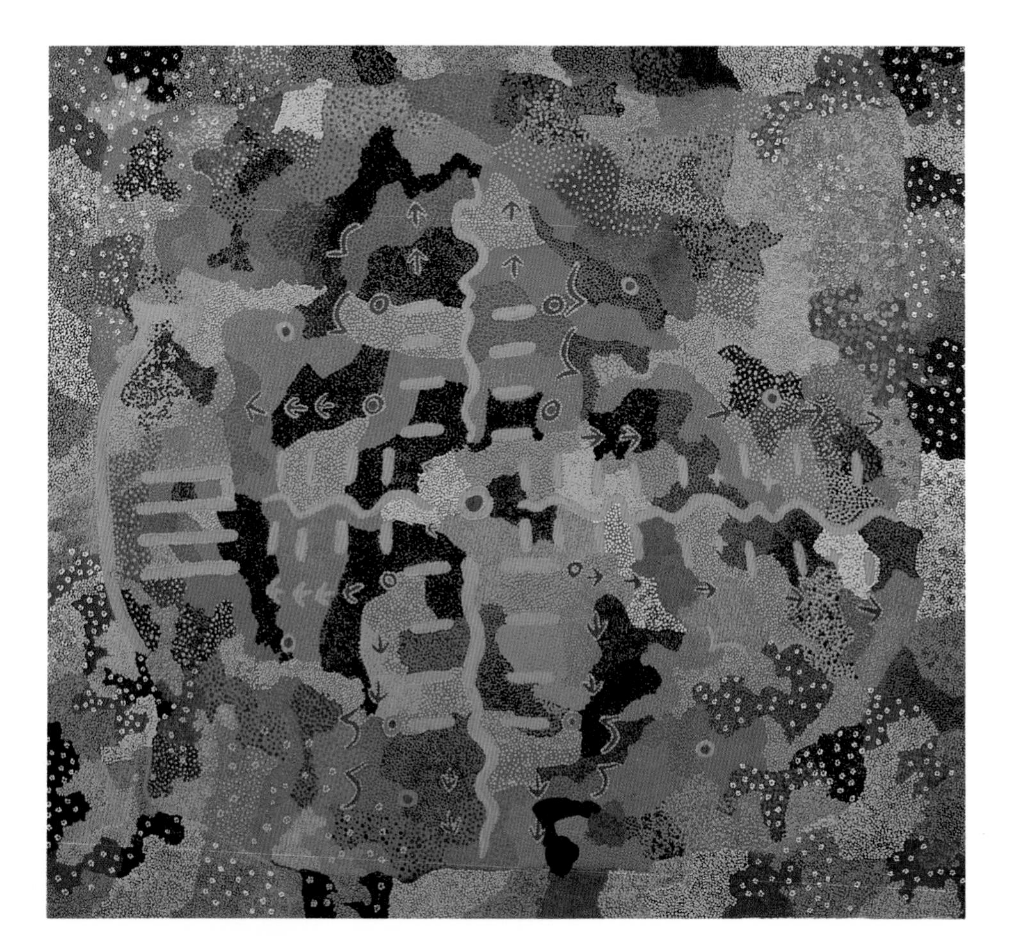

FIG. 160 / CAT. 41
Water Dreaming at Mikanji, 1986. Tilo Nangala, Yuendumu, Central Australia. Acrylic on canvas, 154 × 185 cm.

also seen, in some ways, to *be* burrowing skinks themselves. Here the boundaries between the mythic past and the actual present as non-Aborigines understand them are blurred. This blurring occurs in another way through actual events becoming incorporated in or encompassed by myth, as illustrated in the painting by Lucy, Hilda, and Ruth Napaljarri of Sugarleaf Dreaming at Ngarlu near Mt. Allan (Figs. 159, 159a). In the painting, mythic beings and real people are presented as one. It shows mythical women gathering sugarleaf and dancing a *yawulyu*, a women's ceremony involving the story of a man who took as his wife a woman whom he was not supposed to marry. At the same time, it depicts the birth (to the sisters of the man) of two babies who are actual men living today.

Paintings as Social, Mythic, and Geographic Maps Acrylic paintings demonstrate both the linkages and the separations between people and between people and place. They are pictorial statements of sociality, as well as of geography and Dreamings.

The paintings by the Yuendumu artists Judy Nampijinpa Granites (Fig. 138) and Tilo Nangala (Fig. 160) depict a segment of the Rain Dreaming at Mikanji, a site that is the intersection of several Rain Dreaming tracks. The artists share the same segment of the same Dreaming through their kin relationship, and this accounts for the similarities in the main design elements of their paintings. The painting by the Papunya artist Dick Pantimas Jupurrurla (Fig. 161) portrays the same Rain Dreaming track but at a different site—Kalipinypa in Pintupi country to the southwest of Mikanji.

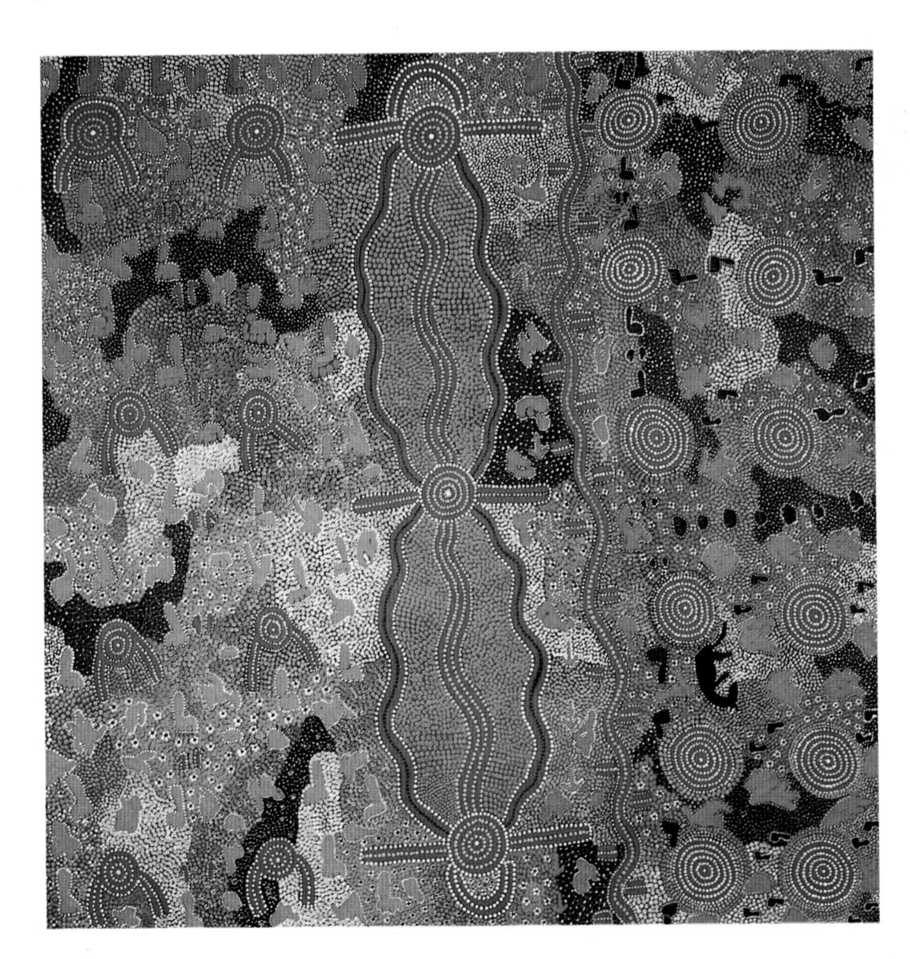

FIG. 161
Water, Lightning, and Bush Food Dreaming at Kalipinypa, 1981. Dick Pantimas Jupurrurla, assisted by Charlie Egalie Japaljarri, Papunya, Central Australia. Acrylic on canvas, 183 × 182.5 cm.

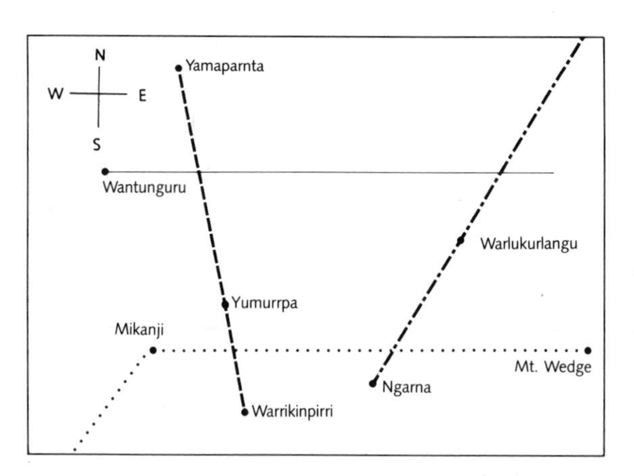

FIG. 162 Selected Dreaming tracks in the Yuendumu region:

——— Flying Ant (*Pamapardu*) from the east to Wantunguru in the west (Fig. 143).

– – – – – – Wild Yam Dreaming (*Yarla*) from Yamaparnta in the north to Yumurrpa and Warrikinpirri in the south (Fig. 157).

–·–·–·–· Blue-tongue Lizard (*Lungkarda*), Initiated Youths (*Maliyarra-maliyarra*), and Emu (*Yankirri*) from the east to Warlukurlangu and Ngarna in the south (Figs. 144, 163).

········ Rain (*Ngapa*) from the southwest and from Mt. Wedge in the east to Mikanji.

While he employs some of the motifs, such as the wavy lines, used by Nampijinpa and Nangala, Jupurrurla combines them in a different way, primarily because he is depicting a different site along the Dreaming track. What this example illustrates is that although the artists may never have met, they are linked to one another in a social relationship because they share the same Dreaming.

Paintings of the same site and same Dreaming sometimes differ in appearance because of their emphasis on different segments of the Dreaming myth. This difference may reflect the social or residential histories of the artists, but it more often is related to gender. Paintings by Dinny Nolan Jampijinpa, for example, often depict the site featured in the two women's paintings discussed above but deal with different segments of the Rain Dreaming associated with the site. These artists have the same class of ownership rights over the site and the Dreaming, and thus are linked together in a special way as men and women. Yet they focus on different segments of the myth, and this is an expression of their separateness.

Several of the paintings illustrated here depict tracks that the ancestor heroes are believed to have traveled in the Yuendumu region. (See Fig. 162 for a diagram of the tracks.) Pamapardu, the Flying Ant, traveled from the east to Wantunguru in the west (Fig. 143); Yarla, the Wild Yam, went from Yamaparnta in the north to Yumurrpa and Warrikinpirri in the south (Fig. 157); Lungkarda, the Blue-tongue Lizard, Maliyarra-maliyarra, the Initiated Youths, and Yankirri, the Emu, came from the east to Warlukurlangu and Ngarna in the south (Figs. 144, 163). The Rain track links Pintupi people in the west to the Warlpiri at Mikanji in the center and the Anmatyerre at Mt. Wedge in the east. With these paintings, the artists are not merely making a statement about themselves and their religious affiliations. They are also affirming their relationships, both in social and pragmatic terms, with the other people who have rights along those tracks. In presettlement days, people depended on these shared relationships for survival during periods of food or water shortage. Today, affirmation of a Dreaming through painting, including acrylics, places the artist within a social group in his own community and within a network of other people at different settlements.

Acrylic paintings are geographic as well as social representations. Paintings by Kaapa Jampijinpa of Papunya and Paddy Jupurrurla Nelson of Yuendumu sometimes show the travels of Warnayarra, the Rainbow Snake, from Winparrku, west of Papunya, to Ngama, near Yuendumu. The mythic track is depicted as the body of the Snake itself. A creek, called Mijilyparnta, today represents this Snake body/track. In this sense the paintings are like schematic maps of the landscape: mythic events are also topographic features. Tim Leura Japaljarri's *Possum Spirit Dreaming* (Fig. 153) portrays the entirety of the artist's country on Napperby Station and many of its topographical features through the events that occurred there in the Dreaming. The relationship between Dreamings and sites is also a basis for interaction between the people associated with them.

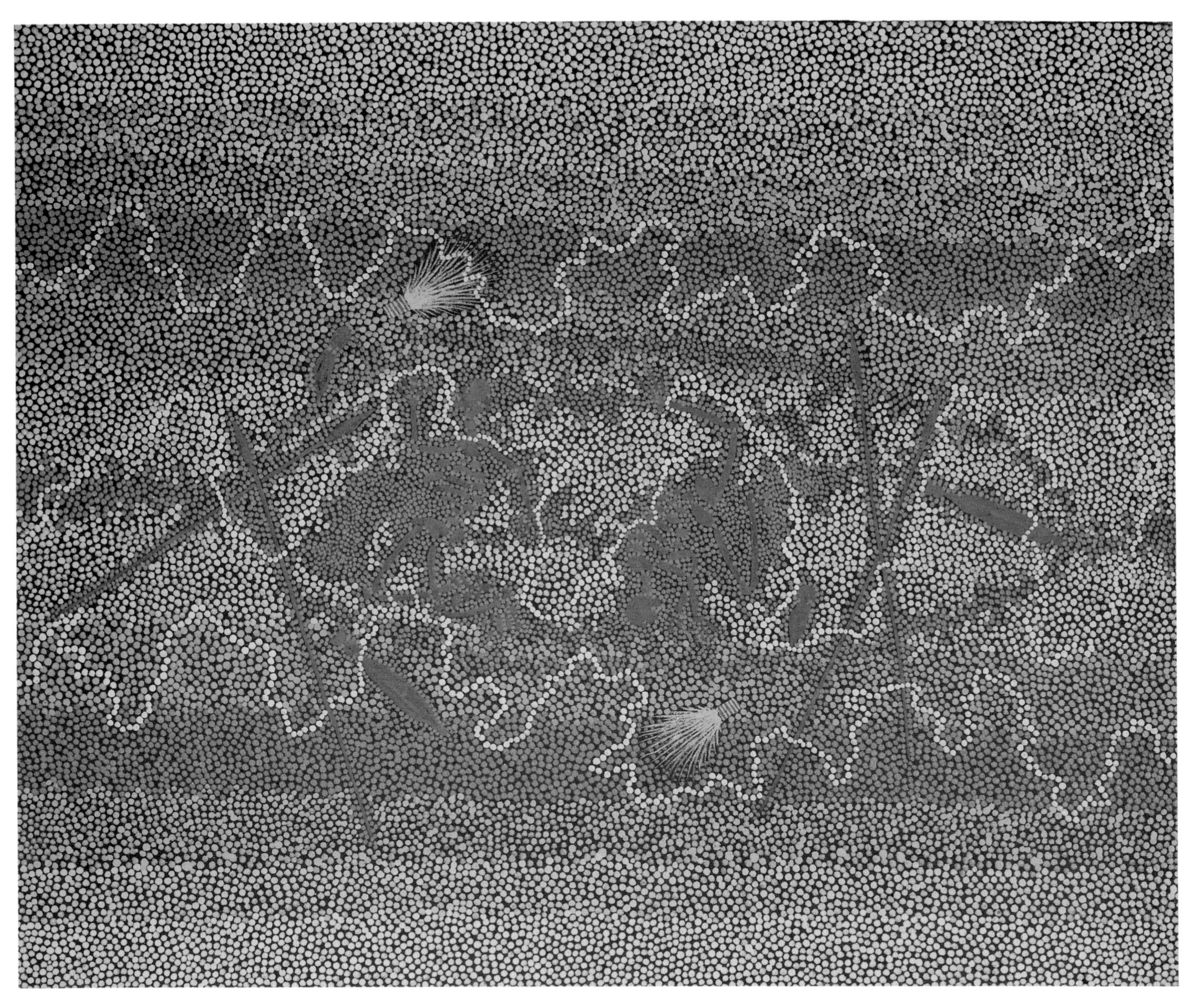

FIG. 163 / CAT. 48
Bushfire Dreaming, 1982. Clifford Possum Japaljarri, Mbunghara, Central Australia. Acrylic on canvas, 81 × 100.8 cm.

An examination of paintings of the same site reveals the segmentation of myth, and it also shows something of the diversity of style and composition in painting. Let us consider, for instance, Kunajarrayi, an important site at Mt. Nicker some two hundred eighty miles west of Alice Springs. The site is the meeting place of at least six Dreamings: Witchetty Grub, Snake, Wallaby, Spider, Wild Yam, and Vine. Some paintings of this site concentrate on one set of events concerning one or two ancestors. *Witchetty Grub Dreaming at Kunajarrayi* (Fig. 164), by Paddy Japaljarri Sims, is dominated by the sinuous lines representing the tracks of a Snake fleeing the area after a fight. The depiction of women gathering Witchetty Grubs, along the edges of the painting, is a minor element in the composition. In contrast, the painting of the same title by Gladys Napanangka (Fig. 166) focuses on this segment of the myth. Another depiction of the site—*Plains Kangaroo Dreaming at Kunajarrayi* (Fig. 165) by Peter Jungarrayi Davis—presents at least four Dreaming figures associated with Kunajarrayi. Social connections are established through the commonality of site, while differences between people are confirmed through the segmentation of myth.

There is a direct relationship between a painting's narrative content and its composition or overall visual effect. When one or more myth segments from one Dreaming and one site are portrayed, the composition of the painting is usually simple and dominated by one or two design elements (Figs. 91, 144). Those paintings that depict segments from several Dreamings at one site tend to be more complex in composition but still have a strong unifying design element (Fig. 164). In more complicated narratives depicting several events from one Dreaming and the convergence of mythic heroes from different sites at one site, the main motifs of the painting compete for visual dominance (as with the wavy lines representing Rain, the straight lines representing Lightning, and the C-shaped form symbolizing Clouds in Fig. 138). The most visually complex—and in the case of some artists, the most visually satisfying—paintings are those that portray events from different Dreamings at different sites (Fig. 143).

FIG. 164 / CAT. 38
Witchetty Grub Dreaming at Kunajarrayi, 1986. Paddy Japaljarri Sims, Yuendumu, Central Australia. Acrylic on canvas, 136 × 108 cm.

Differences in Painting Styles and Techniques Just as there are social and linguistic differences between Western Desert Aboriginal groups, there are also differences in acrylic painting styles. Instead of attempting to explain these differences by referring to environmental or other factors, as some writers have, we will discuss them in terms of the major features that distinguish the various language or "tribal" groups.

Male Pintupi painters tend to favor the use of concentric circles in their work (Fig. 167). These are sometimes joined by straight lines (Fig. 148), with the mythic events or stylized objects shown in and around or superimposed on the background of circles (Figs. 177–78). Warlpiri painters, both male and female, show an abiding concern with symmetry (Figs. 144, 151), a feature repeated in the lining up of participants by height in a ceremony.[36] Anmatyerre and Luritja painters often use dotting as an overlay, which produces a blurring effect (Figs. 153, 155). Some Aranda painters (Fig. 91)

FIG. 165
Plains Kangaroo Dreaming at Kunajarrayi, 1986. Peter Jungarrayi Davis, Yuendumu, Central Australia. Acrylic on tent canvas, 289.3 × 175 cm.

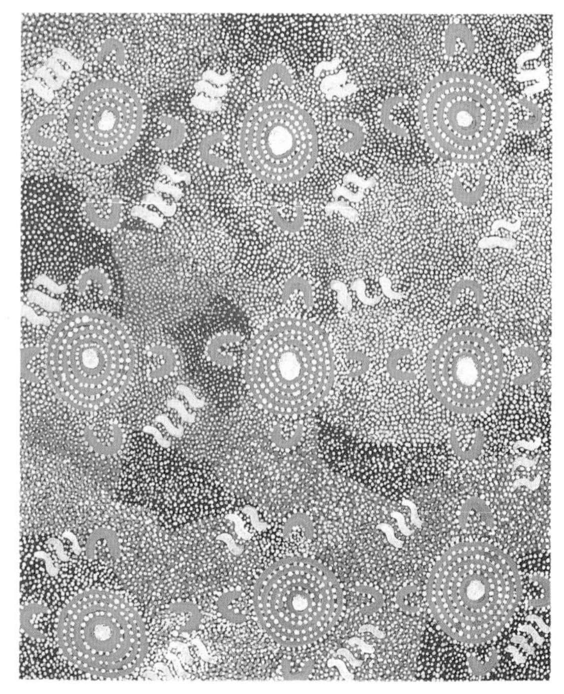

FIG. 166
Witchetty Grub Dreaming at Kunajarrayi, ca. 1986. Gladys Napanangka, Papunya, Central Australia. Acrylic on canvas, 50.4 × 61 cm.

use a stippled background. Walmadjarri painters in the northwest of the desert tend to use a joined-bar design instead of concentric circles and connecting lines (Fig. 141).

It is perhaps more relevant to compare community styles, as it allows us to see some of the local factors that condition the differences between groups. When comparing Papunya with Yuendumu, art dealers and critics sometimes comment that Papunya paintings, including those by Pintupi people from communities further west, are more precise, formal, stylized, and perhaps more "slick," while Yuendumu work is said to be more fluid, freer, and less definite. One explanation for these differences may be that painters of the Papunya movement have been painting for a longer period of time. They do not view painting merely as a process of grafting traditional forms onto canvas.

Another noticeable difference in Papunya and Yuendumu painting style is the use and choice of color. Comments by the artists themselves about the difference in color usage often focus on the competition between the two communities, as in this statement by Michael Nelson Jakamarra, a Warlpiri painter resident at Papunya:

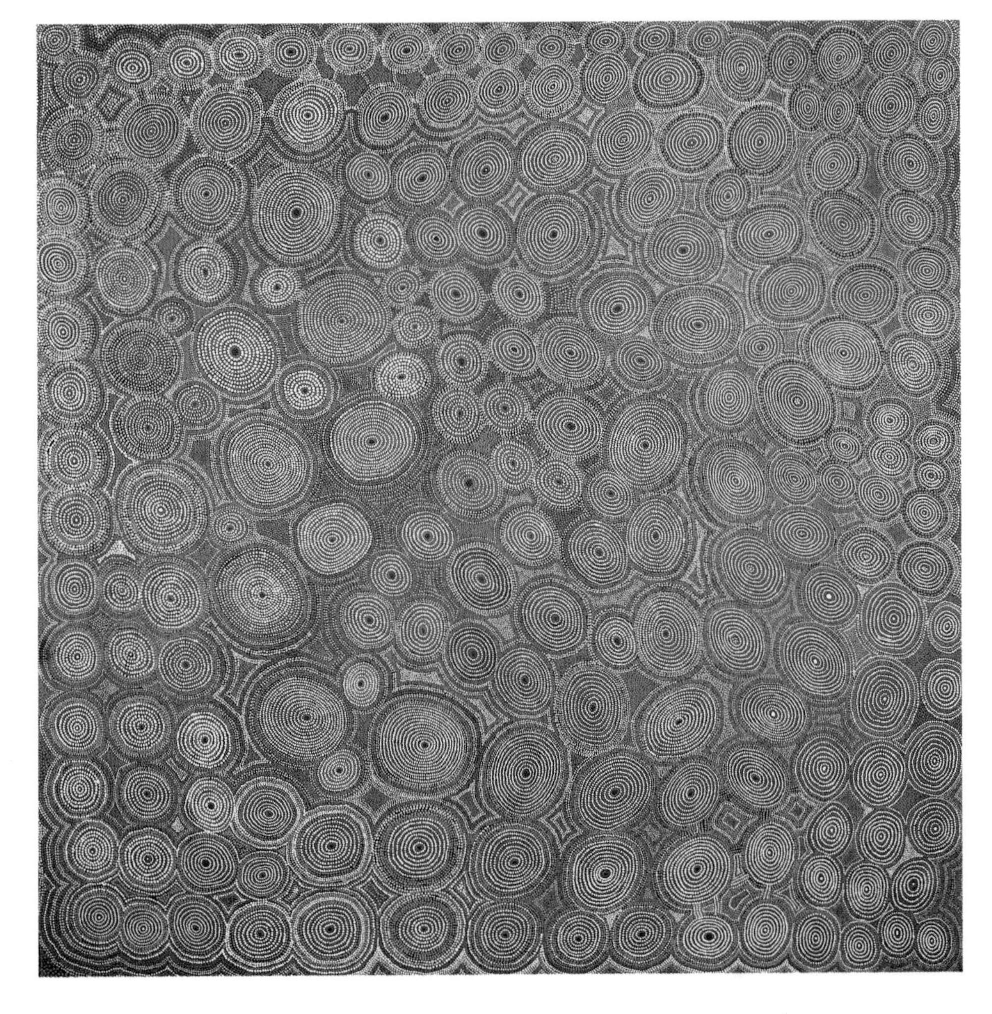

FIG. 167 / CAT. 59
Ceremonial Ground at Kulkuta, 1981.
Anatjari Jampijinpa, Papunya, Central Australia. Acrylic on canvas, 182.5 × 182 cm.

> We tried to join with Yuendumu mob [that is, they tried to get Yuendumu to join the Papunya Tula company], but they reckon they want their own . . . they want to have their own thing, you know. There are a lot of problems, you know. I see a lot of painting from Yuendumu artists. They use some light, you know, very bright colors. A little bit bright. We [Papunya artists] don't use them. We only get four colors and we mix them—yellow, red, black, and white.[37]

The relationship between the artist's age and painting style is most clearly seen at Yuendumu. The older men and women, who are also the ritual heads and the most knowledgeable in religious matters, tend to paint in the traditional style of body and rock painting, emphasizing large and boldly executed design elements (Figs. 164–65, and Cat. 44). Younger painters usually produce stylized, simple designs with fine lines, small elements, and more carefully constructed dotting patterns. This can be seen in Fig. 151, in which much of the painting was done by two younger people.

Painting styles of the two communities are also related to the gender difference in the painting population. Over the period 1985–87, more than seventy percent of Yuendumu's painters were women. In contrast, not one of the 620 paintings done at Papunya in 1971–72 was recorded as being by a woman. Even as late as 1979, the Papunya company had no women listed as artists, although women may have been working on paintings by their male relatives. The art advisers gave canvases to the men, and the men said it was not appropriate for women to paint. Also, the market for acrylic art was extremely limited in the early days, and the men conceivably were acting to protect their own interests by restricting the number of painters. From about 1985 on, however, Luritja and Pintupi (Fig. 166) women from Papunya and communities to the west began to paint more and to sell their paintings through Papunya Tula. At Yuendumu, the issue of which gender should be involved in acrylic painting is still discussed by both men and women. The fact remains, however, that Yuendumu painters are producing at a time when the market is rapidly expanding and unless both men and women paint, the supply cannot be met.

Certain graphic forms commonly identified with women are occasionally included in women's paintings, as in Fig. 156, where the central motif is an interpretation of a design for women's body painting. Mythic segments depicting women's day-to-day activities and their possessions (gathering witchetty grubs or bush plant foods, using digging sticks, and so forth) are also sometimes shown in women's paintings, but they may appear in men's paintings as well.[38] Aside from these distinctions in subject matter, the only other area in which there is a noticeable difference between men's and women's paintings is the size of paintings. At Papunya, the western Pintupi settlements, and Yuendumu, as well as in other areas where acrylic paintings are produced such as Lajamanu and Balgo, women tend to paint on smaller canvases than men. This may be related to the association of large canvases with the ground designs of the men. But it probably has more to do with historical circumstance and the interaction between the Aborigines' and the art advisers' perceptions of what constitutes an appropriate painting size.

At Yuendumu in the early painting period, women painted exclusively on small canvas boards, mainly because the smaller canvases were easier to handle both for artists and for potential buyers ("suitcase size," as one artist put it). The move to larger canvases occurred when the men at Yuendumu began to paint. The men may have chosen to work on larger canvases as a way of differentiating themselves from the women and emphasizing their perceived importance in the painting process. It may also have been assumed by the non-Aborigines who supplied the materials that the men would only be able to execute ground-type designs on similarly large surfaces. (It is important to remember, however, that acrylic paintings have never been restricted to the depiction of Dreaming events used in ground paintings.) By 1987 both men and women were painting on large canvases, primarily because large paintings sell more readily and fetch higher prices in the southern city galleries. (The men did not object to the women's use of large canvases.) Large canvases provide more scope for individual artistic expression and for the depiction of Dreaming themes, and they allow involvement of more people in the production of the painting.

The materials used by artists have changed over time. At Papunya in the early days of the painting movement any available surface was used, including doors, boards, tiles, and cardboard (Fig. 168 and Cat. 58). Yuendumu painters initially worked on small artist boards (averaging twenty by twenty-eight inches). Today painters in both communities, especially when producing works for exhibition and sale through their artists' companies, use large canvases measuring up to seven square feet.

FIG. 168
Women Dreaming at Wilkingkarra, 1971. Turkey Tolsen Jupurrurla, Papunya, Central Australia. Acrylic on wooden door, 36.6 × 38.5 cm.

Changes in style and technique in the work of Papunya and Kintore artists are evident in a number of areas. We have already noted the move away from the inclusion of anthropomorphic elements. The earliest paintings done at Papunya were on dark plain backgrounds with prominent foreground elements consisting of realistic depictions of shields, spears, axes, and, in particular, sacred objects—bull-roarers, *tjurunga*, and string emblems, all of which are used in secret initiation and other ceremonies open only to adult men. Any designs tended to be portrayed on these objects associated with particular sets of myths, so that the works actually were paintings of painted objects.[39] Although many paintings of this type were sold and now exist in public and private collections, they can no longer be exhibited or published without offending Central Australian Aborigines. Papunya painters, and other Central Australian painters, soon realized that the paintings, unlike most traditional media, were permanent works of art and that the artists often had no control over who would see the paintings after they were sold. By 1974 the figured objects had largely disappeared and the designs themselves had become the subject of the paintings. This gave the artists more freedom to interpret the designs and thus more flexibility in constructing the content of the paintings.

The foreground of paintings was deemphasized by filling in the space with dots. Dots had originally been used only for the outlines of design

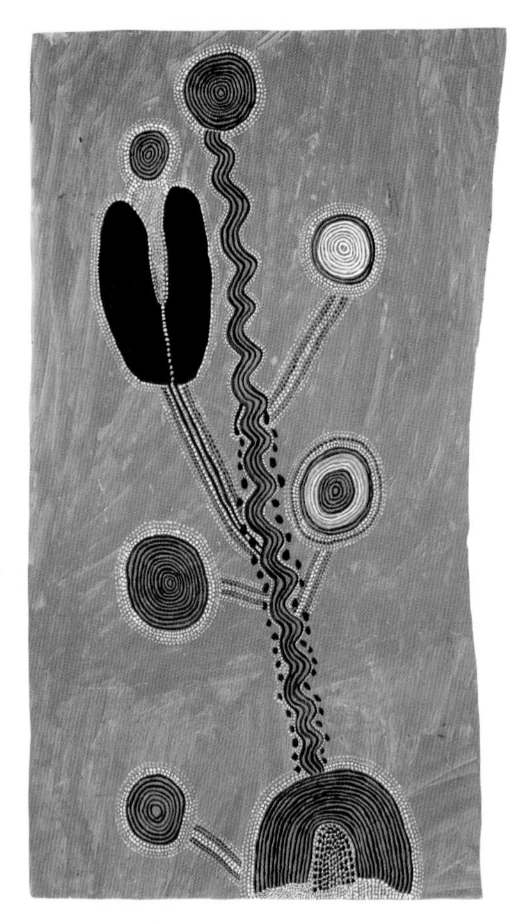

FIG. 169
Old Man Dreaming at Yumari, 1973. Uta Uta Jangala, Papunya, Central Australia. Acrylic on board, 75 × 43 cm.

elements, as shown in the early work by Uta Uta Jangala (Fig. 169). Examples of early Yuendumu paintings show a similar pattern (Fig. 139). The density of dotted lines sometimes creates a feeling of overall dotting, as in the painting by Mick Namarari Japaljarri (Fig. 154).[40]

In some cases, secret versions of designs are now modified in acrylic paintings—full circles have become half-circles, for instance. There have also been changes in the number of symbols used. Some symbols have been omitted altogether, and some design elements have been deliberately obscured by motifs such as smoke or clouds. These all represent attempts to reduce the overt meaning of paintings, thus protecting the artists from accusations by other Aborigines that they have revealed restricted information, and to make the paintings more accessible to non-Aborigines. Further evidence of the interest in appealing to the art market is the increasing use of realistically depicted objects such as boomerangs and insects, reptiles, and other animals (although at Papunya such elements have always been used by some artists).

Yuendumu painting style has changed more rapidly than that of Papunya. This is a function of the shorter period of time in which Yuendumu artists have been producing paintings and the dramatic increase in the market for acrylic art in the last five years. A comparison of the early works of

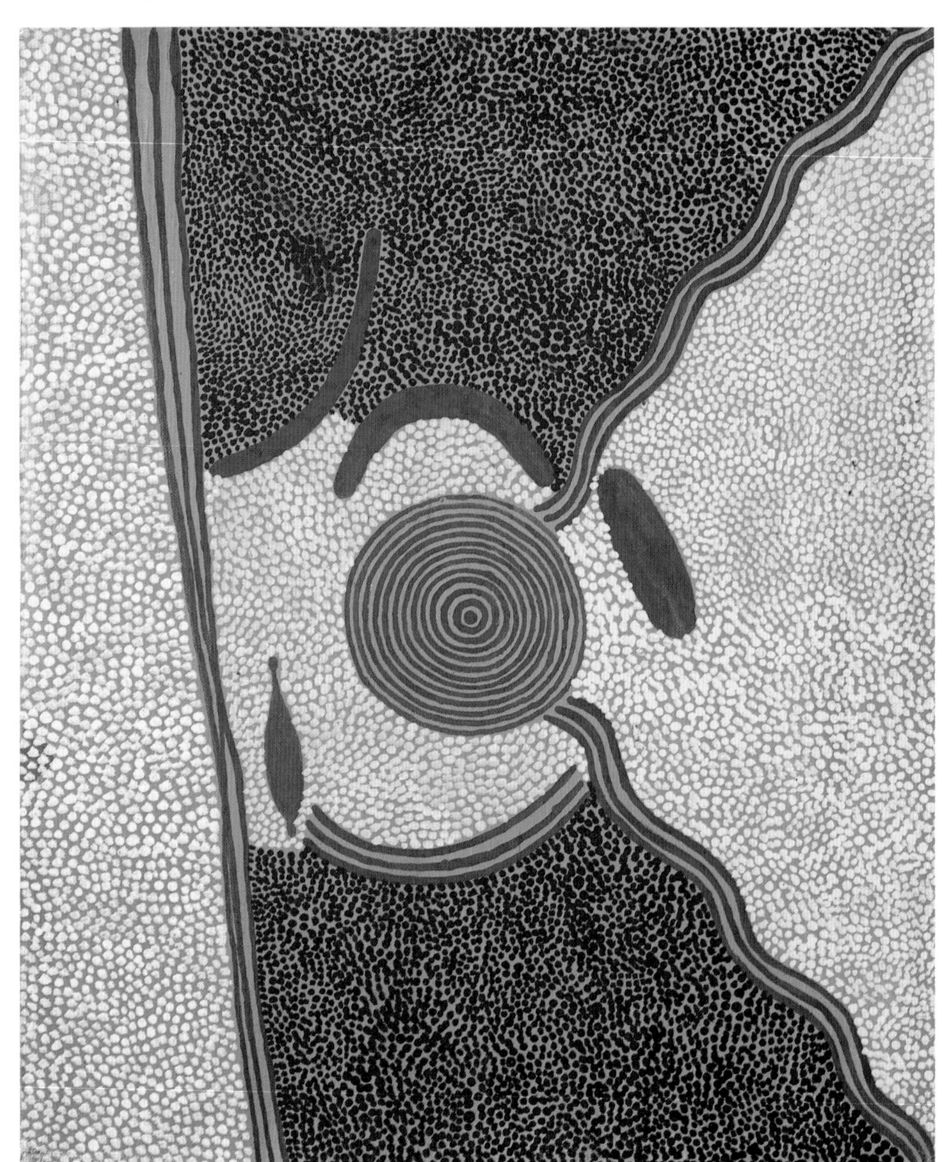

FIG. 170 / CAT. 53
Possum Dreaming at Kurningka, ca. 1977. Tim Leura Japaljarri, Papunya, Central Australia. Acrylic on canvas board, 61 × 50.5 cm.

Yuendumu painters (Figs. 139, 156) with those produced more recently (Figs. 151, 159–160) reveals several general trends:

> Much of the work has become more gracile over time as artists have gained greater control of the acrylic medium (Fig. 151).
>
> While the size of the motifs have often not changed, the scale of the paintings has increased. This permits more complexity in mythic content, and it contributes to a tendency toward less symmetry in the larger paintings (Fig. 159).
>
> Colors are now denser in hue, whereas in earlier paintings they are more transparent. Dots, especially in men's painting, have become smaller, with more definition of shape and intensity of color. There is also a tendency to superimpose color on color through dotting and with the use of different ground colors. This has also made the paintings more visually complex. (Fig. 160).

Changes and perfection of technique can also be seen when examining the work of one artist over time.[41] Compare, for example, the dotting style and use of color in Tim Leura Japaljarri's earlier work (Figs. 170–71) with that of his monumental painting of the Dreamings of the Napperby area (Fig. 153). In the recent work of

FIG. 171
Untitled, 1975. Tim Leura Japaljarri, Papunya, Central Australia. Acrylic on hardboard, 60 × 90 cm.

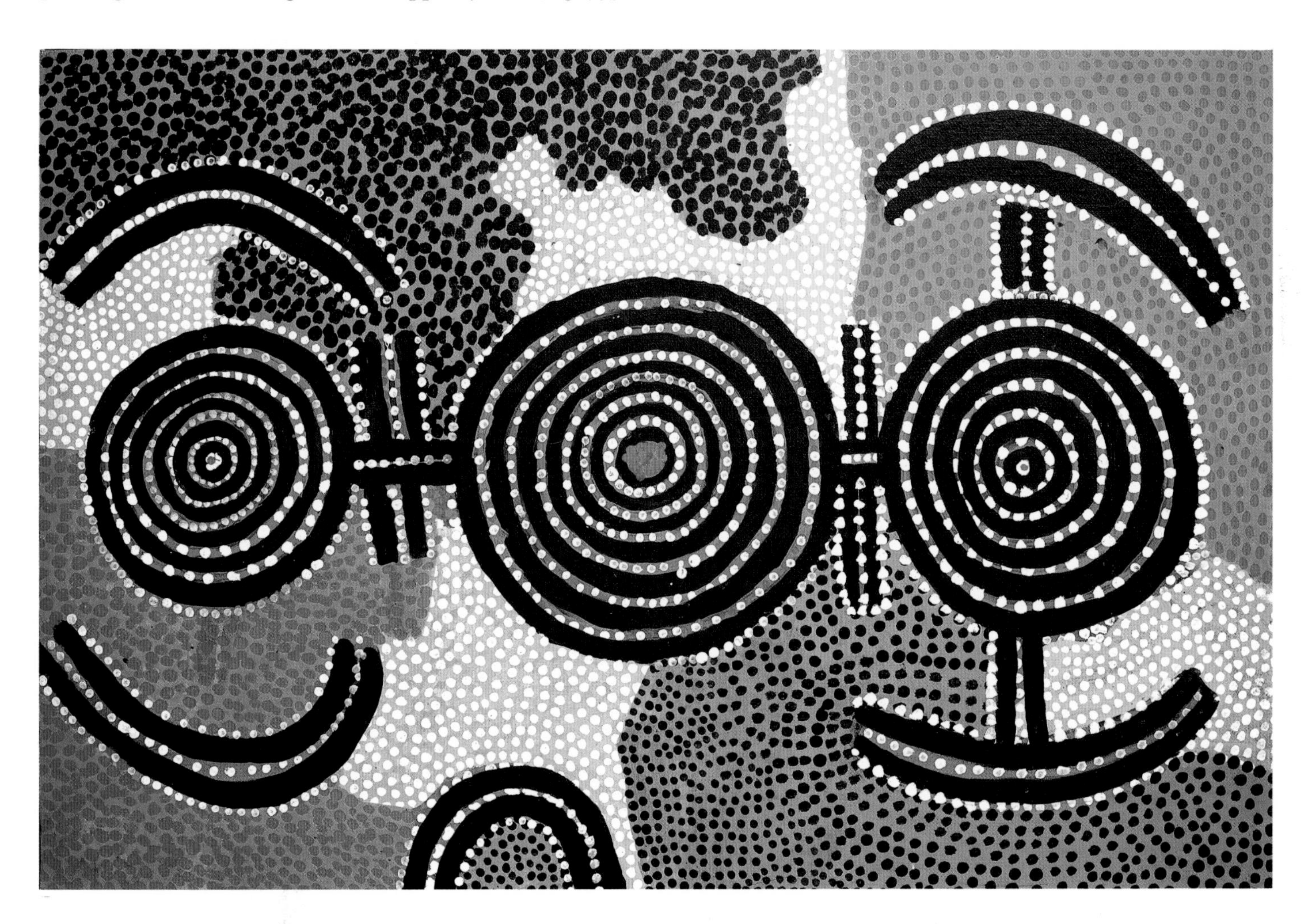

Clifford Possum Japaljarri, color and shading have taken on more importance than in his earlier paintings (compare Fig. 172 with Figs. 163, 173).

Some artists experiment with new styles in a marked departure from their previous work, as in the case of Kaapa Mbitjana Jampijinpa (Fig. 174). Others have developed what began as small-scale concepts into epic statements, evident when comparing the ghostly overlay effect of Tim Leura Japaljarri's *Women's Corroboree* (Fig. 175) with his *Possum Spirit Dreaming* (Fig. 153). Some artists have perfected the dotting technique to a fine-grained level, for example, Tommy Lowry Japaljarri (Fig. 90) and Shorty Lungkarda Jungarrayi (Fig. 176). In looking at the paintings of Uta Uta Jangala, moving from Fig. 169 to Figs. 177–79, we see a change from the use of strong foreground elements with no dotting in the background to very dense, complex works with both prominent foregrounds and busy backgrounds.

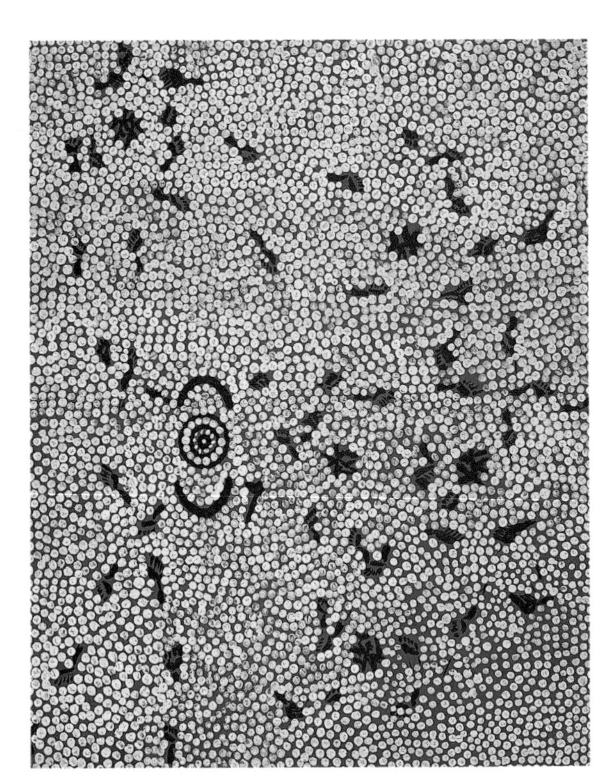

FIG. 172 / CAT. 49
Aralukaja, 1976. Clifford Possum Japaljarri, Mbunghara, Central Australia. Acrylic on board, 50 × 40 cm.

Acrylic Paintings and Non-Aborigines

Acrylic paintings, as we have seen, are merely a new form in which the classical elements of Aboriginal life and religion in Central Australia are expressed. In this sense they have similar functions to the more traditional art forms of body, rock, and ground paintings: they state a person's relationship to those around him, to the land, and to the Dreaming. Yet they also represent a new context of interaction between Aborigines and the larger, white-dominated Australian society.

Revelation of ritual designs, in whatever form, constitutes proof for Aborigines of their identity. In teaching whites about Aboriginal culture, Aborigines will frequently show someone a site, sing a song, or draw relevant designs, saying "You've seen. Now you know." The revelation is proof in and of itself.[42] Aborigines view acrylic painting as a vehicle for teaching whites about their way of life, for proving that they belong to and own the land. To Aborigines, seeing the designs on the paintings is sufficient evidence of the strength and vitality of their culture.

Aborigines are not surprised that others are interested in their acrylic paintings. They consider it only natural that those who are not fortunate enough to be Warlpiri, for example, would want to learn about their culture. Nor do they find it exceptional that whites will pay high prices for the privilege of seeing their ritual designs on canvas, as they, too, must pay for their knowledge. In traditional Aboriginal culture, revelations and the imparting of ritual knowledge have to be compensated for: in certain ceremonies the young men must provide meat for the old men who are their teachers, and people from neighboring groups who want to obtain a particular ceremony must pay those who currently own it.

Acrylic on canvas as a medium for artistic expression allows Aboriginal people to develop their expertise and to maintain their aesthetics while satisfying the non-Aboriginal market. This process is influenced by art advisers and coordinators, by anthropologists and others working in the settlements,

FACING PAGE

FIG. 173 / CAT. 47
Water Dreaming at Napperby, 1983. Clifford Possum Japaljarri, Mbunghara, Central Australia. Acrylic on canvas, 183.5 × 155.5 cm.

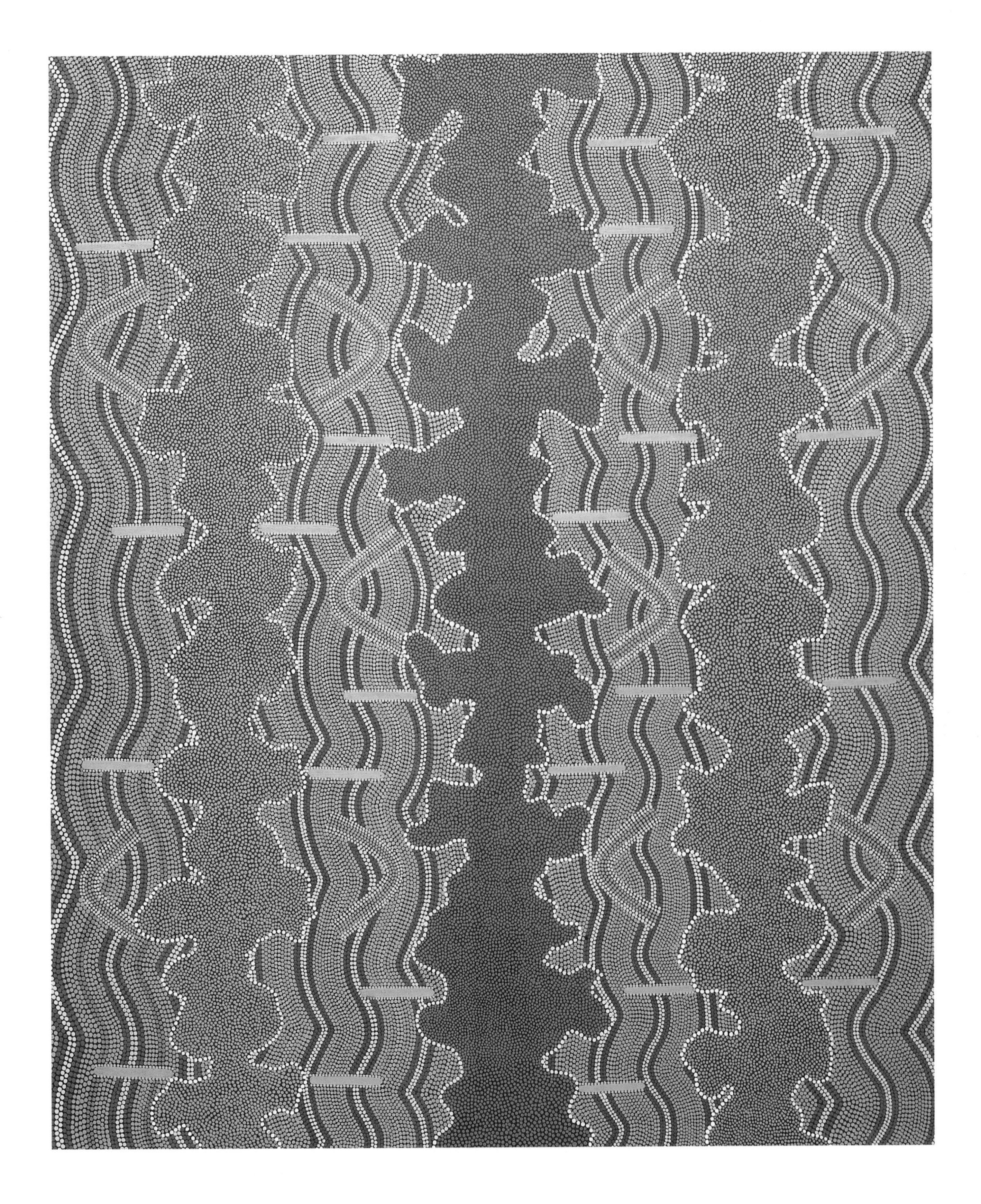

and by agents, art dealers, and critics. As the principal suppliers of canvas and paints, art advisers and other whites are directly involved in the production of acrylic paintings. But they often exert a more subtle influence, one that involves their own aesthetic views and personal interactions with individual painters. They may, for example, give larger canvases to those artists whom they consider more skilled or whose works sell more readily in the market. When a painting achieves outside recognition, it will often be taken as a model to be copied (not in Dreaming content, but in technique and style). Advisers and other non-Aborigines in Aboriginal communities also make important decisions about what is "good" and "bad" in a painting. At times, there is a discrepancy between the aesthetic preferences and objectives of the advisers and those of the painters. The latter respond to their paintings both emotionally and culturally, as they embody the graphic forms of myths and associated sites. To criticize a painting on aesthetic grounds is to criticize the artist's Dreaming—indeed, the artist's very being. To say that a painting is "good" is to compliment its mythic substance and the painter's ability to reproduce it. This is not to say that Aborigines do not have aesthetic standards independent of socio-cultural factors—artists, in fact, constantly comment on the visual qualities of each other's work—but these standards are difficult to elicit.[43]

FIG. 174
Witchetty Grub Dreaming, 1979. Kaapa Mbitjana Jampijinpa, Papunya, Central Australia. Acrylic on board, 38.5 × 55.2 cm.

FIG. 175
Women's Corroboree, ca. 1973. Tim Leura Japaljarri, Papunya, Central Australia. Acrylic on board, 66.2 × 82.4 cm.

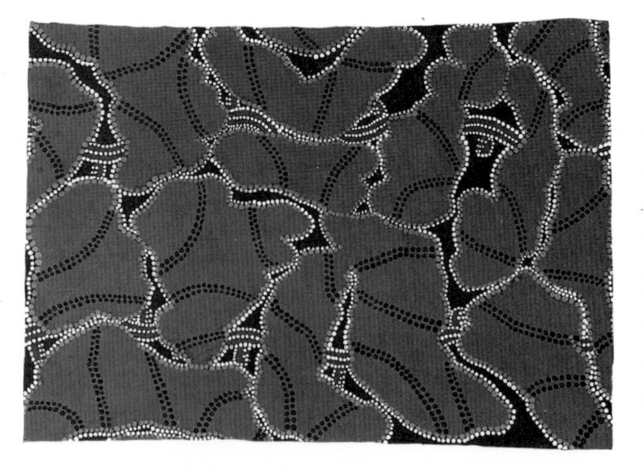

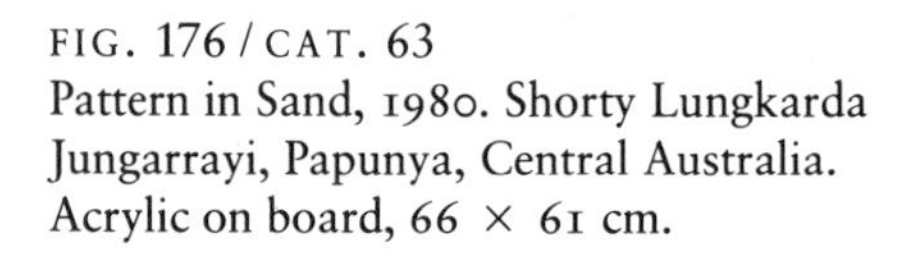

FIG. 176 / CAT. 63
Pattern in Sand, 1980. Shorty Lungkarda Jungarrayi, Papunya, Central Australia. Acrylic on board, 66 × 61 cm.

FACING PAGE
FIG. 177 / CAT. 60
Jangala and Two Women at Ngurrapalangu, 1982. Uta Uta Jangala, Kintore, Central Australia. Acrylic on canvas, 122.5 × 91 cm.

FIG. 178 / CAT. 61
Old Man Dreaming at Yumari, 1983.
Uta Uta Jangala, Kintore, Central Australia. Acrylic on canvas, 242 × 362 cm.

It is clear that the role of whites in the production of acrylic paintings in the desert communities is critical. They provide an impetus; they have the necessary outside contacts to obtain materials for the artists; and they are willing to handle the financial and administrative work (not that Aboriginal people cannot do it, but that they often do not want to). The whites are outside of the Aboriginal social system and thus are perceived by the Aborigines as neutral agents (although in practice this may not be the case). In such a position, the white adviser is also someone who can be blamed when things go wrong.

Two examples serve to illustrate the pivotal role played by white advisers. First, it is unlikely that the Papunya acrylic painting movement would have materialized without Geoff Bardon. He provided the initial motivation, procured and organized the materials, and assisted in promoting the artists and the sale of their works. To the Aborigines, Bardon was the "painting man," and they now refer to his days at Papunya as "Bardon-time." The second example concerns the gender difference in the artist populations at

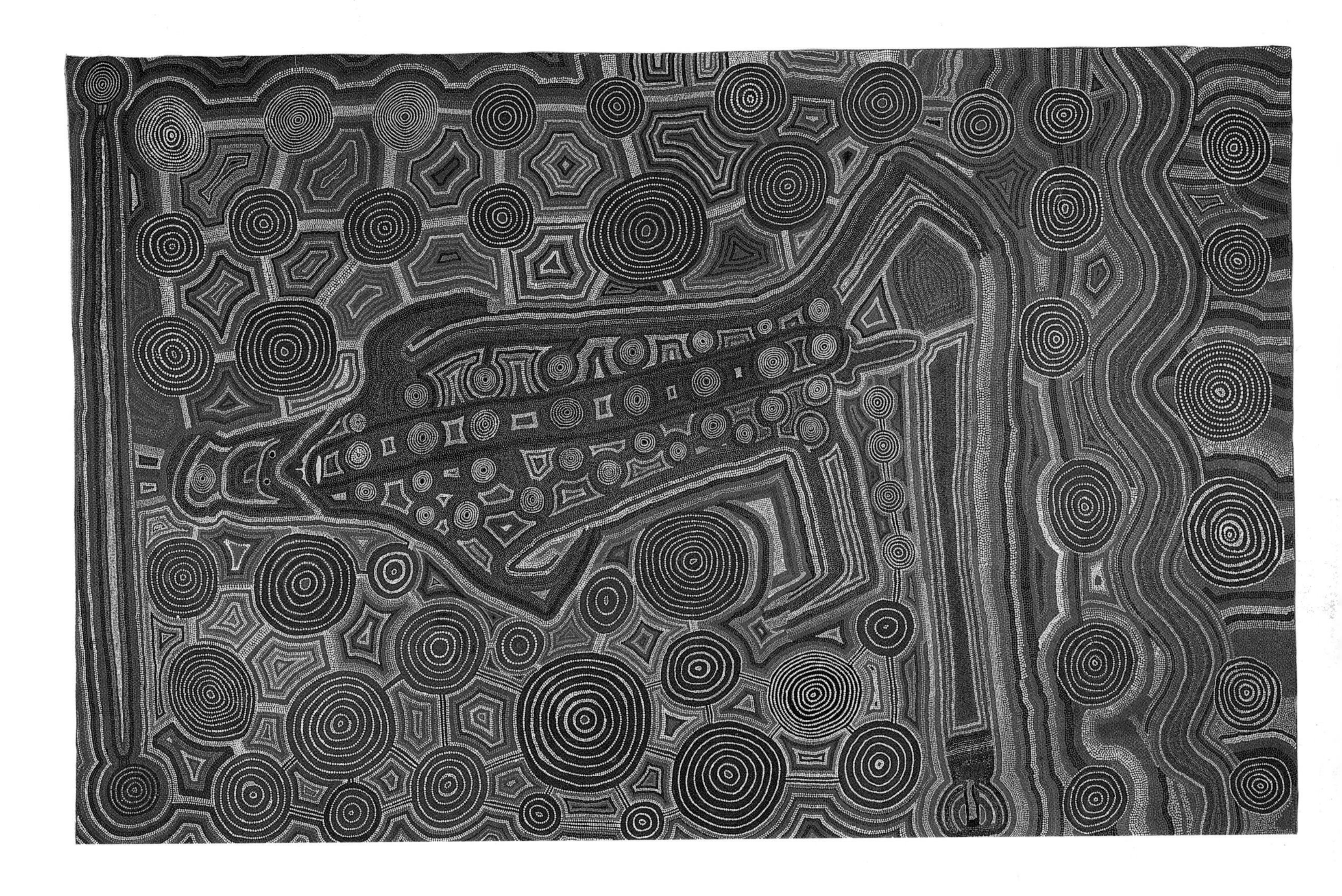

FIG. 179 / CAT. 62
Yumari, 1981. Uta Uta Jangala, Papunya, Central Australia. Acrylic on canvas, 244 × 366 cm.

Papunya and Yuendumu. Although the two settlements have similar backgrounds and are in many respects culturally equivalent, Papunya, unlike Yuendumu, has had few women artists over the course of its painting history. Janet Maughan states: "In comparison with the male painters of the Western Desert, female Aboriginal painters are few. Women's creative energy has often been channeled into other forms (procreation, nurturance, song, dance and ceremony), and where it is expressed visually it is generally classified within the 'craft' tradition rather than an 'art' tradition. This is particularly so in the cross cultural context."[44] This description does not characterize the situation at Yuendumu, where women have been painting since the beginning. The difference in the experience of the two communities becomes more understandable when we examine the involvement of the white advisers.

When Bardon began the school mural project at Papunya, he discussed the Dreamings that were to be portrayed and who should do them with senior Aboriginal men.[45] This was appropriate and expected, given the

FIG. 180
Molly Nampijinpa teaching children to dance, Yuendumu, Central Australia, 1984.

nature of religious life in the region and the importance placed on proper mythic attribution and ownership of the Dreamings. Moreover, it was considered proper that Bardon, as an adult male, should discuss these important matters with the old men and take an active role in the production of their paintings. After Bardon, the major on-site art advisers at Papunya, at least into the mid-1970s, were almost all men (the exception, Janet Wilson, was supervised during her term by Dick Kimber). They were willing to become even more involved in traditional religious matters than Bardon, and this reinforced the acrylic painting movement as basically a male-dominated activity. Since the mid-1980s the coordinator of Papunya Tula has been a woman (Daphne Williams), and it is not accidental that Aboriginal women in the Papunya region are now painting much more than before.

At Yuendumu, women were among the first to do acrylic painting, and they still account for the majority of painters at the settlement. In contrast to the situation at Papunya, non-Aboriginal women have always played a facilitative role, especially in supplying paints and materials, coordinating sales, and assisting with the distribution of money earned.[46] The house of one of these women (Francoise Dussart) was a focal point for women's painting (Fig. 180). Since its founding, the Yuendumu artists company, Warlukurlangu Association, has had a woman (Felicity Wright) as its art coordinator.

None of this is to imply that Aborigines do not have a central role in their painting. They are the ones who control the wellspring that is the essence and form of the entire acrylic movement. White people are not its founders, yet it is clear that they have played and continue to play an essential role.[47]

The Impact of the Acrylic Movement on Western Desert Aboriginal Society

The acrylic movement has clearly had an economic effect on Western Desert Aboriginal communities. The painting business is probably one of the few tradition-oriented activities that provides Aborigines with a cash income. In 1985 at Yuendumu small painted canvas boards sold for about A$40 each. In 1987 larger paintings on canvas sold in the community (to a visitor or a white community worker) for an average of about A$400, of which the artist usually received about three-quarters. At four major exhibitions in Perth, Sydney, Adelaide, and Melbourne in the period 1986–87, the average sale price for the larger Yuendumu paintings was about A$1,800. Of this sum, the gallery or agent received forty percent, and the remaining sixty percent was divided equally between the artist and artist company. The prices of large Papunya paintings tend to be higher, averaging about A$4,500 at exhibitions in the southern cities. In 1987, for example, the works of well-known Papunya Tula artists, such as Clifford Possum Japaljarri, Uta Uta Jangala, and Michael Nelson Jakamarra, have brought as much as A$10,000 to $15,000 each. Such sums, while not large on a countrywide, per-capita basis, make a significant impact on Aboriginal family incomes, which are considerably lower than those of the average white Australian family.

Acrylic paintings have also had a noticeable cultural and social impact. They are frequently used by individual Aborigines to reinforce their stand in certain internal political struggles in the settlements. In one case, a Warlpiri man produced a number of paintings of the same site and Dreaming in order to bolster his position in a dispute with a man of another lineage over who had primary rights to the site. Because he was a skilled artist, whites regularly bought his paintings; this, he contended, was proof of his claim to seniority, as the paintings would not have sold if they were not "true" Dreamings. In another case, involving a controversy over royalty rights in a proposed mining venture, an artist who was the senior owner of a major site in the area claimed that the Dreaming tracks in his paintings also represented the seams of the mineral deposits and that his depiction of them constituted his right to receive any royalties.

While having many other elements in common, acrylic paintings do not share the impermanence of most traditional Aboriginal art forms. All ritual designs executed with natural pigments on traditional media are obliterated following the ceremonial performances for which they were produced. Ancestral designs are evoked only as part of the dramatic form of the ceremony, and presentation of the designs outside this context is not seen as appropriate. Moreover, some designs are too important, too powerful, and therefore too dangerous to be viewed outside the proper setting.

Acrylic paintings, in contrast, are permanent forms of artistic expression. Aborigines quickly realized that whites were buying the paintings to keep them (Fig. 181).[48] At Yuendumu, at least, Aborigines themselves do not think of paintings as valued objects to be hung on the walls of their houses. Paintings are generally not given any special treatment as material items. (In fact, a frequent concern of art advisers is to remove completed paintings from the camps or houses and into safe storage before dogs or children ruin them.) The permanence and sheer quantity of acrylic paintings may eventually result in the transformation of a dynamic ideology into a static and lifeless one.

Although acrylic painting provides a different mode of expression for people's individual creativity, it also to some extent converts religious art into a commodity, thereby alienating the art from religious practice. The acrylic movement could ultimately have negative effects on the socialization of young people into their ritual heritage. They are now exposed to designs on canvas, and they often participate in their creation. Undoubtedly, they are acquiring knowledge and skills that they would normally receive in a completely different context.

Aboriginal painters are now confronted with the alien notion of a form of personal expression that overrides ancestral heritage and obligations. Individual artists are singled out for public recognition, and cooperation with other *kirda* and *kurdungurlu* is displaced. Also, while the context of acrylic painting is understood as different from that of traditional art forms and related to the non-Aboriginal domain, the graphic designs used in the paintings are still seen as powerful, and therefore potentially dangerous, representations. Problems can develop because of the altered nature of individual cooperation and the transformation that designs undergo in acrylic paintings. Such conflicts can pit men against women, *kirda* against *kurdungurlu*, or young against old, and may endanger the long-standing arrangements of control over ritual designs and their transmission. Disputes have arisen in several communities over the issue of artists' rights to paint a given ritual design when they have failed to involve other *kirda* and *kurdungurlu* with whom rights are shared. To not involve the right people in the production of the painting undermines the traditional obligation that each person has to perform particular tasks and to ensure that the painting recounts the myth correctly and does not disclose any secret information. It also leads to conflict over the distribution of money earned from the sale of paintings.[49]

Difficulties have also emerged between young painters and senior members of the community. Senior people may complain, for example, that the young artists have painted ritual designs for which they do not have sufficient rights or knowledge or that they have used designs that are not recognized as "authentic" by the older generation. In the latter case the painters

FIG. 181
Paddy Japaljarri Sims with his painting Bush Plum Dreaming at Kunajarrayi (1986, Yuendumu) at Yuendumu exhibition on Achille-Lauro, America's Cup, Fremantle, Western Australia, 1987.

are told that their artistic compositions do not refer to pictorial arrangements inspired by the Ancestral Beings and are therefore illegitimate. To some extent this represents an attempt by the older people to reserve for themselves the right to dominate the output (and therefore the financial and other rewards) of acrylic paintings on the grounds that they have the exclusive right to transmit knowledge about Dreamings and their graphic forms. Young people, they say, may participate in the production of the paintings, but only as junior partners, until the time that they are judged to be knowledgeable and responsible enough to paint in their own right.

Men and women of different generations and positions in the society also come into conflict over the production of acrylic paintings and their content, in particular over the nature of the ritual designs and their public exposure. Both men and women are concerned about the issue of censorship and the way in which elements in the painting should be disguised in order not to reveal secret or semisecret information. The degree of censorship may vary over time and according to the context and the individuals involved. At all times, the concern of senior members of communities is that the right people do the right paintings and that the graphic forms used refer to symbols that can be seen by all but not necessarily understood. Understanding is only acquired through participation in ritual life, channeled through procedures of social and ritual obligations and payments. The acrylic movement may in some ways subvert this traditional process. On the other hand, the movement has meant that young people are gaining and passing on to contemporary Aboriginal society knowledge that otherwise might be lost.

Some final remarks are in order concerning the individual and Central Australian Aboriginal society in the "acrylic age." In addition to the changes discussed above, it seems certain that the acrylic painting movement has in many cases transformed the "individual who paints" into the "artist." There is what appears to us an increasing identification of and association with paintings not just as depictions of Dreamings, but also as individual creations and professional achievements. This is reinforced by the presentation of paintings in galleries and museums accompanied by identification labels and artists' biographies. Painters such as Clifford Possum Japaljarri and, more recently, Michael Nelson Jakamarra have received widespread recognition. Their works appear in most of the major publications on acrylic painting, and analyses of their work have begun to be published.[50] A retrospective exhibition of Clifford Possum Japaljarri's work is scheduled to open in London in 1988, and both he and Jakamarra have obtained commissions for major public art works (paintings for the Brisbane 1988 World Expo and a floor mosaic for the new Australian Parliament House respectively). A number of people in several communities in Central Australia now spend much of their time painting. Some earn enough from the sale of their paintings to purchase expensive vehicles. The prestige gained by younger successful male painters puts them into potential conflict with the middle-aged men who have important roles in organizing traditional ceremonies. In one case, this situation has led to a painter moving to a settlement away from the more senior members of his group.

Western culture views individual expression as the very definition of art. Artistic movements are looked upon as collections of individual painters rather than embodiments of certain social and cultural forces. White Australians likewise single out individuals within the acrylic movement who in their view qualify as its "stars" or true artists. The variation in the price of paintings, the fact that (at Yuendumu at least) a small number of people are doing most of the paintings, and the trend away from group to individual exhibitions all point to the emergence of the Aboriginal acrylic artist. This is without doubt a function of particularly skilled and gifted individuals having the opportunity to direct and develop their aesthetic capabilities. But it also is indicative of the ultimate control that white Australian society has over the acrylic movement. If non-Aborigines stopped buying the paintings, the Aborigines would stop producing them.

The acrylic movement is in many ways a positive one, for it represents the continuity of a culture and the successful integration of part of that culture into a system that has hitherto actively attempted to destroy it. Whatever internal conflicts and changes their production may bring about, acrylic paintings demonstrate the strength and vitality of Aboriginal culture. They are an important means of transmitting cultural knowledge at a time of great flux and change. The power of the Dreaming does not stop at the museum door.

Perceptions of Aboriginal Art: A History V

PHILIP JONES

OVER THE PAST century perceptions of what is still termed "primitive art" have altered fundamentally. Nowhere has this shift in opinion been more apparent than in the realm of Australian Aboriginal art. In 1919 at a Paris exhibition that included works from Africa, North America, and Oceania (and none from Australia), the organizers characterized the Australian Aborigines as a people without art.[1] Today, while similar works from Africa, North America, and Oceania remain in ethnology museums and in the primitive art and antiquity sections of major galleries, Aboriginal bark paintings and acrylic works are increasingly capturing the attention of individual collectors, art galleries, and museums.

The current wave of interest has been generated by several factors. Aboriginal people themselves have become more interested in bringing their works before a larger audience and in notable instances have developed new art forms. In this they have been assisted, from the middle of the last century, by efforts of anthropologists and others in interpreting Aboriginal culture and art to the wider Australian and international public. Opinions about Aboriginal art have also been influenced by a shift in attitude exemplified by the mid-nineteenth-century Western interest in Oriental art and by the discovery of so-called primitive art by Western artists at the turn of the century.[2]

First Impressions

Alexander von Humboldt made one of the earliest and most successful attempts to induce Europeans to reach beyond the dominant aesthetic of naturalism when observing the newly discovered Pacific region. He advanced the theory that each country possessed its own typical landscape and peculiar form of beauty. Humboldt's *Aspects of Nature*, published in 1808,[3] did much to free European landscape painting from classical conventions of style

FIG. 182
Native Man Standing in an Attitude Very Common to Them All, ca. 1790. Thomas Watling. Watercolor on paper, 21.5 × 33 cm.

and composition. Nevertheless, this revolution in attitudes toward the pictorial depiction of the tropics and the Pacific region did not substantially influence contemporary ethnographic descriptions of their native inhabitants. Despite the objectivity advocated by the Societé des Observateurs de l'Homme prior to the French exploration of the Pacific in the period 1802–1803,[4] the terms that observers applied to the appearance, social behavior, and "arts and manufactures" of Pacific Islanders and Australian Aborigines retained the ethnocentrism of Europe, confident and civilizing in tone. It was not until the publication of Emil Stephans's *Sudseekunst* in 1907 that the two artistic techniques of fidelity to nature and stylization began to be treated as equally valid.[5]

Explorers' and travelers' accounts of the Pacific region both reflected and subsequently reinforced current popular attitudes toward "the savage." The observations contained in these accounts resulted in two popular versions of primitivism.[6] First, "soft primitivism" stemmed from Rousseau's ideal of the "noble savage" living harmoniously in a South Seas Arcadia. Tahiti became the archetype of this paradise, and its people fulfilled the role of "soft primitives," leading easeful lives surrounded by plenty. In contrast, the indigenous people of Australia, Tierra del Fuego, and New Zealand were exemplars of "hard primitivism." While in New Zealand it was the belligerence of the Maoris that qualified them for this category, in the case of Tierra del Fuego and Australia it was the inhabitants' harsh environments and the apparent minimal development of their material cultures that observers stressed (Fig. 182). In the last two cases, the terms "simple," "rude," and "miserable" recur in descriptions of the inhabitants and their societies, even though observers often pointed out that Aborigines appeared as content as other peoples.

Another obvious contrast between "hard" and "soft" primitivism rests in the status that Europeans ascribed to the material possessions of various indigenous peoples. Collections of material culture were a means of documenting a newly discovered country and its people and were inevitably ranked against material gathered from other countries. Artifacts became primary sources in constructing the "great map of mankind." Just as the diffusion of evolutionary traits in plants and animals was charted, so similarities and differences in weapons, utensils, ornament, and invention illustrated the differential advance of civilization. Early European accounts of the Society Islands, Easter Island, and other parts of Polynesia often referred to carvings and decorations and described these with such terms as "elaborate," "well proportioned," and "beautiful." Little reference, in contrast, was made to the art of Australian Aborigines, beyond describing the technical characteristics of the returning boomerang. Food-gathering implements and weapons of warfare and the chase provided sufficient evidence of the "hard primitivism" of the Aborigines—an existence characterized by ceaseless searching for barely sufficient sources of food.[7] To a large extent, Europeans found only what they expected to find in Aboriginal material culture. While the early ethnographic literature recorded the existence of rock engravings and paintings, commentators rarely connected these occurrences with the activities of living people. This was despite the fact that Aborigines of the Hawkesbury and Hunter Rivers, for example, were still painting and carving images on rocks there during the 1840s, fifty years after European settlement.[8]

Sir George Grey's discovery in 1837 of the spectacular rock-painting style of northwestern Australia now termed Wandjina art (Fig. 75) is a telling

FIG. 183
Copy of an Aboriginal painting at Chasm Island, near Groote Eylandt, 1803. William Westall. Pencil and wash on paper, 26.7 × 37.2 cm.

FIG. 184
Ancestral figures, Namarrkon the Lightning Man and spirit people. Nawurlandja, Kakadu National Park, Northern Territory.

example of this attitude. Grey was among the founders of Australian ethnography, and his expeditions brought him into contact with a wider range of Aboriginal art than many of his contemporaries. Despite this, Grey was unwilling to credit Aboriginal people with the artistic capacity to produce the Wandjina paintings: ". . . whatever may have been the age of these paintings, it is scarcely probable that they could have been executed by a self-taught savage. Their origin, therefore, must still be open to conjecture."[9] As a general rule, the less accomplished a rock painting appeared, according to Western conventions of naturalism, the less difficulty commentators had in attributing it to Aboriginal artists. All shared a characteristic inability to approach Aboriginal art on its own terms. Even influential European anthropologists such as E. B. Tylor did little more than note Australian paintings and rock carvings with mild interest: "Travellers in Australia sheltering from the storm in caves wonder at the cleverness of the rude frescos on the cavern-walls of kangaroos and emus and natives dancing . . ."[10]

There is, however, a second fundamental cause of nonrecognition of Aboriginal art. In the first period of Aboriginal-Western contact, the defining media of art—sculpture and painting—were certainly represented in Aboriginal Australia, but these forms were not readily available for Western scrutiny, especially in the densely settled regions of southeastern Australia. Of the five types of Aboriginal art described in this book, only the shields of the Lower Murray River region would have been readily apparent to Europeans during the first fifty years of Australian settlement. A characteristic of Aboriginal material culture in the coastal areas of southeastern Australia was the relative lack of painted objects apart from shields. The use of body paint was widespread across the country, but neither this nor the rock paintings of the southeast approach the fineness of line of rock paintings in the Kimberley, Arnhem Land, or Cape York Peninsula (compare Figs. 48, 184).

Apart from the rock engravings of the Sydney and Hawkesbury districts, and the elaborately engraved trees of inland Victoria and New South Wales, very few examples of sculpture in the round were recorded in the southeast,[11] a fact that immediately distinguished Aboriginal art from that of New Zealand, New Guinea, or the Pacific Islands. Moreover, the geometric designs on wooden artifacts from southeastern Australia were only rarely interspersed with figurative representations (Fig. 185), and Europeans saw no special qualities in this work when compared with examples from the Pacific or New Zealand. One of the most observant European artists in Australia during the 1840s, George French Angas, postponed his sketching of Australian Aborigines and their artifacts after seeing a friend's collection of "beautifully ornamented [Maori] weapons."[12]

It was not until the 1870s that bark paintings were identified as a characteristic form of Aboriginal art, and another forty years passed before Sir Baldwin Spencer made the first substantial museum collection of these.[13] The toas of Lake Eyre appeared as an isolated example only around 1904–1905; the elaborate wooden sculptures of Western Cape York Peninsula were first documented in the 1950s; and Western Desert acrylic painting did not receive commercial exposure until 1972. Despite their occasional publication after the 1890s, the intricate ground designs of the desert inland were seen only by a privileged handful of Westerners until the transformation wrought by the acrylic painting movement in the 1970s. Much of the painted rock art of Central and northern Australia that now attracts popular attention was unknown to Western eyes until the outback became accessible to tourists in the 1960s.

While many observers in southeastern Australia witnessed the public corroborees (ceremonial dances) of Aborigines on the fringes of towns and settlements, by the 1860s the more intense visual drama of restricted ceremonial events was no longer a feature of Aboriginal life in these areas and continued only in Central and northern Australia (Figs. 186–87). What then could Europeans have appreciated as Aboriginal art in the early period? Observers did comment on the way in which Aboriginal people habitually decorated themselves: "Even the poorest and most wretched do not forget to paint their bodies, justifying Martin's remark about the West Australians: 'What they wear is ornament rather than clothing.' "[14] Most European artists depicting Aborigines throughout the first decades of contact observed this characteristic. It can be seen in their surviving work, from Sidney Parkinson's watercolors made on Captain James Cook's first voyage in 1768–71 (Fig. 188) to those made by George French Angas (Figs. 2, 224, and Cat. 75) and Samuel Thomas Gill in the 1840s and 1850s. Artists like Angas, Eugene von Guerard, and Augustus Earle recorded aspects of southeastern Aboriginal art that were fast disappearing as Aboriginal people relinquished their traditions, adopting European dress and artifacts in the process. Angas's publications, and exhibitions of his work held in Sydney, Adelaide, and London

FIG. 185
Design for a wooden grave memorial to Thomas Bungaleen, Kurnai man. Drawn by Simon Wonga (after Smyth 1878).

FIG. 186
Corroboree, South Australia, 1840. John M. Skipper. Oil on canvas, 106 × 152 cm.

during the 1840s, ensured that the Aboriginal customs and material culture of southeastern Australia were known by a far wider audience than before.

European artists only gradually achieved lifelike depictions of the Australian landscape and its people. Accomplished artists such as von Guerard, Nicholas Petit, John Glover, or Benjamin Duttereau, who were trained in the European landscape tradition, took longer to adapt to the new conditions of light, composition, and subject imposed by the Australian environment. Thus the Grecian torsos of Petit's warriors present a marked contrast to the wiry realism of the Aborigines painted by Richard Browne, an untrained artist working outside classical conventions (Fig. 189, and compare Fig. 188).

By the mid-nineteenth century Europeans were at least aware of the range of Aboriginal material culture and of Aboriginal use of pigments, ochres, and other decorations. Despite this, with little exposure to the ceremonial art and rock paintings of Central and northern Australia and with scant understanding of the complexity of Aboriginal belief and social structure, it is not surprising that Europeans remained unimpressed by Aboriginal art. They found no evidence of the Aborigines' capacity to create works visually powerful or accessible enough to modify a dominant Anglo-Saxon aesthetic. Ruskin's famous remark that "there is no art in the whole of Africa, Asia, or America" could equally have applied to European views of Australia. Ironically, at a time when Western ethnocentrism was already undergoing revision in Europe and North America through the transforming influences of Oriental art and Japonisme, attitudes toward Aborigines and their art remained negative within Australia, partly because of the growing concept of "hard primitivism" and the increasing popularity of the social evolutionist theories being developed by Spencer, Darwin, and Huxley. Indeed, as evolutionary theory became accepted, Aboriginal art found its place in scientific and popular thought as no more than a quaint precursor of Western art.

FIG. 187
The Mudlungga dance, a public ceremony, near Killalpaninna Mission, Lake Eyre region, 1901.

FIG. 188
Two of the Natives of New Holland Advancing to Combat, 1768–71.
T. Chambers after Sydney Parkinson.
Engraving, 22.5 × 19 cm.

FIG. 189
Natives Fishing in a Bark Canoe, 1819.
Richard Browne. Watercolor on paper, 32.4 × 27.8 cm.

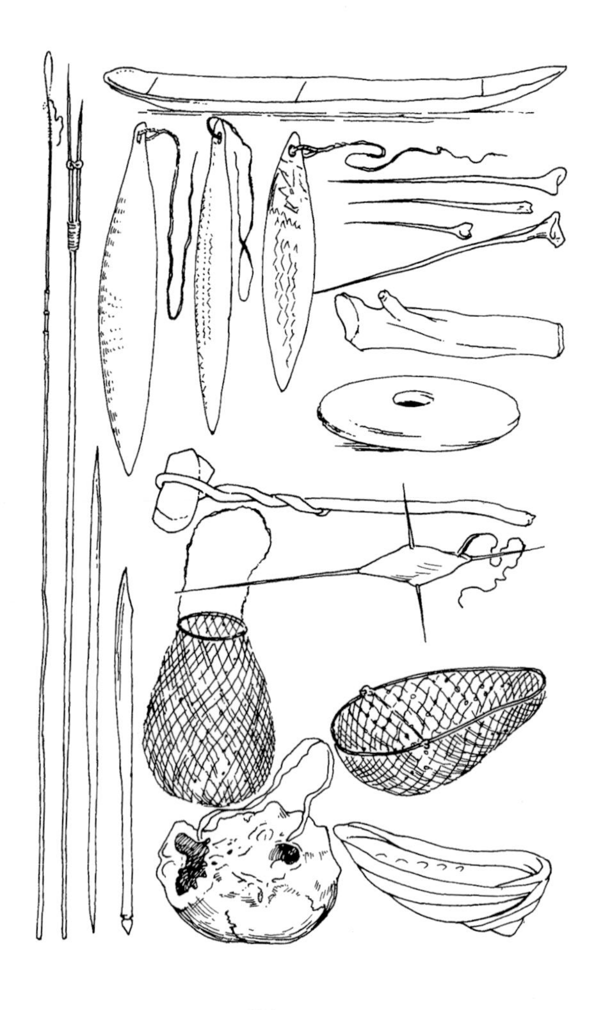

Collectors and Collections

Early collections of artifacts did much to shape Western perceptions of Aboriginal art in the nineteenth century. A curio trade in Australian material did not develop until the second half of the century, but explorers, missionaries, pastoralists, and government officials had been forming collections from the first years of settlement. From Cook onward, explorers were careful to acquire material evidence of the people whom they encountered (Fig. 190). Expedition accounts often provided the first evidence of particular categories of Aboriginal art. The Wandjina paintings published by George Grey and the rock paintings of Ayers Rock recorded and published by Edward Stirling in

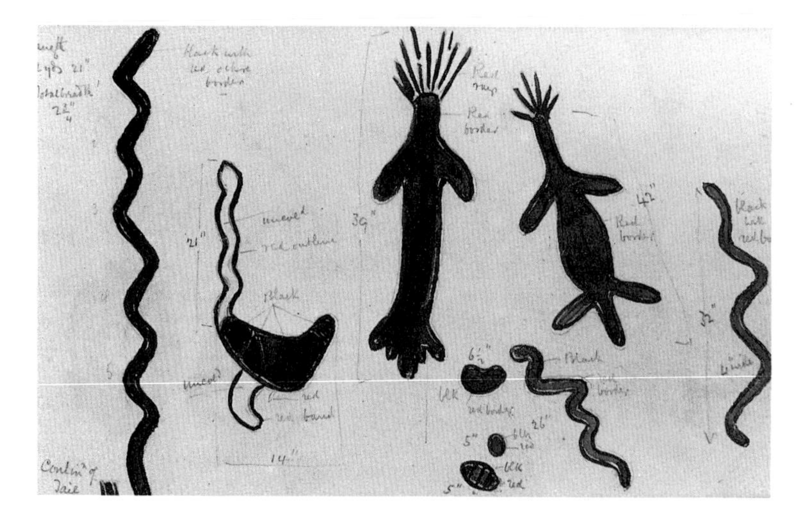

FIG. 190
Native Implements, 1841. Edward John Eyre (after Eyre 1845).

FIG. 191
Sketches of paintings at Ayers Rock, made by Edward Stirling on the Horn Expedition, 1894. Watercolor and pencil on paper, 10 × 17 cm.

1896 following the Horn Expedition (Fig. 191) are notable examples. Missionaries, particularly Lutherans such as Carl Strehlow of Hermannsburg and Johann Reuther of Killalpaninna (Figs. 3, 192), acquired religious objects, which they considered idolatrous, but they were also motivated to investigate and document material culture as part of their effort to understand Aboriginal beliefs and customs. Missionary collections were consequently the most comprehensive and best documented until the advent of investigative field anthropology in the twentieth century. Other collectors, such as government officials working on the frontiers of settlement in northern or Central Australia, acquired artifacts in the course of their administrative and economic dealings with Aboriginal communities. Aboriginal people were attracted to European settlements, among other reasons because of the availability of new commodities such as metal tools, tea, flour, and sugar. In return for these goods, or for other real or perceived advantages, they were often prepared to exchange their artifacts and weapons. In the southern centers, this flow of ethnographica soon diminished to no more than the occasional boomerang or basket as Aboriginal people were forced off their lands and began living semipermanently on town margins.

By the mid-nineteenth century many pastoralists' homesteads contained collections of Aboriginal artifacts displayed in hallways or game rooms. The

FIG. 192
Pastor Johann Reuther in his study at Killalpaninna Mission, Lake Eyre region, ca. 1900.

value attached to such collections had more to do with their symbolic status as trophies than with perceptions of their qualities of beauty, skill, or workmanship. Nevertheless, commentators did occasionally remark upon these qualities, usually stressing the facility with which Aboriginal people manufactured weapons and utensils from apparently meager raw materials.

With the establishment of public museums in Australian cities from 1829, collections of Aboriginal material gradually became the object of investigation by ethnographers and the first anthropologists. By the end of the century, as publications such as Spencer and Gillen's *Native Tribes of Central Australia* joined Smyth's *Aborigines of Victoria* and Howitt's *Native Tribes of South-East Australia*,[15] the extent of variations in Aboriginal material culture across the continent became more obvious. The larger state museums in Sydney, Adelaide, and Melbourne attempted to make their collections as complete as possible. The South Australian Museum in Adelaide achieved the most success, with its director, Edward Stirling, establishing a network of collectors throughout northern and Central Australia during the 1890s and 1900s (Fig. 194). Telegraph station operators such as Frank Gillen

FIG. 193
Sketch of two groups of squatters near Echuca, Victoria, ca. 1862, Tommy McRae (Barnes), (after Smyth 1878), 3 × 10.5 cm.

FIG. 194
Letter from Edward Stirling to telegraph operators requesting native articles for the South Australian Museum, 1890.

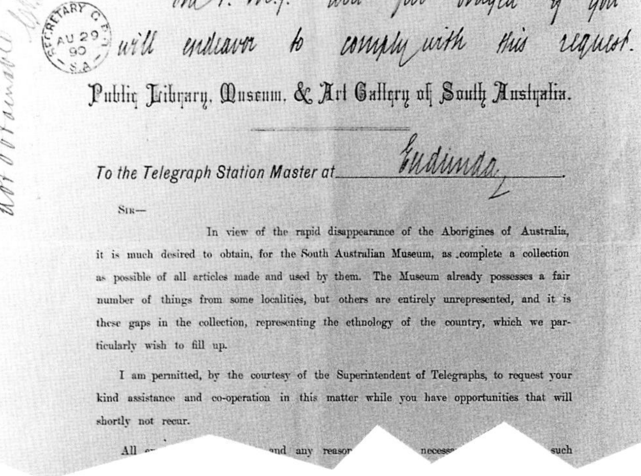

SECRETARY G.P.T. AU 29 90 S.A.

The P. M. G. will feel obliged if you will endeavor to comply with this request.

Public Library, Museum, & Art Gallery of South Australia.

To the Telegraph Station Master at Eudunda.

Sir—

In view of the rapid disappearance of the Aborigines of Australia, it is much desired to obtain, for the South Australian Museum, as complete a collection as possible of all articles made and used by them. The Museum already possesses a fair number of things from some localities, but others are entirely unrepresented, and it is these gaps in the collection, representing the ethnology of the country, which we particularly wish to fill up.

I am permitted, by the courtesy of the Superintendent of Telegraphs, to request your kind assistance and co-operation in this matter while you have opportunities that will shortly not recur.

All … and any reasor… necess… such

FIG. 195
Carved and painted grave posts around the grave of Isadore Tipakalippa, Melville Island, 1986.

(Baldwin Spencer's collaborator), policemen such as Paul Foelsche, and traders such as D. M. Sayers gathered a range of material from remote areas: ceremonial objects, women's net-bags, and even large funerary *pukamani* poles (Fig. 195).[16] By supplying these men with a sufficient honorarium and money to purchase trading goods such as steel tomahawks or sticks of tobacco, Stirling ensured that much rare material was preserved.

Apart from the missionary collections, many of the best-documented collections of Aboriginal art in museums today were assembled by individuals whose training or experience in anthropology or ethnography led them to pursue the social function of material culture in Aboriginal life. The collections of Spencer, Gillen, Walter Roth, Norman Tindale, Donald Thomson, Ronald and Catherine Berndt, Ursula McConnel, C. P. Mountford, Theodor Strehlow, and others are all characterized by a level of detailed documentation that sets them apart from the more random efforts of other collectors and has provided a model for more recent fieldworkers.[17] (Figs. 196, 197.)

FIG. 196
Baldwin Spencer and Francis Gillen's 1901–1902 expedition party at Alice Springs, May 1902. Seated: Gillen, Spencer; standing: Purula, Chance, Jim Kite (Erlikiliakirra).

Aboriginal reactions to this attention from collectors are difficult to assess. Reynolds has written of the various ways in which Aboriginal people turned the presence of Westerners to their own local advantage across Australia, despite the broad negative effects of contact.[18] For Aboriginal informants in remote areas, the attraction of European commodities and food was strong, and these items soon became a medium of exchange. Gillen wrote with characteristic flippancy of his Kaytej informant, Arabinya-urungwina, who

> has fattened on our fare and perhaps never again will he wallow in such abundance. He is fitted out with tomahawk knives, pipes and a good supply of tobacco and says that he is going away into the bush where his lubras will feed him on yams until he recovers from his grief at our departure. He has been of great assistance to us in our work among his tribal brethren . . .[19]

Most anthropologists, from Robert Mathews, Alfred Howitt, and Spencer and Gillen onward, have been accorded kinship status within the Aboriginal groups that they have studied. In many cases these relationships have been extended to take account of their special access to restricted knowledge. This access has involved anthropologists in complex reciprocal relationships entailing more than a simple exchange of European goods or money for artifacts and knowledge. Westerners have, for example, used their influence in wider Australian society to sponsor particular individuals in local or community politics and moves for land rights or to introduce them to a wider market for their art or artifacts.[20]

In another sense, the behavior of anthropologists and fieldworkers undoubtedly provided a diversion for Aboriginal people unaccustomed to such interest from Westerners (Fig. 198). Recalling the early Board for Anthropological Research Expeditions, Tindale observed:

> . . . in a sense we entertained them. Our activities were so strange to them . . . I don't think that the bush ones in the early days ever realised that we were making records of them. They had no idea why white men held boxes up to their eyes when they were talking or asking questions, or looking at ceremonies. That was their [the white men's] *inma*, their ceremonial way of doing it.[21]

There is little doubt that Aborigines often responded creatively to the intense interest in their culture displayed by fieldworkers and collectors. The motives

FIG. 197
Donald Thomson and his assistant "Tiger," with Caledon Bay people in front of Thomson's darkroom, Trial Bay, North East Arnhem Land, July 1935 (after Thomson 1983).

FIG. 198
Recording Aboriginal songs during the Board for Anthropological Research expedition to MacDonald Downs, Central Australia, 1930.

FIG. 199
Bark paintings exhibited at the Ethnological Court of the Garden Palace exhibition, Sydney, 1879–80 (after Strahan 1979).

of these individuals, furthermore, may have varied, but the result was often the same: an efflorescence of artifact production, which sometimes even inspired new forms of Aboriginal art (see Chapter VI). As a rule, though, collectors had fixed ideas about what they wanted to obtain from Aborigines. Comparison with museum collections from other Pacific regions shows that proportionately greater numbers of utilitarian artifacts (weapons and tools) than ornaments or decorative pieces were collected.[22] There is no doubt that, particularly in the nineteenth century, this bias reflected Western preferences as well as patterns of production by Aborigines for the Western market. Museum collections from southern Australia in particular were often "reflections of a century or more of cultural contact, and they were shaped more by the enthusiasms of the collectors and the state of the dealers' market than by contemporary . . . society."[23] The bias toward weaponry supported the dominant and erroneous view of Aborigines as people with little leisure, preoccupied with internecine warfare rather than with ceremonial or artistic life.

This view was to be further emphasized by museum exhibitions and published images such as postcards from the turn of the century onward. In the meantime, the same stereotype was promoted by the international expositions of the second half of the nineteenth century, huge trade fairs that became a feature of colonial expansion by the major Western powers.[24] Aboriginal art was never well represented at these exhibitions. Although the Paris Exhibition of 1855 included six bark paintings, they would have been unlikely to have aroused much comment if they were of a similar quality to those exhibited at the Sydney Exhibition of 1879–80 (Figs. 72, 199–200).[25] In these exhibitions Aboriginal artifacts, like those from other countries, were displayed in a way calculated more to promote the exotic effect of a bristling array of spears or clubs than the appreciation of incised patterns or painted designs. If any works stood out, these were the sculptural figures and masks from Africa and the Pacific. Weaponry was the main category contributed by Australian participants. In some cases, as with the Calcutta Exhibition of 1883–84, Aboriginal weapons served only a decorative function, a fan of spears framing displays of South Australian produce and manufactures.[26] In other cases, such as the Colonial and Indian Exhibition of 1886 in London, participating countries were urged to contribute lifelike dioramas of native life. South Australia's contribution was a remarkably lifelike set of models of Lower Murray River Aborigines (Fig. 201).[27] The scene was a powerful evocation of that enduring image of Australian Aboriginal life: a family intent on the business of survival, without leisure and without art.

If the Western museum-going public had little more than these enduring images of "hard primitivism" with which to form the visual basis of their opinions on Aboriginal art at the turn of the century, the collector and connoisseur was little better served. The Sydney firm of Tost and Rohu and the Adelaide dealer A. E. Marval conducted steady business with museums at the turn of the century.[28] Australian museums also purchased artifacts from

FIG. 200 / CAT. 7
Bird, ca. 1877. Artist unknown, Western Arnhem Land. Ochre on bark, 64 × 31 cm.

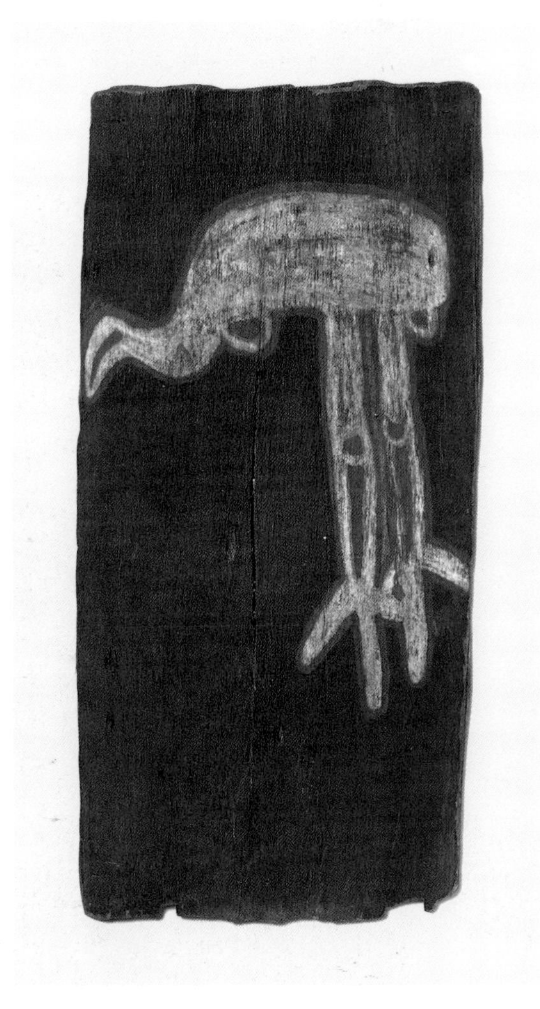

FIG. 201
South Australian Museum exhibit in the Colonial and Indian exhibition, London 1886 (after Hale 1956).

the extensively illustrated catalogues of two international ethnographic dealers, Webster and Oldman, both based in London. These firms played a large part in promoting Aboriginal art to a world market of collectors and connoisseurs during the 1890s and 1900s. The Webster and Oldman catalogues show that the collector's choice in Australian material was still mainly restricted to weaponry, with engraved and painted shields from eastern Australia providing the main decorative component (Fig. 202). Occasional examples of engraved pearl-shell ornaments, painted bark baskets, or woven bags were offered for sale, but these examples were rare.[29] In their pricing levels, also, these catalogues demonstrate the continued low profile of Aboriginal art during the period when the attention of international collectors and art historians was directed more toward Africa and Polynesia.

The rise of museums did little to modify prevailing opinions about Aboriginal art. In the middle years of the nineteenth century there was no more than a vaguely articulated desire to gather representative collections of artifacts from a race of people still perceived by many as essentially homogeneous and undifferentiated. This attitude had already resulted in much rare material of regional significance leaving the country as Australian museums exchanged Aboriginal artifacts for foreign material.[30] After the 1880s, Australian museums followed the British and North American "natural history" model, incorporating four main elements that are still retained by most of the larger Western museums today.[31] Minerals, fossils, animals, and anthropological collections represented coherent evidence of what was described as the "great chain of being," which linked the inert foundation of the earth, through its earliest life forms, to bird and animal species. It represented the progression from the simplest human cultures (Australia and the

Pacific) to the much-admired sophistication of ancient Egypt, popularly regarded as the origin of modern Western civilization.[32]

From its origins as a miscellany of cultural and natural historical material (often derived from the "Royal cabinets" and "cabinets de curiosité" of the sixteenth, seventeenth, and eighteenth centuries), the ethnographic museum acquired a new and powerful relevance as an exemplar of evolutionary theory.[33] It was ". . . the age of reason with implicit faith in the ultimate value of collecting facts and things."[34] That faith was founded in the belief that although the different "races of man" had evolved in a linear, progressive manner from a common ancestor (the widely held notion of monogenesis), evolution was itself subject to fixed laws and stages. These, and the dynamic of the evolutionary process, were investigated by comparing the material culture of those peoples, like the Australian Aborigines and the Polynesians, who appeared to represent different stages of development.[35] The principles of evolution were first applied in earnest to museum ethnographic collections by A. Lane-Fox Pitt-Rivers. In 1851 he began assembling the wide-ranging collection that now forms the basis of the Oxford Pitt-Rivers Museum. Its arrangement by artifact type was complete by the 1880s and stressed the differential advances made by indigenous peoples in technical achievement. Predictably, Aboriginal culture was once again found lacking.

FIG. 202
Page from 1897 Webster catalogue depicting Australian Aboriginal artifacts for sale.

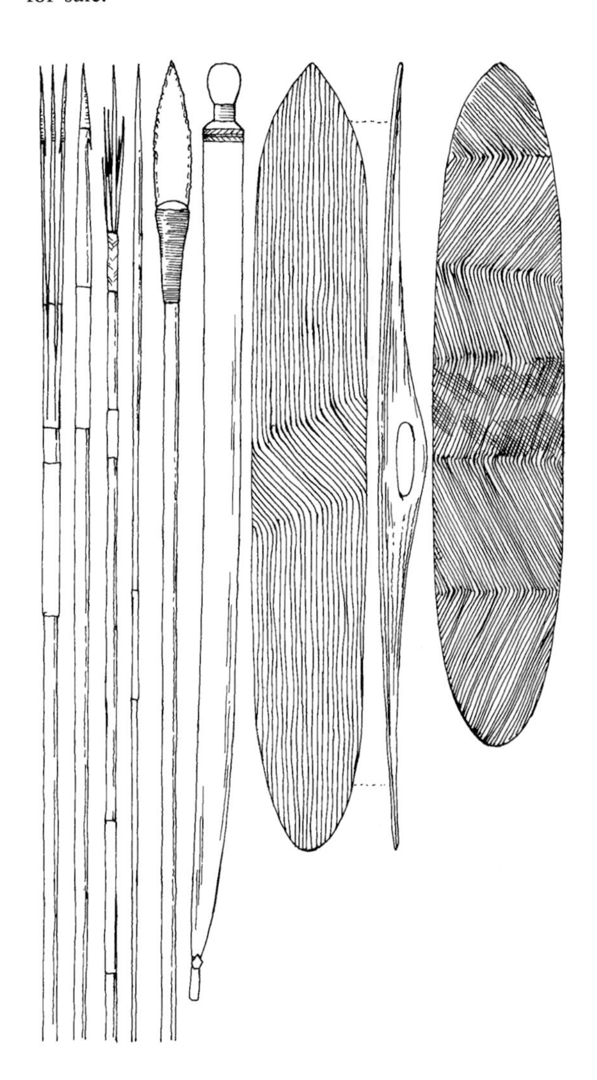

Western Scholars and Aboriginal Art

During the fifty years from 1870 to 1920 several Western scholars approached the subject of "primitive art." Aboriginal art was included in this discussion initially only as data in the development of evolutionary theory. By the 1920s, however, the art began to provoke serious investigation on its own account. In Europe, Pitt-Rivers's general interest in the meaning and origins of primitive art and folk motifs was given more scholarly expression during the 1860s through the work of the German art historian Gottfried Semper.[36] Semper's suggestion that the Greek key, or meander, design derived originally from a simple textile weave was accepted by Colley March, who published the first scientific treatise on the subject in 1889.[37] In the meantime, the Norwegian ethnographer Hjalmar Stolpe gave the subject a wider relevance by postulating that the geometric decoration characteristic of much non-Western art was derived from progressive modifications of naturalistic representations.[38] This theory, also expressed by Henry Balfour of the Pitt-Rivers Museum, was used to account for the appearance of sophisticated Paleolithic cave art in newly discovered sites in the south of France, as well as in Australia. Balfour's 1893 publication on the evolution of decorative art[39] further cemented this view, together with its underlying assumption that evolution had proceeded according to the same principles in all countries and cultures. Despite Franz Boas's criticism of this assumption in 1896, it was not until his publication of *Primitive Art* in 1927 that the application of conventional evolutionary principles to the study of ethnographic art was seriously challenged.[40]

By the last decades of the nineteenth century, ethnographers such as Tylor and Friedrich Ratzel shared the prevailing opinion that Australian Aboriginal art occupied the lowest rung of the evolutionary ladder. There were occasional assessments made independently of this accepted wisdom. Brough Smyth wrote:

> One sees in the simple forms used by the natives of Australia the rudiments of the arts which gave splendour to the palaces of ancient Chaldea. In the richest monuments of the luxurious races that dwelt on the lands watered by the Euphrates and the Tigris the same lines and combinations of lines as those figured here are used and repeated.[41]

As the evolutionary model was increasingly accepted by ethnographers and anthropologists, it became clear that the people typified in the previous century as exemplars of "hard primitivism" would become the standard by which achievements of other cultures were to be measured. This conclusion was inevitable, given the acceptance by Darwin and his adherents of an apparently self-evident truth: that mankind's evolutionary development led necessarily to cultures such as those of nineteenth-century Western Europe or North America, technologically sophisticated civilizations built upon literary traditions of knowledge.

Although both Darwinian theory and the more generalized "chain of being" hypothesis were mainly concerned with the emergence of the human species, the pervasiveness of the taxonomic approach affected nineteenth-century ethnologists as much as it did zoologists or geologists. The divisions between peoples (or races, as they were more commonly known), animals, plants, and minerals were made according to similar criteria of appearance and behavior, and rankings were made accordingly. The same process of classification applied within a culture: Edward Curr's word lists of Australian languages and Howitt's *Native Tribes of South-East Australia* are examples.[42]

FIG. 203
Distribution of longitudinal zigzag designs incised on wooden artifacts. One of a series of distribution maps produced by Daniel S. Davidson (after Davidson 1937).

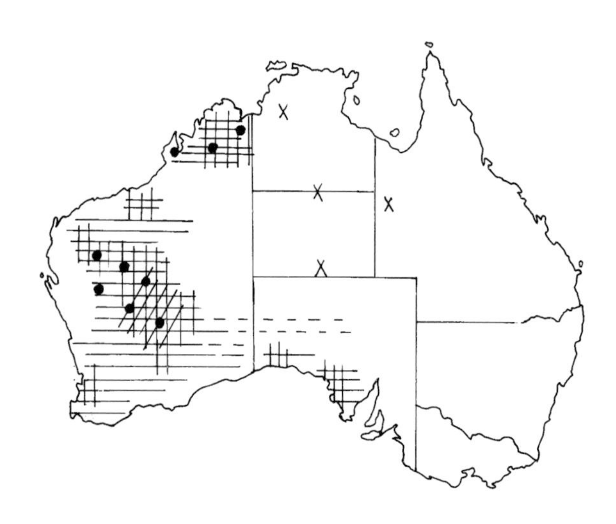

From the 1920s the notion of uniform evolution had to contend both with Franz Boas's "historical particularism" and with the increasing popularity of the diffusionist theory that informed his work and was later propounded by scholars such as Alfred L. Kroeber, Elliott Smith, and Clark Wissler. Diffusionist theory was to have most relevance for Australia through the work of the American ethnographer Daniel S. Davidson. His application of the "culture-area" concept to decorative traits in Aboriginal art resulted in the first comprehensive survey of the subject in 1937, *A Preliminary Survey of Australian Decorative Art*.[43] As with Tindale's tribal map of Australia, prepared during the same period, Davidson's map of the distribution of art styles within distinct culture areas helped to focus scholarly and public attention on Aboriginal art as a field of study in its own right (Fig. 203).

The work of several scholars illustrates the new attention that Aboriginal art began to receive from the 1930s onward. The first Australian Chair of Anthropology had been established at the University of Sydney in 1926, and it was not until over a decade later that significant numbers of students and graduates in this profession began to study Aboriginal art. Among the earliest was Olive Pink, whose fieldwork findings during the 1930s still remain unpublished. Another Sydney graduate, Ursula McConnel, undertook fieldwork among the Wik people of Cape York Peninsula and published in scientific and art-history journals. Her work analyzed design in both ceremonial and secular material culture. Her Cape York studies were complemented by those of Donald Thomson, who also extended his inquiries to Arnhem Land and Central Australia. The process of synthesis that Davidson began was continued until the 1970s by another Sydney student, Frederick McCarthy of the Australian Museum in Sydney. McCarthy was the first museum curator in Australia to be trained in social anthropology. His studies concerned continent-wide trends and art styles and released much previously inaccessible data, initially to the museum-going public but also to a wider readership, including the increasingly influential group of lay connoisseurs. Since the 1940s the work of Ronald and Catherine Berndt, also graduates of A. P. Elkin's University of Sydney Anthropology Department, has involved the more analytical and descriptive concerns of Australian social anthropology. Their pioneer studies of Aboriginal art have proceeded alongside broad ethnographies covering most aspects of Aboriginal life, including explications of mythology and its associated symbolism. The Berndts' work underlines the pervasiveness of certain key themes and motifs within Aboriginal culture and has again stressed regional variation across the continent. Their concern to reach a wide audience has resulted in popular works of synthesis on Aboriginal culture as well as publications aimed at the art world.

FIG. 204
Aborigines making crayon drawings during the Board for Anthropological Research expedition to Mt. Liebig, Central Australia, 1932.

Elkin coordinated a great deal of the first professional research into Aboriginal art during the 1930s and 1940s and was himself responsible for several important studies. His first chapter of *Art in Arnhem Land*, a popular but scholarly account of the subject coauthored with the Berndts in 1950, presented a masterly synthesis of his students' work, detailing the main attributes of Aboriginal art and its complex relation with both sacred and secular life. He also took an active interest in exhibitions of Aboriginal art during the 1940s and 1950s.

Although the study of Aboriginal art by professional anthropologists graduating from Sydney did not commence in Australia until well into the 1930s, fieldworkers and physical anthropologists based in Adelaide were active from the late 1920s. The Board for Anthropological Research expeditions, undertaken annually in Central Australia from 1926 until World War II, yielded a significant corpus of Aboriginal art in the form of crayon drawings made by Aborigines who had previously made only ground, rock, or body paintings (Fig. 204).[44] These crayon drawings were collected mainly by Norman Tindale of the South Australian Museum and by C. P. Mountford. Mountford published a large number of these drawings during the 1930s, foreshadowing his later involvement in documenting a variety of Aboriginal art forms—from the rock engravings of South Australia and the watercolor art of Albert Namatjira to the painted rock art and bark paintings of Arnhem Land. Tindale obtained the first significant collection of Groote Eylandt bark paintings in 1921–22 and the first well-documented crayon drawings at Hermannsburg in 1929. His excavations at the Devon Downs rock shelter in the same year provided the first firm archaeological evidence of the antiquity of Aboriginal rock art. Tindale's 1932 paper on "Primitive Art of the Australian Aborigines" (based on his observations of the crayon-drawing artists) was one of the first to discuss the interpretations that tradition-oriented Aboriginal artists placed on their own work.[45]

Another important scholar, W. E. H. Stanner, remains largely unpublished in the field of art. His other published writings have, nevertheless, heavily influenced the way in which the present generation of scholars regard Aboriginal art and culture. Stanner focused on the complex articulation between Aboriginal artistic life and the sacred and secular domains of adult life. He also imparted a strong historical sense to analyses of Aboriginal social practice, to the extent that commentators no longer speak of bark painting, for example, as a traditional (and therefore ahistorical and timeless) art but describe it as an activity firmly located in time and space.[46]

The "Discovery of Primitive Art"

It is now more common for museum curators to ascertain the names and personal details of Aboriginal artists whose works they collect. This is a relatively recent development; no such effort was made until the late 1940s, despite academic interest in the forms and styles of such art during the previous fifty years. The reason for this neglect lies in the history of attitudes toward Aboriginal art, and toward "primitive art" in general. Until recently commentators have tended to stress the functional, religious significance of the art and its symbols and motifs, rather than its aesthetic qualities. Today the assumption that the Aboriginal artist is motivated by religious or magico-religious impulses and not by aesthetic considerations has largely been abandoned in favor of the view that these two aspects cannot be separated.

The earlier view first found expression in relation to the cave art of southern France. The images of bison at Lascaux were interpreted as drawings made for the primary purpose of capturing these animals; the beauty of the images was regarded as incidental to this primary function.[47] The consequent opinion that there were no true individual artists in tribal societies was supported by anthropologists, who tended to regard these societies as collectivist entities, undifferentiated by divisions of labor or talent. More specifically, the findings of anthropologists and archaeologists suggested that Aboriginal art revealed highly formalized, intensely local, and long-established styles that apparently constrained the limits of individual expression. Following his Arnhem Land expedition of 1912, Baldwin Spencer recorded that "the natives very clearly distinguished between the ability of different artists . . . the majority of those [bark paintings] that I collected and [that] now hang in the National Museum at Melbourne are regarded as first-rate examples of first-rate artists."[48] Despite such observations, Aboriginal artists rarely received individual recognition until the 1950s and were usually given only the status of anonymous craftspeople.

A change in attitude came only as Westerners have become exposed both to more Aboriginal art and to the accompanying insights into the culture that produced it. The art historian Robert Redfield describes this development in the following way:

> . . . every established art is an expression of a style, which is a language, in which the forms are found, the qualities are set forth. In coming to see the style, the persisting structure of available forms, we are helped to see the work as art. We are helped also to begin to make the discrimination of better and worse, or of more or less successful achievement. In the arts of the West, we have already some ability in these languages of form. For the exotic arts we have to learn them. It follows . . . that the exhibition of primitive art which presents together several objects in the same stylistic tradition gets us along faster in our appreciation and understanding than that exhibition which shows us one object beside one other object of another tradition.[49]

One of the first expressions of a more enlightened attitude to the subject within Australia was made by the Berndts in their 1957 catalogue accompanying *The Art of Arnhem Land* exhibition in Perth. It included descriptions of eighty paintings and sculptures and gave relevant details for twenty-three artists, including name, linguistic group, and moiety. The Berndts wrote:

> To people of European descent, the art of 'First Australians' often appears exotic, bizarre, or even crude . . . this gap is largely because we do not understand the symbolism involved, nor the context of that symbolism. In other words, we do not have the clues which would help us to interpret it.[50]

This change in attitude toward the aesthetic qualities of Aboriginal art took many years to develop. A gradual appreciation of the power of the aesthetic impulse in primitive art had one of its first expressions in the findings of nineteenth-century scholars working within evolutionary theory. Semper, who had posited in the 1880s that primitive art arose from the purely technical processes of making particular artifacts, left room for the notion that the aesthetic sense operated as a transforming agent.[51] Nevertheless, these early studies were dominated by the notion that the stylizations of primitive art reflected an inability to copy nature satisfactorily.

A full sixty years before the "discovery" of primitive art by Western artists in 1904–1905, the German museologist Philippe von Siebold had underlined the ethnographic museum's potential for inspiring Western artists, designers, and art lovers.[52] The international expositions, and the new ethnographic museums themselves, undoubtedly played a part in widening the perceptions of Western artists and the public in the decades before the events of 1904–1905.[53] The expositions provided an opportunity for the public to compare the ethnographic material of different cultures, and for the first time this material was displayed next to Western art and artifacts. While for some the contrast may have had an alienating effect, leading to "the replacement of romantic notions of the primitive by a bourgeois esthetic of technical achievement,"[54] others were stimulated by this striking juxtaposition of new images and symbols. The image of the "savage" became more real with the display of his weapons, artifacts, masks, and carvings. The art critics Paul Guillaume and Paul Munro wrote in 1925 of the powerful effect of such exhibits on the public and on artists particularly, at the turn of the century:

> . . . highly civilized and very tired brains feel the need to adore the rough force of the primitive, to dream of the noble savage and to attribute to him mythical virtues. The fetish gives them the excuse to dream of mysterious forests, of strange incantations, of Negro warriors . . . of an existence free from all conventions.[55]

By the 1880s Matisse was a regular visitor to the Trocadero Museum in Paris, which contained some Australian material deriving from the 1879 Paris Exposition. The 1889 Universal Exposition provided Gauguin and van Gogh with their first taste of primitive art.[56] Yet such influences were clearly overshadowed by the direct effect that Orientalism and Japonisme exerted on Western styles of art and design: primitive art was to wait in the wings until 1901 when the artist Vlaminck began collecting African art for its beauty rather than its ethnographical value.[57]

There is no doubt that the "discovery" of tribal art by avant-garde artists in the first decade of this century heralded a new period of interest in its creative and imaginative aspects. Despite this fact, Aboriginal art remained almost unknown. The "great audacity of taste" displayed by such artists as Picasso, Vlaminck, Braque, Duchamp, and Matisse was mainly directed toward Africa at the outset and toward a restricted domain—the sculptural forms of masks and figures.[58] Despite the Cubists' preoccupation with experiments in dimension and perspective, the X-ray paintings of Aboriginal art remained unknown and unexploited.

With few exceptions, these artists overlooked the inherent conservatism of ethnographic art. They saw it as an exciting source for innovation in their own work rather than a culture-bound form of expression that relied on repetition and regularity of style to convey clearly recognizable messages between artist and audience.[59] The call made by Ernst Grosse in 1897 for a more balanced acknowledgment of the "indispensable social element in artistic behaviour among nonliterate peoples, and . . . for a scientific rather than an aesthetic approach to its study"[60] was generally unheeded until the 1920s. The French poet and art critic Guillaume Apollinaire provided a partial exception. In 1912 he published an article titled "Exoticism and Ethnography," inspired by the Trocadero Museum collections. This was one of the first aesthetic evaluations by an established art critic on the "inferior" art of the "savages." Apollinaire did not refer to Australia in this article, and it was to be another thirteen years before Margaret Preston made the same claims for Aboriginal art.[61] Apollinaire followed his 1912 article with a wide-ranging discussion of primitive art published in *Le Mercure de France* in April 1917, incorporated within his album *Sculptures Nègres* published in the same year.[62] By the time of the publication of Guillaume and Munro's *Primitive Negro Sculpture* in 1926,[63] aesthetic and functional considerations were starting to balance each other in Western assessments of primitive art. As H. B. Chipp has observed: "this [Guillaume and Munro's] book was the first systematic study of the inherent qualities of the objects themselves. It thus marked a new phase in the study of primitive art, when it began to be considered as a major art."[64]

Most art historians who have approached the subject have stressed the importance of the "discovery" of primitive art by Vlaminck, Picasso, and other avant-garde artists in 1904–1905 and have tended to trace later developments in Western perceptions of the art from this period.[65] There are dangers in endowing this event with too much significance and thus overlooking other currents and trends affecting Western perceptions. Although there was certainly a wide gap between the scientific concerns of the anthropologists of the late nineteenth century and the aesthetic concerns of the avant-garde artists, practitioners in both fields shared many concerns and clearly influenced each other. On a superficial level, for example, Haddon's pioneer 1894 work *The Decorative Art of British New Guinea*, with its new proposition of a primitive art aesthetic, shared common ground with apparently unrelated Western art vogues of the period such as Art Nouveau or some forms of English illustration, with their common emphases on stylized, geometric, and natural forms.[66]

At the turn of the century the two pursuits of anthropology and art were also linked by a common search for origins and first causes that pervaded the social sciences. This inquiry was precipitated by the implications of the acceptance of Darwin's evolutionary theory on the one hand and of Freudian theory on the other. The convergence between the "cult of the savage," engaged in by anthropologists and ethnologists, and the "cult of childhood," pursued by the new profession of psychology (as well as by artists of the period), was later given expression by Apollinaire, "[who] hinted at the primitive impulse of his generation in a letter to André Breton: 'In order to reach far, one must first return to first principles' . . ."[67] Tylor had written as early as 1892 that

> [the] painter's and sculptor's art seems to have arisen in the world from the same sort of rude beginnings which are still to be seen in children's attempts to draw and carve. The sheets of bark or skins on which barbarous tribes have drawn men and animals, guns and boats, remind us of the slates and barn doors on which English children make their early trials in outline.[68]

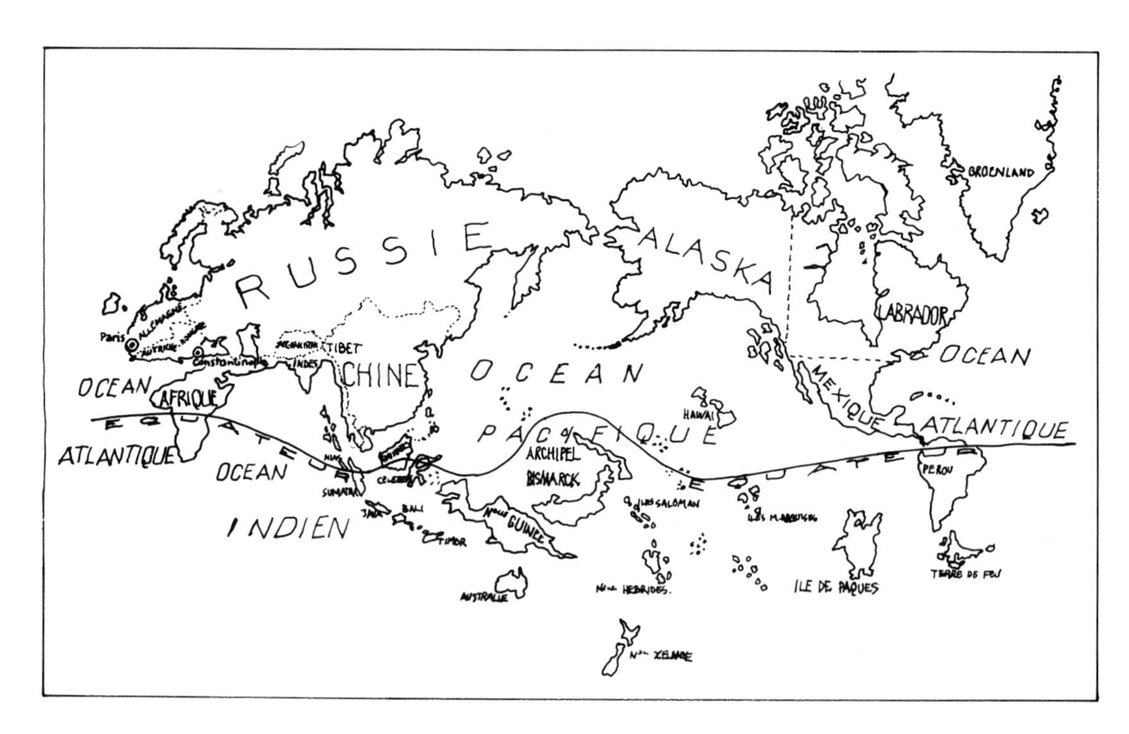

FIG. 205
Surrealist map of the world. Published in *Variétés*, Paris 1929.

The decade of the Surrealists, the 1920s, saw the publication of several books discussing economic, religious, and psychological aspects of primitive society as factors influencing the style and production of art. German authors such as Herbert Kuhn, Eckart von Sydow, and Ernst Vatter were all concerned to define a worldview that might place primitive art in context. If, as the art historian Paul Rubin suggests, the art of Oceania became attractive to Western artists only after this level of analysis had made it conceptually accessible, Australian Aboriginal art was nevertheless still out of reach and undesirable. The motifs of Aboriginal art were largely passed over by the Surrealists as they had been by the Cubists. The 1929 Surrealist Map of the World shows Australia dwarfed by Easter Island and New Guinea (Fig. 205). Despite their fascination by images evoking the unconscious, the Surrealists showed little interest in Aboriginal art. The work of Paul Klee may provide an exception. He was attracted to Inuit (Eskimo) art, with its depictions of the various dimensions of apparently empty and limitless space, and he may have observed the same qualities in Aboriginal art. He would have had access to reproductions of bark paintings from Spencer's collection, which were published in European art magazines of the 1930s, and some examples of his work resemble Groote Eylandt paintings.[69]

Rubin may have understated the efforts made by avant-garde artists to understand the cultural background to African art. Nevertheless, his emphasis on the conceptual difficulties that non-Western art presented may contain part of the explanation for the consequent lack of appeal that Aboriginal art held for Western artists and the Western public, until its motifs began to be interpreted and popularized from the 1930s. Otherwise, the reasons lie in the fact that until its wider exposure through exhibitions and publications, Aboriginal art remained relatively unknown, even in Australia.

Exhibitions and Critical Attention: 1929 to 1961

The first primitive art exhibition of any size was held at the Galerie Devambez in Paris in 1919. Organized by Paul Guillaume, it purported to be comprehensive in scope and included works from Africa, Polynesia, Melanesia, and North America. Significantly, Australia was not represented, a fact accounted for in the exhibition catalogue written by the art critics Henri Clouzot and André Level.[70] Their assessment of the art objects followed the model popularized in the international expositions and confirmed by Haddon during the 1890s. They classified the exhibition pieces

> . . . in terms of their plastic values—the more geometric pieces being the more esteemed—and the supposed state of savagery of the groups that produced them. At the very bottom of the scale lies Australia, which according to them [Clouzot and Level] is totally ignorant of art and whose sole display of genius would be the invention of the boomerang.[71]

During the following decade this attitude toward Australian art came under pressure as the attention of the avant-garde art movement shifted decisively to the Pacific, largely through the preoccupations of the Surrealists and Dadaists with symbolism and "magic art." As Christian Zervos, editor of the influential *Cahiers d'Art*, remarked in 1927: "What happened twenty years ago with Negro sculpture is what is happening at present with Melanesian and pre-Columbian art . . ."[72] In 1929 the March–April issue of the magazine was devoted entirely to Oceanic art. Art historian Philippe Peltier has observed that this coverage meant that "[for] the first time a complete panorama of the arts of the Pacific, or at least what was known of them, was presented. Polynesia retained its leading position."[73] The authors included Australia in the discussion, again as an exemplar of the least sophisticated of art-producing cultures.

Before the first major exhibition of Aboriginal art in Melbourne in 1929, this art was widely regarded as being so far removed from the sophistication of Western culture that it was rarely discussed as art at all. The publication in 1897 of Thomas Worsnop's *The Prehistoric Arts, Manufactures, Works, Weapons etc. of the Aborigines of Australia*[74] offered an exception to this view. Worsnop's interest in Aboriginal art may have been stimulated in the late 1880s by his attending what was possibly the world's first exhibition of Aboriginal art as "art." (Standard museum exhibitions of Aboriginal material culture rarely contained any references to Aboriginal "art." Terms such as "ornament" or "decoration" were most common.) This exhibition, characteristically entitled *Dawn of Art*, was held in Adelaide. It consisted of eighteen "original sketches and drawings by Aboriginal natives of the Northern Territory executed without the aid of a master" and was organized by John George Knight, deputy sheriff of the Palmerston (Darwin) Gaol, during one of his periods of leave in Adelaide (Fig. 206). The colored

FIG. 206
Detail of pencil drawing from the *Dawn of Art* exhibition, Adelaide, late 1880s, 32 × 50 cm.

pencil drawings of animals and birds are reminiscent of the delicately painted rock art of the Arnhem Land region, and their fineness of line must have surprised Adelaide's art lovers. The five artists represented in the exhibition were from different groups in the Darwin region and either worked at the Palmerston Gaol or were incarcerated within it. The drawings, preserved in the South Australian Museum, represent the earliest surviving examples of their kind from northern Australia.

It was to be another forty years before the National Museum of Victoria (now the Museum of Victoria) in Melbourne exhibited a comprehensive selection of Aboriginal material under the title *Primitive Art*, in July 1929. By this time the term "primitive art" had acquired its own, pejorative connotations.[75] Apart from its historical significance, the 1929 exhibition was notable in several ways. First, the venue itself was appropriate, as the former director of the National Museum of Victoria, Baldwin Spencer, had contributed significantly to the promotion of Aboriginal art by collecting, publishing, and exhibiting what is now recognized as one of the most significant assemblages of bark paintings.[76] Second, the exhibition was organized by the influential Bread and Cheese Club, a group of Melbourne art-establishment figures including Charles Barrett; Robert Croll, later to be involved in the "discovery" of the Aboriginal artist Albert Namatjira; Alexander Kenyon, an engineer and coauthor of the exhibition catalogue; and George Aiston, a former mounted police trooper in South Australia. Aiston was a storekeeper on the remote Birdsville Track in the Lake Eyre region where the toas were made, and he had firm opinions on the authenticity of these objects (see Chapter VI). An accomplished ethnographer, Aiston had coauthored *Savage Life in Central Australia* in 1924 with George Horne, another member of the Club.[77] For the 1929 exhibition he escorted two Wangkangurru men from the Birdsville Track region to Melbourne to demonstrate artifact manufacture, including the production of ceremonial headgear (Fig. 207). This was the first occasion of any direct Aboriginal involvement in an exhibition of this kind, and it generated considerable public interest (Fig. 208). The *Herald* newspaper reported on the event:

> Made up in ceremonial fashion, their bodies fantastically decorated with feather-down and their heads impressively adorned, they squat in front of a newly constructed mia-mia [hut], chipping boomerangs, making native string from rabbit fur, and powdering red ochre with primitive grindstones . . . Ethnologically however, there are more important exhibits than Jack and Stan. Among them is the fine collection of bark drawings, a feature of the display. Many of these are the work of the fierce Alligator River tribes, whose artists evidently included cubists and impressionists.[78]

FIG. 207
Jack Noorywauka demonstrating woodcarving techniques at the *Primitive Art* exhibition, Melbourne, 1929.

The Melbourne exhibition presented a range of Aboriginal art: carved trees from New South Wales, spears and shields, painted ceremonial boards from Groote Eylandt, reproductions of rock paintings from Victoria, some of the bark paintings collected by Baldwin Spencer and Paddy Cahill in 1912, and even the design for a wooden grave memorial (Fig. 185). It was not unusual for Australian museums to display a similar range of ethnographic material. What was new in this exhibition was the definition of the material as "art." The newspaper reports of the exhibition show that this notion, although something of a novelty, was not beyond the public's appreciation. The *Herald*'s reference to Cubists and Impressionists was matched by a comment in The *Leader*:

> It is in bark painting that the Australian aboriginal reaches his highest achievement . . . The facility of execution and appreciation of design in some cases are surprising. In the Northern Territory the bark paintings reached their greatest development in intellectual realism.[79]

FIG. 208
Visitors to the *Primitive Art* exhibition, Melbourne, 1929.

Elsewhere in the world, there were several exhibitions of ethnographic art during the 1930s. Of these, an exhibition at the 1933 Berlin Kunstgewerbe Museum[80] and the 1935 exhibition of *The Art of Primitive Peoples* at the Burlington Fine Arts Club in London were perhaps the most significant. Neither exhibition contained any Australian material. Commentators retained the view that the significance of primitive art lay less in its aesthetic merit than in its capacity to inspire Western artists and thinkers through its proximity to the most elemental forms of human expression, an attribute that endowed it with the allure of innocence and simplicity. The theme of primitive art as an uncomplicated, naïve expression from which Westerners could derive inspiration was reinforced in 1935 by George Stevens, who wrote:

> Primitive art is the most pure, most sincere form of art there can be, partly because it is deeply inspired by religious ideas and spiritual experience, and partly because it is entirely unselfconscious as art; there are no tricks which can be acquired by the unworthy, and no technical exercises which can masquerade as works of inspiration.[81]

It was this theme that the painter Margaret Preston (Fig. 253) stressed during the 1930s in her efforts to promote an "indigenous art of Australia":

> In wishing to rid myself of the mannerisms of a country other than my own, I have gone to the art of a people who had never seen or known anything different from themselves . . . These are the Australian Aborigines and it is only from the art of such people in any land that a national art can spring.[82]

Preston's enthusiasm for an indigenous art based on what she considered to be art of the stone age extended well beyond her own painting to include other forms more accessible to the public: fabrics, ceramics, even a dado for a child's bedroom. As early as 1925 she advocated the use of Aboriginal decorative motifs in homes, cafes, and theaters, stressing "the need of fresh stimulus and a return to simple symbols."[83]

Designers and decorators only began responding to these sentiments on any scale during the 1940s and 1950s, when the influence was seen in a range of material from tea towels and curtain fabrics to caravan interiors and theater set designs.[84] In fact, this period not only saw Western artists and designers incorporating Aboriginal art within their own work; images of Aboriginal people themselves were appropriated by the advertising industry to promote products ranging from shirts to motor cars. (This practice was not new: Aboriginal images had been used to promote products such as eucalyptus oil and laundry soap as early as the 1880s.) These forms of appropriation rarely matched Preston's own high standards of design, and the result has often been a devaluation of Aboriginal art together with the Western public's image of Aboriginal culture itself. Preston has been criticized for her view that Aboriginal art needed "the all-seeing eye of the

Western artist to adapt it to the 20th century."[85] Certainly, her crusade to bring Aboriginal art into the homes of white Australians was largely directed by this rationale. Nevertheless, it appears that, in one sense at least, she was correct. There are not many examples of Aboriginal art that have been absolutely untouched by the influence of a Western aesthetic.

Preston's contribution extended well beyond the popular domain. She contributed four of the mere half-dozen articles on Aboriginal art published between 1916 and 1942 by *Art in Australia*, a leading art journal of the country.[86] Her scholarly commentary on Aboriginal art also reached an international audience. She wrote the introduction to the Aboriginal art section of the *Art of Australia 1788–1941*, an exhibition sponsored by the Carnegie Institute in New York that toured the United States and Canada in 1941–42. This exhibition consisted of eleven bark paintings and three pen drawings by the Aboriginal artist Tommy Barnes (also known as McRae), dating from the 1860s (Figs. 193, 209). Although the art was displayed as something of a "prehistoric" adjunct to the main body of Australian paintings, this was nevertheless the first occasion that Aboriginal material had been exhibited outside Australia as "art," and for this Preston may take much of the credit.

FIG. 209
Buckley's Escape, and other scenes, ca. 1865. Tommy McRae (Barnes), Victoria. Pen and ink on paper.

In 1941 the Sydney department store David Jones held an exhibition that owed a lot to Preston. The exhibition of more than two hundred fifty items was composed of three main sections: Aboriginal art works, Western artifacts influenced by Aboriginal design, and Western art works depicting Aboriginal themes. The Aboriginal art included reproductions of rock paintings, rock engravings, ground paintings, artifacts of "material culture" (including weapons, utensils, and sacred objects), and crayon drawings from the South Australian Museum collection. Among the artifacts were numerous exhibits of pottery and other craftwork, Arunta designs from the Hermannsburg region adapted for women's dress materials and ornaments, and a re-creation of a lounge room incorporating Aboriginal motifs.[87]

Two years later, in May 1943, the first full-scale Australian exhibition of primitive art opened in Melbourne. The organizers, the National Museum of Victoria and the National Gallery of Victoria, could justly claim to have assembled the largest and most representative collection of non-Western art objects yet seen. As well as painted and carved Australian material, it included works from New Guinea, Africa, Melanesia, Polynesia, North and South America, Asia, and western Iran. If not as well represented as in the 1929 Melbourne exhibition, the Australian material in the 1943 exhibition covered a diverse range. There were eighteen items displayed: five pen drawings, four bark paintings (three collected by Spencer), a Wandjina painting and a copy of a rock painting ("reminiscent of late Paleolithic rock pictures of eastern Spain"), a painted Queensland shield and a carved Victorian shield ("note the effect of light and shadow bringing out alternately either diamond or square patterns"), two small beeswax animal sculptures ("some of the scarce examples of plastic art in Australia"), and three engraved *tjurunga*, or ceremonial boards. The exhibition thus provided the first public exposure of Aboriginal sculpture to art connoisseurs and, by giving prominence to Aboriginal *tjurunga*, focused critical attention on the artistic qualities of sacred (and usually restricted) religious objects.[88]

In his introduction to the 1943 exhibition catalogue, the art historian Leonhard Adam noted the burgeoning Western interest in primitive art, ascribing this both to the developing recognition of its aesthetic qualities and to the increasing interpretative role played by the two "scientific" professions of anthropology and psychology.[89] Adam rightly considered that these twin factors—aesthetics and religious or social context—had together raised the profile of Aboriginal art.

This improved status was not in evidence three years later in 1946 when the *Arts of the South Seas* exhibition opened at the Museum of Modern Art in New York. The exhibition was stimulated by the United States's growing interest in the Pacific region following its wartime involvement there. It confirmed Australia's reputation as the most backward art-producing culture. Australian art was allotted the final, peripheral place in Ralph Linton and Paul Wingert's catalogue accompanying the exhibition and did not figure at all in their introductory discussion of art styles of the region. More generally, Linton and Wingert joined Leonhard Adam in noting the increased interest by Westerners in the cultural background of primitive art generally, and of Oceanic art in particular, since the initial "discovery" of African art by the avant-garde movement at the turn of the century.[90]

In stressing that non-Western art should not be assessed in purely aesthetic terms, Linton and Wingert (together with Adam) were assuming that Western art *could* be interpreted in this way—as art for art's sake. It has taken the efforts of art theorists such as E. H. Gombrich, who have argued that Western art is just as bound by the necessity to incorporate religious and social iconography and cannot be purely aesthetic, to counter this view.[91] In the meantime, however, a false dichotomy emerged between aesthetic and cultural considerations. This distinction gained credence during the 1940s and exerted a considerable influence upon perceptions of Aboriginal art.

Adam was the main proponent of this distinction within Australia. For him the "primitive artist" was motivated primarily by religious rather than aesthetic considerations.[92] He shared the opinion of the avant-garde artists that the naturalistic style was the earliest and purest form of non-Western art, and he noted the considerable appeal to Westerners of the apparent naïveté of this art: ". . . all these different types of primitive art seem to have one feature in common, which makes all the difference when compared with modern European art, namely, the *spontaneity* and absolute *sincerity* of the primitive artist."[93] But in accepting that the highest forms of Western art in the Renaissance tradition, such as landscape painting, were motivated primarily by aesthetic considerations and in describing such art as art for art's sake, Adam ignored the fact that Western art also relied heavily on nonrepresentational elements. This flawed logic caused Adam, and other critics such as Stevens and Sir Herbert Read, to exclude primitive art from consideration in the same terms as the mainstream art of the West. As Adam put it in 1948: "A good test of art for art's sake is landscape painting. Generally speaking, it does not occur in primitive art . . ."[94]

One consequence of this general approach was that Aboriginal art remained in ethnographic museums rather than in art museums during the 1930s and 1940s. The effect was also reinforced by anthropologists and other fieldworkers in Australia, who stressed the religious and social function of Aboriginal art. Publications by Tindale, Mountford (despite his later stance), Elkin, McConnel, Pink, Roheim, and the Berndts all contributed to the prevailing view that authentic Aboriginal art was undertaken only with sincerity and serious intent and that art for art's sake—with its associations of pure aestheticism—was inapplicable as a description. As Ronald Berndt wrote in 1973: "No Aboriginal art is introvert, planned solely as an exercise in individual expression or a dissertation on the mental or emotional state of a particular artist."[95] The ethnographer and collector Mountford later became one of the only specialists in the field to dissent from this view, believing that Aborigines painted and carved their artworks primarily for art's sake. Another was the European artist Karel Kupka, who considered that Arnhem Land bark painters were "expressionists," with "sovereign artistic freedom."[96] Few would now agree with these views.

Mountford's efforts in this regard can be seen as part of his drive to have Aboriginal art recognized on the same terms as Western art. His mistake was to assume that any true artist, Aboriginal or Western, painted purely for art's sake. In his introduction to the catalogue accompanying expatriate Australian artist James Cant's exhibition of reproductions of Aboriginal rock paintings in London during 1950, Mountford supported this artificial distinction between aesthetic and cultural considerations: "Although, for many years, I studied the art of the Australian aborigines . . . my approach had been that of the scientist. I was but dimly aware of their artistic merit."[97] Ten years later, in his introduction to the Aboriginal art section of the 1960 Adelaide Festival of Arts souvenir catalogue, Mountford was more forthright: "All the bark paintings in this exhibition are examples of 'art for art's sake,' of an activity that gives pleasure, but not gain, to the artist."[98] In making this claim Mountford overlooked the details of his own transactions with Aboriginal artists. Although he rarely recorded details of his payments to Aboriginal artists, most of Mountford's bark paintings were commissioned, as he freely admitted: "To obtain examples of their art I asked the men to make a bark painting for me, seldom mentioning a subject. When at the end of the day, the artists brought the completed paintings to my tent, they explained the myth they had illustrated and the meanings of the designs they had used."[99]

Regardless of theoretical deficiencies, Mountford achieved more success than any other individual in promoting Aboriginal art in exhibitions in Australia, Europe, and North and South America during the 1950s and 1960s. His role in first collecting and then interpreting and popularizing the bark paintings of Arnhem Land has been noted earlier. As leader of the combined American-Australian Scientific Expedition to Arnhem Land in 1948, he acquired a large collection of bark paintings, many of which formed the basis of Aboriginal collections in Australian art museums. Others were lodged in North American museums where they have since stimulated interest in the field. The impact of Mountford's collections on national and international perceptions of Aboriginal art is comparable to that resulting from Spencer's 1912 collection.

Mountford's stance on the "art for art's sake" issue can be seen partly as a reaction against the analytical trend in Australian professional anthropology of the period. This trend was set in process by Radcliffe-Brown at the Sydney University Department of Anthropology during the 1920s and led to detailed studies by such scholars as Pink, McConnel, Stanner, Thomson, and the Berndts. Foreign-based Australianists such as Helmut Petri, Phyllis Kaberry, Geza Roheim, Frederick Rose, Nancy Munn, and Karel Kupka were also beginning to publish their results. Mountford occupied an ambiguous position between the two disciplines of art history and anthropology, and although regarded as a gifted amateur in both fields, he nevertheless became the greatest of all popularizers of Aboriginal art. As early as 1935 he had been involved with Norman Tindale of the South Australian Museum in collecting crayon drawings by Aboriginal people who had had only the briefest contacts with Western culture.[100] Mountford published this material during the 1930s and 1940s, and like other fieldworkers of the time, he stressed the anthropological significance of the works rather than their aesthetic appeal. His 1938 paper, "A Contrast in Drawings Made by Australian Aborigines Before and After Initiation," is one of the earliest Australian publications to document the impact of initiation on Aboriginal artists.[101] On the other hand, Mountford's interest in and promotion of the art of Albert Namatjira (see Figs. 245–47) from 1939 onward reflected his interest in the aesthetics of Aboriginal art, divorced from any attempt at other sorts of analysis. His association with Namatjira resulted in several popular editions of a book on the artist, published in 1944 by the Bread and Cheese Club of Melbourne, and helped to bring Namatjira enormous popularity. In a period when Aboriginal affairs were becoming heavily influenced by the belief that a distinctive Aboriginal culture was fading fast before Western influence, the federal government's policy of assimilation was accepted by most Australians as a solution. Namatjira's art became a symbol of this policy's viability. The Art Gallery of South Australia's 1939 acquisition of his *Haast's Bluff* (*Ulumbaura*) marked the first purchase of an Aboriginal painting by any major art museum.[102]

Many critics, Mountford included, regretted the passing of "true" Aboriginal art but praised Namatjira for crossing the cultural and aesthetic divide between primitive symbolism and Western landscape painting. The radical significance of Namatjira's art as an overt example of the potency of symbol and myth in Western landscape painting was lost on such commentators.[103] Mountford and other commentators believed that through his use of Western forms, and by painting for art's sake, Namatjira had excluded himself from the ranks of true Aboriginal artists. His watercolor landscapes were regarded as "assimilation art." Writing after Namatjira's death, the artist and curator Tony Tuckson observed that "Namatjira gained greater recognition than any of the others because in Western eyes his work was the least Aboriginal."[104] This fundamental popular misinterpretation of Namatjira's work has been exposed in several recent studies that have highlighted the importance in his work of the recurrent and classical Aboriginal theme of mythological place.[105] Tuckson also overlooked the fact that for many European and American artists and connoisseurs in the 1950s who were still unfamiliar with the bark-painting genre, the work of Namatjira and the Aranda school represented a distinctively Aboriginal form.

Despite its characterization by critics as nontraditional, Namatjira's work was vital in blurring the false distinction between evaluations of Aboriginal art made mainly on aesthetic grounds and those made primarily according to anthropological criteria. Large numbers of people who purchased or appreciated Namatjira's work undoubtedly regarded it as a vernacular expression of a Western art form. Nevertheless, the knowledge that this work (which hung as reproductions on living-room walls throughout the country during the 1940s and 1950s) was by an Aborigine prepared the way for later public acceptance of more distinctly traditional forms of Aboriginal art.

Public interest in Aboriginal art quickened during the 1940s with the 1941 David Jones exhibition, the 1943 *Primitive Art* exhibition in Melbourne, and another David Jones Art Gallery exhibition in 1949. This latter exhibition of Arnhem Land art collected by the Berndts was visited by large numbers of people, and according to Ronald Berndt it provided the turning point in the Australian public's attitudes toward Aboriginal art. Namatjira's influence also undoubtedly played a part in the success of that exhibition, for through him the public had become aware not just of an individual Aboriginal artist but of a distinct school of artists. This awareness no doubt contributed to the growth of critical appreciation.

These large exhibitions of the 1940s were followed during the 1950s by others that mainly reflected a bias toward northern Australia. The chief exception was the continued exposure given to Albert Namatjira and the Aranda watercolorists in a number of exhibitions at venues ranging from Rex Battarbee's Alice Springs gallery and the Anthony Hordern Gallery of Fine Art in Sydney to the 1956 Melbourne Olympic Village. This last exhibition, organized by the National Museum of Victoria, included the work of Aranda artist Cordula Ebaturinja, one of the first Aboriginal women to receive recognition as an artist. One of her paintings, *Mt. Hermannsburg*, was purchased during the Olympics by Prince Phillip for the Royal collection at Buckingham Palace.

Other exhibitions during the 1950s were more concerned with Arnhem Land art—a result of the expeditions mounted by Mountford and the Berndts. In 1950 Mountford collaborated with James Cant on the exhibition in London of reproductions of Aboriginal cave paintings.[106] In the following year the Jubilee Exhibition of Australian Art in London included fourteen bark paintings, four cave painting reproductions, and six carved figures, all from Arnhem Land.[107] During 1953 Mountford was responsible for a major exhibition in Adelaide, *Aboriginal Bark Painting and Objects of Native Culture*. It contained a wide variety of Aboriginal art, similar to the range exhibited in the 1943 Melbourne *Primitive Art* exhibition.[108] Arnhem Land art received even greater attention during the late 1950s with a major traveling exhibition of thirty-one bark paintings from the South Australian Museum's collection, organized by Mountford. This was shown during 1957–58 in London, Edinburgh, Zurich, Göteborg, Paris, and Cologne and was accompanied by a catalogue prepared by Mountford and introduced by Herbert Read. Both stressed the "primal" quality of the art, and Read attributed its "unique significance" to the fact that it represented "the art of a living race comparable in its social and cultural development to the prehistoric men of the Stone Age."[109] Also in 1957, Ronald and Catherine Berndt mounted *The Art of Arnhem Land* exhibition during the Festival of Perth. Its significance lay not only in its scholarly presentation and coverage of contemporary and historic trends in Arnhem Land art but in the prominence given to individual Aboriginal artists and their location within artistic schools and traditions.[110]

Despite the local success of these exhibitions, their critical approval and wider impact relied heavily on the interest of important figures in the Australian art world. The list of non-Aboriginal artists contributing to the 1941 David Jones exhibition shows how many recognized artists were actively interested in the cause of Aboriginal art.[111] Of these, Margaret Preston was undoubtedly the leading figure, through her art as well as her writings on the subject. After the 1940s, Preston's place as an active promoter of Aboriginal art was taken by several individuals working within the discipline of anthropology: McCarthy, Mountford, Elkin, and the Berndts. All these individuals collected, discussed, and popularized Aboriginal art through exhibitions and publications. Despite the friendships between McCarthy and Preston or Mountford and Cant, and despite the 1956 Commonwealth bequest of Arnhem Land bark paintings to state galleries, Aboriginal art had still to receive the patronage and approval of major art institutions in Australia. It was left to two Sydney art figures, Tony Tuckson and Stuart Scougall, to promote Aboriginal art within the Australian art establishment.

Tuckson was well placed to do this. An artist himself, he was employed as curator of paintings at the Art Gallery of New South Wales. Scougall practiced as an orthopedic surgeon in Sydney and collected contemporary Australian art. Both men wanted to see Aboriginal art exhibited as art rather than as ethnographica. In 1958 and 1959 Tuckson and Scougall mounted expeditions to Arnhem Land and the northern coast, with the prime aim of collecting Aboriginal art. On the 1959 trip they were accompanied by Dorothy Bennett, later to become a major collector and a significant figure in the Aboriginal art-marketing business.

The Tuckson-Scougall expeditions were the first to have the acquisition of Aboriginal art, rather than anthropological data, as their primary aim. The trips were partly funded by the Art Gallery of New South Wales, which received a small number of acquisitions directly from Tuckson on his return. The most significant acquisitions, though, were donated to the gallery by Scougall: a collection of seventeen Melville Island *pukamani* poles, or grave posts, collected in 1958, followed by a specially commissioned series of bark paintings from Yirrkala in 1959. The grave posts formed a dramatic exhibit at the gallery that immediately became the center of controversy. The *Bulletin* critic, Douglas Stewart, had doubts as to the objects' status as art:

> . . . the 17 grave-posts make a somewhat bizarre display . . . and most people, admitting that the poles are delightful in themselves, will wonder if the proper place for them is not the [natural history] museum . . . These Melville Island posts, although they have definite artistic merit of an elementary kind, are really more in the nature of ethnological curiosities than works of art.[112]

Tuckson prepared a major traveling exhibition of Aboriginal art gathered on his and Scougall's historic expeditions. This toured state art galleries during 1960–61 with widespread success. The accompanying book was a major publication of particular significance in that it was a combined production by artists and anthropologists.[113]

The Recent Period: Growing Aboriginal Involvement

The touring exhibition arranged by Tuckson, and the inclusion of Aboriginal art in the inaugural 1960 Adelaide Festival of Arts program, signaled the beginning of the Australian art establishment's serious acceptance of Aboriginal art, as well as the art's wider popular appreciation. The period of the early 1960s also saw the first regular supply of Aboriginal art to southern city venues—which made it possible for collectors to acquire Aboriginal art without venturing to Central Australia or beyond.

The Arnhem Land mission had been supplying their city shops with bark paintings during the previous ten years or so, but it was not until the early 1960s that Aboriginal art was vigorously marketed.[114] The clientele patronizing these outlets was drawn from local residents and a small but increasing number of foreign tourists as well as buyers from Australian art galleries, museums, universities, and trade and cultural organizations. This diversity highlighted a dilemma: how to rationalize the numerous but more easily satisfied requirements of the tourist market with the rigorous standards set by the academic and art worlds. The need for regularity in marketing procedures and for a uniform system of payment to Aboriginal artists and the wider promotion of their work was recognized by the federal government's Department of Aboriginal Affairs. In 1971, four years after the Australia-wide referendum establishing the political and social rights of Aborigines as Australian citizens, the department founded the Aboriginal Arts and Crafts Company to manage the growing art and artifact industry.[115] The 1970s saw a proliferation of government departments and institutions established to regulate various aspects of Aboriginal affairs—health, social security, law, politics, and art and academia. The latter two areas were catered to by the founding of the Australian Institute of Aboriginal Studies in 1961 and the Aboriginal Arts Board in 1973. This meant that Aboriginal art was becoming influenced as much by the activities of government instrumentalities as by those of museums or private entrepreneurs. The major exhibitions of the 1970s and early 1980s reflect this fact.[116]

Paradoxically, the involvement by Aboriginal people of Arnhem Land and Central Australia in the wider Australian economy led indirectly to the outstation movement—a return to traditional lands away from large government-controlled population centers, which was made possible by the local economic independence brought by social-welfare payments and access to government services. The art and artifact industries of Arnhem Land and Central Australia took a new direction as a result of this movement and the desire of many Aboriginal people to supplement their income from welfare payments. Government-appointed art advisers have exerted considerable influence on local art styles and techniques of remote communities throughout Central and northern Australia.[117] As noted in Chapter IV, their role has extended beyond that of supplying artists with painting materials and mar-

FIG. 210
Galarrwuy Yunupingu (left), Daymbalipu Mununggurr (second to right), and Dadaynga Marika (right), discussing the Gove land rights case with their counsel, Canberra, September 1970.

keting the works to suggesting designs and influencing composition and choice of colors.

During the late 1970s and the 1980s the appointment of Aboriginal people to key administrative positions on government boards and instrumentalities involved in Aboriginal affairs raised the profile of Aboriginal art both within Australia and internationally. Large exhibitions such as *The Art of Aboriginal Australia*, which toured Canada in 1976, and *Aboriginal Australia*, on view in Melbourne and Perth in 1981, proceeded under the aegis of the Aboriginal Arts Board, chaired in each case by prominent Arnhem Land Aboriginal men.[118] As the chairman's preface to the 1981 exhibition catalogue made clear, Aboriginal people increasingly regard the national and international exposure of their art as a means not only of keeping Aboriginal art "strong" but of helping other people "to see this country in the Aboriginal way."

Aboriginal art, always an implicit statement of local identity and politics in Aboriginal society, assumed a far greater political role following the emergence of the land-rights debate after Justice Blackburn's historic decision in the Milirrpum v. Nabalco Pty Ltd. and Commonwealth of Australia case of 1968–71 (Fig.210).[119] In certain land claims, for example, claimants have been expected to express their traditional rights to the land by painting, singing, or dancing the stories associated with it (Fig. 211). During the 1970s the land-rights debate proceeded alongside community concern and government action on environmental and heritage issues affecting Aboriginal rock art and sites of significance. Legislation establishing governmental responsibility for these issues was enacted across Australia during the 1970s and focused community attention on Aboriginal art.

FIG. 211
Sandy August Liwirriwirri giving evidence in the Cox River land claim hearing, June 1982.

Greater Aboriginal involvement in administration of Aboriginal art has also meant that new forms of art have received attention. In the first years of the Aboriginal Arts Board the emphasis rested more on traditional expressions. The Papunya Tula Artists Company and the Aboriginal Artists Agency, founded in 1972 and 1978 respectively, are designed primarily to safeguard the interests of tradition-oriented Aboriginal artists. Painters of Arnhem Land and of the Western Desert, such as Turkey Tolsen Jupurrurla (Fig. 168), Narritjin, and Banduk Marika (Figs. 213, 249), were the first Aborigines to receive artist-in-residence positions at southern galleries. The performing arts, notably Aboriginal dance companies operating with federal government support in the 1980s, also reflect this bias toward traditional art forms.

Since 1980, the appointment of southern and urban Aboriginal people to key administrative positions has led to greater prominence of Aboriginal art from these areas and less emphasis on traditional, classic forms of art. An increasing proportion of grant money has been diverted to Aboriginal printmaking and video-making, for example, and as a consequence ethnographic museums have begun collecting in areas once regarded as the sole province of art galleries.[120] These fields of art provide opportunities for Aboriginal people in urban and remote areas to strengthen or to reforge their links with tradition. In turn, Aboriginal artists from more remote areas, such as the printmaker Jimmy Pike from inland Western Australia and the Bathhurst Island or Indulkana printmakers, have been commercially successful.

Aboriginal art today possesses all of the trappings of a major art movement: a variety of diverse, often competing schools of art; a bureaucratic and administrative structure that regulates marketing and stimulates production;

a network of collectors comprising individuals and public institutions; and an increasingly appreciative public informed by an attentive media. There is no doubt that Aboriginal art, by engaging with the wider art world and market, has in turn assumed several of the market's characteristics. Aboriginal artists and groups of artists compete for prominence and funding in much the same way as their Western counterparts. Artists like David Malangi, who received neither payment nor recognition for painting the design used on Australia's first dollar bill until after the notes were issued and circulated through Arnhem Land in 1966 (Fig. 212), could not be so easily forgotten today.

Notwithstanding obvious changes during the past two decades, and indeed over the past two centuries of Western presence in Australia, Aboriginal art retains its distinctive link with land-based mythology and tradition. At the same time, it displays a flexibility and dynamism that confounds predictions made as recently as the 1960s of its atrophy and decline. The dynamic qualities of Aboriginal art and its capacity for innovation and adaptation have become widely accepted.

FIG. 212
Design by David Malangi (left third of image), Central Arnhem Land, on the Australian $1 note, 1966.

VI Survival, Regeneration, and Impact

PETER SUTTON, PHILIP JONES, AND STEVEN HEMMING

FOR MOST OF the nineteenth and early twentieth centuries, the outside world's perceptions of Aboriginal art had been emerging against a darkly pessimistic background. It was assumed that Aboriginal society and culture would continue to decline rapidly and would soon be extinct. That assumption proved to be wrong. Aborigines in the remoter parts of Australia, especially, maintained much of the fabric of their former cultures, even though they were drawn irreversibly—however marginally—into the world system. Elsewhere, in places where Aborigines' cultures had been more radi-

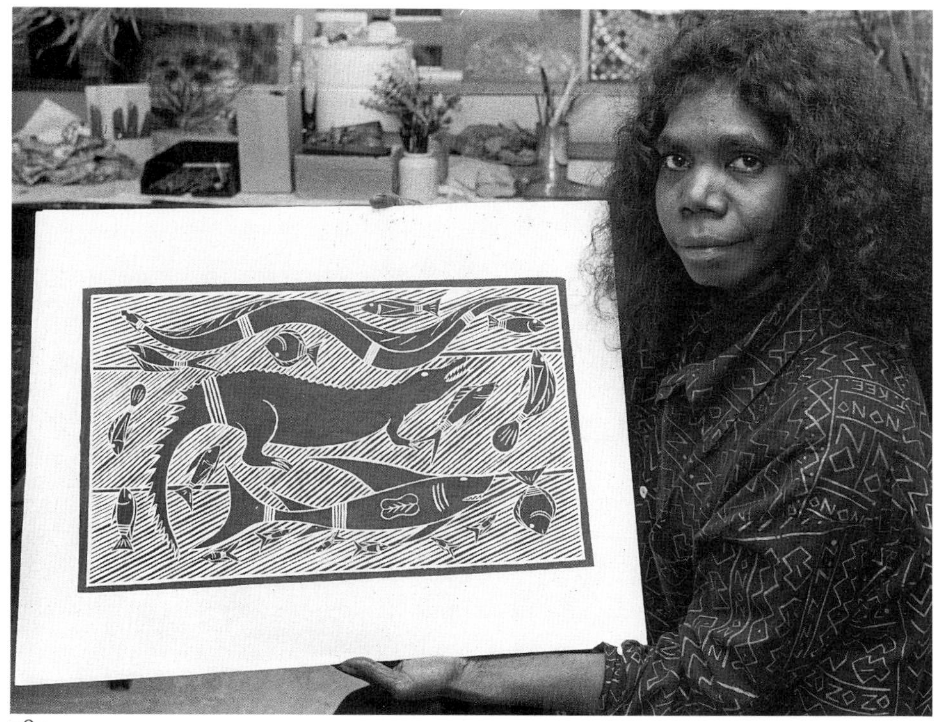

FIG. 213
Banduk Marika, artist-in-residence, Flinders University of South Australia, 1986.

FIG. 214
Tracks, 1987. Lin Onus, Victoria.
Acrylic on canvas, 114 × 180 cm.

FIG. 215
Lin Onus, Melbourne, 1987.

cally transformed by colonization and assimilation, their numbers regained strength after the 1930s, and a wave of cultural revitalization among so-called detribalized Aborigines gradually began spreading from the 1960s onward. This movement was especially marked in the arts. The more traditional forms of Aboriginal art that did survive in remote Australia actually persisted to enjoy an astonishing efflorescence and to have an impact not only on the work of non-Aboriginal artists but also on that of urban Aboriginal artists whose own traditions—often very different ones—had mainly become a thing of the past.

The Aboriginal artistic traditions of the monsoon belt in northern Australia and those of the desert center frequently managed to continue more or less unchanged in outward form, even while their media and their wider social and cultural contexts were dramatically changing. Other traditions, particularly those of eastern and southern Australia, either became extinct or declined to a point where only a handful of individuals still knew some remnant of them by the 1970s. In a small but increasing number of cases these dead or dying practices have been reemerging among the descendants of their original practitioners, revitalized by the wider Aboriginal cultural renaissance of the 1970s and 1980s.[1] Other contemporary Aboriginal artists have preferred to innovate rather than simply to resume past practice, making more thoroughgoing use of new technology and the industrial world's art styles, while still identifying their own work as lying within an Aboriginal framework (Figs. 213–14, 234, 236–37, 251). At the same time, Aboriginal art has had an unprecedented influence not only on the styles but, more recently, on the intellectual approaches of a few non-Aboriginal painters, sculptors, and ceramists. In this chapter we examine examples of these three processes of survival, regeneration, and impact.

The Oldest Continuous Art Tradition?

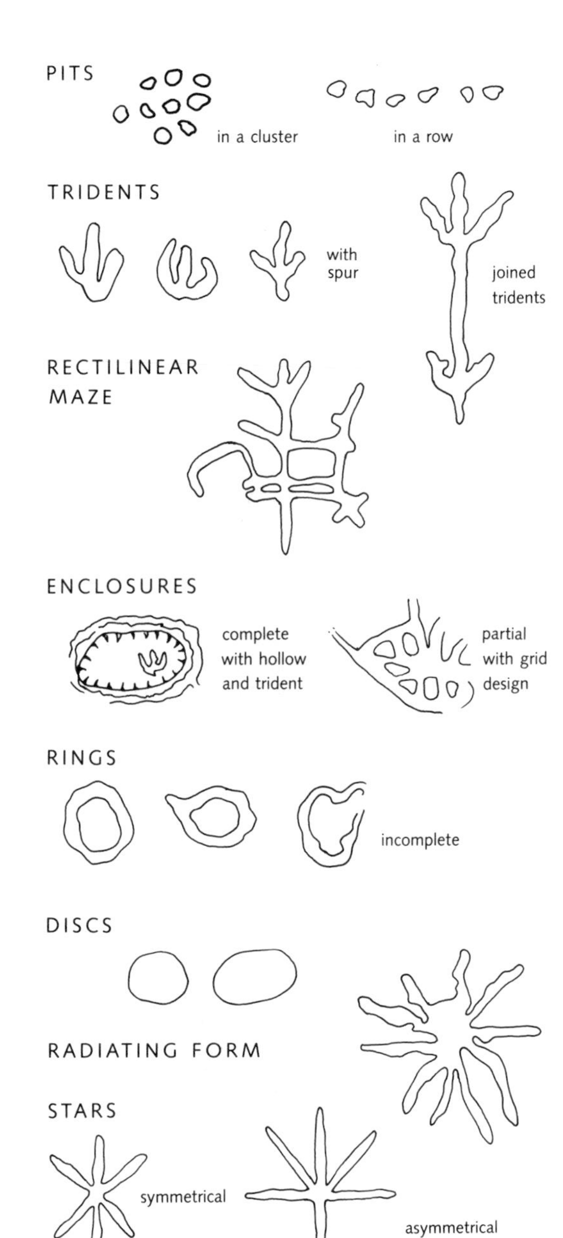

FIG. 216
Rock engravings, Cape York Peninsula (after Rosenfeld et al. 1981).

It has been asserted more than once that the world's oldest continuous surviving artistic tradition is that of the Australian Aborigines. This idea appeals to the average jaded urbanite in its ready evocation of warm, even romantic, feelings about the allegedly lost naturalness of human life in remote antiquity. This response may be understandable, but it remains decidedly odd in view of the fact that tradition-based Aboriginal art—at least as we know it from the past two hundred years—is among the most hierarchically controlled and least spontaneous in the modern world. This is not to detract from the art but merely to point out that Arcadia may not have been free. The conservative artistic systems of Arnhem Land and Central Australia recorded by anthropologists are marked by a very firm system of control—over designs and over who may execute them—by senior members of those societies.[2] These authorities believe that the designs came from the Ancestral Beings and cannot, or should not, be changed.

Even given this conservatism, it is still phenomenal that Aboriginal art has shown the great continuity that it has. In 1967 archaeologist Carmel Schrire[3] dated ochre-grinding implements in a Western Arnhem Land rock shelter to a period more than 20,000 years before the present. This was in one of the great rock-art provinces of the world—one believed to be very ancient, although secure dates for actual paintings have yet to be established.[4] (The practice of rock painting there has continued well into the present century.) But the use of paint, at least, is known to extend well back into remote times in Australia. For many years the wall markings at Koonalda, South Australia, inferentially dated to 24,000 B.P., were considered to be Australia's oldest art, although their status as art has been thoroughly questioned.[5] From 1968, fully modern human skeletal remains have been found at Lake Mungo in New South Wales and radiocarbon dated as up to 30,000 years old (Fig. 1). One man's bones, dated to 30,000 B.P., had been red-ochred.[6] As in the case of Western Arnhem Land, the use of ochre as a pigment had been demonstrated for the earliest known phase of human occupation in Australia.

In 1974 archaeologist Andrée Rosenfeld excavated engravings in a Cape York Peninsula rock shelter and was able to assign them a minimum age of 13,000 years on the basis of radiocarbon dating (Fig. 216).[7] The engravings were in a basic style that, with significant variations, may also be found in Central Australia and elsewhere on the continent.[8] In a number of their design features and techniques, they resembled the rock engravings in northern South Australia—which had for decades been recognized as important and probably of great antiquity.[9] This widespread stylistic complex is often referred to as Panaramitee, after one of the earliest reported sites.

In 1988 dramatic new results from a process known as cation-ratio dating provided concrete assessments of the ages of a number of engravings in the Panaramitee style from a South Australian station (ranch) near Man-

FIG. 217
Dolomite outcrops, near Mannahill, South Australia.

nahill, where dolomite outcrops dot the stony plain (Fig. 217). Physical geographer Ronald Dorn and rock-art researcher Margaret Nobbs collaborated to measure the age of desert varnish on the engravings. The designs, dominated by circles, bird and animal tracks, and a variety of arcs and other lines, include many of the same motifs recorded widely for Central Australia in sand drawings, ceremonial body decoration, artifact decoration, and other forms since the nineteenth century (Fig. 218). They also include many of the same distinctive motifs found in the toas from the nearby Lake Eyre region (Fig. 238) and in the Western Desert acrylic paintings after 1970 (see Chapter IV). Figure 219 shows a section of these engravings where Dorn and Nobbs

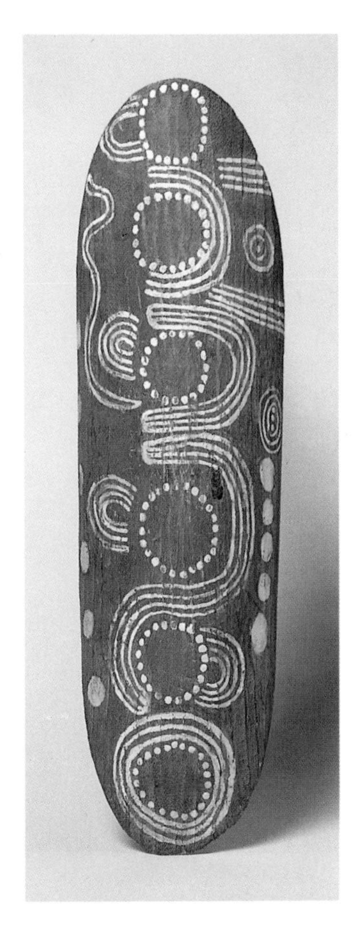

FIG. 218 / CAT. 68
Imbarra Dreaming, pre-1912. Artist unknown, Central Australia. Pipe clay and ochre on wood, 61 × 18 cm.

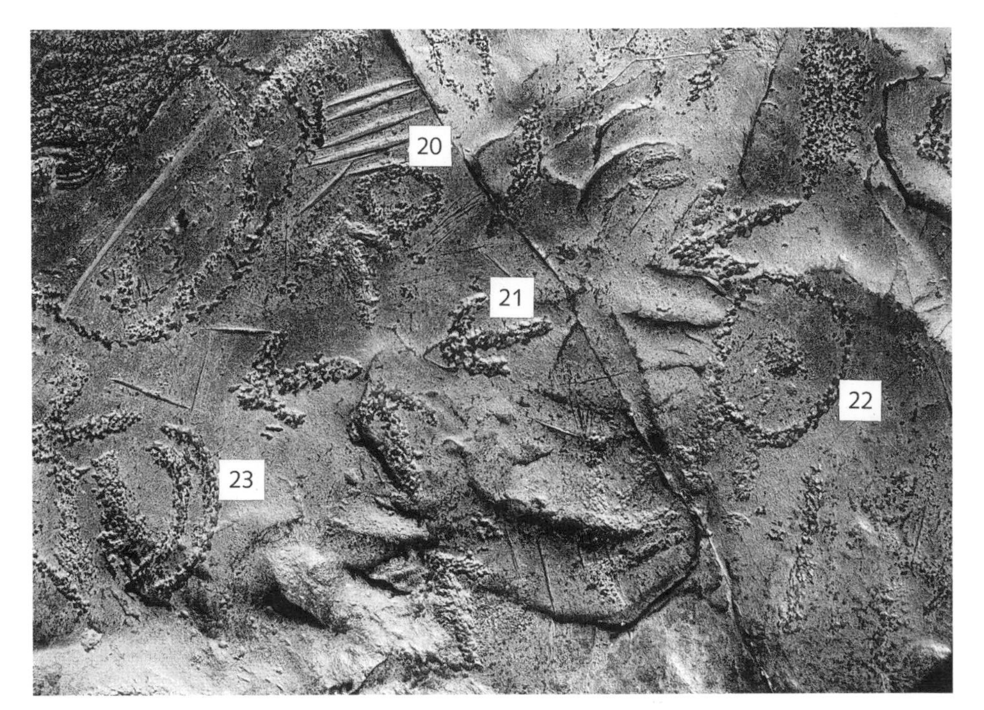

FIG. 219
Rock engravings 16,100–31,400 years old, near Mannahill, South Australia.

made tests for dating. Tag 20 marks a set of abraded grooves dated at more than 16,100 years B.P. Tag 21 marks one of the "bird" track motifs so abundant in the area, this one dated at more than 25,600 years B.P. Tag 22 designates a circle with a round motif in its center; the outer circle is dated at more than 24,800 years B.P. But the oldest date so far obtained for an engraving of this type in Australia is marked by Tag 23, the concentric-arc motif so commonly recorded in Central Australia in historic times.[10] These particular concentric arcs are dated at more than 31,400 years B.P.

Are the modern acrylic paintings lineal descendants of this kind of tradition, or are they merely works recently inspired by observations of rock art of this type? In the Mannahill area, the dated engravings actually range between 31,400 and 1400 B.P., and we know that for people such as the Pintupi and Warlpiri—from further north and west in Central Australia—such designs have been a daily part of their cultural practice since records of such events began in the last century. So the likelihood of contemporary Aboriginal art from Papunya, Yuendumu, or Indulkana being neoclassical, or a recent revival of lost art forms based on observations of rock art, is very slim indeed. For Central Australia, at least, it does seem true that Aboriginal art *is* the world's oldest continuous living artistic tradition.

That region has, however, also been one of the last to receive major impacts from the outside world. Many parts of the center of Australia were untouched by Europeans until as late as the 1950s and 1960s, and most of it remains uninhabited even in the 1980s. There may, in 1988, still be some Aboriginal people living beyond contact with the rest of the world in the fastnesses of the desert heartlands of Western Australia. In many other parts of the continent the story has been entirely different. In southeastern Aus-

FIG. 220
Spear-shield, ca. 1840. Artist unknown, Lower Murray River region. Bark and ochre, 91 × 24 cm.

FIG. 221
Spear-shield, ca. 1850. Artist unknown, Lower Murray River region. Wood and pipe clay, 92 × 26 cm.

FIG. 222 / CAT. 74
Spear-shield, 1932. Clarence Long, Lower Murray River region. Bark, ochre, and pipe clay, 67 × 26 cm.

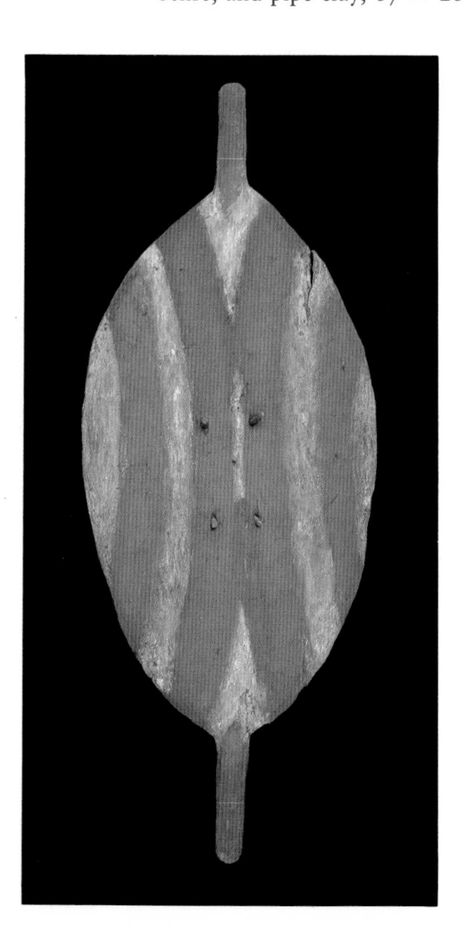

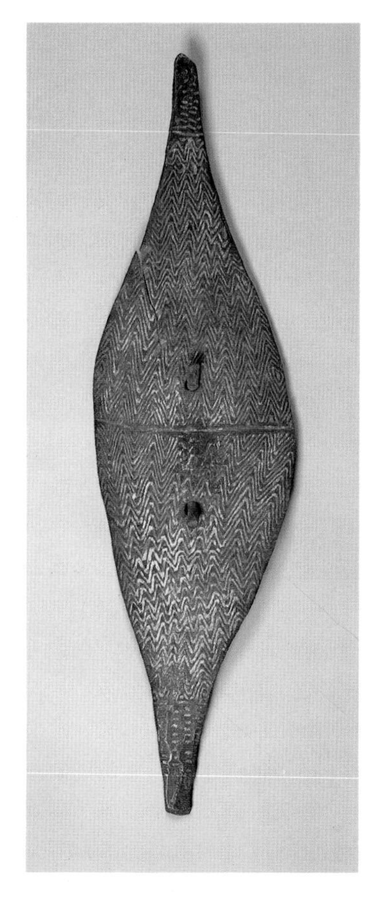

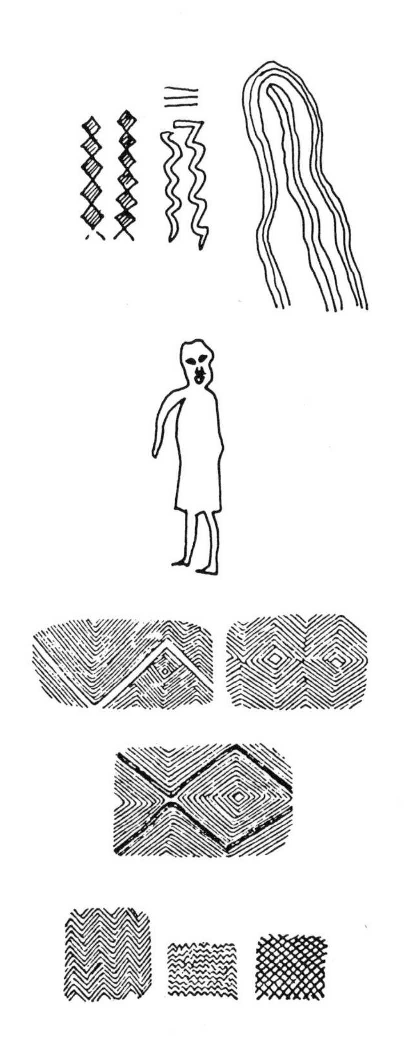

tralia the major processes have been those of decline, decimation, and subsequent revitalization. Here we focus our attention on one part of that region—the Lower Murray River—by way of example.

FIG. 223 / CAT. 73
Parrying shield, ca. 1880 (detail). Artist unknown, Lower Murray River region. Wood and pipe clay, 85 × 9.5 cm.

FIG. 224 / CAT. 76
Native Weapons and Implements, 1844. George French Angas, South Australia. Watercolor on paper, 49 × 34 cm.

FIG. 225
Common designs on weapons, southeastern Australia, mid-19th century (after Smyth 1878).

Death and Regeneration

British settlement of the Lower Murray River began in 1836 with the establishment of the colony of South Australia. This region, like so much of temperate southeastern Australia, had none of the elaborate painting traditions that characterized the far north of the continent. What it did have, however, was a rich tradition of wood engraving. The nineteenth-century art of the southeast is best represented by weapons and other artifacts that Aboriginal people engraved and painted in a variety of highly localized designs. Their shields, decorated by painted arcs and bars and mainly geometric engravings, are perhaps the richest example of their visual art now surviving (Figs. 220–25, and Cat. 72–73). Lower Murray rock art, of unknown antiquity, includes simple representations of shields of a similar form

FIG. 226
Warrior with Bark Spear-shield, ca. 1844. William A. Cawthorne, Lower Murray River region. Watercolor on paper, 34 × 28 cm.

FIG. 227
Fending off Spears with Shield, ca. 1844. William A. Cawthorne, Lower Murray River region. Watercolor on paper, 18 × 27 cm.

FACING PAGE

FIG. 228
Clarence Long (left) holding a parrying shield, and Gollan Seymour, Point McLeay, South Australia, ca. 1933.

FIG. 229
John Lindsay (left) teaching woodcarving, Glossop, South Australia, 1985.

FIG. 230
Spear-shield, 1987. Paul Kropinyeri, South Australia. Bark and ochre, 91 × 24 cm.

to those in use in the nineteenth century. The British artists William A. Cawthorne (Figs. 226–27) and George French Angas (Fig. 224 and Cat. 75) carefully recorded the distinctive forms and colors of Lower Murray shields in their delicate watercolors of the 1840s. Without these artists' records, knowledge of the ephemeral painted designs of this particular tradition would be very thin indeed.

The shield-making tradition of the Lower Murray region continued in a modified form until the 1930s and 1940s. By the turn of the century, the geometric engraved designs of the nineteenth century had long been superseded by more figurative designs achieved with metal tools rather than the original possum-teeth engravers.[11] The painted designs used on bark spear-shields appear to have survived the longest. The South Australian Museum examples made by Clarence Long in 1932 are probably the last of these painted shields to have been produced (Fig. 222).[12] An undecorated parrying shield made by Long in the early 1930s and now in the museum's collection (Fig. 228) is representative of shields from the period when engraved and painted designs on wooden shields were no longer being used. Long was one of the last initiated men of the Lower Murray; if the designs had not been forgotten by the 1930s, then Long and men like him had made the decision that the designs could no longer be used, perhaps because of their sacred nature.[13]

The 1980s have seen a renewed interest in the art of shield-making in the Lower Murray, but it does not represent a direct continuation of that region's tradition. While the artists are all descended from Lower Murray people, their knowledge of shield-making has come almost entirely from European records of Aboriginal culture or from material in the South Australian Museum collection. Aboriginal wood carvers John Lindsay (Fig. 229) and Colin Cook began a revival of nineteenth-century traditions at Gerard in the Lower Murray region in 1983 by approaching the museum and asking for copies of records of early Murray River tools and weapons. Using their skills and knowledge of local woods, they produced a set of accurate replicas of these objects and donated them to the museum's collection. Paul Kropinyeri has also made Lower Murray spear-shields using similar sources and the carving skills he learned from older Aborigines in his youth in the 1950s (Fig. 230). In a period when the strengthening of Aboriginal identity is a central ideal in southeastern Aboriginal communities, the revival of Lower Murray arts and crafts is becoming an important part of the process. These developments have followed several decades in which wooden works by Aborigines of the Lower Murray region were largely restricted to hunting clubs, which they used themselves, and returning boomerangs, which they sold to the curio and tourist market.

In contrast, the coiled basketry of the Lower Murray area has survived and adapted to the changes brought about since the arrival of the British there in 1836. Basketry was originally used in many forms: carrying containers, fish scoops, coffins, mats, clothing, and a variety of other objects.[14] The Lower Murray people used sedges growing along the banks of the Murray River and

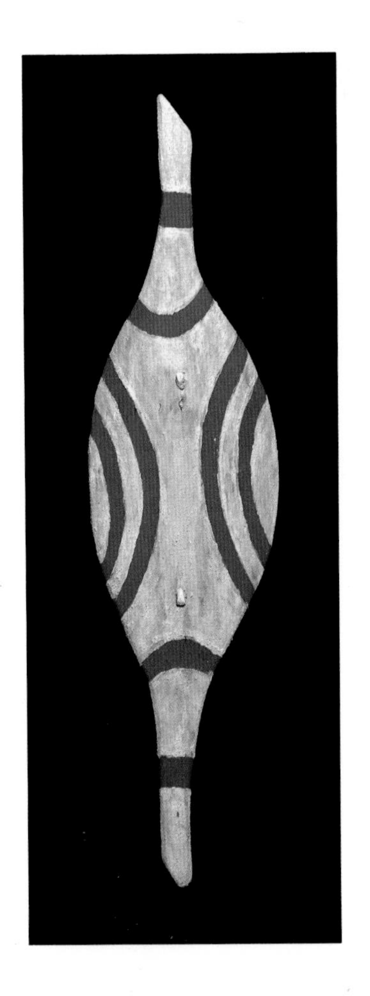

FIG. 231
Coiled carrying basket, 1900. Artist unknown, Lower Murray River region. Sedge, 40 × 23 cm.

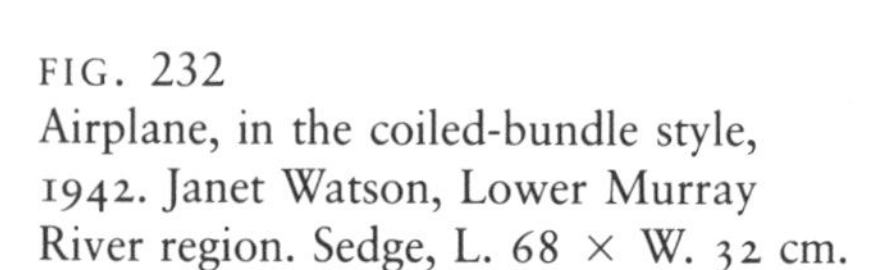

FIG. 232
Airplane, in the coiled-bundle style, 1942. Janet Watson, Lower Murray River region. Sedge, L. 68 × W. 32 cm.

the shores of the lakes and Coorong. The traditional technique, which has survived to the present day, is a coiled bundle with a simple loop stitch. The different groups in the region had distinctive styles, employing different types of sedges. One of the most characteristic styles, from the Kingston area, incorporated red-colored sedges in a spiral pattern (Fig. 231). Among the most striking examples of innovation in Lower Murray basketry is an airplane in the Kingston style made by Janet Watson in 1942 (Fig. 232). Dorothy Kartinyeri, who was responsible for passing on the basket-making tradition to younger people in the region, also experimented with shapes that could be created from the medium. She conducted a workshop in 1982, and from this Ellen Trevorrow (Fig. 233) and Yvonne Koolmatrie have continued the tradition and taught it to others in the community. They have made pieces for the South Australian Museum's collection and sell some of their work locally, but their primary interest is in encouraging basket-making as a social activity rather than as a commercial enterprise.

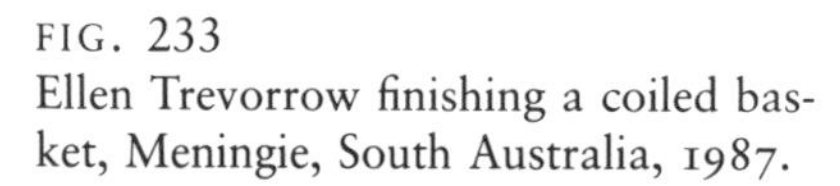

FIG. 233
Ellen Trevorrow finishing a coiled basket, Meningie, South Australia, 1987.

The New Ngarrindjeri Art

The peoples of the Lower Murray, at one time identified by a large number of local clan and language-group designations, are now generally known as Ngarrindjeri. Bluey Roberts is probably the most prolific of the Ngarrindjeri artists and is best known for his carved emu eggs (Fig. 234) and decorated weapons such as boomerangs (Fig. 235). The Emu depicted in Fig. 234 is a Dreaming figure and represents the spirit of the young Bird inside the egg. It comes from his father's country on the west coast of South Australia. The diamond patterns on the Emu are based on classic Ngarrindjeri designs, selected by Roberts from early written sources and from objects in the South Australian Museum. The animals that appear on the other side of the shell—the Cod, the Turtle, and the Snake—belong to the Lower Murray River region. This is the country of Roberts's mother and the area with which he most closely identifies himself. His decorated boomerangs are perhaps the most striking examples of his art style. He burns and incises the designs on the surface of large ornamental boomerangs made of eucalyptus, achieving a relief effect. Two examples are illustrated in Fig. 235. *Spirits from the Bush* depicts the animals and insects that Roberts is familiar with from his early life spent in Aboriginal camps on the fringes of rural towns. In *Camping Places of My Ngaatjis* (*ngaatji* is the Ngarrindjeri word for totem), the camping places of the Dreaming animals are represented by the circles, crescent moons, and other motifs in the design.

Harvey Karpany is a Ngarrindjeri painter who has experimented with acrylic color but prefers the effect produced by black and white—which enables him to produce a dream-like quality in his paintings, an attempt to forge a link with the Dreamings of his ancestors. He has developed a unique style that in some ways resembles silhouettes and animated-film illustration. A recurring theme in Karpany's paintings is that of a young person learning

FIG. 234
Carved emu egg, 1983. Bluey Roberts, Lower Murray River region, H. 13, Diam. 8 cm.

FIG. 235
Decorated boomerangs: *Spirits from the Bush* (top, L. 74 × W. 8 cm) and *Camping Places of My Ngaatjis* (bottom, L. 64 × W. 9 cm), 1986. Bluey Roberts, Lower Murray River region. Wood.

from an elder—as illustrated here in *The Fisherman* (Fig. 236), in which a young man is shown learning the skills of fishing and attempting to prove himself as an adult. Jacob Stengle, an oil painter active in the Ngarrindjeri community, finds inspiration for his work in the traditions of his people and in the spectacular country around him on the shores of Lake Alexandrina. Like the works of Bluey Roberts and Harvey Karpany, his paintings are largely his impressions of Ngarrindjeri Dreaming Stories set against the background of the local, natural environment (Fig. 237). Donald Smith, a Ngarrindjeri painter who uses acrylics, admits to being influenced strongly by the Namatjira school. His painting illustrates the influences of other Aboriginal art traditions on the new Ngarrindjeri art. Some Ngarrindjeri artists, like Kerry Giles, are working in the new areas of poster art and silk-screen printing. Giles is trying to develop a unique but obviously Aboriginal style in her designs and to use it to make statements about Adelaide's urban environment and the relations between Aboriginal and white society.

These Ngarrindjeri artists are not well known outside their immediate region, and their works do not generally fetch the high prices of the fine-art market. Their eclectic, innovative styles place them in the historical role of reconstituting a distinctive Aboriginal culture while drawing significantly, and even heavily, on the conventions of other Aboriginal art traditions and the popular and commercial art of the dominant industrial society in which they live. Other cultural groups across the southern and eastern parts of Australia have been responding in a similar way, and over roughly the same period of time. In the major cities of Sydney and Melbourne, some of the work of urban Aboriginal artists has achieved recognition in the fine-art market. Like the Ngarrindjeri, however, most urban and rural Aboriginal artists have had to struggle with the commonly held non-Aboriginal view that their innovations represent a loss of authenticity. Ethnographic museums, which in the past played such a key role in denying the validity of new forms of Aboriginal art, are now playing a reverse role by promoting that art's value and significance.

FIG. 236
The Fisherman, 1985. Harvey Karpany, Lower Murray River region. Ink on paper, 27 × 21 cm.

Attitudes Toward Innovation

Most major Australian museum exhibitions of Aboriginal material culture were left largely unaltered from the time of their installation in the early part of this century until the 1970s and the 1980s.[15] One reason for this lack of change was the persistence of taxonomic arrangements within ethnographic galleries, which discouraged innovation and the introduction of new forms of Aboriginal art such as watercolors or Western Desert acrylic paintings. A second, less obvious, reason was the conviction that the museums' obligations lay with traditional Aboriginal culture and that this responsibility was fulfilled once a representative range of the "authentic" art and artifacts of the culture had been established in museum galleries. This

FIG. 237
The Creation of the Coorong, 1987. Jacob Stengle, Lower Murray River region. Oil on canvas board, 62 × 50 cm.

attitude was firmly grounded in the belief that the Aborigines were a people without change in an unchanging environment.

In the 1860s ethnographers began to explore the range of Aboriginal material culture, social behavior, and religious belief. By the turn of the century there were several publications based on this work that described aspects of the main categories of Aboriginal art: body decoration, wood carving, sculpture, engraved *tjurunga* (ceremonial boards), rock paintings and engravings, and bark paintings. The person who first drew attention to the innovative and less well-known forms of Aboriginal art, however, was Thomas Worsnop, the amateur ethnographer and town clerk of Adelaide. Not bound by the taxonomic rigidities of nineteenth-century ethnography, Worsnop sought to explore the many variations of Aboriginal art across the continent. His study, published in 1897, provided descriptions and illustrations of both traditional and less conventional examples of Aboriginal art, including bark paintings, ink drawings, and wooden and clay sculptures.[16] An elaborately carved walking stick with strong Western influence was allotted the same space as a rock painting and a carved shield.

Worsnop's appreciation of the unusual and innovative in Aboriginal art was not shared by Australian museums; taxonomic categories of classification did not readily admit the emergence of new species or phenomena. Variations in style and motifs across the continent were recognized in exhibitions and publications, but they were usually attributed to the influence of cultural diffusion rather than to independent, local invention. By the time the major museums had installed their permanent exhibitions of Aboriginal culture in the early 1900s, it was assumed that the full range of types and styles of Aboriginal works had been located and described. The new permanent exhibitions sometimes incorporated small displays showing Aboriginal adaptations of Western materials, but these displays served only to reinforce the perception that Aboriginal culture had remained unchanged until its collision with Western culture. Objects that departed stylistically from their indigenous prototypes—such as headdresses constructed of European string, axes made from footplates of telegraph poles, glass spearheads, and even metal boomerangs—focused the public's attention on Aboriginal culture as something passive and degraded by contact, rather than possessing its own dynamism.

The diversity of Aboriginal response to Western presence across the breadth of the Australian continent is only now being uncovered. Whether this response took the form of resistance or accommodation, from the moment of contact Aboriginal people were quick to recognize the adaptability of Western materials such as metal, glass, and cloth. The incorporation of Western themes into songs and ceremonies and of Western symbols and motifs into wood carvings and rock paintings is evidence of the extent to which Aboriginal people were actively engaging with Western culture while retaining their own worldview.[17] This process, repeated elsewhere in the colonized world, was rarely noted by Western commentators until recent times.[18] In any event, it was overshadowed during the 1920s and 1930s by the observable fact that Aboriginal people and their cultures were still undergoing great stress in many areas across Australia. At that time, few observers accurately gauged the resilience of Aboriginal cultures or could have anticipated the resurgence of Aboriginal art over the coming decades. In a period when most images of Aboriginal art were reaching the wider public through the output of Western artists such as Margaret Preston, Kubler's judgment of the situation seems apt:

> Works of art are symbolic expressions . . . The triumph of one culture over another is usually marked by the virtual cessation of the art of the vanquished, and its replacement by the art of the conqueror. When the offending objects and monuments finally cease to correspond to any living behaviour, they be-

come symbolically inert. They then are 'safe' to play with in recombinations emptied of previous vital meanings, as in tourist souvenirs, antiquarian reconstructions, or archaizing revivals.[19]

As a result of this attitude, innovations or adaptations in Aboriginal art were not generally perceived as such until relatively recently. Commentators rarely considered the possibility that Aboriginal people had actively responded to the presence of Westerners and to Western taste either by modifying existing art forms or by producing entirely new ones. Instead, the tendency was to ignore innovations or adaptations, or else to conclude that such occurrences had previously been overlooked "by science" (thus explaining their absence from museums or publications).

There is no doubt that in much of southern and eastern Australia "the art of the vanquished" barely survived beyond the first few decades of contact. The picture was different for the rest of Australia. In some cases, as with bark paintings, Aboriginal people actively responded to Western presence by modifying existing art forms. In others—the wooden and clay sculptures of northern and Central Australia, for example—the response was to produce an entirely new range of art forms. In turn, Western reactions to these initiatives were ambivalent, ranging from the nonrecognition of poker-work carvings to the acceptance of bark paintings as an already existing but unrecognized type of art. Before Baldwin Spencer's and Paddy Cahill's collections reached the National Museum of Victoria after 1912, bark painting was virtually unrepresented in Australian museums.[20] Over the next fifty years Australian museums acquired more than five thousand bark paintings, and by the 1960s they had become instantly recognizable as Aboriginal art. During this period, as bark paintings continued to appear in southern centers from previously unrepresented communities, the assumption of museum curators and collectors appears to have been that they were uncovering undocumented centers of this art form rather than new sources of recently motivated production. Aboriginal communities that had only occasionally painted on bark were now applying themselves to it with vigor and an eye to commercial return, but that fact was either overlooked or considered of little importance. Also disregarded until relatively recently was the increasing influence of the Western market on the bark-painting movement and a consequent observable decline in artistic quality of works in some communities.[21]

The Western market has been operating in Arnhem Land in one form or another for most of this century since Spencer and Cahill "commissioned" the Museum of Victoria's earliest bark painting collection from 1912 to 1920. The next Westerners to exert an influence there were Christian missionaries: Margaret Matthews at Goulburn Island, from 1921 to 1928; Harold Shepherdson of Elcho Island and H. L. Perriman of Groote Eylandt, from the mid-1920s; and Wilbur Chaseling of Yirrkala, from 1935. All encouraged production of bark paintings, both as "useful toil" for unoccupied Aboriginal men residing on the missions and as a means of supplementing mission income. C. P. Mountford's 1948 Arnhem Land expedition, during which Aboriginal men and women were employed to produce paintings and artifacts in exchange for money or gifts, gave further impetus to production. Yet it was not until the 1970s, several years after a bark-painting design by the Aboriginal artist David Malangi had appeared on Australia's first one-dollar bill (Fig. 212), that anthropologists gave serious attention to analyzing the stylistic and social changes stimulated by engagement with Western markets.[22]

Western attitudes to Aboriginal sculpture reveal an even greater disregard for that culture's capacity to innovate and adapt. In his study published in 1897, Worsnop had given serious consideration to the possible influence of other cultures on Aboriginal art, ranging from the fanciful speculation surrounding George Grey's records of Wandjina paintings in northwestern Australia to the European influence on wood-carving traditions. It was not until fifty years later, with Ronald and Catherine Berndt's analysis of Indonesian influence on the wooden sculptures of Arnhem Land,[23] that such

FIG. 238 / CAT. 79–93
Toas of the Lake Eyre region, ca. 1904. Artists unknown. From 19 to 57 cm.

FIG. 239 / CAT. 94, 95
Two dogs from Killalpaninna, ca. 1904. Artists unknown, Lake Eyre region. (Left: *Color of White Stone*, spinifex resin and ochre, L. 19.3 cm; right: *Big Eater*, spinifex resin and gypsum, L. 20.5 cm.)

discussion was revived among scholars. The Berndts, nevertheless, were among the first to observe that Aboriginal innovation did not depend on outside influence and stimulus but was at least partly a characteristic of the culture.[24] On the other hand, it is only in the recent past, for example, that research among Central Australian or Arnhem Land communities has revealed the dynamism and interaction of painting schools. Commentators have generally been reluctant to explore the nature of the relationship between evolving forms of Aboriginal art and Western influences. This diffidence undoubtedly stems from the accepted view of Aboriginal culture as static and tradition bound.

The Toas as Innovations

Events surrounding the "discovery" of the Lake Eyre sculptures (Figs. 238–39) in the early part of this century exemplify the conservative attitude of Westerners toward Aboriginal art that prevailed until recently. At the time the objects became known to the South Australian Museum in 1906, there was not room for the view that the toas and dog sculptures of Lake Eyre were a new form of Aboriginal art.[25] The fact that the previous forty years of ethnographic investigation in the Lake Eyre region had revealed no trace of such an art form and that the Aborigines who produced the toas had been living at, or in contact with, a Lutheran mission station since 1867 did not sway the opinion of the museum's director and curator of ethnology, Edward Stirling. He remained convinced that the toas were authentic artifacts of precontact Aboriginal Australia: they had simply been "revealed" by their collector Pastor Johann Reuther (Figs. 3, 192) as "a class of articles which are new to this museum and unknown I believe elsewhere."[26]

This opinion assumed the place of the toas and dog sculptures in traditional Aboriginal life of the region against a significant weight of evidence. It has now been established that these objects were unknown to ethnographers in the nineteenth century. The records of two ethnographers and a scientist who visited Reuther at Killalpaninna in 1900, 1901, and 1903 contain no reference to the toas, although they refer to Reuther's ethnographic collection and to artifacts in the region generally. More significantly, Reuther's fellow missionary Otto Siebert, an accomplished ethnographer who worked in the region from 1884 to 1902, contended that Aboriginal people did not traditionally make such objects and that the objects were probably a recent innovation.[27]

Stirling's attitude toward Aboriginal culture obliged him to consider the toas as traditional artifacts and to accept Reuther's judgment that they were utilitarian objects—way markers used by Aborigines in the desert regions of Lake Eyre. Like many other ethnographers, Stirling looked upon traditional Aboriginal culture as static and timeless. For Stirling, an invention or hoax was the only other possible explanation for the existence of the toas, and he was not prepared to consider that possibility. Other commentators were, however. In 1920 the ethnographer Alexander Kenyon expressed his reservations in a letter to the director of the South Australian Museum: "I trust you have noted my doubts about the genuineness of those implements. In Melbourne there is a continued supply of spurious implements from the same locality."[28] In another private communication, George Aiston, an ethnographer who had lived for twenty years among Aboriginal people from the Killalpaninna Mission, went even further, stating that the toas were "a thing totally unknown to any of the tribesmen in this country" and referring to "the great Toa hoax."[29] There is no evidence to support Aiston's contention not only that the toas were a hoax but that their manufacture was supervised by one of the teachers at Killalpaninna who "suggested the designs."[30] But we do know that of the two schoolteachers at Killalpaninna from 1903 to 1905, one, Harry Hillier, was a gifted artist who had already sold ethnographic collections overseas, and the other, Theodor Vogelsang, was a skilled carpenter who instructed Aboriginal people in carpentry at the mission. Hillier's meticulous watercolor drawings of the toas and other objects in Reuther's collection were used to promote the collection to museums in Germany and Australia. Both Hillier and Vogelsang could have influenced the production of the toas, just as Geoff Bardon encouraged and directed the initial stages of the Papunya art movement seventy years later.[31]

The question about the origin of the toas only arises because Reuther, like other ethnographers and commentators of the period, did not consider it necessary to record details of individual artists or craftspeople, believing that Aboriginal art was an unchanging, homogeneous product. Reuther's constant battle to sway the hearts and minds of his Aboriginal congregation on the mission had convinced him of the immutability of Aboriginal culture and social practice.[32] With few exceptions, his only acknowledgment of the individual character and associations of the toas was to record the tribal group for

FIG. 240
Elias Palkalina, with Joseph Antjalina and Pastor Bogner (right) Killalpaninna, Lake Eyre region, ca. 1915.

FIG. 241
Toby (center), one of Pastor Johann Reuther's informants, near the Killalpaninna Mission, Lake Eyre region, ca. 1915.

which each toa had relevance. The fourteen volumes of information compiled by Reuther during his eighteen years on the mission contain few references to the identities of individual Aboriginal artists—only an occasional oblique reference to "the native concerned" or "the owners of the legends."[33] More tangible evidence is provided by a museum curator's note inked on the Dog Charm (Cat. 96), which reads, "Made by Elias Palkalina." This man (Fig. 240), together with other elders on the mission such as Toby (Fig. 241), Emil Kintalakadi, and Elisha Tjerkalina, were Reuther's main ethnographic informants and all may have participated in the production of toas.

More compelling evidence as to the Aboriginal origin of the toa collection rests in the mythological references encoded in each toa. This information, recorded by Reuther,[34] shows how each of the toas combines a visual depiction of both landscape and Dreaming, in much the same way as bark paintings and Western Desert acrylic paintings do. The travels and exploits of the main characters in the Dreaming Stories associated with the toas and the dog sculptures recur in the ethnographies collected in the Lake Eyre region both before and after the manufacture of these objects.[35] Analysis of the toas' symbolism has shown that the sculptures refer to sites along the interconnecting mythological paths of at least eighty-five Dreamings,[36] covering an area of one hundred thousand square miles in the Lake Eyre region. Much of this area was regarded by early Western observers as desert wasteland, an opinion that has not greatly altered over the succeeding decades. Today there are no more than two or three hundred permanent residents there, but when Western settlers first arrived in the region in the

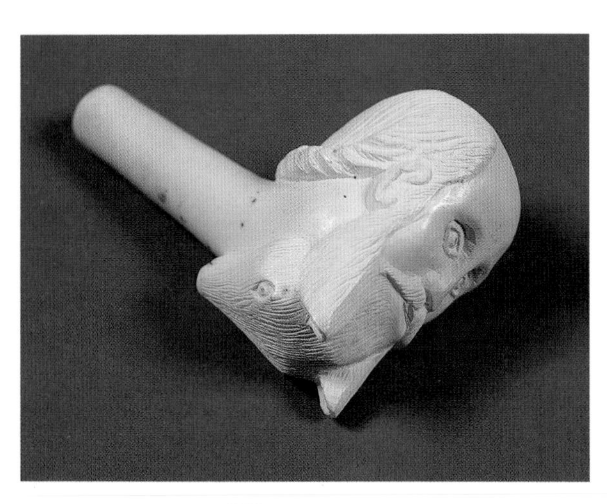

FIG. 242
Gypsum pipe bowl, ca. 1920s. Jim Kite (Erliakiliakirra), Central Australia, L. 9 cm.

1860s it supported an estimated three thousand Aborigines. (It is not surprising that, as with Western Desert paintings, the overwhelming majority of toas refer in their symbolism and mythology to the main water sources of the region.) There is little doubt, given the extent of his own commitment to recording the languages and traditions of Aboriginal people at Killalpaninna, that Reuther paid greater attention to the mythology and symbolism of the toas than to their sculptural forms or the details of their manufacture.[37]

Evidence further suggests that Reuther was keen to gather a large collection for sale, following interest expressed in his artifacts by ethnographers who visited the mission in 1900 and 1903. The reaction by Aborigines at Killalpaninna to Reuther's desire to assemble a collection will never be fully known. The result, though, was to encourage a level of creativity and innovation among Aboriginal people on the mission that led to the production of a series of objects now recognized as significant examples of Aboriginal art. Indications are that the toas and most of the other artifacts in Reuther's collection were made at the mission between 1903 and 1905, before being offered to the South Australian Museum in 1906 for the sum of £500. (The museum purchased the collection in 1907 for £450.)

Reuther retired from Killalpaninna in 1906; with his departure and that of Hillier and Vogelsang, the toa-making tradition apparently came to an end. Although Reuther's successor, Pastor Wolfgang Riedel, recorded the word *toa* in his dictionary of the Diyari language, the only other toas that found their way into museum collections after 1906 appear to have been those collected at Killalpaninna by Hillier or Vogelsang during Reuther's time there.[38] The mission closed in 1915, and the Aboriginal people who had become dependent on it moved elsewhere. The Reuther toas were incorporated in the South Australian Museum's permanent exhibition of Aboriginal culture, which opened to the public in 1914. They were presented not as art but as utilitarian objects. The opportunity to portray a graphic example of Aboriginal artistic innovation sixty years before the Papunya school of Western Desert painters emerged had passed without discussion.

More Sculpture from Central Australia

Other opportunities soon presented themselves, however. The gypsum sculptures of Jim Kite (Erliakiliakirra), an Aranda man from the Alice Springs area, became known to museums during the 1920s. Kite was one of two Aboriginal guides who accompanied Spencer and Gillen on their 1901–1902 Central Australian expedition.[39] His artistic ability first became evident to Gillen after they reached Alice Springs on their northward journey. Gillen explained the circumstances in his diary entry of May 11, 1901:

> I accidentally skipped the two preceding pages and rather than leave them blank I requested Erlickilyka [sic] otherwise the 'Subdued' to fill in the pages with examples of his artistic skill . . . he thought I wanted him to fill in the

whole book and he has spent the whole day industriously trying to do so—it's an example of original drawing by our Australian natives and I have decided to let them stand . . . Spencer is hugely delighted and the hills fairly rang with his laughter.[40]

Kite's later sculptural work, comprising carved gypsum pipe bowls (Fig. 242), decorative vases, and figures of men and animals, is distinguished by a fineness of line and technique lacking in his earlier drawings. His skill brought him considerable local fame during his later years in Central Australia, but he remained unrecognized as an artist until recently. Kite's work corresponded in form with the Reuther dogs, the more figurative toas, and the sculpted human and anthropomorphic sandstone figures produced by a Queensland Aboriginal woman, Kalboori Youngi (Fig. 243). Unlike Kite, Youngi did achieve artistic recognition during her lifetime: Leonhard Adam described her work as an exceptional example of Aboriginal sculpture in the round, works of "naïve, almost early Gothic simplicity," and Roman Black observed that Sydney artists had hailed the Youngi sculptures as "the work of creative genius."[41]

Few of the works on Aboriginal art published in this century have acknowledged the fact that a significant corpus of Aboriginal sculpture has been recorded since the early nineteenth century. Examples include the non-portable forms of carved Melville and Bathurst Island grave posts, the small beeswax figures of North East Arnhem Land, the clay figures of Youngi and unidentified Aboriginal stockmen of northern Western Australia, the carved gypsum and wooden figures of Central Australia, and the early examples of carved wooden figures and other constructions recorded for Southeast Australia. Perhaps one reason for the lack of attention given to this genre is that since the 1940s Aboriginal people in Central Australia have produced quantities of carved material explicitly for the tourist trade. The quality of this work has varied widely, and it has rarely attracted attention from museums or anthropologists. One exception is Frederick Rose, an anthropologist who during his 1962 fieldwork at Angas Downs in Central Australia observed the impact upon Aboriginal art of both the emerging tourist industry and the introduction of Western materials. As in other parts of Central Australia, Aborigines at Angas Downs had begun to use heated fencing wire to produce poker-work designs on carved wooden animals and artifacts (Fig. 244). Rose considered that these naturalistic, sculpted animals were relatively new art forms, and he was able to document the rise of particularly skilled artists whose sculptural work contrasted markedly with the cruder work of others. He also noted that "traditional forms of design [i.e. formalized or traditional geometric designs] have tended to persist although performed with a different technique. On the other hand new types of design have emerged . . ."[42]

As with the toas, the poker-work phenomenon, although rarely achieving the same artistic heights, illustrates the dynamism of Aboriginal responses when confronted with Western culture. Kubler's proposition that the

FIG. 243
Sandstone sculpture, ca. 1935. Kalboori Youngi, Queensland, L. 11, H. 7.5 cm.

FIG. 244
Carved bird, poker-work design. Date and artist unknown, Central Australia.

art of indigenous peoples tends inevitably to diminish in quality after contact with Western culture and technology is insupportable in the case of Aboriginal Australia. As Rose observed:

> It has frequently been remarked . . . that as a result of contact with the white man the traditional art of the Aborigines tends to become degraded. In the sense that the old techniques are not practised so much as in the time before the influence of the white man made itself felt, this is correct. On the other hand the advent of the white man has provided wide possibilities for experimentation which had not existed before. The tragedy is not so much that the traditional art and techniques are lost but that the artistic potentialities of the Aborigines under the new conditions are not realised. What is most remarkable is not that the old methods are lost but the virility that is shown in grappling with new problems under most unfavourable conditions.[43]

Ironically, it took the expertise of one Aborigine in what has traditionally been regarded as one of the highest forms of Western art—landscape painting—to demonstrate this virility to an Australian and international public. The life and work of Albert Namatjira (Figs. 245–47) has been

FIG. 247
Albert Namatjira (center), with his father, wife and child, ca. 1945.

partially reassessed in the 1980s through exhibitions, publications, and documentary films. These commentaries have brought attention to an aspect of Namatjira's work that was overlooked in previous studies and went largely unrecognized during his lifetime: that is, Namatjira painted with Western materials and techniques, but he was adapting and appropriating the symbolism of Western landscape painting for his own purposes. His paintings are firmly grounded in Aboriginal tradition, mythology, and place, and in this sense he was wrongly characterized during his own lifetime as a "wanderer between two worlds."[44] As Daniel Thomas has written:

> We now cannot but see Namatjira's paintings as a way of reaffirming his tribal territorial knowledge while simultaneously sharing with outsiders his pride in his land's great beauty. Further, we now perceive the repetition of similar rocks and similar ghost gums as a way of converting them from once-off observations to timeless symbols . . .[45]

Despite recent recognition of the pervasive Aboriginal content in his work (and in the work of other painters of the Hermannsburg watercolor school), Namatjira is still often regarded as a talented individual into whom artistic life was breathed, as it were, by the Melbourne artist Rex Battarbee. Too little account has been taken of the fact that Namatjira was already a skilled artist before Pastor Albrecht bought him his first set of paints at Hermannsburg in 1934 and before Namatjira accompanied Battarbee on the artist's first painting trip to nearby Palm Valley in 1936. Namatjira had been producing poker-work designs since at least 1932, and the South Australian

FACING PAGE

FIG. 245
A drawing from the 1934 sketchbook of Albert Namatjira, Central Australia. Pencil on paper, 28.5 × 22.5 cm.

FIG. 246
Scene at Amulda, James Range, 1941, Albert Namatjira, Central Australia. Watercolor on paper, 27.5 × 38 cm.

Museum holds a 1934 ink-and-pencil sketchbook that predates his watercolor work (Fig. 245). In comparison with drawings made by other Aboriginal people on the mission at the time, Namatjira's sketches confirm that he was already well advanced as an artist.[46] His mastery of landscape painting, together with his clear ambition, placed Namatjira at the forefront of public attention from the time of his first solo exhibition in Melbourne in December 1938 until his death twenty-one years later.

During his heyday Namatjira was regarded as an Aborigine who represented the potential for success of the federal government's assimilation policy. With his own income, house, and truck, and the bestowal of full citizenship rights in 1957 (ten years before such rights were extended to all Aboriginal people), Namatjira appeared to many to have relinquished his Aboriginal traditions. But Namatjira's story in fact underscores one of the defining characteristics of Aboriginal art: its capacity to adapt, to borrow, and to innovate. The many forms taken by Aboriginal art today are further evidence of this characteristic. It may be possible, for example, to obtain in the one Aboriginal art shop in Central Australia a Western Desert acrylic painting, an Aranda watercolor landscape, a boomerang, a carved animal with poker-work designs, and a plaited stock-whip—all made by the same Aboriginal artist.

Airports, Kitsch, and Authenticity

Is yesterday's airport art tomorrow's masterpiece? Not very often, perhaps, but in certain cases we cannot resist feeling it is true—true enough to render simple distinctions like "fine art" versus "craft" at best outmoded ways of summarizing much more complex responses to the vast variety of things that people make.[47] The impulse behind such distinctions is that many of us are bent on fending off too-ready acceptance of cheaply won imitations of the more honest, intelligently unpredictable works that we regard as worth protecting. Yet this kind of distinguishing activity is coming to be endangered. In the late 1980s the quality of the work may mean less, or in extreme cases even nothing at all, while the position of the artist may mean more, or everything, not only to a postmodern critic but even to an art dealer.[48] The implications of this for the art establishments are profound. For Aboriginal artists, it may simply mean that members of metropolitan cultures are rising above their precious, hothouse perceptions of value and moving toward less narrow and obsessively visual criteria for quality in art. One thing is probably certain: some notion of value, and a practice of discrimination based on perceived quality, will persist.

For much of this century, the "primitive art" market has given highest monetary value to objects that are aesthetically pleasing to connoisseurs, relatively uncommon, documented, and "authentic." Authentic objects are often regarded as those that enjoy the "sincerity" of a precommercial, pre-Christian tribal cultural origin. This particular criterion for quality is now, more than ever, under a cloud. Sincerity in art is, happily, a metaphor, just as the definition of primitivism in Western art as "a retreat from false sentiment" is a metaphor.[49] But the reason why art is not really a universal language is that metaphors are not, in fact, always shared. They depend on an act of creation in the receiver, as well as in the transmitter. This cannot always be guaranteed.

Herbert Read hoped that the student of art might rise above the different senses of "beauty" entertained by different cultures and regard as art *all* the manifestations of the sense of beauty experienced by members of those cultures, refusing a privileged position to those manifestations that merely appealed to the hypothetical student and simply distinguishing "between the genuine and false."[50] But how does one really do this? The yardstick of "contaminated versus uncontaminated" (by external forces) simply will not do, as we shall see.

Some pre-European Aboriginal art is gauche and unappealing from an outside aesthete's perspective, while some contemporary works made expressly for the tourist market may be regarded by the same kind of person as brilliant works of dangerously inventive power and serious intellectual fiber. Both may still be "full of conviction" to the very same admirer of art. While both kinds of work may come from artists who live within an unquestioned Aboriginal religious framework, conviction itself may never have been an issue for their makers, however. Aboriginal artists are rarely concerned with the issue of belief, and almost never with that of belief in belief. Many artists in the Aboriginal tradition are, though, concerned with art as evidence, as proof, and as an educational medium for establishing to others the facts of the Dreaming.

In postmodern circles an ironic mode may even be almost obligatory if an artist's work is to be accepted,[51] yet an Aboriginal artist may proceed without the detachment of a mode of irony and certainly in most cases does so without cynicism. This is especially true of the more tradition-oriented artists. Urban artists like Trevor Nickolls (Fig. 74), on the other hand, may well employ irony and bitter humor in their work.[52] But the difference between these two kinds of artistic approaches is not merely one of sincerity versus irony. The irony of the urban artist may be as sincere in its own way as the conviction of the painter of Dreamings. And the underlying difference is one of detached comment (recent urban art) versus symbolic narrative (traditional art).

In the urban case, there are usually two primary texts: the art object and its message. The latter is often an articulate political message or at least a meaning that the artist is frequently prepared to interpret in language. Urban Aboriginal artist James Simon says: "What I do is think of a word sometimes like racism, destruction, something like that and I just use that word as the foundation for the whole painting, do the painting around that word."[53] In traditional Aboriginal art there is basically only one public text: the story, or spirit, or animal represented and its representation. The artist does not say things like: "In this painting I am trying to show the relation between power

FIG. 248
Untitled, 1971–72. Welwi (Wuyulwuy), Eastern Arnhem Land. Ochre on bark, 55 × 46 cm.

FIG. 249
Djanda and Water Hole, 1986. Banduk Marika, North East Arnhem Land. Linocut, ink on paper, 54 × 29.5 cm.

centered in the gerontocracy and what has happened to young people in my society." Meaning is not made exterior to its representation, and the message is not distinct from the myth or image itself. There is a quantum gap between this kind of mythic interpretation and an ethics-based overt analysis of the social order. In the 1980s, however, objectification of the social order is as authentically Aboriginal in Sydney as embeddedness in a mythic order is in remote Papunya or Ramingining.

To a large extent, though, authenticity in art has become a Western myth.[54] If "authentic" merely means that a work purportedly by artist X is indeed by artist X, then it is a harmless factualism. But if it means that the only real, true, and proper Aboriginal art is that which was made beyond the influence of capitalist markets, Western governments, and the influence of outside art traditions, it is of little relevance to most of what attracts attention as Aboriginal art. Australia's major art and ethnographic museums, as well as its more prominent private collectors of Aboriginal art (Fig. 260), have long collected works that according to that orthodox view of authenticity would be defined as inauthentic.

In the Australian case, that view has been referred to as an attempt to "pickle Aborigines in the past."[55] A major turning point in the destruction of this myth in Australia was the exhibition *Koori Art '84*, which was held in Sydney in 1984 and presented the works of twenty-five contemporary Aboriginal artists, most of them urban-based.[56] Although the artists used Western materials and a variety of styles derived from both Western and traditional Aboriginal sources, according to one commentator "the Aboriginality of the majority of works was unmistakable."[57] This was, after all, the focal idea of the exhibition. A successor to this exhibition was actually called *Art and Aboriginality 1987*.[58] This phase has involved not the defense of a tradition against foreign inroads but the construction of a new tradition out of a variety of materials, underpinned both by official funding and by a relatively new conception: Aboriginality.

As pointed out earlier in this book, a pan-Aboriginal movement is a postcolonial phenomenon. Until the colonial period, Aborigines knew only a restricted number of neighbors, being unaware of the entirety of the continent on which they lived. Groups did not live in total isolation, however. It is well established that particular Aboriginal traditions were subjected for many centuries to exotic influences, not only those of neighboring Aborigines, but in the case of northern Australia also those of Asian and Melanesian peoples. Aborigines were never hermetically sealed off from waves of artistic influence, with the possible exception of post–Ice Age Tasmania and Kangaroo Island in the far south. If authentic art is the uninfluenced, most Aborigines had none. Still, Aboriginal art forms have adapted and changed most radically with the inroads of the colonists and the more subtle subsequent reach of the Australian state, sometimes declining into repetitive rigidity and "slickness" (Fig. 248), for example, or exploding into far more highly developed levels of nuance, variation, and visual complexity.[59] In spite of conservative Aboriginal ideology, the creators of the art have not in practice equated truth with a simple reproduction of the past.[60]

What does make for authenticity in Aboriginal art? A customer in the South Australian Museum shop one day was asking the manager if some carved boomerangs there were "authentic." The artist who made them, Bluey Roberts (Fig. 235), was in the shop and overheard the conversation. He approached the customer and asked: "Well, am I authentic?" To question the authenticity of the work was to question the Aboriginality of its maker. The only definition of "authentic Aboriginal art" that we regard as defensible is similar: it is art made by Aboriginal people.[61]

FIG. 250
Sun Lizard, 1984. Fiona Foley, Sydney. Aquatint with dried lizard, 40 × 15 cm.

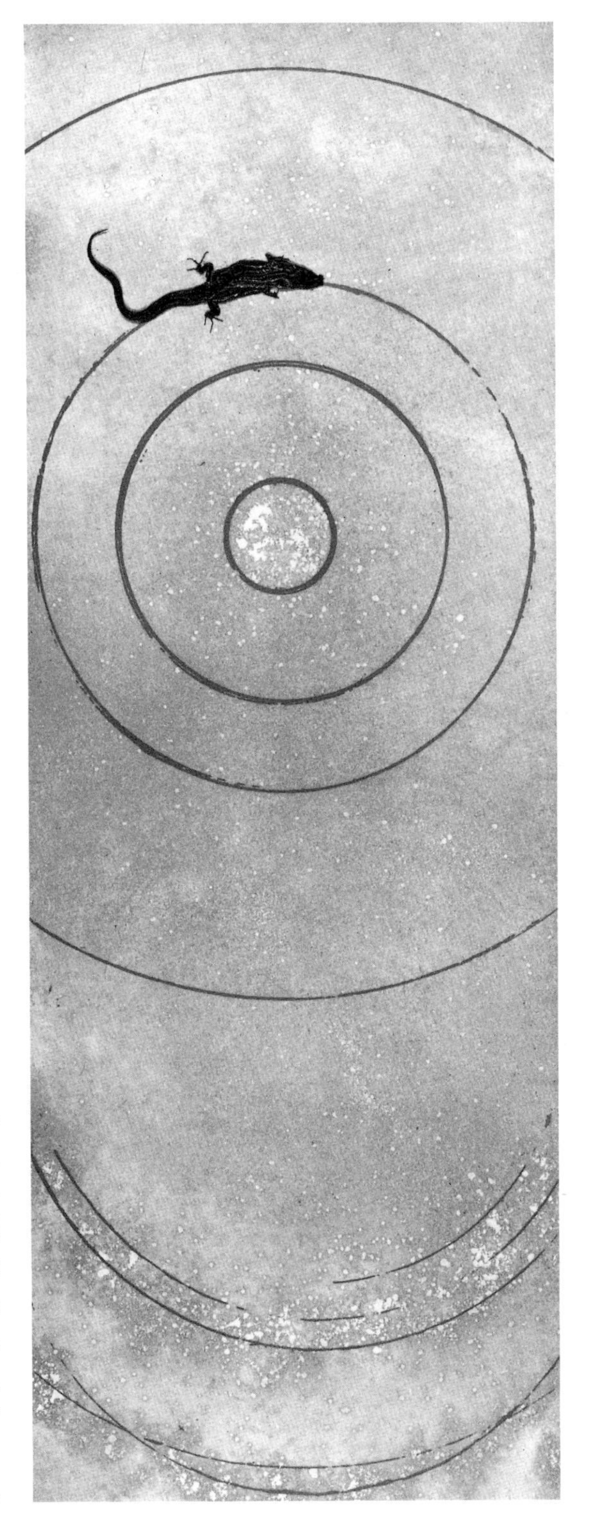

Rugs, Prints, Pots, Posters, and Photographs

Beginning in the 1960s and expanding dramatically in the 1980s, Aboriginal art has extended its repertoire into new media, especially woven and printed fabrics, printed works on paper (Figs. 249–51), ceramics, and photography (Figs. 5, 46). Most of these forms have historically been relegated to the craft or industry category. But increasingly successful efforts to elevate specific examples of such work from craft to art have resulted in such an assault on the conventional craft-art distinction that it is now in ruins—in Australia at least. All artifacts are on various continua of productive skill, mechanization, intellectual density, or usefulness, and it seems fruitless now to try and subsume this complexity under a simple two-way distinction.

From 1948 wool has been spun by hand and woven into rugs, scarves,

FIG. 251
Aboriginality, 1986. Byron Pickett, Western Australia. Serigraph, 34 × 50 cm.

and other items at Ernabella in Central Australia by Aboriginal women advised by M. M. Bennett, Winifred Hilliard, and others.[62] Batik has also been produced at Ernabella and, much further north, at Utopia since 1978. This has been a product of the interest and artistic talents of Aboriginal women and the advice and organizational skills of non-Aboriginal women resident in those communities. Since 1969, when Madeleine Clear introduced woodblock printing at Bathurst Island, the Tiwi people have been producing printed fabrics (mainly silk-screened), which are exported for sale around the world.[63] In Melbourne and later in Adelaide, Aboriginal administrator John Moriarty and his partner and wife Roslynne Moriarty have since 1982 created and marketed a wide range of printed fabrics using Aboriginal designs.[64] Their exceptional success in this field is partly a product of crisp, distinctive designs, business acumen, and a wave of interest in "Australiana" textile printing.[65] Lawrence Leslie of Moree, New South Wales, has recently printed silk-screened designs on fabric in collaboration with traditional owners of totemic designs in Central Arnhem Land, exemplifying a growing tendency for urban and rural Aboriginal artists to establish connections with Aborigines whose traditions have better survived history. The painter Trevor Nickolls attributes the kindling of Aboriginal content in his own work to a period spent working in the Northern Territory (Figs. 74, 252).[66]

Pottery is not indigenous to Australia. The first substantial introduction of pottery to an Aboriginal community was Michael Cardew's work at Bagot in Darwin in 1968.[67] This work continued, and at Bathurst Island Aboriginal people still produce pottery that finds its way onto the market. The only

Aboriginal ceramic artist who has achieved any fame is Thancoupie of Cape York Peninsula:

> Clay at Weipa was sacred. We only used it for ceremonial purposes and each colour had a meaning . . . We didn't need pottery because we had shells to drink from and tea-tree bark and leaves to wrap and cook food in. The idea of having my hands in clay and working with it making art was somehow strange but exciting. I thought of pots then as just for using in the kitchen—it was only much later I realised that clay would be my art, and also my legends.[68]

Thancoupie has produced ceramic sculptures of a consistently robust and rounded form, in a narrow range of glazes and decorated with coarsely applied linear designs frequently related to traditional mythology.

Aboriginal people have taken photographs since at least the early part of this century,[69] but only in the 1980s have several individuals emerged as recognized photographers. These include Tracey Moffat (Fig. 5) and Polly Sumner (Fig. 46). Moffat is also one of a small but growing number of Aboriginal filmmakers.

FIG. 252
Untitled: Landscape with Rocks, 1982. Trevor Nickolls, Sydney. Acrylic on canvas, 51 × 76.4 cm.

FIG. 253
Aboriginal Art, 1949. Margaret Preston, Sydney. Color stencil on black card, 21.8 × 30.2 cm.

FACING PAGE

FIG. 255
Advertisement for children's nightwear, Melbourne, 1987.

FIG. 256
Kakadu. In the Beginning, 1987. Ken Done, Sydney. Oil on canvas, 77 × 202 cm.

FIG. 254
Rangga, 1941. Frances Burke Fabrics, Melbourne. Screenprint on cotton, W. 125 cm.

Impact on Other Artists

In 1925 Margaret Preston, "the noisiest and most energetic personality among the Australian post-impressionists," was the first to promote publicly the use of Aboriginal designs in non-Aboriginal painting, printmaking, textiles, and pottery (Fig. 253).[70] Although she claimed an importance for the "mystic" properties of Aboriginal art, Preston is also reported as having said that the student of Aboriginal art should ignore the myths it illustrates: "Mythology and religious symbolism do not matter to the artist, only to the anthropologist."[71] Indeed, for many years the major influence of Aboriginal art was in what was called "applied Aboriginal art"—the appropriation of specific motifs from Aboriginal traditions for use in curtains, table mats, ashtrays, and other utilitarian objects. In the 1930s and 1940s Preston, Michael O'Connell, Frances Burke, Douglas Annand, Gert Sellheim, William Constable, and a host of lesser lights applied Aboriginal motifs to painting, printmaking, and the design of fabrics, murals, pottery, menu cards, and even theater sets and postage stamps.[72] An eclectic approach often combined designs from quite distant traditions, and forms were used as abstract patterns in repetitive decorative ways, as in Frances Burke's Rangga design (Fig. 254), or were contained in depictions of Aboriginal implements or scenes, as in Allan Lowe's earthenware vase of 1936 now in the Australian National

Gallery. Much of this effort was based on a desire to evolve a truly indigenous Australian fine-art and applied-arts tradition.[73]

Although Preston continued until the 1960s to produce prints and paintings that reflected her love of Aboriginal designs, particularly those of Arnhem Land, the 1950s and 1960s saw little new in the way of Aboriginal influence on other Australian art. Arthur Boyd gave X-ray features to animals in some of his paintings and Ian Fairweather is said to have been influenced by bark paintings in his highly calligraphic works of the same period,[74] but Fairweather's work, like that of Tony Tuckson, actually shows little specific and overt evidence of the Aboriginal influence that has been claimed for it.[75] Also in the 1960s are occasional cases of Aboriginal influence in the art of Thomas Gleghorn, Jon Molvig, and Clifton Pugh,[76] but in most cases these are simple transfers of design features without much serious engagement with the world of Aboriginal thought and values. This is the phenomenon most readily criticized as "appropriation" and "cultural colonialism" by those disposed to use such phrases.

Suddenly, beginning in the 1970s but especially in the mid- and late 1980s, there is an avalanche of Aboriginal influence on non-Aboriginal art and on commercial design and advertising (Fig. 255) in Australia. There is not enough space here to list all the examples, but we can single out two distinguishable approaches that emerge from this period. The first is a more or less sophisticated extension of the Preston phenomenon, its visual vocabulary expanded greatly by access to major rock-art sites such as those in the Alligator Rivers region and Cape York Peninsula and by the discovery of Western Desert acrylics. Ken Done's painting (Fig. 256) is a recent example.

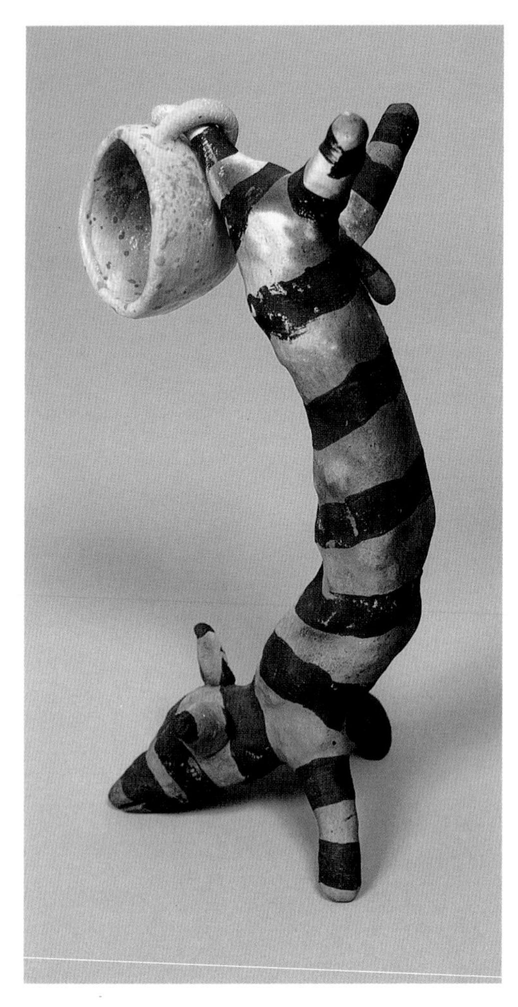

FIG. 257
Domestic Tail II, 1986. Philippe Lakeman, Adelaide. Ceramic, H. 35 cm.

His is essentially a quotational approach: Aboriginal art is referred to by quotation in a work that itself lies happily within the contemporary, Western-oriented art scene. Philippe Lakeman's playful ceramic dogs (Fig. 257), based on the Lake Eyre dogs collected by Reuther (Fig. 239), are similarly quotational. The art of Imants Tillers—and to some extent that by Susan Norrie—is a similar case in its use of Western Desert roundels, but his work is also accompanied by a vigorous social and political commentary on the place of Aborigines in Australian society.[77]

Perhaps even further from the Preston phenomenon is Tim Johnson, a non-Aboriginal artist, who sometimes paints collaboratively with Western Desert artists and whose work is heavily influenced by their traditions as well as by Asian art (Fig. 258). Johnson would certainly distance himself from the "appropriators" of Aboriginal art. His expressed respect for Aboriginal culture and willingness to accept in principle the possibility of truth for Aboriginal myth and the Dreaming are part of an assertion that he has experienced a certain amount of cultural convergence with Aboriginal thought.[78] Another non-Aboriginal artist, Juan Davila, has attacked Johnson, Tillers, and James Simon in a recent paper:

> Like moths to the art flame, the models of rapprochement expressed in [their] words are of an aesthetic and politically regressive nature: the collector, the

FIG. 258
Tun Huang, 1987. Tim Johnson, Sydney. Acrylic on linen, 147.5 × 177 cm.

FIG. 259
"See Australia First," 1987. Ann Newmarch, Adelaide. Silk-screen print, 44 × 47 cm.

> entrepreneur, the romantic explorer . . . And the works of Johnson, Simon and Tillers, in the shadow of institutions like the [Sydney] Biennale and its museographical walls, are still speaking from inside the authority and prestige of a colonising tradition too . . . In the work of these three artists . . . there is an operation which selects from reality only those items which function to patch together the illusion of a reconciled society . . .[79]

The work of Adelaide artists Ann Newmarch and David Kerr represents a second case in which non-Aboriginal artists have absorbed lessons from Aboriginal art, not in the Prestonian manner, not merely quoting images from another culture, and not, it would seem, under any particular program concerned with reconciliation. Both artists are in regular contact with Aboriginal people and are acutely aware of the kind of critique Davila and others may make of any work that shows evidence of Aboriginal influence. In Newmarch's art there is a strong grasp of the relation between snake scales and tire tracks, for example, which recognizes the layers of meaning, ancient and modern, that lie on the desert landscape of Central Australia (Fig. 259). Tire tracks are regularly repetitive, like snake tracks in sand; they also have to do with scarring, particularly in Newmarch's vision. Her use of dotting acknowledges the prior Aboriginal presence and the Aboriginal aesthetic of shimmering fragmentation, which again is like snake scales, like the actual vegetation patterns of the Australian bush, and, in some ways, like tire tracks, too. And the litter and dead cars of the outback are markers—microcosms—of the impact of the world economic system on the remotest of places.[80]

What these particular post-1960s works represent here is the increasing sophistication with which non-Aboriginal artists are absorbing influences from Aboriginal art. A better understanding of the cultural background and specific religious and aesthetic values of Aboriginal art, combined with a heightened sense of their own position as artists in Australian politics, has enabled some recent borrowers from the Aboriginal tradition to translate complex responses to Aboriginal art into elements of their own vision of things.

This raises the question of the persistence of Aboriginal art as a distinctive category. As we have seen in this chapter, the art produced by Aborigines has been influenced by white Australian culture, and it is also true that the works of white Australians are increasingly enjoying a reverse influence from Aboriginal art. Yet this process can only represent true cultural convergence if elements larger and deeper than mere motifs or materials become shared. Such elements would include tenets of worldview, understanding of landscape, and, perhaps the most problematic of all, greater social integration between Aborigines and other Australians. Thus far, social integration in Australia has mainly been privileged in one direction—integration into the dominant, essentially Western order. This Western dominance is not merely an offshoot of population numbers, cohesiveness, and economic power. It is also ideological. Australia's Western tradition, in spite of perennial self-doubt, seeks to transcend localism, to ingest and interpret other cultural forms, and to aim for a kind of universal account of the world and its peoples. This is a major obstacle to any cultural convergence with Aborigines that might be in the offing. Aboriginal culture, also persistent, resists Westernization in its equally perennial emphasis on the specific and local. True cultural convergence across this kind of gap, even if it were possible, must be a very long way off.

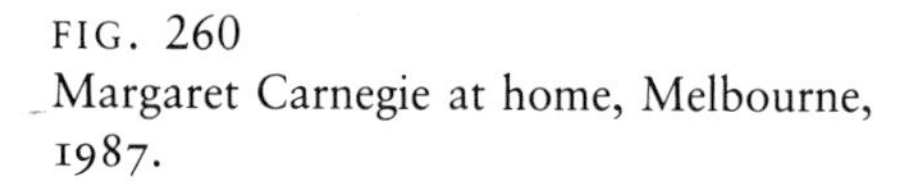

FIG. 260
Margaret Carnegie at home, Melbourne, 1987.

Postscript

PETER SUTTON

IN THIS BOOK and the exhibition that it accompanies we have focused mainly on the kind of Aboriginal art that is firmly rooted in the classical, pre-European past of Aboriginal tradition, even though we have demonstrated the continuing vitality of that tradition over much of Australia. We have done so at a time when Aborigines in the cities are beginning an explosive creative period in the arts, and while the pattern of that explosion is still emerging. At the time of writing, for example, there is still no substantial written study of urban Aboriginal art on which one might draw for interpretations or even information of any depth. The relationship of this art to classical forms is by no means simple. Nor is it just a slightly modified extension of the same tradition.

In that sense we have left a vacuum, which must now be filled by another kind of exhibition and another book. We have begun at the beginning, with the mature traditions that will continue to be seen as foundational, though not limiting, to the story of Aboriginal art. We have concentrated on the key elements of those foundations: the cosmological, the aesthetic, and the social and cultural systems that underpin classical Aboriginal art. These systems, understood by city-dwellers in a form largely simplified by the factors of upbringing, time, or geography, are now objectified as "culture," and they continue to exert an influence on urban Aboriginal art and indeed on the art of non-Aborigines as well.

We have tried to break new ground by concentrating on a few key matters of depth and avoiding the temptation to survey a little of everything across this large field. But there is still a quantum gap between the literature available on Aboriginal art and that which deals with the vastly better-known traditions of, for example, Renaissance Europe or Moghul India. In Australia there are no major university courses available on Aboriginal art, while many such courses on European art are offered. Few scholars work on the subject. Without a substantial and sophisticated literature it will remain difficult to design appropriate courses and to tempt talented scholars into the field. Philip Jones's chapter here on the history of Aboriginal art scholarship, which is the first of its kind, shows that an important beginning has been made but that thus far the record is thin. Much of the literature on Aboriginal art will continue to come from anthropologists. This is understandable, in the sense that the more exotic kinds of Aboriginal culture remain difficult to comprehend without the kind of comprehensive learning process anthropologists call fieldwork. The fact that much of the Aboriginal art literature has come from anthropologists in the past also means that the field will continue to attract those who have chosen a social-science paradigm within which to work.

But now that Aboriginal works have begun to be accepted into the fold of the art world, we must expect them also to be studied, written about, and exhibited under many other paradigms as well. In this book we have tried to ignore the conventional division of labor that exists between museum anthropologists and art curators or art historians. We actually find that division counterproductive, believing that art criticism and art history have much to gain from a grasp of social theory and the craft of ethnography, while anthropology has just as much to gain from recognizing the value of aesthetic, stylistic, and historical analyses of the objects people make. In saying that, we are not suggesting that only the academic disciplines can offer a satisfying or deep basis for the appreciation of Aboriginal art. But the most powerful and rewarding Aboriginal works come out of a combination of rigor and passion that is inevitably intellectual, as well as sensuous, and that requires commitment to intellectuality both from the artists and from those observers who would try to appreciate their works. Most of us are novices in this process.

CATALOGUE

Unless otherwise noted, works of art are in the collection of the South Australian Museum. Height precedes width in the dimensions given for each work. The consultations with Aboriginal people that are referred to in the catalogue descriptions were conducted by the authors in 1987. Titles of works were in most cases not assigned by the artists, who until recently did not give formal titles to paintings or sculptures. Titles given here were established either by existing documentation or were devised by the authors of this book.

Paintings on Bark and Board

1 / Fig. 49

The Sea-dogs, 1954

Big Tom (1880–1958), Melville Island
Ochre on bark, 31 × 80.5 cm (A47122)

During our consultations at Milikapiti, Melville Island, senior Aboriginal people identified the style of this bark painting as "not from here, from Arnhem Land," but, in fact, it was painted at Milikapiti on August 17, 1954, by a Tiwi man. This is not typical of Melville Island art style, either in 1954 or in the 1980s.

At the close of the creation period, Kirinua asked all the dogs if they preferred to live on the land or in the sea. They divided according to preference. Depicted here are the Sea-dogs, who live on a sandbar near the entrance of Snake Bay. In the center is the mother, surrounded by her twelve sons, all of them unusual in that they are portrayed with two rather than four legs in profile. Two dogs have been erased at the upper right.
Published: Mountford 1958

2 / Fig. 121

Sun Woman in Her Hut, 1954

Tjamalampuwa (ca. 1895–ca. 1956), Melville Island
Ochre on bark, 58 × 47 cm (A47088)

The Sun Woman, Wurriyupungala, is shown seated in her bark hut at Wurriyupi. For further details, see text pp. 76–77.
Published: Mountford 1958

3 / Fig. 122

Sun Woman at Wurriyupi, 1954

Big Tom (1880–1958), Melville Island
Ochre on bark, 95 × 40 cm (A47107)

The Sun Woman is depicted traveling across the sky with her blazing torch of bark. For further details, see text pp. 76–77.
Published: Mountford 1958

4 / Fig. 128

Crocodile Woman at Mundinyu, 1954

Big Tom (1880–1958), Melville Island
Ochre on bark, 89.5 × 44 cm (A47089)

The two sisters Wilindhuwila and Numanirakala camped at Mundinyu before they made their home at Wilindhu and Numanira respectively. For further details, see text p. 78.
Published: Mountford 1958

5 / Fig. 78

The Death of Purrukuparli, 1954

Marruwani (1916–after 1954), Melville Island
Ochre on bark, 89 × 24 cm (A47085)

A representation of the most famous traditional story of the Melville Island region. For further details, see text p. 50.
Published: Mountford 1958

6 / Fig. 72

Copulating Couple, ca. 1877

Artist unknown, Western Arnhem Land
Ochre on bark, 50 × 13 cm, Macleay Museum (P991)

The Macleay Museum, Sydney, holds the ten oldest surviving Aboriginal bark paintings, of which this and Cat. 7 are two. Cox 1878 published descriptions and line drawings of the paintings and identified this one as a pair of frogs. Those familiar with the representation of copulation in Aboriginal art agree that what is shown here, however, is an "unpacked" frontal view of heterosexual intercourse (see Figs. 73–74). An Aboriginal person consulted about the painting at Kalawadjbarra, Western Arnhem Land, considered the male figure to be Namarrkon (Lightning) because the figure's feet resemble axeheads (see, for example, Cat. 22).

Cox 1878:155 reports that this bark painting and the nine others in the Macleay Museum collection were "obtained from the natives on Essington Island, on the north coast of Australia." In the 1960s the words "Essington Island" were written on the face of this painting. (They were removed during conservation treatment for the present exhibition.) No place of this name is known to have existed, although there was a Port Essington in Western Arnhem Land.

O'Donnell 1980 has suggested that Cox only published the paintings and that Alexander Morton actually collected them and brought them to Sydney in November 1878, along with eleven other bark paintings collected for the Australian Museum, which were destroyed by fire in 1882. This theory does not correspond with the date of Cox's address to the Linnaean Society on August 26, 1878, at which he exhibited the barks.

Published: Cox 1878; Cooper et al. 1981
Exhibited: Linnaean Society of New South Wales, Sydney, 1878; *Aboriginal Australia*, traveling exhibition, 1981

7 / Fig. 200

Bird, ca. 1877

Artist unknown, Western Arnhem Land
Ochre on bark, 64 × 31 cm, Macleay Museum (P997)

Cox 1878 identified this bird as a cassowary, but that species does not occur in Western Arnhem Land. Aboriginal people consulted about the work at Oenpelli and Kalawadjbarra, Western Arnhem Land, stated that it may be a beach-dwelling bird (*gadigadi*) or a bustard.

Published: Cox 1878; Stanbury 1978; Isaacs 1984
Exhibited: Linnaean Society of New South Wales, Sydney, 1878

8 / Fig. 53

Saltwater Turtle, ca. 1884

Artist unknown, Western Arnhem Land
Ochre on bark, 83 × 63.5 cm (A45559)

One of five bark paintings collected by Captain F. Carrington at Field Island, near the mouth of the South Alligator River, Western Arnhem Land, in 1884 and now in the collection of the South Australian Museum (A4973, A45557–9, A45561). The paintings were taken from the ceilings of bark shelters in use by the Aborigines at a time before major encroachments by the European economy (Carrington 1890 and N. B. Tindale pers. comm. to S. Hemming 1980).

Aboriginal people at Oenpelli consulted about this work gave the Aboriginal name of Field Island as Kardangarl and suggested that the artist may have been Nawumirrili, a man of Bunitj kunmokurrkurr, nakangila subsection, Yirritja patrimoiety, and Gaagudju language.

Published: Worsnop 1897; Mountford 1957b; Carroll, 1977
Exhibited: Royal Geographical Society, Adelaide, 1887

9 / Fig. 55

Spirit Called Auuenau, 1912

Artist unknown, Western Arnhem Land
Ochre on bark, 149 × 33 cm
Museum of Victoria (19896)

Collected by Sir Baldwin Spencer at Oenpelli in 1912 (see Mulvaney and Calaby 1985:250,303–304). The label beneath the painting reads: "A night-walking being living amongst the hills in the country of the Geimbio [Kundjeyhmi] tribe, and said to eat dead Aborigines. The head projection represents a warning rattle, and the tail-like structure, lightning. The knobbed projections from his joints are said to be bones of the dead." This description is basically the same as that given in Spencer 1915:118; a slightly expanded version appears in Spencer 1914:435 and 1928:806–807, where the vertical strokes above and below the hands and behind and under the feet are identified as maggots. Spencer 1913:39, the original field-notebook page, provides some additional information—for example, this spirit sings out "Udu du du du!" This source also confirms the spelling of the subject's name as "Auuenau," as opposed to the "Auunau" of Spencer 1914:Fig. 80 and the "Auenau" and "Aunenau" of Spencer 1928:806, Fig. 523.

Published: Spencer 1914, 1928; Berndt (ed.) 1964
Exhibited: National Museum of Victoria, ca. period 1915–1960s

10 / Fig. 56
A Spirit Being, 1914

Artist unknown, Western Arnhem Land
Ochre on bark, 117 × 48 cm, Museum of Victoria (20055)

The label beneath the painting reads: "Frontal and side views are combined and from the elbows hang dead men's bones. The figure is possibly a Namandi, who was sometimes a human ghost, antagonistic to man. Representations such as this were made by artists to illustrate a story or personal experience. Gagadju tribe, Oenpelli, Western Arnhem Land, No. 20055, Spencer Collection, 1914." The register entry, however, describes the painting as being collected by Patrick Cahill for Spencer. Cahill was a buffalo shooter and farmer at Oenpelli and, after Francis Gillen, was Spencer's most important collaborator (see Mulvaney and Calaby 1985:301–302). The register also notes that the subject is Nudjerabipi (Cahill's spelling, Nudjer-ar-be-pe), the "debil debil" (spirit) that eats dead natives.
Published: Black 1964

11 / Fig. 94
Fruit Bats, period 1921–28

Artist unknown, Western Arnhem Land
Ochre on bark, 91 × 41 cm (A34826)

These fruit bats, known as "flying foxes" in Australian English, are shown hanging upside down from branches. This is a common theme in sacred performances across northern Australia. Aboriginal people consulted about this painting at Oenpelli identified the ceremonial body paint designs on the bats as Yirritja moiety (top two rows) and Duwa moiety (bottom row). The theme is locally associated with the ceremonies Kunapipi and Wubarr.

Collected by Margaret Mary Matthews, missionary at Goulburn Island from 1921 to 1928. Matthews came from a family of missionaries (see Cato 1976). The relevant language group was given by Matthews as Mau (Maung).
Published: Mountford 1939c
Exhibited: Museum of Modern Art, New York, 1946

12 / Fig. 93
Kangaroo with Young, period 1921–28

Artist unknown, Western Arnhem Land
Ochre on bark, 35 × 78 cm (A45635)

Aboriginal people at Oenpelli suggested that the species depicted here is a long-tailed kangaroo known locally as *ngabutj*. They identified the body-paint design on the kangaroo as Yirritja moiety, which is associated with Wubarr ceremony. The painting was collected by Matthews (see Cat. 11) at Goulburn Island in the period 1921–28.
Published: Mountford 1939c
Exhibited: (probably) Museum of Modern Art, New York, 1946

13 Ceremonial Object, period 1921–28

Artist unknown, Western Arnhem Land
Ochre on bark, 42.5 × 81 cm (A45883)

This is another painting collected by Margaret Matthews, from "opposite Goulburn Island" and from an Aboriginal group identified as Maung-speaking. Matthews described the work as a ceremonial object, or "Murin Walk." *Murin* is Mardayin, a category of sacred objects and ceremonies. Senior Aboriginal men at Oenpelli stated that the painting represents a body-paint design used in Mardayin ceremony; the design is Yirritja moiety and Spider (Karrh). No further details may be discussed here, as the topic is too ceremonially dangerous. The image itself, however, may be published.

14 Ceremonial Object, 1930s

Artist unknown, Western Arnhem Land
Ochre on bark, 40.5 × 113.5 cm (A26341)

Registered in 1938 as coming from Arnhem Land. The painting's intended meanings are now obscure. Mountford (1939c) thought the design had possibly "been derived from a fish motif." Aboriginal people consulted at Oenpelli

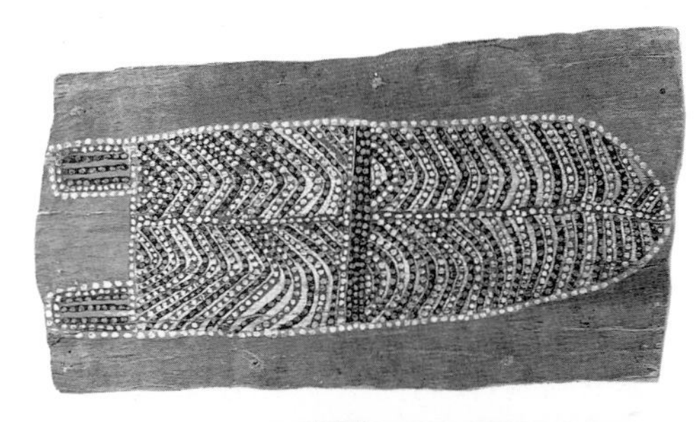

13

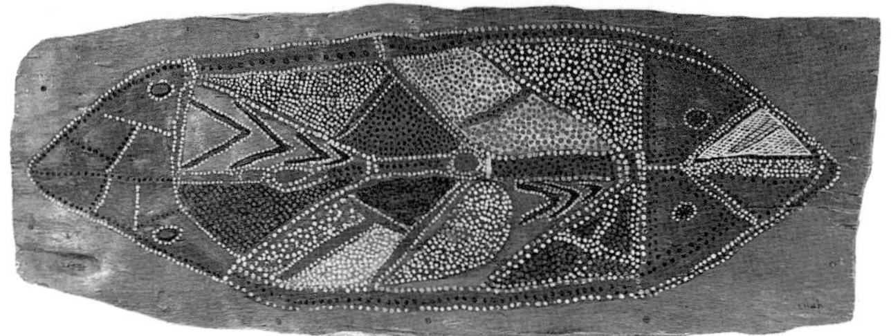

14

thought it might be a cheeky yam, known in Gunwinggu as *mandanik*, which had been smashed with a mallet.
Published: Mountford 1939c

15 / Fig. 120

Ceremonial Crocodile, ca. 1970

Yirawala (1903–1976), Western Arnhem Land
Ochre and charcoal on bark, 45 × 101 cm (A62167)

This representation of the Saltwater Crocodile (Namanjwarre, Kinga) stresses the ceremonial connotations of the subject through its use of Duwa moiety cross-hatching (*rarrk*) and rectilinear internal borders (*rungkal*), according to Aboriginal people consulted at Oenpelli. The 1971 documentation of this work by the collector Sandra Holmes reads in part: "The crocodile in the Dreaming time was once a man . . . on his head the spikes represent storm centres over water holes in the Dreaming country of the Crocodile. The crocodile is associated with magic that kills—and there are some old drawings of him half man half crocodile with long finger nails that always indicate the magician."

16 / Fig. 104

Crocodile Hunting Story, ca. 1979

Mick Gubargu (b. 1925), Western Arnhem Land
Ochre and charcoal on bark, 270 × 92 cm (A66795)

Nawalabirk was a renowned crocodile hunter. One day he found crocodile tracks and followed them to a deep water hole. Assisted by his wife Djadbelbel and his younger brother Njoryuwuk, he made a strong rope. He then swam down into the water hole and tied the rope around the crocodile's neck and tail. Back on the bank, he began to pull the crocodile ashore, but it awoke, lashing its tail and sweeping Nawalabirk into the pool, where it ripped him to pieces. As his bereaved wife and son stood weeping on the bank, his younger brother, who had always coveted his brother's wife, called out: "Goodbye brother, it's all right. The crocodile has eaten you, but I will look after our wife and son."

One of the largest bark paintings in existence, this dramatic work exhibits several important features typical of Arnhem Land art: the depiction of the same figure at two different times (tying the rope and after death), the use of the dismemberment theme, and the dorsal orientation of the body (see text pp. 64–79).
Exhibited: South Australian Museum, early 1980s and 1986–87

17 / Fig. 99

Lumarluma, ca. 1970

Yirawala (1903–1976), Western Arnhem Land
Ochre on bark, 104 × 54 cm (A62163)

Lumarluma is a mythic figure associated with thunder and storms, and particularly with the area of Maningrida-Milingimbi, northern Arnhem Land. His flatulence sounded across the country like a conch horn. He was a cannibal. He was, in some accounts, also a Whale. A dominant figure in the mythic founding of Mardayin ceremonies, he traveled overland, naming the creatures he found and creating songs and dances about them. He cut Mardayin designs into his skin, as shown in the painting.

Further details are contained in Sandra Holmes's extensive documentation of this painting in Holmes 1972. Also see Berndt and Berndt 1970.

18 / Fig. 79

Mimi Spirits, ca. 1970

Yirawala (1903–1976), Western Arnhem Land
Ochre on bark, 90 × 48 cm (A62166)

For a description of this painting, see text pp. 50, 53.
Published: Satterthwait 1978

19 / Fig. 103

Spirit Figure, 1972

Attributed to Dick Nangulay (b. 1920), Western Arnhem Land
Ochre on bark, 37 × 57 cm, Art Gallery of South Australia (729PA3)

Collection documentation entitles this work "The Lightning Spirit" and cites the artist as unknown. Aboriginal people consulted at Oenpelli, however, suggested that it probably is a Mimi spirit and attributed the work to Dick Nangulay on the grounds of style and subject. Peter Cooke, former art advisor at Maningrida, independently makes the same attribution. The painting is an unusual example of a figure shown mainly in profile.

20 / Fig. 77

Lightning Figure, 1986

John Mowandjul (b. 1952), Western Arnhem Land
Ochre and charcoal on bark, 65.5 × 39.5 cm (A65163)

Namarrkon, the Lightning Man, lives in a sacred water hole near Nimbuwa rock in Western Arnhem Land and responds with angry thunder if humans come too close to his home. In the wet season, he sits among the clouds flashing lightning from his head. This type of figure is one of the most frequently painted subjects in Western Arnhem Land art. In some cases the figure is female rather than male, is related to different sacred sites, and has axes protruding from the knees and elbows. The axes are the instruments by which Lightning cleaves trees and people.

21 / Fig. 58

Female Lightning Figure, ca. 1974

Bilinyarra Nabegeyo (b. ca. 1920), Western Arnhem Land
Ochre on bark, 55 × 34 cm (A66796)

When the artist was shown a photograph of this painting in 1987, he found it interesting but did not recognize it as his own work. He described the subject as "Lightning, but girl-one." The center section, which resembles a simplified sacred design, is "just a normal body." The stripes below the face are "just the neck part." The vertical stripes at the pelvis are a pubic string cover, of a type once worn by Aborigines.

22 / Fig. 92

Female Lightning Figure, 1982

Djawida (b. ca. 1935), Western Arnhem Land
Ochre on bark, 64 × 156.5 cm, Private Collection

The artist's name, written on the back of the bark probably by someone else, is given as "Jawiada," who is most likely the Djawida known from various sources. The back of the painting also gives the word "Namorrgon," the masculine form of the Gunwinggu word for lightning (*namarrkon*). The figure is clearly female, however.

This work is a dramatic example of the folding of a human-like figure into a rectangular frame, which avoids the more standard splayed arrangement of the body.

23 / Fig. 123

Catfish Dreaming, 1987

Jimmy Wululu (b. 1936), Central Arnhem Land
Ochre on bark, 41 × 139.5 cm (A65406)

This painting, which appears abstract to many viewers, represents the fine rib-bones of the eel-tail Catfish, a Dreaming for which the artist has custodianship.

24 / Fig. 127

Catfish and Whitefish Dreaming, 1954

Artist unknown, Central Arnhem Land
Ochre on bark, 24 × 103.5 cm (A61768)

Collected by A. A. Abbie, this unusual bark painting was executed at or near Maningrida by a Burarra person. The back of the work bears the words "Dreaming 1 Catfish + 2 White fish. Fishe's (sic) mouth + teeth," and the date 1954. The hole represents the mouth (Abbie 1969). A strikingly similar work from the same area, now in the Australian Museum, Sydney, defines this form as a representation of a hollow-log coffin (Fig. 126). The same form is found in *The Time of the Dream* by David Malangi (Allen 1975).
Published: Abbie 1969.

25 / Fig. 80

Sacred Places at Milmindjarr', 1982

David Malangi (b. 1927), Central Arnhem Land
Ochre on bark, 107 × 79 cm (A67850)

For a description of this painting, see text p. 53.

26 / Fig. 12

Tortoise, Honey, and Spikerush, 1952

Birrikitji Gumarna (ca. 1898–1982), North East Arnhem Land
Ochre on bark, 57 × 62 cm (A47618)

Collected by C. P. Mountford at Yirrkala in 1952, this painting depicts the totemic lagoon of Freshwater Tortoise at Kulwitji. The dots and diamonds in the upper left panel represent drowned bees and honey respectively, both of which floated to the surface of the lagoon after a hive was submerged there. The leaves of the spikerush growing in the lagoon are shown as diamonds at the upper right quadrant and upper half of the lower left quadrant. The six parallel lines in the bottom section of the lower left quadrant symbolize the fish trap constructed by the totemic hero Lanytjung. In the center of the lower right panel is a Freshwater Tortoise. The meanders represent its wake, and the diamonds and dots in the same panel are bubbles rising to the surface as the Tortoise feeds on the bottom.
Published: Mountford 1956

27 **Journey of the Yirritja Dead,** 1952

Attributed to Wakuthi Marawili (b. 1921), North East Arnhem Land
Ochre on bark, 29 × 44 cm (A47702)

Although not among the most spectacular bark paintings, this type represents an important, early phase in the development of a form that has become less lively and more predictable since the 1960s. Aboriginal people consulted at Yirrkala attributed the painting to Wakuthi Marrawili. Mountford, who collected the painting at Yirrkala in 1952, did not record the artist's name.

A recently deceased man is shown surrounded by mourning women in the lower left panel. On the lower right, the dead man is in his grave; below him are three men beating music sticks and singing, while one man plays the drone tube. On the extreme right is a line of women singing and dancing a mortuary ceremonial. The remaining panels depict the journey of the dead man's spirit to its resting place.
Published: Mountford 1956

28 Turtle and Oystercatcher, 1952

Mawalan Marika (1908–1967), North East Arnhem Land
Ochre on bark, 43 × 20 cm (A47665)

Part of the Djang'kawu Sisters mythological series, this painting concerns the song the Djang'kawu composed about a Hawksbill Turtle and a bird that is a species of Oystercatcher, shown here seated on a rock. The Turtle (upper panel) is transformed into a boulder, which is submerged at high tide, and the Oystercatcher is portrayed as a pillar of rock in the sea. The cross-hatched panels represent the sea breaking over the totemic rocks. The relevant site, said by Mountford's informants to be in the region of Waipingboi, was identified by Aborigines as being at either Wultju or Manhala.
Published: Mountford 1956

29 / Fig. 81

Squid and Turtle Dreamings, 1972

Liwukang Bukurlatjpi (b. ca. 1927), North East Arnhem Land
Ochre on bark, 92 × 52 cm (A67540)

For a description of this painting, see text p. 55.

30 / Fig. 116

Space Tracking Station, 1967

Munggurrawuy Yunupingu (ca. 1907–1979), North East Arnhem Land
Ochre on masonite, 92 × 60 cm (A66759)

The central conical form in this painting is a traditional form with multiple meanings, including that of ceremonial ground. Here it represents the rockets tracked by the ELDO tracking station established at Gurlkurla. The non-Aborigines working at the station are represented by the pale-colored people inside the rocket; their leader is shown at the top wearing a crown. The black people symbolize human beings who were transformed into totemic Kangaroos, Flying Foxes, and Dogs, who remain at Gurlkurla forever.

31 / Fig. 15

Possum Story from Djarrakpi, ca. 1967

Narritjin Maymurru (1922–1982), North East Arnhem Land
Ochre on masonite, 89 × 40 cm (A66758)

Written documentation for this painting was supplied by an unknown Aboriginal person: "This bark also tells about a man called Maymuru a man from the beginning—these two possimas [possums] are just walk up and down and three birds which sings special at night on their tree tops [the T-shaped forms]. And besides these trees are some creatures that always sings through the day. On each corns [corners] of on this bark there are four holes for these four possimos and this bark painting tells many stories about this one bark painting. Also these tracks of these creatures also tells their stories too and now they can tell this story from a place call Djarrakpi and now Marngalili [Manggalili] tribe is still useing this law and their painting that Maymuru gave of his people and the bark paintings they sale now is its many stories to and releagens [religions] too. And also Barrima the big boss of the very beginning gave these laws and stories."

32 / Fig. 57
Canoe and Figures, 1922

Attributed to Taimundu (ca. 1879–1940s), Groote Eylandt
Ochre on bark, 22.5 × 15 cm (A12866)

This work is one of a group of bark paintings in the South Australian Museum collected by anthropologist Norman B. Tindale. It was acquired by Tindale on April 16, 1922, at Yetiba (Yadikba) on the Emerald River, Groote Eylandt. At that time Aborigines there had had only minimal contact with Europeans. Tindale was the second field anthropologist to assemble a bark painting collection; he was preceded by Baldwin Spencer, who collected bark paintings at Oenpelli in 1912.

Tindale (1987) noted that the Aborigines "were very fond of decorating their possessions, and during the rainy season, the 'Wet,' they spent hours lying in shelters made of stringybark sheets. A constant activity is the painting of pictures of all kinds on the smooth under-surface at arm's reach above them." In his journal Tindale records that on the day he acquired this painting he was drawing on paper and Aboriginal men fetched pieces of bark and painted them (see Fig. 9). He considers the work as possibly that of Papatama, but "probably the work of Taimundu, which was never so finished as those executed by Papatama." (Tindale 1987.)

33 / Fig. 83
The Kestrels, 1948

Manggangina Wurramara (1919–1984), Groote Eylandt
Ochre and manganese on bark, 68.5 × 33 cm,
Art Gallery of South Australia (701PA14)

For a description of this painting, see text pp. 55–56.
Published: Mountford 1956, 1966b

34 / Fig. 95
Two Crabs, 1948

Dakilarra Wurramara (d. ca. 1950), Groote Eylandt
Ochre and manganese on bark, 36.5 × 93 cm, Art Gallery of South Australia (701PA16)

The northern Australian mud crab grows to a large size and is considered to be a great delicacy. At Groote Eylandt, as well as many other places in Aboriginal Australia, it is also celebrated in myths, songs, and dances. The Crab is said to have left Groote Eylandt's Amakula river and gone to the mainland; it is also still present in a spring on the island (Mountford 1956a:31–33). Here, the male is on the right, the female on the left.
Published: Mountford 1954, 1956a, 1966b; Severin 1973; Isaacs 1980

35 Orion and the Pleiades, 1948

Minimini Mamarika (1900–1972), Groote Eylandt
Ochre and manganese on bark, 76 × 32 cm, Art Gallery of South Australia (701PA46)

Above are the wives of the fisherman called Burumburumrunya, seated within their circular grass hut. Below, in the T-shaped form, are the three fishermen (across the top of the T is the constellation known as Orion's Belt in European mythology). Below them are the fishermen's fire, two parrotfish, and a skate. All of these are also stars: those in the circle above are the Pleiades, and those in the T-formation, the constellation of Orion.
Published: Mountford 1954, 1956a, 1966b; Poignant 1967; Isaacs 1980
Exhibited: Art Gallery of South Australia, 1960; Worcester Art Museum, England, 1966; Allentown Art Museum, Pennsylvania, 1966

36 / Fig. 86

Crane and Freshwater Shrimp, ca. 1909

Artist unknown, Borroloola, Northern Territory
Ochre on wood, 24 × 60 cm (A45906)

Written in ink on the inside of this box lid is the word *Crane*. John Bradley (1987) provides information on the significance of this designation, based on his discussions with Aboriginal authorities from Borrolooola: The bird is identified as the crane species known as Brolga (*kurdarrku*), shown here chasing a freshwater shrimp (*majika*). The Brolga is a major Ancestral Being for the Mambaliya-Wawukarriya semimoiety and is closely associated with restricted Kunabibi rituals and with various public funeral rites related to the release of a deceased person's spirit back into the country. Brolga's power name is Burangkul. The Brolga Dreaming is associated with two lagoons in the Borroloola region—Wubunjawa and Lurriyarri—located on the plains west of the Wearyan River.

37 / Fig. 85

Black Bream, ca. 1909

Artist unknown, Borroloola, Northern Territory
Ochre on wood, 23 × 38.5 cm (A45910)

For a description of this work, see text pp. 56–57.

Acrylic Paintings

38 / Fig. 164

Witchetty Grub Dreaming at Kunajarrayi, 1986

Paddy Japaljarri Sims (b. ca. 1916), Central Australia
Acrylic on canvas, 136 × 108 cm (A65164)

Kunajarrayi (Mt. Nicker) is a site near the Western Australian border, about ninety miles west of Yuendumu. It is the intersection of at least six Dreamings and an important ceremonial center. In this painting the clusters of small U-shaped symbols around a concentric circle on the left edge of the painting represent women of the napaljarri and nungarrayi subsections digging for Ngarlkirdi (Witchetty Grub). The women watch a fight between two Witchetty Grub brothers, one of whom turns into a snake before traveling to another site near Yuendumu. The fight and the transformation into the snake are depicted by the sinuous lines.

39 / Fig. 144

Burrowing Skink Dreaming at Parrikirlangu, 1986

Darby Jampijinpa (b. ca. 1910), Central Australia
Acrylic on canvas, 145.3 × 94.2 cm, Duncan Kentish

For a description of this painting, see text pp. 118–19, 121.
Exhibited: Kintore Gallery, Adelaide 1986

40 / Fig. 138

Water Dreaming at Mikanji, 1986

Judy Nampijinpa Granites (b. 1934), Central Australia
Acrylic on canvas, 92 × 111 cm, Eric H. Pinkerton and Josie A. Pinkerton

Mikanji is a small water hole west of Yuendumu, the point of convergence of several Ngapa (Water/Rain) Dreaming tracks from sites in Warlpiri, Anmatyerre, and Pintupi country. In the Jukurrpa (Dreamtime), the meeting of these Dreamings at Mikanji caused a great storm to rage across the land. After the storm had passed, green shoots and wild fruits began to grow, which attracted the mythological Emu Men who were traveling from the east. See Fig. 138a for a description of the elements depicted in the painting.
Exhibited: Blaxland Gallery, Sydney, 1987

41 / Fig. 160

Water Dreaming at Mikanji, 1986

Tilo Nangala (b. 1944), Central Australia
Acrylic on canvas, 154 × 185 cm, Private Collection

This painting is of the same site and Dreaming as that depicted in Cat. 40. The two artists, Nangala and Nampijinpa, share the same mythological segment through inheritance from their respective fathers. For further details on Cat. 40 and 41, see text pp. 121–22.
Exhibited: Gallery Gabrielle Pizzi, Melbourne, 1987

42 / Fig. 157

Wild Yam Dreaming at Yajarlu, 1986

Paddy Jupurrurla Nelson (b. ca. 1925), Central Australia
Acrylic on canvas, 77 × 85.5 cm (A68811)

Yarla (Wild Yam Dreaming) traveled from Yajarlu near New Haven Station, north of Papunya, to country around Yumurrpa, southwest of Yuendumu and near Mt. Singleton. The roundels are the sites where the ancestor stopped and the long curved lines, the traveling paths.

43 / Fig. 143
Five Dreamings, 1984

Michael Nelson Jakamarra (b. 1946), assisted by Marjorie Napaljarri, Central Australia
Acrylic on canvas, 122 × 182 cm, Gabrielle Pizzi

In this painting the artist depicts five Dreamings to which he has various relationships. The horizontal line is Pamapardu (Flying Ant) Dreaming at Yuwinji, west of Vaughan Springs. The circles at the lower left and the upper right with radiating wavy lines represent Possums at Jangankurlangu and Mawurji respectively. The snake figure is Warnayarra, the Rainbow Serpent at Yilkirdi, near Mt. Singleton; the animal tracks at the lower right are those of the Two Kangaroo (Marlujarra) ancestors at Yintarramurru. Also at the lower right are circles representing Mirrawarri, a Rain Dreaming site near Mt. Doreen. The Sydney artist Imants Tillers incorporated the design of this work into one of his own paintings (see Art Gallery of New South Wales 1986).
Published: Aboriginal Law Bulletin No 17, December 1985; Brody 1985; Art Gallery of New South Wales 1986
Exhibited: National Gallery of Victoria 1985; Art Gallery of New South Wales, 1986; Institute of Contemporary Art, London, 1987; Contemporary Art Centre, Adelaide, 1988

44 Bush Potato Dreaming, 1986

Mary Nungarrayi (b. ca. 1942) and Lady Nungarrayi (b. ca. 1933), Central Australia
Acrylic on canvas, 140 × 95 cm, Private Collection

Ngarlajiyi is a wild tuber (*Vigna lanceolata*) that resembles a small potato. Here napaljarri and nungarrayi women are shown digging for the plant. The four roundels of the square represent individual plants; the lines joining the circles are the roots. The U-shaped forms are women digging, and the central roundel, the women's campsite.
Exhibited: Editions Gallery, Fremantle, Western Australia, 1986; Blaxland Gallery, Sydney, 1987

45 / Fig. 159
Sugarleaf Dreaming at Ngarlu, 1986

Lucy Napaljarri (b. ca. 1926), Hilda Napaljarri (b. ca. 1941), Ruth Napaljarri (b. ca. 1940), Central Australia
Acrylic on Canvas, 173 × 187.5 cm, Tim and Vivien Johnson

Ngarlu is near Mt. Allan Station, east of Yuendumu. The primary Dreaming for the site is Yanyirlingi (Sugarleaf), a plant with sweet nectar that is eaten by Aboriginal people. The depiction of this Dreaming is complex and has several levels of meaning. Women are shown both gathering Sugarleaf and performing a *yawulyu*, or women's ceremony, associated with the Dreaming. In addition, an actual event—the birth of two jampijinpa boys to two nungarrayi sisters—at a camp near Ngarlu is shown. The Dreaming story concerns an illicit relationship between a man of the jungarrayi subsection and his classificatory mother-in-law, a napangardi. The man happened to pass by while the woman was urinating. He desired her and began to spin hairstring for a pubic tassel, singing love songs while he did so. This had the intended result of drawing her to his campsite at Ngarlu.
Exhibited: Editions Gallery, Fremantle, Western Australia, 1986

46 / Fig. 151
Bush Cabbage Dreaming at Ngarlu, 1986

Cookie Stewart Japaljarri (b. ca. 1940), Alma Nungarrayi Granites (b. 1955), and Robin Japanangka Granites (b. 1952), Central Australia
Acrylic on canvas, 120.5 × 237.5 cm, Duncan Kentish

This Dreaming of Yajakurlu, a bush food that grows near creeks, is from Ngarlu, near Mt. Allan (see Cat. 45). In the Jukurrpa (Dreamtime), the wind blew the Yajakurlu seeds from Yirdikupuurda (a site near Mt. Dennison, northeast of Yuendumu) to many different sites, including Yakurlpu, a water hole near Ngarlu. The three roundels represent both the plants and the sites in the Dreaming story. The roots and seeds of the plants are shown along the radiating lines. Around the plants are U-shaped forms and adjacent lines that represent people and their digging sticks.

Cookie Stewart Japaljarri, the senior owner of the Dreaming, mapped out the main design; the two other, younger artists, who were living with Japaljarri and his family at the time, helped execute the dotting and the plant motifs.
Exhibited: Kintore Gallery, Adelaide, 1986

47 / Fig. 173

Water Dreaming at Napperby, 1983

Clifford Possum Japaljarri (b. ca. 1943), Central Australia
Acrylic on canvas, 183.5 × 155.5 cm, Flinders University Art Museum (2028)

This painting shows the Water Dreaming traveling from the west into Anmatyerre country. The site is Yantanji on Napperby Station, northwest of Alice Springs. This Water Dreaming, along with Emu Dreaming and others, is depicted in the Maliyarra-maliyarra initiation ceremonies in this area. The wavy background lines are both rain and water on the ground; the larger blue and brown lines in the foreground are clouds; and the U-shaped and straight lines represent people painted for a ceremony.
Published: Brody 1985; Maughan and Zimmer 1986; Australian Government Information Service 1986
Exhibited: Royal South Australian Society of Arts, Adelaide 1984; National Gallery of Victoria, 1985; Royal Melbourne Institute of Technology Gallery, 1985; Kintore Gallery, Adelaide, 1986; Flinders University Art Museum, 1987; South Australian College of Advanced Education Gallery, Underdale, 1987

48 / Fig. 163

Bushfire Dreaming, 1982

Clifford Possum Japaljarri (b. ca. 1943), Central Australia
Acrylic on canvas, 81 × 100.8 cm, Art Gallery of South Australia (846P12)

This is part of the Fire Dreaming that crosses Anmatyerre, Warlpiri, and Pitjantjatjara territory. In this segment of the Dreaming story, two brothers kill and eat a sacred Kangaroo. This angers their father Lungkarda, the Blue-tongue Lizard, who sends a bushfire to burn them to death. The brothers are shown in the center of the painting as skeletons next to their weapons and the brush bundles with which they tried unsuccessfully to extinguish the fire. The background colors represent fire and smoke. See the discussion of this story in Kimber 1981.
Published: Postcard (Aboriginal Artists Agency, Sydney)
Exhibited: Art Gallery of South Australia 1984, 1986

49 / Fig. 172

Aralukaja, 1976

Clifford Possum Japaljarri (b. ca. 1943), Central Australia
Acrylic on board, 50 × 40 cm (A67223)

In the Dreaming depicted here, two men made camp at Aralukaja, a water hole on Napperby Station. They argued over whether to go hunting, and one man chased the other with a stone axe. The concentric circle and the U-shaped forms above and below it represent the men's camp; the surrounding footsteps depict the chase. The tracks at the far right of the painting reappear in Cat. 50, where the story continues.

50 / Fig. 152

Five Dreamings, 1976

Clifford Possum Japaljarri (b. ca. 1943), Central Australia
Acrylic on board, 50 × 40 cm (A67224)

This is a mythologically complex painting and shows the artist's skill at incorporating a large amount of information in a small space. Segments of five major Dreamings are depicted here, all of which either focus on Anmatyerre country around Napperby Station or across that area and together represent the mythic network of hundreds of people.

The dispute between the Dreaming characters that began in Cat. 49 continues in this painting and concludes with one man catching and killing the other with his axe. The vertical line of four roundels in the middle of the painting are the travels of the Honey Ant ancestors to Yulamu (Mt. Allan) and Yuendumu. The dog tracks to the right represent Maliki, the Dingo ancestor traveling from Western Australia through Pikilyi (Mt. Dorren Station) and Ngarlu, near Mt. Allan, before going further east. The Dingo alternates between animal and human—hence the mixture of animal and human tracks. (The Dingo as a human is involved in the story in Cat. 45, where it is depicted by the footprints at the top of the painting.) Crossing the painting from right to left is the Mala (Hare Wallaby) ancestor traveling from Warlukurlangu (the Bushfire site of Cat. 48), near Yuendumu, to Napperby Creek and into the Tanami Desert. Finally, a mythological nungarrayi woman travels through the area from country far to the south to Lajamanu, or Hooker Creek, about four hundred miles northwest of Alice Springs. See 152a for a description of the elements in the painting.

51 / Fig. 149

Man's Love Story, 1981

Clifford Possum Japaljarri (b. ca. 1943), Central Australia
Acrylic on canvas, 52 × 41.5 cm, Tim and Vivien Johnson

Commissioned by Sydney artist Tim Johnson when he was acting art advisor for Papunya Tula in July 1981, this painting shows the jungarrayi man depicted in Cat. 45 making his hair string on a spindle and singing love songs to attract a napangardi woman to his campsite.

52 / Fig. 153

Possum Spirit Dreaming, 1980

Tim Leura Japaljarri (ca. 1939–1984), assisted by Clifford Possum Japaljarri, Central Australia
Acrylic on canvas, 213 × 701 cm, Mrs. Douglas Carnegie O. A. M. and Sir Roderick Carnegie

This monumental painting was apparently done principally by one man, Tim Leura Japaljarri, in only a few week's time. It was commissioned by Geoff Bardon for a film on Western Desert painting, which was never made. Bardon asked the artist for a "real painting . . . a really good one . . . your story, your country" (Bardon n.d.). Japaljarri requested a large canvas and Bardon sent him a twenty-three foot roll of canvas.

The painting encompasses most of the Dreamings over which the artist had rights and many of the ones that pass through his country on Napperby Station. These include Wild Yam, Water, Sun and Moon Love Story, and Old Man Dreamings. (Many aspects of these Dreamings can also be seen in other paintings by Japaljarri.) In this painting, the integrating theme is the artist's primary Dreaming, the Possum ancestor. The background dotting reflects visual qualities of the landscape: sand, earth, leaves, clouds, and smoke. See 153a for a description of elements in the painting.
Published: Diggins 1987; Bardon 1981
Exhibited: Australian Perspecta, 1981; Art Gallery of New South Wales, 1986; National Gallery of Victoria, 1987; Auckland City Art Gallery, 1988

53 / Fig. 170

Possum Dreaming at Kurningka, ca. 1977

Tim Leura Japaljarri (ca. 1939–1984), Central Australia
Acrylic on canvas board, 61 × 50.5 cm, Flinders University Art Museum (1458)

In this painting the artist reminisces about the hunting days of his father and grandfather, both of whose Dreaming was Possum. The central roundel represents a small rock shelter at Kurruka on Napperby Station. Shown around this site, clockwise from the upper left, are a boomerang, a U-shaped form representing a person setting, a shield, a U-shaped form symbolizing a windbreak, and a spear-thrower. The vertical lines to the far left are spears.
Published: Maughan and Zimmer 1986
Exhibited: Royal Melbourne Institute of Technology Gallery, 1985; Flinders University Art Museum, 1987; South Australian College of Advanced Education Gallery, Underdale, 1987

54 / Fig. 150

Kulijarra, 1981

Tim Woods Jampijinpa (b. ca. 1930), Central Australia
Acrylic on canvas, 80.3 × 99.2 cm, Art Gallery of South Australia (827P18)

No information is available on this painting.

55 / Fig. 155

Bushfire Dreaming, ca. 1976

Johnny Warangula Jupurrurla (b. ca. 1925), Central Australia
Acrylic on hardboard, 61.5 × 63 cm (A66892)

This painting is a good example of the artist's use of dotting overlays. The Dreaming is Fire and the site is Lungkarda (home of the Blue-tongue Lizard). As the Lizard traveled around the land, he burned off the grass with fire fanned by his breath. It is from this that the present-day Blue-tongue lizard gets his habit of flicking out his tongue and hissing. The fires ended with the coming of rain storms from Kalipinypa, which nourished the abundant growth of bush foods that Lungkarda ate.
Published: Cooper et al. 1981
Exhibited: National Gallery of Victoria, 1981

56 / Fig. 154

Wallaby Dreaming, 1982

Mick Namarari Japaljarri (b. ca. 1930), Central Australia
Acrylic on canvas, 101.7 × 102.4 cm, Art Gallery of South Australia (847P19)

The design of this painting apparently is based on the impression made in the ground by a sleeping wallaby. The story may be one of those in the Tingarri ceremonial cycle.
Exhibited: Art Gallery of South Australia, 1986

57 / Fig. 148

Kangaroo and Shield People Dreaming at Lake Mackay, 1980

Timmy Japangardi (b. ca. 1942), Central Australia
Acrylic on canvas, 186 × 155 cm, Tim and Vivien Johnson

Most of the details of this painting are restricted. The Kangaroo Dreaming is part of the Tingarri ceremonial cycle. The Kangaroo ancestor's tracks visible at the top of the painting depict his travels from site to site. The artist's country, Lake Mackay, a large dry salt lake in Western Australia, is represented here in classic Pintupi style. Water, flowing on the ground after big rains, is symbolized by the wavy lines around the edges of the painting; the unconnected roundels in the middle are trees and the golden colored patches, sandhills. The connected roundels are both campsites and soakages. Elements of this work were used by the Sydney artist Imants Tillers in his 1987 painting for the Bicentennial Pavilion in Centennial Park, Sydney.
Published: Australian Government Information Service, 1986

58 Lake Mackay, 1980

Timmy Japangardi (b. ca. 1942), Central Australia
Acrylic on pine board, 125 × 12 cm (A67255)

This work depicts several Dreaming sites in the artist's homeland at Lake Mackay.

59 / Fig. 167
Ceremonial Ground at Kulkuta, 1981

Anatjari Jampijinpa (b. ca. 1929), Central Australia
Acrylic on canvas, 182.5 × 182 cm, Tim and Vivien Johnson

Kulkuta is southwest of Sandy Blight Junction in Western Australia. It is a major water soakage and an important site for the Tingarri ceremonies. The painting depicts a ceremony at the site and the site itself. The larger circles are the older men, who are decorating the young men, shown as the smaller circles, for the ceremony. At the Hobart and Brisbane exhibitions, Tim Johnson showed *Ceremonial Ground at Kulkuta* and a painting of his own based on a photograph of Anatjari painting the work.
Published: Brody 1985
Exhibited: Yuill-Crowley Gallery, Sydney, 1983; Tasmanian School of Art Gallery, Hobart, 1984; Institute of Modern Art, Brisbane, 1985; National Gallery of Victoria, 1985

60 / Fig. 177
Jangala and Two Women at Ngurrapalangu, 1982

Uta Uta Jangala (b. ca. 1920), Central Australia
Acrylic on canvas, 122.5 × 91 cm, Tim and Vivien Johnson

This painting portrays the actions of a man and two women at Ngurrapalangu, a site southwest of the Kintore Ranges near the Northern Territory-Western Australian border. The three "hills" at the top of the painting are a man of the jangala subsection and two women, a nangala (his sister) and a napanangka (the sister of his mother's father). The roundels represent caves at the site, while the other shapes and the dotting depict hills and vegetation in the area.
Published: Australian Government Information Service 1986

61 / Fig. 178
Old Man Dreaming at Yumari, 1983

Uta Uta Jangala (b. ca. 1920), Central Australia
Acrylic on canvas, 242 × 362 cm, Art Gallery of South Australia (844P11)

Most of the details of this painting are restricted, but in general it depicts the punishment received by an old jakamarra man who had intercourse with his mother-in-law, a

nangala. Yumari is the name of the site and the Pintupi word for *mother-in-law*. The trail of the old man can be traced for 125 miles from Kamperapa (northern Ehrenburg Ranges) in the east along the latitudinal ridges of parallel sand dunes to Yumari. The linked roundels in the background represent rock holes and campsites where the events in the story occured. In the center of the painting are six ovoid forms symbolizing rocks at the Yumari site.
Exhibited: Royal South Australian Society for the Arts, Adelaide, 1984

62 / Fig. 179

Yumari, 1981

Uta Uta Jangala (b. ca. 1920), Central Australia
Acrylic on canvas, 244 × 366 cm, Aboriginal Arts Board

The description of the meaning of this painting is the same as that for Cat. 61.
Published: Murphy 1983
Exhibited: Sao Paulo Biennale, 1983; Nieman-Marcus Australian Festival, Dallas and San Francisco, 1986–87
(Not in exhibition.)

63 / Fig. 176

Pattern in Sand, 1980

Shorty Lungkarda Jungarrayi (ca. 1920–1987), Central Australia
Acrylic on board, 66 × 61 cm, Mrs. Douglas Carnegie O. A. M. and Sir Roderick Carnegie

The Dreaming story for this painting is unknown, but it is similar to others painted by the artist, which are of Goanna Dreaming.
Exhibited: National Gallery of Victoria, 1988

64 / Fig. 90

Two Men Dreaming at Kulunjarranya, 1984

Tommy Lowry Japaljarri (ca. 1935–1987), Central Australia
Acrylic on canvas, 121.5 × 183 cm, Duncan Kentish

The country depicted in this painting is southwest of Kintore. Two ancestral Watikujarra (two men) who were *nangkaris*, or traditional Aboriginal doctors, were traveling in the area. They found some *minykulpa* (very strong native tobacco) and sat down on some sandhills to eat it. It was so strong that they died, sprawled out on their backs with their legs wide apart on the sand. Their bodies began to urinate. The urine flow was so great that the ground became saturated and a great salt lake was formed. The lake exists today and is called Kumpukurra (bad urine). After the lake was formed the Two Men came to life and traveled over this area, having further adventures. The large roundels are the lakes; the circle at the bottom left with surrounding oblong lines is the tobacco plant.

65 / Fig. 91

Witchetty Grub Dreaming at Mt. Zeil, 1986

Theo Brown Jakamarra (b. ca. 1939), Central Australia
Acrylic on canvas, 122.5 × 122.5 cm (A65165)

This painting concerns a myth associated with Maku (Witchetty Grub) Dreaming at Lajarrka, or Mt. Zeil, the highest mountain in the MacDonnell Ranges. The Dreaming ancestor stopped at this site on his way west from the Alice Springs area. The central roundel represents the site Lajarrka; the small crescent shapes are the grubs, and the small circles, the leaves on the tree on which they feed.

66 / Fig. 141

Jila Japingka, 1987

Peter Skipper (b. ca. 1929), Central Australia
Acrylic on canvas, 181.5 × 120.5 cm, Duncan Kentish

Fitzroy Crossing, where the artist lives, is in the northwestern part of the Western Desert region. People there have only recently begun to produce acrylic paintings. In this work, Peter Skipper utilizes the joined-bar design typical of artifact decoration from the area.

The painting encodes a complex story of the origins of a series of water holes and underground streams (*jila*) focused at a place called Japingka. During the creation period, a large group of traveling ancestors of the pajarri subsection group visited the area. After being at Japingka for some time, they lay down, water welled up around them to form the *jila*, and the men then turned into a large mythological snake, who is still resident at the site.

The joined-bar forms are stylized sandhills. The central motif is Jila Japingka, with its four extensions representing other water holes and rain coming from different directions. The four small roundels at the upper right represent Pajpara, secret water holes open only to initiated men. See Fig. 141a for a description of elements in the painting.

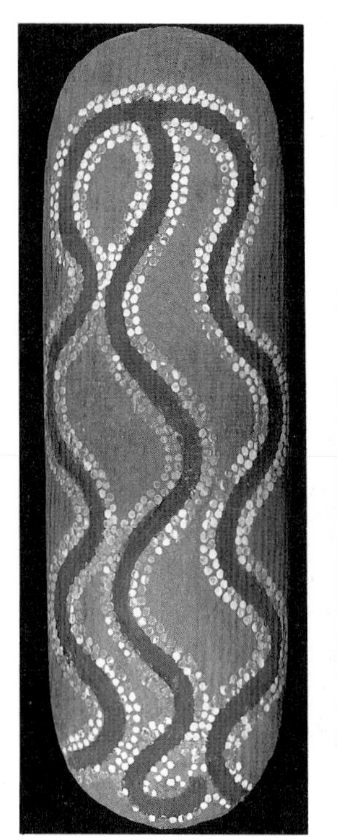

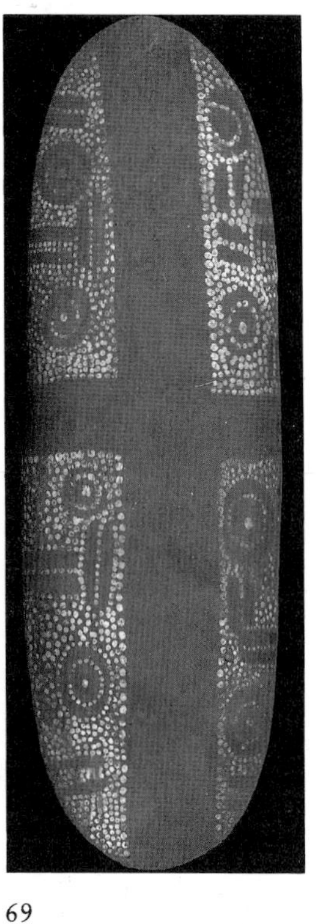

67 69 70

67 Shield, pre-1902

Artist unknown, Central Australia
Earth pigments on beanwood, 69 × 23 cm (A2208)

The design on this shield is probably of Water Dreaming. No other information is known.

68 / Fig. 218
Shield, Imbarra Dreaming, pre-1912

Artist unknown, Hermannsburg, Central Australia
Pipe clay and ochre on wood, 61 × 18 cm (A541)

This shield is from the Luritja group and was purchased at Hermannsburg mission, west of Alice Springs, probably around the turn of the century.

69 Shield, Flying Ant Dreaming, pre-1980

Artist unknown, Willowra Station, Central Australia
Earth pigments (?) on beanwood, 86.5 × 29 cm (A67051)

This shield was used in post-initiation instruction of young men of the Anmatyerre group. The design was deliberately rubbed off by Aborigines after the ceremony to desanctify it and make the image safe for all to see.

70 Shield, pre-1964

Artist unknown, Macdonald Downs, Central Australia
Earth pigments on beanwood, 69 × 25 cm (A55381)

This shield was obtained by a Lutheran missionary after a ceremony involving Alyawarra people in Central Australia.

71 / Fig. 38
Hare Wallaby Dreaming, 1976

George Jangala (b. ca. 1925), Central Australia
Acrylic on beanwood, 76 × 25 cm (A67050)

This Dreaming comes from the area of eastern Lake Mackay and runs south to Ayers Rock.

72 Spear-shield, 1855

Artist unknown, Mannum, South Australia
Wood and pipe clay, 84 × 24.5 cm (A2283)

72 73

This is a very early example of a spear-shield and shows the characteristic style of carving the designs with an engraver made from an animal tooth. The designs are composed of a combination of concentric lozenge shapes.

73 **Parrying shield,** ca. 1880

Artist unknown, Lower Murray River region, South Australia
Wood and pipe clay, 85 × 9.5 cm (A2290)

The surface of this shield is decorated with incised designs that have been filled in with white pigment. The incisions do not show the characteristic scoop patterns of the oldest shields, which were carved with an engraver made from an animal tooth. The designs consist of several separate panels on the surface of the shield, each being filled with a combination of chevron and zig-zag motifs.
Published: McCarthy 1974

74 / Fig. 222
Spear-shield, 1932

Clarence Long (ca. 1870–1941), Lower Murray River region, South Australia
Bark, ochre, and pipe clay, 67 × 26 cm (A17537)

The design and shape of this shield are based on the artist's memories of shields he had seen in his youth. Tindale commissioned this shield as part of his attempt to record and collect the material culture of the Lower Murray River region.

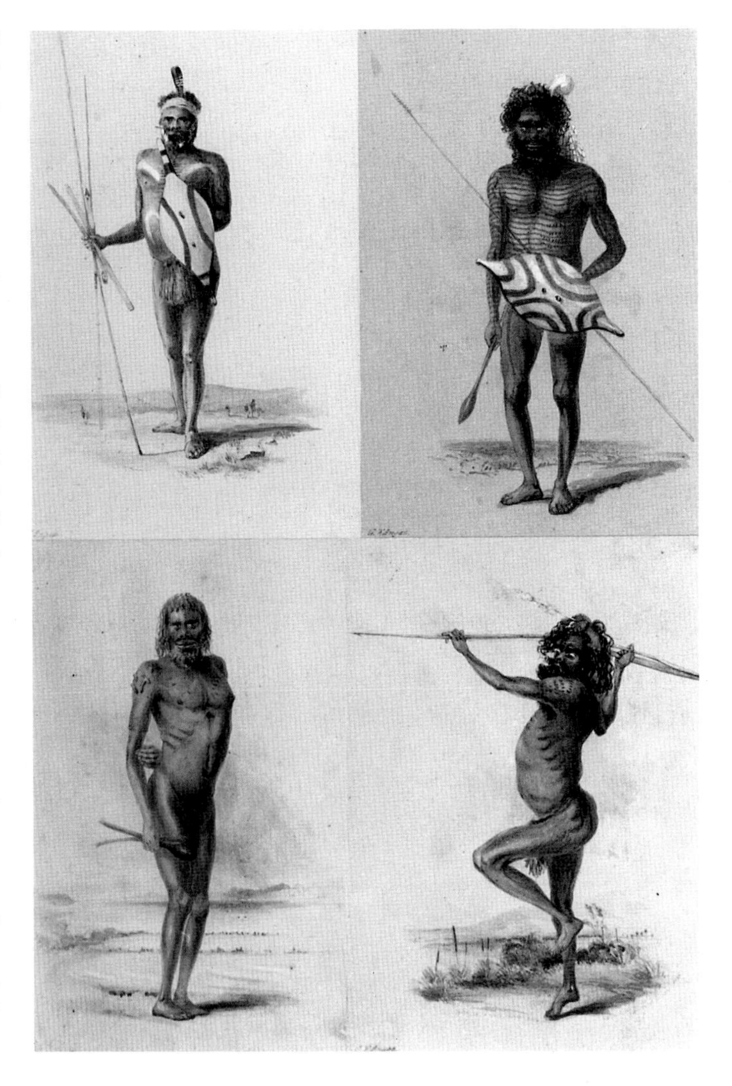

Watercolors

75 **Portraits of the Aboriginal Inhabitants,** 1844–45

George French Angas (1822–1886), Adelaide, South Australia
Watercolor on paper, composite of four images: 24.5 × 16; 24.5 × 17; 24.5 × 17.5; 24.5 × 17.5 cm (AA8/2/8)

Top left (I): Warrior of the Adelaide Tribe. An Aboriginal man decorated for a fight, with body paint of red and white ochre. He is wearing a pubic covering and a head ornament of possum-fur string, into which is stuck a tail feather of the black cockatoo. His weapons are a wooden shield, spears, spear-thrower, and clubs.
Top right (II): Warrior of Mt. Barker. Painted with stripes of red ochre, this Aboriginal man wears a head ornament of down feathers of the black swan.
Bottom left (III): Patyinni Coorung. A young Milmendura Aborigine of the Coorong coated with red ochre and fat as part of initiation rites.
Bottom right (IV): Mintalta, Coffin's Bay. A warrior of the Nauo people, near Port Lincoln, about to hurl a barbed spear.
Published: Angas 1846a; Ellis 1978; No. I, Ross 1986; No. IV, Tindale and George 1971, Baillie 1978
Exhibited: Adelaide, 1845, 1912; Sydney, 1845; London, 1846, Adelaide 1986–87

76 / Fig. 224
Native Weapons and Implements, 1844

George French Angas (1822–1886), Adelaide, South Australia
Watercolor on paper, 49 × 34 cm (AA8/2/2)

These weapons and implements used by the Aborigines of the Adelaide Plains and Hills, Lower Murray River and Lakes regions, include shields, spears, spear-throwers, clubs, and ornaments. In the center is a warrior poised to hurl a grass-tree spear with a spear-thrower.
Published: Angas 1846a; Baglin and Robinson 1968; Edwards 1972; Cooper et al. 1981; Smith 1985; Moyal 1986
Exhibited: Adelaide, 1845, 1912; Sydney, 1845; London, 1846; Melbourne and Sydney, 1981

77 / Fig. 47

Aboriginal Inhabitants, Implements, and Domestic Economy, 1844

George French Angas (1822–1886), Adelaide, South Australia
Watercolor on paper, 49 × 34 cm (AA8/2/11)

Portrayed here are shields, nets, baskets, and various utensils made by the Aborigines of the Adelaide Plains, Lower Murray and Lakes regions, and southeastern part of South Australia. In the center are two fishermen in a bark canoe on the Murray River.
Published: Angas 1846a; Baglin and Robinson 1968; Edwards 1972; Cooper et al. 1981
Exhibited: Adelaide, 1845, 1912; Sydney, 1845; London, 1846

78 / Fig. 2

Aboriginal Inhabitants, 1844–45

George French Angas (1822–1886), Adelaide, South Australia
Watercolor on paper, composite of four images: 24 × 15; 24 × 15; 24.5 × 15; 24.5 × 17 cm (AA8/2/7)

Top left (I): Natives of the Country South of Lake Hawden. The taller figure is carrying a basket characteristic of the region.
Top right (II): Nainnirmey: Murray River Boy. This youth is wearing an animal-skin cloak and carrying a throwing club.
Bottom left (III): Murray River Boys. The two boys are fishing for freshwater crayfish, probably by dangling a piece of meat as bait.
Bottom right (IV): Milliltie: A Man of the Battara Tribe, Northwest of Port Lincoln. He is wearing a kangaroo-skin cloak.
Published: No. IV, Angas 1846a; No. III, Dutton 1974
Exhibited: Adelaide, 1845, 1912; Sydney, 1845; London, 1846

Sculpture

79 / Fig. 238

Snake Skeleton Creek, ca. 1904

Artist unknown, Killalpaninna, Lake Eyre region
Wood, gypsum, and ochre, H. 43 cm (A6153)

A toa of the Diyari people depicting a creek that the Dreaming ancestor Billipilpana noticed was shaped like a snake skeleton he found on the nearby plain. The toa represents the backbone and ribs of a Snake. The red dots are trees on the lower part of the plain.
Published: Stirling and Waite 1919; Morphy 1977c; Jones and Sutton 1986
Exhibited: South Australian Museum, various times in the period 1916–1982 and 1986–87 (Cat. 2)

80 / Fig. 238

Cracks on the Dry Plain, ca. 1904

Artist unknown, Killalpaninna, Lake Eyre region
Wood, gypsum, and ochre, H. 42 cm (A6194)

A toa of the Ngamani people representing a plain on Cooper Creek that the Dreaming ancestor Darana named after Ngurluwarila, one of his Dogs. The red stripes are the cracks on the plain in the dry season and the white band, the plain.
Published: Stirling and Waite 1919; Jones and Sutton 1986
Exhibited: South Australian Museum, various times in the period 1916–1982 and 1986–87 (Cat. 29)

81 / Fig. 238

Where Two Creeks Join, ca. 1904

Artist unknown, Killalpaninna, Lake Eyre region
Wood, gypsum, vegetable fiber string, and ochre, H. 48 cm (A6146)

A toa of the Wangkangurru people showing the Wirkaripudla plain where two creeks join, which was discovered by the Dreaming ancestor Godagodana. The white tip of the toa represents the plain; the red dots, the stones lying on the plain; the yellow body of the toa, the soil of the plain; and the black stripes, the two joined creeks.
Published: Stirling and Waite 1919; Jones and Sutton 1986
Exhibited: South Australian Museum, various times in the period 1916–1982 and 1986–87 (Cat. 41)

82 / Fig. 238

Sleeping Emu, ca. 1904

Artist unknown, Killalpaninna, Lake Eyre region
Wood, gypsum, and ochre, H. 57 cm (A6150)

A Diyari toa representing a place where the Dreaming ancestor Karuwontirina once saw two Emus sleeping behind a bush. The toa depicts an Emu; the yellow dots represent its ribs.
Published: Stirling and Waite 1919; Morphy 1977c; Jones and Sutton 1986
Exhibited: South Australian Museum, various times in the period 1916–1982 and 1986–87 (Cat. 76)

83 / Fig. 238

Wild Ducks Quacking, ca. 1904

Artist unknown, Killalpaninna, Lake Eyre region
Wood, gypsum, and ochre, H. 29.3 cm (A6478)

A Diyari toa of a plain where the Dreaming ancestor Kirlawilina once saw two wild Ducks opening their beaks to quack. The toa, in the form of a Duck's head, represents the plain.
Published: Stirling and Waite 1919; Jones and Sutton 1986; *The Adelaide Review*, March, 1986
Exhibited: South Australian Museum, various times in the period 1916–1982 and 1986–87 (Cat. 85)

84 / Fig. 238

Hill Caves where the Girls Hid, ca. 1904

Artist unknown, Killalpaninna, Lake Eyre region
Wood, gypsum, and ochre, H. 19 cm (A6241)

A Diyari toa depicting a hill where the Dreaming ancestor Kirlawilina implored his uncle to let him chase after the Girls who lived there. The toa, in the shape of a human head, represents this hill. Its eyes, mouth, and nostrils represent the hills where the Girls hid.
Published: Stirling and Waite 1919; Jones and Sutton 1986
Exhibited: South Australian Museum, various times in the period 1916–1982 and 1986–87 (Cat. 89)

85 / Fig. 238

Plucked Hair from Beards, ca. 1904

Artist unknown, Killalpaninna, Lake Eyre region
Wood, gypsum, ochre, and human hair, H. 34 cm (A6259)

A Diyari toa representing a plain (white knob) where the

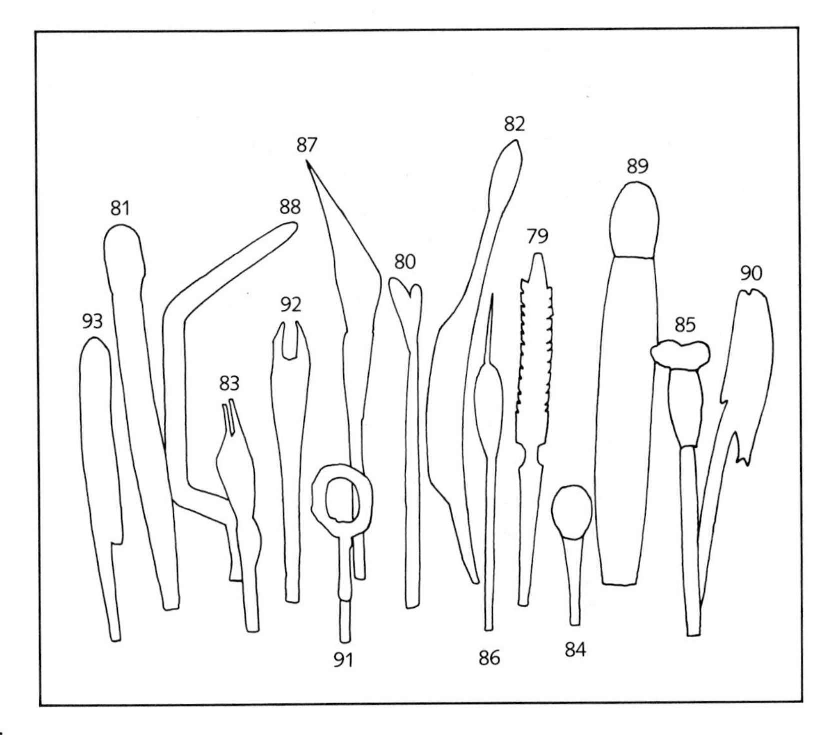

Dreaming ancestor Darana and his men plucked out the hair of their beards. Reuther recorded that this toa also depicts the plain where Kirrapajirka, in the form of a bird, lost his tail feathers.
Published: Stirling and Waite 1919; Jones and Sutton 1986
Exhibited: South Australian Museum, various times in the period 1916–1982 and 1986–87 (Cat. 96)

86 / Fig. 238

Prickly Bushes on the Plain, ca. 1904

Artist unknown, Killalpaninna, Lake Eyre region
Wood, gypsum, ochre, and bone, H. 38 cm (A6182)

A Diyari toa depicting a plain (bulbous section) overgrown with prickly Palpuru bushes (red dots), where the Dreaming ancestor Mardabuluna camped. He found people there who used finely pointed emu bones to extract prickles from their feet.
Published: Stirling and Waite 1919; Jones and Sutton 1986
Exhibited: South Australian Museum, various times in the period 1916–1982 and 1986–87 (Cat. 135)

87 / Fig. 238

Pelicans Standing, ca. 1904

Artist unknown, Killalpaninna, Lake Eyre region
Wood, gypsum, and ochre, H. 52.5 cm (A6117)

The toa of the Thirrari people, representing a lake where the Dreaming ancestor Mandramankana once saw many Pelicans standing. The top of the toa depicts a Pelican's head; the white band represents the lake.
Published: Stirling and Waite 1919; Morphy 1977c; Jones and Sutton 1986; *The Adelaide Review*, March 1986
Exhibited: South Australian Museum, various times in the period 1916–1982 and 1986–87 (Cat. 124)

88 / Fig. 238

Bends in Cooper Creek, ca. 1904

Artist unknown, Killalpaninna, Lake Eyre region
Wood, gypsum, and ochre, H. 47 cm (A6149)

A Thirrari toa representing a crooked part of Cooper Creek that the Dreaming ancestor Patjalina noticed on his travels. The white dots are gum trees standing in the bed of the creek.
Published: Stirling and Waite 1919; Jones and Sutton 1986
Exhibited: South Australian Museum, various times in the period 1916–1982 and 1986–87 (Cat. 216)

89 / Fig. 238

Deep Waterhole on Cooper Creek, ca. 1904

Artist unknown, Killapaninna, Lake Eyre region
Wood, gypsum, and ochre, H. 51.5 cm (A6134)

A Thirrari toa of a sandhill on Cooper Creek where Patjalina went while hunting. The white knob and the dots on it represent the sandhill covered with bushes; the black lateral stripe, a deep water hole at the base of the sandhill, and the black vertical stripe, Cooper Creek. The dots surrounding the vertical stripe depict gum trees growing in the sand (yellow border) around the creek.
Published: Stirling and Waite 1919; Jones and Sutton 1986
Exhibited: South Australian Museum, various times in the period 1916–1982 and 1986–87 (Cat. 228)

90 / Fig. 238

Fish Dead from Brackish Water, ca. 1904

Artist unknown, Killalpaninna, Lake Eyre region
Wood and ochre, H. 39.3 cm (A6213)

A Diyari toa representing the many dying fish that the Dreaming ancestor Pitikipana once found at Lake Kirlawilpa (Killalpaninna, site of the Lutheran mission). The water had become too brackish for the fish, and Pitikipana gathered them up and spread them on the shore to dry in the sun.
Published: Stirling and Waite 1919; Morphy 1977c; Jones and Sutton 1986
Exhibited: South Australian Museum, various times in the period 1916–1982 and 1986–87 (Cat. 268)

91 / Figs. 35, 238

Plain Ringed by Sandhill, ca. 1904

Artist unknown, Killalpaninna, Lake Eyre region
Wood, reeds, vegetable fiber string, and gypsum, H. 22 cm (A6245)

A Diyari toa depicting a small plain, ringed by a sandhill, where the two Dreaming ancestors, the Putantara, camped. Reuther noted that this site was used as a camping place after rain had fallen.
Published: Stirling and Waite 1919; Jones and Sutton 1986
Exhibited: South Australian Museum, various times in the period 1916–1982 and 1986–87 (Cat. 276)

92 / Fig. 238

Hero Dead with Mouth Agape, ca. 1904

Artist unknown, Killalpaninna, Lake Eyre region
Wood and ochre, H. 33 cm (A6277)

A Wangkangurru toa depicting the plain where the Dreaming hero Wadlulana died with his mouth open, like a yawning man. A broken tree trunk on this plain symbolized this event and was avoided by Aborigines in Reuther's time. The white knob represents the plain overgrown with bushes (red dots).
Published: Stirling and Waite 1919; Jones and Sutton 1986
Exhibited: South Australian Museum, various times in the period 1916–1982 and 1986–87 (Cat. 309)

93 / Fig. 238

The Cracked Bowl, ca. 1904

Artist unknown, Killalpaninna, Lake Eyre region
Wood and ochre, H. 36 cm (A6287)

A Diyari toa representing a plain where the Dreaming ancestor Wittimarkani gathered grass seed in her wooden bowl. As she placed the bowl on her hip to carry it back to camp, it slipped to the ground and cracked. The red stripes represent the cracks in the bowl and on the plain itself, and the dots symbolize the bushes or holes in the ground.

Published: Stirling and Waite 1919; Jones and Sutton 1986
Exhibited: South Australian Museum, various times in the period 1916–1982 and 1986–87 (Cat. 348)

94 / Fig. 239

Big Eater, ca. 1904

Artist unknown, Killalpaninna, Lake Eyre region
Spinifex resin and gypsum, L. 20.5 cm (A68461)

A female Dog belonging to Darana, the Dreaming ancestor of the drought.
Published: von Leonhardi 1908; Jones and Sutton 1986
Exhibited: South Australian Museum, 1986–87 (Cat. 424)

95 / Fig. 239

Color of White Stone, ca. 1904

Artist unknown, Killalpaninna, Lake Eyre region
Spinifex resin and ochre, L. 19.3 cm (A68457)

A Dog belonging to the Dreaming ancestor Pirnaworankana.
Published: von Leonhardi 1908; Jones and Sutton 1986
Exhibited: South Australian Museum, 1986–87 (Cat. 427)

96 **Charm for Finding Lost Dogs,** ca. 1904

Elias Palkalina (ca. 1856–ca. 1930), Killalpaninna, Lake Eyre region
Wood and spinifex resin, H. 59 cm (A6056)

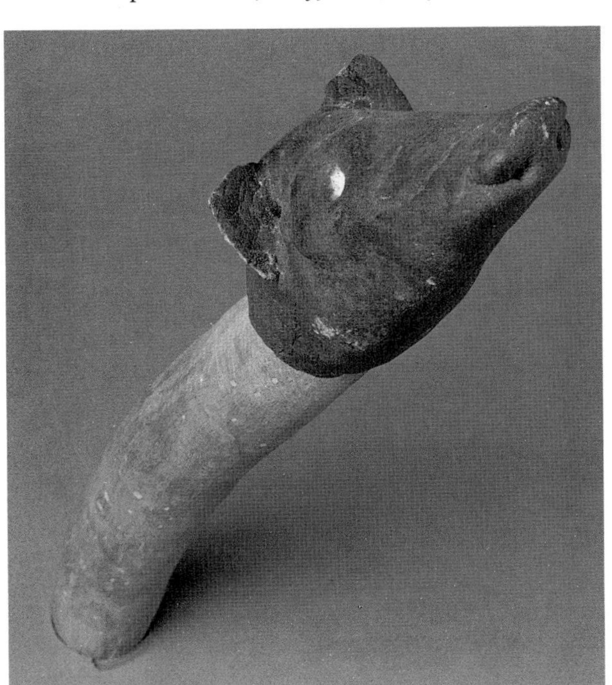

Reuther wrote of this object: "When a dog has run away, this sign is set up in the vicinity of the camp to the accompaniment of a sacred ceremonial song. It is believed that the dog will then come back again." (Reuther 1981 vol. 12: 211)
Published: von Leonhardi 1908

97 / Fig. 18

Saarra, the Seagull Hero, 1962

Artist unknown, Western Cape York Peninsula
Wood, ochre, charcoal, nails, burlap, and leather, 132.5 × 46 cm, National Museum of Australia (1985.100.1)

Saarra (also known as Shivri and Chivirri) is a hero figure traveling north to Torres Strait, moving along Western Cape York Peninsula. He is Seagull. Seagulls go north each year to nest in Torres Strait. Saarra is particularly associated with the area north of Aurukun, around Weipa and Mapoon. A detailed version of the story from a Mapoon perspective is given in McConnel 1957:20–27; a more southern version appears in McCarthy 1978.
Published: Cooper et al. 1981
Exhibited: *Aboriginal Australia* traveling exhibition, 1981

98 / Fig. 19

Bonefish Man from Archer River, 1962

Arthur Pambegan, Jr. (b. 1936), Western Cape York Peninsula
Wood, nails, bark, cockatoo feathers, bush string, ochre, and black pigment, 72 × 56 cm, National Museum of Australia (1985.100.24)

This is Bonefish (Bony Bream), spearing bonefish at night by holding aloft a bark torch. The totemic center for Bonefish is Walkaln-aw, on the Archer River. In this representation Bonefish wears the distinctive horizontally banded ceremonial paint of the Winchanam ceremony—a ceremony that is especially associated with the Archer River and its peoples, even though an initiation ceremony under this same title is widespread in the region. The red, white, and black horizontal stripes, similar to the paint worn by dancers in the ceremony, derive from the Peewee bird. A dispute between Bonefish and his sister Mangrove (an edible variety) over who should cook some meat resulted in her hitting him with a yamstick and his spearing her in the head, before they separately descended into the earth to create their respective totemic centers. For a more detailed version of this story, see McConnel 1957:38–41.
Published: Berndt, Berndt, and Stanton 1982

99 / Fig. 21

The Older Apalach Brother, 1962

Attributed to Uki Pamulkan (1912–1980) and Don Tybingoompa (b. 1918), Western Cape York Peninsula
Wood, nails, ochre, horsehair(?), and xanthorrhea(?) resin or beeswax, 118.5 × 40 cm, National Museum of Australia (1985.100.48)

See Cat. 100.

100 / Fig. 21

The Younger Apalach Brother, 1962

Attributed to Uki Pamulkan (1912–1980) and Don Tybingoompa (b. 1918), Western Cape York Peninsula
Wood, nails, and ochre, 84.5 × 19.5 cm, National Museum of Australia (1985.100.49)

The two Apalach men, sometimes said to be brothers, traveled south from Love River to Kendall River, discovering the totemic centers, creating the clan estates and their clans, and bestowing various languages on the clans' members. They eventually fought and split up, one returning to the north, the other traveling further south. The full version of their name is Pungk-Apalach (Knees-Clear Water, in Wik-Ngathan) or Pul-Uchan (Two Initiates, in Wik-Mungkan). Apalach (Clear Water) refers to the settling of sediments in the sea at the end of the wet season, when it becomes easier to see and spear fish and rays. The sparkling of this clear water is marked by dots both on this sculpture and on the bodies of performers of the associated ceremony. The ceremony, and therefore the people from the area between Love River and the north side of Kendall River, are also known as Apalach. Apalach dots are distinguished from Winchanam (Archer River) dots by being smaller.

The use of the term *pungk* (knees) is probably a reference to the fact that novices in Uchanam (Ochangan-tharran) ceremony have to crawl like infants when they emerge reborn as men—*uchan*, initiate, is cognate with a term for *knee* in other Aboriginal languages. Marking of knees is also generally pronounced in sculptures of this region. See text pp. 27–29 and Sutton 1978, Appendix 2.
Published: Cooper et al. 1981
Exhibited: *Aboriginal Australia* traveling exhibition, 1981

101 / Fig. 22

Shark from Cape Keerweer, 1962

Lesley Walmbeng (1941–1971), Western Cape York Peninsula
Wood, ochre, and plastic buttons(?), 30 × 61.5 cm, National Museum of Australia (1985.100.76)

This is a forepart of Freshwater Shark, focus of a major totemic cult ceremony, local mythology, and clan totemism in the Cape Keerweer area. Several Shark totemic centers exist in the Cape Keerweer area. Shark is a significant feature of the Apalach mythology and ceremony, which link clans of the area between Love River and Kendall River. The dotting on the Shark is that of Apalach (Clear Water) and is the same as that painted on performers in this ceremony. This type of estuarine shark is a food source; there are many traditional regulations and prohibitions concerning its preparation and consumption, although some of these restrictions have been relaxed in recent times.

102 / Fig. 23

Crippled Boy of Thaa'puunt, 1962

Jackson Woolla (b. 1930), Western Cape York Peninsula
Wood, ochre, nails, glass beads, bone, horsehair, and resin or beeswax, 74.5 × 21.5 cm, National Museum of Australia (1985.100.63)

A little Boy lived on the coast at Pupathun, a totemic center for Children in the lower Kendall River area. His ceremony was Puch (Cloudy Water), and his language Wik-Keyangan. He came into conflict with the Yamstick people and went inland to the middle Kendall River, taking Theelichany (Shark) with them. He went to a forbidden place and thus became crippled, hence his shape. He lives in a swamp called Thaa'puunt(iy), in the mangroves on the middle Kendall. Totemic centers for Children and for Shark are both there. Note that the knees on this figure are small panels of wood actually nailed onto the body of the sculpture.
Published: Berndt and Phillips 1973; Cooper et al. 1981
Exhibited: *Aboriginal Australia* traveling exhibition, 1981

103 / Fig. 24

Wallaby from Thawungadha, 1962

Attributed to George Ngallametta (1941–1986), assisted by MacNaught Ngallametta (b. 1938) and Joe Ngallametta (b. 1945), Western Cape York Peninsula
Wood, ochre, nails, and resin, 68 × 11 cm, National Museum of Australia (1985.100.7)

This Wallaby belongs to the site Thawungadha (also known as Thaa'kungath) on the lower Holroyd River. The ceremony in which it is featured is Wanam, a regional cult ceremony similar to Chivirri, Winchanam, Apalach, and Puch in areas further north. See von Sturmer 1978 for further details.
Published: Cooper et al. 1981
Exhibited: *Aboriginal Australia* traveling exhibition, 1981

BIOGRAPHIES OF THE ARTISTS

Many of the works listed in the Catalogue have no known makers. Even where the names of artists are available, records of their lives vary greatly in the amount and quality of information provided. People born beyond the reach of missions or other settlements, for example, usually have no birthdate recorded. Biographies are given only for those artists whose works appear in the exhibition.

Many of the biographical classifications used here are peculiar to Aboriginal Australia or to particular regions of the country. They are important to the artists' identities as members of groups or social categories that in part define their position within Aboriginal society. While some of the information is derived from other published works on Aboriginal art, much of it is the result of primary investigations by the authors (North Australia: Peter Sutton; Central Australia: Christopher Anderson and Françoise Dussart; Elias Palkalina and G. F. Angas: Philip Jones; Clarence Long: Steven Hemming).

Format of the Biographies

Most of the artists listed have both Aboriginal and non-Aboriginal names. The most frequently used or official name appears first, followed by other known names. The artist's dates, if known, and gender appear after the name. The subsections of Western Desert painters are often cited as if they were surnames. Here, the subsection is listed alphabetically, with a cross reference to the main entry under the artist's non-subsection name. The classifications used in the biographies are defined as follows:

Subsection One of eight basic divisions of society in much of northern and Central Australia. These divisions are mainly relevant to ceremonial organization and to kinship groupings and their rules governing interaction between kin.

Also cited as Misspelled names or other names not considered by the authors to be valid or established alternatives. In some cases, these names are linguistically more accurate than the established spellings.

Residence Most frequent home base of artist, where known. Many artists move frequently between several nearby residential centers. When the actual residence is not known, the collection point of the work is given.

Region The broad cultural region of origin of the artist.

Country Clan land or set of sites to which the person has spiritual and historic ties.

Moiety One of two basic divisions of society (here the patrimoiety, unless matrimoiety is specified; this variation depends on region). This division is important for marriage rules and ceremonial organization. In most Aboriginal moiety systems, one's spouse must come from the opposite moiety, not from one's own. Semimoiety is a division equivalent to two halves of a moiety, or the combination of two pairs of subsections.

Clan In much, but not all, of Aboriginal Australia, the basic land-holding descent group. The Western Arnhem Land variation (*kunmokurrkurr*) is specified, where known. In North East Arnhem Land the clan is also the language group.

Language The person's language of formal affiliation, thus in many areas also the language-group identity of the person (frequently, "tribe"). The term does not mean simply "language spoken."

Totems Entities with whose spiritual essence a person is identified—for example, the Dreamings of a clan, or the key Dreaming on whose track one has been conceived. Precise significance varies by region.

Anatjari (M, b. ca. 1929)
Subsection: jampijinpa
Also cited as Anitjari Tjampitjinpa, Anatjari Number One
Residence: Kiwirrkura, outstation of Kintore
Region: Central Australia
Country: south of Jupiter Well, Western Australia
Language: Pintupi

Acrylic painter

Angas, George French (M, 1822–1886)
Residence: South Australia, New South Wales

Watercolorist. Angas was trained in Britain as a natural history artist and traveled to South Australia in 1844. He spent six months making watercolor drawings of Adelaide and Lower Murray River Aborigines and landscapes. Angas published and exhibited watercolors of Australia and New Zealand in London in 1846. In 1847 he visited South Africa and published another volume of drawings. His interest in natural history led to his appointment as Secretary of the Australian Museum, Sydney, from 1853 to 1860.

Big Tom (Malummarringita, Tawarlawi, Puririlimpirlila; M, 1880–1958)
Also cited as Malu-nari-nida
Residence: Milikapiti (Snake Bay) in 1954
Region: Melville Island
Country: Malawuwila
Language: Tiwi
Totem (matrilineal): Housefly (Mantupani)

Painter who produced a number of works on bark at Mountford's request in 1954.

Brown, Theo (M, b. ca. 1939)
Subsection: jakamarra
Residence: Papunya and Ambangara outstation
Region: Central Australia
Country: Mt. Zeil area
Language: Aranda
Totem: Witchetty Grub

Acrylic painter

Bukurlatjpi, Liwukang (M, b. ca. 1927)
Also cited as Lewukang
Residence: Mainly Galiwin'ku (Elcho Island) and homeland center called Dholtji
Region: North East Arnhem Land
Moiety: Yirritja
Clan: Warramiri (dialect group: Djaangu)

Bark painter

Darby (M, b. ca. 1910)
Subsection: jampijinpa
Residence: Yuendumu
Region: Central Australia
Country: Ngarliyikirlangu, north of Yuendumu
Language: Warlpiri
Totems: Emu, Bandicoot

Acrylic painter

Djawida (M, b. ca. 1935)
Subsection: nawakadj (?)
Also cited as Djoyita, Jawiada, Djawida Nargorlgorle
Residence: Namugardabu, Kudjekbinj outstations
Region: Western Arnhem Land
Clan: (*kunmokurrkurr*): Djalama (?)
Language: Gunwinggu (Kunwinjku)

Bark painter. The name Jawiada on the back of Cat. 22 probably, rather than conclusively, refers to this man.

George (M, b. ca. 1925)
Subsection: jangala
Also cited as George Tjangala
Residence: Yumunyturrngu
Region: Central Australia
Country: West of Haasts Bluff
Language: Wenampa
Totems: Hare Wallaby, Acacia Seed, Fire Shield-maker

Acrylic painter

Granites, Alma (F, b. 1955)
Subsection: nungarrayi
Residence: Yuendumu
Region: Central Australia
Country: Kunajarrayi, Mt. Nicker, southwest of Yuendumu
Language: Warlpiri
Totems: Snake, Witchetty Grub

Acrylic painter

Granites, Judy (F, b. 1934)
Subsection: nampijinpa
Residence: Yuendumu
Region: Central Australia
Country: Warnipiyi; Warlukurlangu, southwest of Yuendumu
Language: Warlpiri
Totems: Creeper, Water, Fire, Flying Ant

Acrylic painter

Granites, Robin (M, b. 1952)
Subsection: japanangka
Residence: Yuendumu
Region: Central Australia
Country: The Granites, northwest of Yuendumu
Language: Warlpiri

Acrylic painter

Gubargu, Mick, (M, b. 1925)
Subsection: balang
Also cited as Kubarku, Kubarkku, Ubargu
Residence: Gubumi
Region: Western Arnhem Land
Moiety: Duwa
Clan (kunmokurrkurr): Kulmarru
Language: Gunwinggu (Kunwinjku)

Bark painter

Gumarna, Birrikitji (M, ca. 1898–1982)
Also cited as Beritjitji, Birigitji
Residence: Yirrkala, Garngarn
Region: North East Arnhem Land
Country: Garngarn
Moiety: Yirritja
Clan: bottom Dharlwangu (Nungbururndi) (dialect group: Dhay'yi)

Bark painter

Hilda (F, b. ca. 1941)
Subsection: napaljarri
Residence: Yuendumu
Region: Central Australia
Country: Coniston Station and Mt. Allan area
Language: Warlpiri/Anmatyerre
Totems: Sugarleaf, Kangaroo

Acrylic painter

Jakamarra, see Brown, Theo; Nelson, Michael

Jampijinpa, see Anatjari; Darby; Woods, Tim

Jangala, see Uta Uta

Japaljarri, see Leura, Tim; Lowry, Tommy; Namarari, Mick; Possum, Clifford; Sims, Paddy; Stewart, Cookie

Japanangka, see Granites, Robin

Japangardi, see Timmy

Jungarrayi, see Davis, Peter; Lungkarda, Shorty; Spencer, Jimija

Jupurrurla, see Nelson, Paddy; Warangula, Johnny

Kennedy, Lucy (F, b. ca. 1926)
Subsection: napaljarri
Residence: Yuendumu
Region: Central Australia
Country: Coniston Station and Mt. Allan area
Language: Warlpiri/Anmatyerre
Totems: Sugarleaf, Kangaroo

Acrylic painter

Lady (F, b. ca. 1933)
Subsection: nungarrayi
Residence: Yuendumu
Region: Central Australia
Country: Jila, Chilla Well, northwest of Yuendumu
Language: Warlpiri
Totem: Hare Wallaby

Acrylic painter

Leura, Tim (M, ca. 1939–1984)
Subsection: japaljarri
Also cited as Tim Leurah Tjapaltjarri, Timmy Leura Tjapaltjarri
Residence: Napperby Station and Papunya
Region: Central Australia
Country: Nurta, area on Napperby Creek
Language: Anmatyerre
Totems: Possum, Yam, Fire

Acrylic painter

Long, Clarence (Milerum; M, ca. 1870–1941)
Residence: Point McLeay, South Australia
Region: Lower Murray River, South Australia
Country: Coorong, South Australia
Language: Tangane
Totem: White-faced Heron

Shield-maker. One of the last initiated men of the Lower Murray region, Long worked with Norman Tindale of the South Australian Museum recording many aspects of Lower Murray Aboriginal culture and producing representative artifacts from the area.

Lowry, Tommy (M, ca. 1935–1987)
Subsection: japaljarri
Also cited as Tommy Larry Tjapaltjarri
Residence: Kiwirrkura, outstation of Kintore
Region: Central Australia
Country: Patjar, Clutterbuck Hills, far to the southwest of Kintore
Language: Pintupi, Ngardajarra
Totem: Two Men

Acrylic painter

Lungkarda, Shorty (M, ca. 1920–1987)
Subsection: jungarrayi
Also cited as Shorty Lungkata Tjungarrayi
Residence: Papunya, Kintore
Region: Central Australia
Country: south of Lake MacDonald
Language: Pintupi
Totem: Blue-tongue Lizard

Acrylic painter

Malangi, David (Daymirringu; M, b. 1927)
Residence: Yathalamarra, via Ramingining
Region: Central Arnhem Land
Clan: Manharrngu (other clan identifications recorded: Liyagalawumirri and Urgiganjdjar)
Language: Djinang
Moiety: Dhuwa

Bark painter whose work was used as the basis of part of the design of the Australian dollar note in 1966 (see Bennett 1980). Malangi's works were collected and published by Kupka 1965 and Allen 1975; also see Ward 1986, McDonald 1986.

Mamarika, Minimini (M, 1900–1972)
Also cited as Mini-mini, minimini
Residence: Umbakumba in 1948
Region: Groote Eylandt
Clan: Warnindilyakwa
Language: Anindilyakwa
Totems: Rose 1960:378 records that his totems were "mamariga" and "angandiljuba," the same as those of "dajamunda" (see Taimundu)

Bark painter. A prolific artist who is well represented in collections made by Adam 1951:164 and Mountford 1956a:13 (also see Gunn 1973).

Marawili, Wakuthi (M, b. 1921, some sources give ca. 1930)
Residence: Yirrkala area
Region: North East Arnhem Land
Country: Baniyala
Moiety: Yirritja
Clan: Mardarrpa (dialect group: Dhuwala)

Bark painter

Marika, Mawalan (M, 1908–1967)
Also cited as Mauwulan, Mawalung
Residence: Yirrkala during 1950s, 1960s
Region: North East Arnhem Land
Country: Yalangbara
Moiety: Dhuwa
Clan: Rirratjingu (dialect group: Dhaangu)

Well-known bark painter in his lifetime and father of a number of other artists, all of whom have borne the surname Marika.

Marruwani (M, 1916–after 1954)
Also cited as Malony, Maruwani
Residence: Milikapiti (Snake Bay) in 1954
Region: Melville Island
Country: Thamalampi (also given as Mantiyupi)
Totem (matrilineal): Housefly (Mantupani, also given as Yilupurrungwari and Kutampini)
Language: Tiwi

Painted on bark for Mountford in 1954. Born at Cockle Point, Melville Island.

Mary (F, b. ca. 1942)
Subsection: nungarrayi
Residence: Yuendumu
Region: Central Australia
Country: Yarrunkanyi, Mt. Hardy, west of Yuendumu
Language: Warlpiri
Totems: Hare Wallaby, Initiated Man

Acrylic painter

Maymurru, Narritjin (M, 1922–1982)
Also cited as Naradin
Residence: Yirrkala, Djarrakpi
Region: North East Arnhem Land
Country: Djarrakpi
Moiety: Yirritja
Clan: Manggalili (dialect group: Dhuwala)

Eminent bark painter and maker of painted sculptures. Artist in residence, Australian National University 1978. Member of a family of active painters, among them his son Banapana.

Mowandjul, John (M, b. 1952)
Subsection: balang
Also cited as Mawundjal, Mawurndjurl, Mawandjul, Mowundjal
Residence: Momeka
Region: Western Arnhem Land
Moiety: Duwa
Clan: Kurulk
Language: Kunkurulk (also cited as Gunwinggu [Kunwinjku])

Bark painter

Nabegeyo, Bilinyarra (M, b. ca. 1920)
Subsection: nakangila
Also cited as Bilinjara, Billinyara, Bilinjarra Nabekeyo, Bob Bilinyarra Nabegeyo
Residence: Oenpelli area (for example, Kalawadjbarra)
Country: Mandilbareng
Matrimoiety: Namardku
Patrimoiety: Yirritja
Semimoiety: Yarrikarnkurrh
Clan (kunmokurrkurr): Djalama
Language: Gunwinggu (Kunwinjku)

Bark painter. Remembers the 1948 expedition on which Mountford collected numerous bark paintings at Oenpelli. Member of a family of painters, including his sons Bruce and Mukguddu.

Namarari, Mick (M, b. ca. 1930)
Subsection: japaljarri
Also cited as Mick Numerari Tjapaltjarri, Mick Numieri Tjpaltjari, Mick Namari
Residence: Nyunmanu, outstation of Kintore
Region: Central Australia
Country: Nyunmanu, Munpi area
Language: Pintupi
Totem: Kangaroo

Acrylic painter

Nampijinpa, see Granites, Judy

Nangala, see Tilo

Nangulay, Dick (also Ngulayngulay; M, b. 1920)
Subsection: nawakadj (also given as nawamud)
Also cited as Nguleingulei, Ngulaiengulai, Murrumurru
Residence: Marlgawo, Gumarrirnbang, Oenpelli, Gurruhgurr
Region: Western Arnhem Land
Country: Lohrlo, also given as Kukadjerri, Liverpool River Plateau, and as Yaymini
Matrimoiety: Namardku
Semimoiety: Yarrikarnkurrh
Clan (kunmokurrkurr): Bularlhdja
Language: Dangbon (also given as Gunwinggu [Kunwinjku])

Bark painter. He has worked as a crocodile shooter and on a timber camp in the Jim Jim area. Listed in McDonald 1986.

Napaljarri, see Hilda; Kennedy, Lucy; Ruth

Nelson, Michael (M, b. 1946)
Subsection: jakamarra
Residence: Papunya
Region: Central Australia
Country: Mt. Singleton, west of Yuendumu
Language: Warlpiri/Luritja
Totems: Possum, Snake, Two Kangaroos, Flying Ant, Yam

See Art Gallery of New South Wales 1986:273 and Nairne 1987:217–19.

Nelson, Paddy (M, b. ca. 1925)
Subsection: jupurrurla
Residence: Yuendumu
Region: Central Australia
Country: Yumurrpa to Warrikinpiri area, southwest of Yuendumu
Language: Warlpiri
Totems: Wild Yam, Snake

Acrylic painter

Ngallametta, George (M, 1941–1986)
Also cited as Wanycham, Ngalamata, Minpadya, Ngallapoorgum
Residence: Aurukun
Region: Western Cape York Peninsula
Country: Thawungadha, Holroyd River area
Language: Kugu-Uwanh
Totems: Jackass (Konkon, Chinpu), Jewfish (Nga'a Umbi), Scrub Turkey (Minh Thukan), Jabiru (Minh Monte)

George, MacNaught, and Joe Ngallametta had the same parents and thus the same Aboriginal clan names and the same country and totemic interests in the Holroyd River area of Western Cape York Peninsula. Their regional ritual affiliation is Wanam.

Ngallametta, Joe (M, b. 1945)

See George Ngallametta for details. A preeminent exponent of Wanam ritual in the Aurukun area of Western Cape York Peninsula.

Ngallametta, MacNaught (M, b. 1938)

See George Ngallametta for details. A major exponent of sacred dancing in Western Cape York Peninsula.

Nungarrayi, see Granites, Alma; Lady; Mary

Palkalina, Elias (M, ca. 1856–ca. 1930)
Residence: Killalpaninna Mission, Lake Eyre in 1886–ca. 1905
Region: Northeastern South Australia
Language: Diyari

Palkalina was literate and a baptized Christian. He is recorded as the maker of the Dog Charm (Cat. 96) and probably also made several toas.

Pambegan, Arthur Koo'ekka, Sr. (M, 1895–1972)
Residence: Aurukun
Region: Western Cape York Peninsula
Country: Archer River area
Language: Wik-Mungkan
Totem: Willy Wagtail

Occasional sculptor and senior celebrant in Winchanam ceremony. He was a major informant for anthropologist Ursula McConnel. See McConnel 1957.

Pambegan, Arthur Koo'ekka, Jr. (M, b. 1936)

See Arthur Pambegan, Sr., for details. Occasional sculptor, who with his father made a number of the sculptures collected at Aurukun in 1962 by Frederick McCarthy, including the rack of Bonefish and the Flying Foxes (not in this exhibition). Senior celebrant for Winchanam ceremony.

Pamulkan, Uki (M, 1912–1980)
Also cited as Pam-alkanha, Ku'miitha, Thaypan-kumpa, Koomeeta, Merkella
Residence: Aurukun
Region: Western Cape York Peninsula
Country: Ithananga area, lower Knox River
Language: Wik-Ngatharra
Totems: Taipan (Thaypana, a Snake), Rainbow (Ngooya), Dog (Ku'a)

Occasional sculptor. Apalach ceremonial group and clansman of Don Tybingoompa (see below).

Possum, Clifford (M, b. ca. 1943)
Subsection: japaljarri
Residence: Ambanghara outstation near Papunya
Region: Central Australia
Country: Napperby Creek area
Language: Anmatyerre
Totems: Possum, Fire, Water, Kangaroo, Snake

Acrylic painter

Ruth (F, b. ca. 1940)
Subsection: napaljarri
Residence: Yuendumu
Region: Central Australia
Country: Coniston Station and Mt. Allan area
Language: Warlpiri/Anmatyerre
Totems: Sugarleaf, Kangaroo

Acrylic painter

Sims, Paddy (M, b. ca. 1916)
Subsection: japaljarri
Residence: Yuendumu
Region: Central Australia
Country: Kunajarrayi, Mt. Nicker, southwest of Yuendumu
Language: Warlpiri
Totems: Snake, Witchetty Grub, Star, Initiated Man

Acrylic painter

Skipper, Peter (M, b. ca. 1929)
Residence: Fitzroy Crossing
Region: Western Australia
Country: Japingka/Mangkajakura sites area in Great Sandy Desert, southeast of Fitzroy Crossing
Language: Walmadjarri
Totem: Barn Owl

Acrylic painter

Stewart, Cookie (M, b. ca. 1940)
Subsection: japaljarri
Also cited as Paddy
Residence: Yuendumu
Region: Central Australia
Country: Mt. Allan and Mt. Dennison areas
Language: Warlpiri/Anmatyerre
Totems: Kangaroo, Seed, Possum

Acrylic painter

Taimundu (M, ca. 1879–1940s)
Also cited as dajamunda
Residence: Yetiba (Yadikba) in 1922
Region: Groote Eylandt
Country: "dalimbo" (Rose 1960)
Moiety: No. 2
Language: Anindilyakwa
Totems: "mamariga," "angandiljuba" (Rose 1960)

Painted on bark for Tindale at Groote Eylandt in 1922. Tindale recorded his tribe as Ingura and his country as located in the southwest of Groote Eylandt. He is shown on the left in Fig. 9. The individual in this photograph was also identified by Rose's informants in 1948 as Dan (namadjabmadja), which appears to be a mistake. They agreed with Tindale that the painter on the right is Papatama ("babaduma," see Rose 1960:207).

Tilo (F, b. 1944)
Subsection: nangala
Residence: Yuendumu
Region: Central Australia
Country: Coniston Station area and Warlukurlangu, south of Yuendumu
Language: Warlpiri
Totems: Water, Flying Ant, Fire

Acrylic painter

Timmy (M, b. ca. 1942)
Subsection: japangardi
Also cited as Timmy Payungu, Tim Pyungu Tjapangati
Residence: Kintore and Kiwirrkura outstation
Region: Central Australia
Country: Central west fringe of Lake Mackay
Language: Pintupi
Totem: Kangaroo

Acrylic painter

Tjamalampuwa (M, ca. 1895–ca. 1956)
Also cited as Tjamalampua, Jamalampua, Jamalumpua
Residence: Milikapiti (Snake Bay) in 1954
Region: Melville Island
Country: Tikalaru, Imalunap, Pukutarrantju; some sources say Thikalawila
Language: Tiwi
Totem (matrilineal): Scaly Mullet (Takaringini)

Executed a number of bark paintings for Mountford at Milikapiti in 1954. His photograph appeared in *National Geographic* magazine (Mountford 1956b). A photograph identified as "Tjamalumpua" in Mountford 1967 is not Tjamalampuwa but Summit Tipungwuti, according to those who knew both men.

Tybingoompa, Don (Korngempa; M, b. 1918)
Also cited as Thaka Don, Thaypan-kumpa, Ku'-miitha, Pam-alkanha
Residence: Aurukun and Kendall River
Region: Western Cape York Peninsula
Country: Ithananga area, lower Knox River
Language: Wik-Ngatharra
Totems: Taipan (Thaypana, a Snake), Rainbow (Ngooya), Dog (Ku'a)

Occasional sculptor for ritual purposes. Apalach ceremonial group.

Uta Uta (M, b. ca. 1920)
Subsection: jangala
Also cited as Uta Uta Tjangala, Uta Uta Tjungala, Wuta Wuta Tjangala, Uata Uata Tjangala No. 2
Residence: Kintore
Region: Central Australia
Country: Yumari, site south of Lake MacKay
Language: Pintupi
Totem: Old Man

Acrylic painter

Walmbeng, Lesley (M, 1941–1971)
Also cited as Wikmunea (Wikmanaya), Teentanycha, Kanthanya
Residence: Aurukun and Love River
Region: Western Cape York Peninsula
Country: (father's) Warpanga, Thawala-nhiina (Cape Keerweer area); (mother's) Thoekala (lower Love River)
Language: Wik-Ngatharra
Totems: Marsupial Mouse (Thiinychiinya), Freshwater Shark (Elayepanya), Spear (Kalka), Small Carpet Snake (Peela), Salmon (Kurrawa), Knee (Pungka)

Skilled wood carver. Several of the 1962 McCarthy collection pieces now in the National Museum of Australia are attributed to him. Main ritual affiliations are Apalach and Thu'a.

Warangula, Johnny (M, b. ca. 1925)
Subsection: jupurrurla
Also cited as Johnny Warrangula Tjupurrula, Johnny Warankula Tjupurrula, Johnny Warrangula Tjaparula, Johnny W. Tjupurrula, Jonny W

Residence: Papunya
Region: Central Australia
Country: Kalipinypa, north of Sandy Blight Junction
Language: Luritja
Totems: Water, Yam, Fire

Acrylic painter

Woods, Tim (M, b. ca. 1930)
Subsection: jampijinpa
Residence: Papunya in late 1970s
Language: Pitjantjtjaarra

Acrylic painter

Woolla, Jackson (M, b. 1930)
Also cited as Porelembin
Residence: Aurukun and Kendall River
Region: Western Cape York Peninsula
Country: on Kendall River, just inland
Language: Wik-Ngathana
Totem: Blowfly (Wul)

In the 1980s an active maker of weapons, small sculptures, and other items for the Aurukun craft outlet. His main ritual affiliation is Keyelpa (Pucha).

Wululu, Jimmy (Gaykamangu; M, b. 1936)
Subsection: bulany
Residence: Ramingining area
Region: Central Arnhem Land
Country: Djiliwirri
Moiety: Yirritja
Clan: Daygurrgurr
Language: Gupapuyngu (Manbirri)
Totem: Wild Honey (Niwurda)

Bark painter and sculptor

Wurramara, Dakilarra (M, d. ca. 1950)
Also cited as Banjo Takalara, Tatalara
Residence: Umbakumba in 1948
Region: Groote Eylandt
Clan: Probably Warnungangkwurrakba
Language: Anindilyakwa

Painted on bark for Mountford at Umbakumba in 1948. Possibly the man "dagalara" (Bickerton Island, totems: "jinigarga" and "jingarna" [a Snake]) identified by Rose's informants in 1948 as being in one of Tindale's 1925–26 photographs. See Rose 1960:206.

Wurramara, Manggangina (M, 1919–1984)
Also cited as Big Macka, Manganina Wurramara
Residence: Umbakumba in 1948, Angurugu at later dates
Region: Groote Eylandt
Clan: Warnungangkwurrakba
Language: Anindilyakwa

Active bark painter. Moved from the Groote Eylandt middle-period style of a few images on a wide, black ground to the late-period style of more completely filled surfaces and red-and-yellow color combination.

Yirawala (M, 1903–1976, some sources give 1894–1976)
Subsection: nabulanj
Also cited as Yirwala, Yirrwala; both phonologically more accurate than the Anglicized "Yirawala"
Residence: mainly Croker Island, also Marrkolidjban
Region: Western Arnhem Land
Country: around Marrkolidjban
Moiety: Duwa
Clan (kunmokurrkurr): Born
Language: Gunwinggu (Kunwinjku)

Probably Australia's most famous bark painter. His work was collected and promoted during his lifetime by Sandra Holmes, whose collection of 140 of Yirawala's bark paintings was purchased by the Australian National Gallery in 1976. See Holmes 1972, 1976; listed in McDonald 1986.

Yunupingu, Munggurrawuy (M, ca. 1907–1979)
Also cited as Mungeraui, Munggarawi, Munggerrawuy Yunupingu
Residence: Yirrkala area
Region: North East Arnhem Land
Moiety: Yirritja
Clan: Gumatj I (dialect group: Dhuwala)

Bark painter and father of Galarrwuy (James) Yunupingu, a famous figure in Aboriginal political and legal history since the early 1970s (see Fig. 210). Listed in McDonald 1986.

NOTES

INTRODUCTION

1. The more recent surveys include McCarthy 1974, 1979; Cooper, et al. 1981; Berndt, Berndt, and Stanton 1982; Isaacs 1984.
2. As suggested, for example, by Vivien Johnson 1987.
3. See Chapter VI. A summary of most of these aspects of the toas is found in Jones and Sutton 1986.
4. E.g. *kuruwarri* in Warlpiri (Western Desert fringe area), *dirmu* (*pirmu*) in Murrinh-Patha (Port Keats), *miny'tji* in Yolngu (North East Arnhem Land), *pichath* in Wik-Ngathan (Cape York Peninsula).
5. See Maquet 1971; Barnes, Brock, and Marrie 1982. The latter authors suggest that Aboriginal works are metamorphosed into "art" by scholars, collectors, curators, and the art market.
6. Horton 1978.
7. Smith 1980. Butlin 1983 argues that it may have been much higher.
8. Maddock 1974: 22–23.
9. Although some anthropologists maintain the utility of the term with respect to Aborigines, most scholars argue that in so far as it refers to a politically unified group, it does not apply to Aboriginal Australia.
10. Sutton 1978: 171–78.
11. McCarthy and McArthur 1960.
12. For a summary of this shift and a fuller treatment of traditional Aboriginal politics, see Hiatt 1986; Sutton and Rigsby 1982.
13. Reynolds 1981: 99.
14. Broome 1982: 61.

CHAPTER I

1. Roberts 1978:5.
2. Stanner 1963:231.
3. The majority of bark paintings, acrylic paintings, and sculpted figures that are held in museum and private collections and come from remoter parts of the country belong to the old religious traditions, which center on geography. Many contemporary urban and rural Aboriginal works are not representations of Dreamings but nevertheless often have strong emphases on local geography. For a Eurocentric view of landscape art, see Clark 1949.
4. Stanner 1963:213. Good examples of this type of traveling story are those told by Paddy Sims in Warlukurlangu Artists 1987:47,115.
5. On the functions of the myths, see Hiatt 1975, 1983; Maddock 1982; Sutton (in press); and Jones and Sutton 1986. The latter provides an extended discussion of myths in relation to a body of Aboriginal sculptures.
6. Stanner 1963:227.
7. Stanner 1963:215.
8. These renditions often borrow only the effect of a traditional design: transverse bands, for example, may be placed on limbs, but this is not a precise reflection of Western Arnhem Land style in which the bands usually mark joints. Moreover, it represents a different intellectual approach to the nature of the body (see Chapter III). In the 1960s European-Australian artist Byram Mansell similarly painted amalgams of Groote Eylandt canoes and stick figures, Western Arnhem Land X-ray anatomy, desert dotted circles, and southeast Australian zigzags and alternating hatches (see Black 1964: Figs. 103–106). All these artists have taken an eclectic approach for similar reasons: they wish to establish a distinctive Australian and/or Aboriginal identity.
9. "Old people" is a common expression of respect, in Aboriginal circles, for the more tradition-oriented people of almost any age and for living elders and deceased ancestors. Tradition-oriented Aborigines are seen by many urban Aborigines as symbols of their own ancestry. Some urban Aboriginal artists state that by drawing on living styles from other regions they are rebuilding their own identity, e.g. Meeks 1987; also see Chapter VI. This sustenance from ancestral sources is itself highly traditional in character.
10. Morphy 1980:26–27.
11. Morphy 1980:28.
12. Morphy 1977, and see other Morphy references.
13. E.g. Kupka 1965:154 refers to the "rough, bulky forms in wood" of Cape York Peninsula as "true sculpture." Also see Berndt and Phillips 1973:199; Morphy 1981; Berndt, Berndt, and Stanton 1982:97.
14. See McConnel 1935, 1953.
15. McCarthy kindly made available for this study his unpublished report on the dances and artifacts (1978). There is also one small painted wooden turtle from Aurukun, ca. 1963, at the Australian Museum (E 70222).
16. E.g. the *Stingray* by Jackson Woolla and the *Dugong* by Cecil Walmbeng in the collection of the South Australian Museum (both 1987).
17. Wuungk songs are sung in funerary rites and in healing and fighting events. They are intensely territorial and rights in them are jealously guarded. They are essentially controlled by women. The two women photographed by Donald Thomson at Aurukun in 1933, shown here as Fig. 27, are dressed for Wuungk (Welepany, in Wik-Ngatharr language).
18. People here are traditionally multilingual. The sister on the north side of the river sang in Wik-Ayangenych (Andjingith), even though the clan of that area has Wik-Ngatharr as its language.
19. In fact, one member of the clan owning Pulthalpampang has offspring at Coen, some one hundred twenty-five miles away. Whether this predates the development of this particular segment of the myth is difficult to establish.
20. Shining, and particularly iridescent, objects are commonly held to be specially powerful and attractive/dangerous in Aboriginal traditions. Pearlshell, oily snake scales, rainbows, rainbow lorikeets (birds), and quartz crystals, which refract light into the spectrum, are typically associated with the Rainbow Serpent, fertility, water, and power.
21. Maquet 1979:30–31.

22. Stanner 1963:61.

23. Munn 1973a: 173; Morphy 1980. Port Keats painting is stylistically related to Western Desert art. See Fig. 87, but especially Fig. 88. For a detailed treatment of the circle in Aboriginal art, see Morphy 1980.

24. Meeks 1987.

CHAPTER II

1. Marabottini 1969:200.

2. The first Governor of New South Wales wrote that the Aborigines of the Sydney area were "not without notions of sculpture" (Phillip 1789:106), but neglected to expand on what those notions might consist of. For the first century and more after British settlement in 1788 most published descriptions of such objects said virtually nothing about them apart from their physical appearance.

3. E.g. Jones 1856; Racinet 1869.

4. Cf. Peltier 1984:102.

5. See Rubin 1984 for the most recent major account of modernist primitivism.

6. See Mack, Dean, and Frost 1950 for an excellent retrospective account of the modernism of the early twentieth century.

7. Rubin 1984:74.

8. Cf. Stanner 1977.

9. It will, however, take more than book-learning to produce the Aboriginal-based cultural renaissance that some Australians have predicted and hoped for. Cf. Coombs 1986 and comments on this by Sutton 1987b; also note Langer 1967:263: "To understand the 'idea' in a work of art is therefore more like *having a new experience* than like entertaining a new proposition . . ."

10. See Berndt, Berndt, and Stanton 1982; Isaacs 1984; Hill and McLeod 1984.

11. Boas (1927) 1955. Cf. Rubin 1984:5,74, who points to the problems and continuing irksome usefulness of the term *primitive art* in some circles.

12. Boas (1927) 1955:72–75, and see Halverson 1987 for a comprehensive review of the alleged child/primitive art relationship.

13. Aboriginal religion is not an open system. Induction into the mysteries is controlled by the few, usually defined as the most senior. See further Chapter 1.

14. Cf. Rubin 1984:18–19. Yet this is perhaps too neat. Conceptual and perceptual elements do occur mixed together in Aboriginal and many other art traditions. Morphy, it should be noted, rejects the "reductive" description for Aboriginal art, claiming that the art system is "generative." Morphy 1977a.

15. Rubin 1984:18,75.

16. Sacred objects in the desert regions, grindstones and pounders left at key exploitation sites, rock art, and some personal items of magical or other significance were commonly looked after for long periods. More easily renewable and portable artifacts—and, in more recent times, manufactured goods ranging from audio cassette players to offroad vehicles—typically have had short lives. This is one of several traits that have led others to regard Aboriginal culture as nonmaterialistic.

17. A seeming paradox here is that early Papunya acrylic painters encountered trouble because they depicted decorated sacred objects in their work, and these objections were relaxed when they removed the outlines of the objects, leaving only the designs. The source of secrecy here, though, lay perhaps not in the substrate of the object, or the designs, but in the design-covered object as a whole.

18. See Catalano 1977.

19. In fact, with few exceptions, probably none of them were. The patterns of Central Australian ground drawings reproduced in McCarthy 1974 and Black 1964 are mainly irregular in outline. Concentric squares appear in incised designs of the western region of Central Australia (see Strehlow 1964; Peterson 1981) and rectangles generated by the site-path framework (see text below) are common internal features of Aboriginal designs in Arnhem Land and the desert Center.

20. Bardon 1979:19; Crocker 1987:28.

21. See Carrington 1890; Tindale 1925; Spencer 1928; and Cat. 32. Paintings on bark are recorded in early times for other regions as well: for Tasmania, see Peron and Freycinet 1807, 1816; for Victoria in 1861, Smyth 1878, vol. I:292; for Bathhurst in New South Wales in the period 1839–44, Meredith 1844:91–92. For photographs of decorated bark shelters, see Jelinek 1979:320; Morphy 1981.

22. See Reser (1978) 1981.

23. Photographic sequences showing the preparation of bark paintings may be found in e.g. Edwards and Guerin 1969; Groger-Wurm 1973; Hill and McLeod 1984; Jelinek 1979; Kupka 1972. Many museum conservators recommend the removal of the supporting rods.

24. Bark paintings from Port Keats post–1960 tend to be octagonal, looking like an original quadrilateral that has had its corners cut off. Those from the Kimberley are often hexagonal, having the top two corners of the quadrilateral removed, and framing with an arc the typical Wandjina or similar figure, which itself often has an internal arc-shaped frame about the head; see Fig. 76.

25. See Tindale and George 1971:28; Crawford 1968:127.

26. Snakes appear coiled more often in Western Arnhem Land bark paintings than in those from North Central Arnhem Land. Coiled snakes do appear in Arnhem Land rock art. See Mountford 1956a:138. Meandering and coiled snakes are both common in Western Desert acrylic painting.

27. Hiatt 1975.

28. See Mountford 1956a:225. For a similar treatment of the same subject see Berndt and Berndt 1970: between 158 and 159.

29. See Gombrich 1972; Mundkur 1983.

30. Cooper and Chalfant 1984. Is it the subject matter that crucially defines graffiti? Are Rembrandt's etchings of coupling couples graffiti? We do not think so. Would they be graffiti if Rembrandt had drawn them on the wall of the subway? Perhaps, as context is crucial to the definition. But that would not have detracted from their power as images, nor, these days, from the possibility that they could end up in an art museum. See discussion of Basquiat in Nairne 1987.

31. Images of people urinating and defecating occur constantly in Western graffiti, and even belong to the fine-art tradition as exemplified by both Old and Modern Masters such as Rembrandt and Dubuffet (see Schwartz 1977: B186, B187, B190; Merkert and Krueger 1980:363–64). Rembrandt's more erotic works would certainly have been at least risqué in times past; in fact, their subject

matter was sufficient to prevent their acceptance as genuine Rembrandts for many years. A rare photograph of erotic paintings on the bark walls of a single men's shelter in North Central Arnhem Land appears in Morphy 1981.

32. Luke Taylor (pers. comm. 1987) comments that Western Arnhem Land artists do say that sometimes they just paint animals, but it is very hard to tell when the image is just an animal or, in fact, an ancestor.

33. Stanner 1963:56.

34. Davidson 1964; Gombrich 1972:87.

35. See Crawford 1968; Davidson 1936: Frontispiece; Arndt 1962a,b; Edwards 1979:117; Mountford 1956a (color plate opposite 267).

36. See Munn 1970 and cf. Munn 1973a:126.

37. See Morphy n.d.; Taylor 1984.

38. See Morphy 1980:26. Note also that the symbolization of mythic character X or sacred water hole Z by motifs P and Q is commonly an intention of the Aboriginal artist, but at least one other intention is to paint in one's own cultural and local Dreaming or clan style, thus bringing into play the complex of knowledge that arises from the artist's "discursive practice" or "latent discourse" (Foucault 1972:193–94).

39. Mountford 1958:29–30, plates 2B,2C. Mountford's spellings have been corrected here, and elsewhere in this book, for several reasons: the languages he worked in were basically unknown to him; his linguistic training was minimal; he suffered from partial deafness through the period of collecting represented here; and the languages he recorded have since been studied intensively by trained professional linguists, whose works have been consulted.

40. Typewritten documentation on the back of the painting, by the collector, Sandra Holmes. Mimis are common subjects for Western Arnhem Land bark paintings and they are well known to the anthropological literature. See e.g. Berndt and Berndt 1970:18,51; Carroll 1977.

41. Thomas 1986:26.

42. This is not necessarily a mark of a good painter in this part of the world. See Fox 1982.

43. Further details of the story from various vantage points in Arnhem Land are contained in e.g. Warner 1937; Berndt 1952; Keen 1978. The latter especially makes the visual imagery and the details of the myth coherent, but in a way that cannot be revealed here because of religious restrictions on the explanations.

44. South Australian Museum documentation contains the details of eleven site names and the clans to which they are said to have been allocated. All the site names are said to mean "Squid" in the various languages of the clans. The authorship of this documentation is not stated.

45. A.K. Chase has kindly supplied details of this event, which he witnessed.

46. Mountford 1956a.

47. For a more detailed account, see Mountford 1958:71. Aboriginal words here in the Anindilyakwa language retranscribed after Waddy 1984, by kind permission.

48. Bradley 1987. This document covers several other ca. 1909 Borroloola paintings in similar detail, including the other published here as Fig. 86/Cat. 36.

49. Cf. Elkin 1972; Maddock 1969; Bern 1974.

50. In my own case this goes even a little further: one of my grandmothers worked in the factory whose biscuits were originally retailed in this box, and probably during the same year (ca. 1908 or 1909) it was sent off to Borroloola. The bark painter's relationship to materials is much more personal, though: bark and pigments come from particular places (and via people) known personally to the artist, not from some generalized market. At the same time, the trees and ochres belong to defined groups of people, under Aboriginal law, so the bark and pigments resonate not only with personal meanings but also with communally based ones. This level of appreciation is usually impossible for the stranger who views or buys the painting in some distant city.

51. A point made by Langer 1967:230, and one that arises out of semiotics and information theory, as well as aesthetics.

52. Cf. Michaels 1987:141 on Western Desert acrylics and the question of series.

53. Much of the Port Keats work, and some from all regions, has been painted on plywood, masonite, artist's board, or other such surfaces. Roland Robinson is said to have probably introduced such portable painting to Port Keats in 1954 (see Kupka 1965:138–39). Remarks here about the styles of bark paintings cover similar work in these other media.

54. Anthropologists have earned themselves the reputation of being "cold" (Breton in Kupka 1965:8), and of being aesthetic philistines (see the comments of Rubin 1984:74 note 6) in relation to the objects produced by so-called tribal and other cultures. To be fair, their counterparts in the art world have until recently done little better, responding mainly to the outward forms of such art and in terms that often read all kinds of Eurocentric myths about primitiveness into the art. Both camps are now showing signs of convergence towards a middle paradigm in which both aesthetic response and knowledge of cultural context matter greatly. Neither can be experienced profoundly without the other (cf. Elkin 1950:6–7).

CHAPTER III

1. Stanner 1963:62.

2. This Murrinh-Patha (Murinbata, Port Keats) word also refers to bark paintings and generally to repetitive patterns such as checks, stipples, and spots in both traditional items and imported goods. Michael Walsh, pers. comm. 1987.

3. Stanner 1963:63.

4. Morphy 1986.

5. Power and Danger are never really dissociated in Aboriginal thought. See Keen 1978:339.

6. A painter's local public status as an artist, though, may be based on a good deal more than skill—for example, on seniority in clan affairs or regional ceremonial life.

7. Cf. Langer 1967:229–30.

8. Morphy 1986.

9. E.g., for the Pintupi of Australia's Western Desert, see Myers 1987:Ch.4.

10. Adolf Loos said in 1898 that "All art is erotic" (cited by Gombrich 1984:61), but this sweepingly reductive sense of the term is not what is intended here.

11. See Jones and Sutton 1986; Brook 1986a,b; 1987; Sutton 1986, 1987a; Smith 1987; Carter 1987; Jones 1987b.

12. This includes ceremonial posts made by women in Central Australia, of the type used in public performances of *yawulyu* (a women's ceremony) at communities such as Warrabri and Yuendumu. In these particular cases the posts may be openly stated to be phalluses. In general, though, the erotic connotations of this form are more implicit than explicit, and most examples of the form are magical or sacred in context.

13. Sexual relationships are always political in traditional Aboriginal society, cf.Schebeck 1986:223–24.

14. See Jones and Sutton 1986:Fig. 15 for three examples of double knobs and crossbars.

15. See Jones and Sutton 1986: Figs. 1,14,83.

16. Stanner 1963:64. See also Munn 1973a:67–68,86,138,172, 1973b; Morphy 1980.

17. Thus the apparent contrast between Western Desert and Arnhem Land art is less firm than it may seem: both have an underlying commitment to a perpendicular view (to which there are of course exceptions). The site-path design (see Chapter I and this chapter) also forms an underlying unity across much of Australia, a kind of deep structure principally associated with the sacred domain.

18. Cited in Gombrich 1984.

19. One of the key distinctive features of the look of Aboriginal art is its avoidance of the double-tapered eye shape common in Oceanic, American Indian, Asian, and ancient Egyptian art. Aboriginal eyes are shown almost entirely as small round spots or circles. The circle itself is a typically Aboriginal form; the arabesque is not. In other art traditions, the eyes can be interpreted as sets of paired arabesques.

20. Running figures are common in the so-called Mimi style of Western Arnhem Land, the very similar Bradshaw figures of northwestern Australia, and the rock art of the Adelaide hills. Chaloupka 1977; Crawford 1968, 1977; Lewis 1984; S. Hemming pers. comm. 1987.

21. Clark (1956) 1976: Figs. 220–24. We draw attention to these possible comparisons of Aboriginal and European traditions because many readers of this book will have some grounding in the European tradition, while only a few will be knowledgeable about Aboriginal art. Comparisons across traditions, like those within a tradition, add to our perception of individual works, where we know something of both traditions. Awareness of variation—contrast, resemblance, counterpoint—can lead to discernment, and thus to heightened perception.

22. Richter ca. 1965:104–107.

23. For exceptions see e.g. Berndt and Berndt 1951: pls.8–9; Berndt 1976; Kupka 1965: opp.47; Holmes 1972:77.

24. Phalluses are recorded as objects used by dancers in both men's and women's ceremonies. For Arnhem Land and Western Cape York Peninsula, see Kupka 1965: opp.36; McConnel 1953: pls. V:d and VII:e.

25. See Morphy 1977a,b.

26. Taylor 1986, which is part of a much larger work (Taylor 1987).

27. Mountford 1958:41–42. A remarkably similar interpretation was applied to a North East Arnhem Land bark painting, now in the Macleay Museum (P2041), by an Arnhem Land elder (it also has a row of circles).

28. Representational, in the sense described in Munn 1973a. For another highly geometric, hatched approach to depicting Catfish, see the Melville Island painting in Mountford 1958: pl. 10c.

29. Some bark paintings look like the acrylics (Figs. 43–44,88), but they are a minority.

30. Symmetry may also, however, have been a key avenue for its temptation to vulgarization or at least loss of spontaneity; see Michaels 1987. For some, the occasionally neat symmetry of the Papunya and Mt. Allan painters, in particular, has made many of their works seem like table-cloth decoration.

31. See Stirling 1896; Munn 1973a:65–67; Morphy 1977c:82; Bardon 1979:18–19; Peterson 1981:46 (reproduced in Brody 1985:11); Maughan 1986:16.

32. E.g. Maughan and Megaw 1986. Perhaps the fullest and most accurate rendition in this genre is Warlukurlangu Artists 1987, which also offers both Warlpiri and English versions of the myths. Note also, however, the comments of the anonymous translator in Warlukurlangu Artists 1987:2: "The sense of understanding obtained from reading the translations then is to a large extent spurious, and is analogous to the feeling that one can understand the paintings by use of the keys which have been provided. The keys 'identify,' at one level, some of the features in the paintings. These keys are not intended to 'explain' the paintings—full understanding of the designs comes only to full members of Warlpiri society—but rather to indicate to the reader that these are paintings loaded with meaning. The translations [of the narratives] serve a similar function. Both translations and keys provide only an imperfect, infinitestimal glimpse into the complexities of Warlpiri religion and society." Also see Michaels 1987:136.

33. See Michaels' comments on the look in 1987:141.

34. Bardon's comments, although brief, do broach these subjects, see 1979:19–23,28,36. Some critics reviewing art exhibitions do too.

35. Michaels 1987:140.

36. The numbers of examples are about evenly distributed between Papunya/Kintore and Yuendumu. The sources for this comparison were the paintings published in Bardon 1979; Brody 1985; Crocker (ed.) 1983; Crocker 1987; Maughan and Megaw 1986; Warlukurlangu Artists 1987; the collection of the South Australian Museum; and a large number of paintings held in various other public and private collections.

37. This gradation was already marked before the emergence of the acrylic painting movement, in designs on sacred objects. See Taylor 1979:43. (This unpublished work is for restricted access only, as it comprises an analysis of earlier published records of sensitive religious material.)

38. A principled exception to this is is the placement of a roundel at one end of a long, narrow rectangle, with a doubled-back snake filling the remainder of the space; see Turkey Tolsen's *Brown Snake* (1979) in Maughan and Zimmer 1986: 119 for an example.

39. Principled exceptions to this include *Man's Water Dreaming* by Old Walter Jampijinpa (Bardon 1979:25), *Rainbow Storm Dreaming* by Kaapa Mbitjana Jampijinpa (Bardon 1979:69), and Cat. 45 in Maughan and Zimmer 1986:122 by David Corby.

40. Munn 1973a:214–15 provides the underlying reason why this is so: women's narratives tend to concentrate on the rhythms of family life, centered on the camp, while men's emphasize the rhythms of nomadic movement from site to site, following game and water holes. Women's narratives—and use of roundels—thus

emphasize particular sub-parts of the social and geographical macro-picture. See further Munn 1973:110 and discussion below.

41. For an example of non-matching connectors, which yield an unusual triangular arrangement of roundels, see the door by Paddy Japaljarri Stewart in Warlukurlangu Artists 1987:109. Cf. Stirling 1896; Tindale 1932: 39 (Fig. 1).

42. Davidson 1937:93.

43. Munn 1973a: Ch.5.

44. Myers 1987; cf. also Sharp 1958:159 who has a similar basic analysis for Cape York Peninsula.

45. Tillers 1983:15. Tillers, however, considers the infinite, continuous grid of Western Desert art to be what he calls the "dot-screen," whereas we consider it to be the site-path framework.

46. Fifteen of the thirty-four door panels (counting double doors as two panels) of the Yuendumu school are clearly divisible into two sub-paintings. This may be partly a function of size and the associated fact that two painters may have worked towards the middle from each end of the panels. Smaller paintings from Yuendumu rarely evince this kind of break.

47. Bardon 1979:20,23.

48. Michaels 1987:137. The Yuendumu school doors were painted in 1983 and are published in Warlukurlangu Artists 1987.

49. See note 34, above; for a published encapsulation of the styles, see Peterson 1981.

50. Characteristic of, but not peculiar to, these regions. Each of the sub-regions discussed here produce examples of all these particular design types.

CHAPTER IV

1. State and national galleries have been adding Aboriginal bark paintings to their collections since the 1950s.

2. This is not to say that acrylic artists in Central Australia have in any way been influenced by Western art styles. Most of the artists are nonliterate and rarely travel beyond their remote home territories.

3. The most comprehensive bibliographies are those of Marrie 1987 and Maughan and Zimmer 1986. Major works on acrylics include Bardon 1979; Brody 1985; Kimber 1978, 1982; Maughan 1986; Megaw 1981, 1982, 1984, 1986. Kimber 1982 provides an especially good summary of the acrylic movement.

4. We have chosen to include information on Yuendumu in part because there are no detailed descriptions of Aboriginal acrylic production from Papunya's first decade of painting and because Yuendumu was the site of fieldwork for Françoise Dussart, one of the authors of this chapter. Dussart spent from 1983 to 1985 at the community conducting research for a Ph.D. in anthropology from the Australian National University.

5. Also see Chapter I for a description of the concept of the Dreaming. Many non-Aborigines mistakenly believe that the Dreamtime refers exclusively to a time long before the present. This has contributed to the equally erroneous belief that Aboriginal religion is static and oriented to the past.

6. There are only two types of language in the region: the Arandic on the east and the closely related Kukatja, Warlpiri, Pitjantjatjara, and Walmadjarri on the west.

7. For some Western Desert groups (particularly, the Warlpiri, Anmatyerre, and Pintupi), there is a form of social organization and classification that anthropologists call the subsection system. This system classifies people according to kin relationships into sixteen categories (eight for men, all beginning with the letter *J* or *Tj*, and eight for women, all beginning with *N*). These categories, which in Aboriginal English are called 'skin names,' are used as a kind of surname and as terms of address. In writing artists' subsection or 'skin' names, we have used *J* instead of *Tj*, hence, Japaljarri instead of Tjapaltjarri. The latter form has been used in orthographies where *j* was used for the sound *y*. Yuendumu people prefer to have their skin name put before any surname they might have; painters of the Papunya movement tend to put their skin names last.

8. Berndt 1974:22.

9. Here we use the term *classical* to refer to Aboriginal traditions and practices as they existed, not in any timeless sense but rather just prior to significant non-Aboriginal influence. In this chapter we occasionally use the past tense in referring to some aspects of Aboriginal culture. This reflects the fact that in some areas of the region that we are discussing, Aboriginal life is now very different and some traditions no longer exist.

10. Munn 1973a:58–88.

11. The earliest ethnographic descriptions of Central Australia include many fine examples of these forms of artistic expression (see, for example, Spencer and Gillen 1899, 1927). It should be noted, however, that much of the illustration in these early works is of restricted material.

12. Drawings collected by Tindale and Mountford are in the collections of the South Australian Museum and State Library. M.J. Meggitt, an anthropologist working with Warlpiri people north of the Tanami Desert in the 1950s, also collected crayon drawings, now in the Australian Institute of Aboriginal Studies, Canberra. Nancy Munn collected crayon drawings from Yuendumu during her fieldwork there in the 1950s. In addition, Ronald and Catherine Berndt, working primarily in the western and northern areas of Central Australia after the Second World War, collected hundreds of similar drawings. These are in the University of Western Australia's Anthropology Museum, and some have been published in Berndt, Berndt, and Stanton 1982.

13. Cf. Thomas 1986; Sutton 1987b.

14. See Raggett 1980; Bardon 1979.

15. John Kean pers comm. 1987; also see Billy Stockman Japaljarri 1976.

16. Hogan 1986. The Papunya school retained a collection, which is now largely dispersed. Bardon himself also bought a large number of paintings. He published a book (Bardon 1979) on the acrylic movement and, with his brother James Bardon, made several films on the subject.

17. Sales levels in the first decade of acrylic painting at Papunya were generally low. Tourists and other non-Aborigines were not familiar with the new art form and considered it somehow "inauthentic." At one exhibition in Sydney in 1976, only two out of about seventy paintings sold over a period of two months, despite extensive advertising and an elaborate opening (Kimber pers. comm. 1987). Without the support of Robert Edwards, Dick Kimber, Pat Hogan, Jennifer Isaacs, and others in securing financial and institutional support, Papunya art—and hence the whole acrylic movement—may not have survived.

18. The name derives from a hill near Papunya which is a Honey

Ant Dreaming site. Papunya Tula operated out of a one-room tin shed at the settlement and a small gallery/office at Alice Springs.

19. Myers 1986.

20. This interview was recorded in what is colloquially referred to as "stockman English." To preserve both the meaning and character of this language, only minor changes have been made in the transcription. We thank John Kean and Clifford Possum Japaljarri for allowing us to use this material, which is hitherto unpublished.

21. See Warlukurlangu Artists 1987.

22. See Michaels 1987.

23. The name comes from Warlukurlangu, an important Fire Dreaming site south of Yuendumu.

24. These figures from documentation records of paintings were made available by the Warlukurlangu Association and Felicity Wright.

25. Michael Nelson Jakamarra to John Kean, Papunya, April 1984.

26. The listing of a single artist fits in more with non-Aboriginal notions of the artist-as-individual. It also represents an Aboriginal adaptation to the white system of cash receipt, individual welfare checks, bank books, and so forth. This is also true for Papunya, according to some reports.

27. Megaw pers. comm. 1987.

28. Michael Nelson Jakamarra to John Kean, Papunya, April 1984.

29. Paddy Carrol Jungarrayi to John Kean, Three Mile Outstation, near Papunya, April 1984.

30. For descriptions of these standard elements, see Munn 1973a; Peterson 1981.

31. This is a widespread phenomenon for much of Australia. For an example from further south, see Jones and Sutton 1986. It is also used in some bark painting.

32. Kimber pers. comm. 1987.

33. We refer to "the painters of the Papunya movement" because most of the acrylic painters that began at Papunya no longer live there.

34. Clifford Possum Japaljarri to John Kean, Alice Springs, March 1984.

35. Darby Jampijinpa to Françoise Dussart, Yuendumu, July 22, 1987. Translated from the Warlpiri. This translation has not been rendered in the colloquial language as have the transcriptions of artists' comments given elsewhere in this chapter.

36. Cf. Stanner 1963:62–64.

37. Michael Nelson Jakamarra to Françoise Dussart, Papunya, July 28, 1987. Translated from the Warlpiri. See note 35 above.

38. At Yuendumu, especially in the early days of acrylic painting, there were minor style differences between men's and women's paintings—for example, men used larger and thicker dots. Several Warlpiri symbols are almost exclusively used by either men or women.

39. This was possibly the case because Bardon asked the men to do "special" paintings for him. Bardon 1979:15.

40. Some of the early Papunya paintings have hatched backgrounds similar to those of bark paintings. (Fig. 81.)

41. See Crocker 1987 and Maughan and Zimmer 1986 for further discussion and illustration of particular artists' work over time. It is worth noting that most discussions do not attempt to tie in aspects of the artists' life history. We suspect that this would be a fruitful analysis. For instance, Tim Leura Japaljarri's work as a stockman on Napperby Station allowed him to travel over his own territory at a time when many Aboriginal people were being taken away from their country and put into centralized settlements; this gave him a perspective and source of inspiration and knowledge for his art unavailable to some acrylic artists. On the other hand, the necessary historical information on artists is often difficult to come by, as it is not Aboriginal style to give long, introspective, and analytical autobiographical accounts.

42. See Morphy 1983a.

43. The artists also comment—usually in confidence—on the skills of their colleagues. One man complained that a *kurdungurlu* who had worked on a painting with him had "buggered it up" by not doing it neatly and skillfully.

44. Maughan 1986:23.

45. Bardon 1979:14.

46. There is a long history of women anthropologists in this area, among them, Olive Pink in the 1930s, Nancy Munn in the 1950s, and Françoise Dussart in the 1980s.

47. Similar roles have been played by others in Australian Aboriginal art—for example, Pastor Johann Reuther in the case of the toas (see Chapter VI).

48. Some artists have drawn parallels between the acrylic paintings and Central Australian *tjurunga*, or incised stone objects, which were one of the few permanent material objects in Aboriginal society.

49. In one case at Yuendumu, an artist did not want a visiting anthropologist to buy one of her paintings because she knew that it would be taken back to a nearby settlement where there were other Aborigines with rights in the same Dreaming. The artist was concerned that having done the painting and received money for it, she might be accused by them of not recognizing their rights.

50. See Nairne 1987 on Michael Nelson Jakamarra.

CHAPTER V

1. Peltier 1984:109.

2. Some commentators (for example, Tuckson 1964) have characterized this attitudinal shift as a progression from the "perceptual" to the "conceptual." This distinction has been convincingly dismissed by Gombrich, who stressed that ". . . it is precisely because all art is 'conceptual' that representations are recognizable by their style." (Gombrich 1962:76.) Concepts and symbols are embodied to varying degrees in the art of any culture. In mid-nineteenth century Europe and North America (as well as many parts of Asia) the dominant mode of expressing a worldview was by the convention of naturalism; the symbols, concepts, and forms embodied in so-called primitive art were mediated in an entirely different manner.

3. Humboldt 1808 (trans. 1849); Humboldt's contribution is discussed in Smith 1985:205–212.

4. Degerando (1800) 1969.

5. Stephans 1907.

6. Smith 1985; Lovejoy (1936) 1960. Nevertheless, first impressions counted for a lot in the eighteenth century and exerted a

substantial independent effect. (These early accounts also contributed to the ferment of ideas later to be distilled in Spencerian social evolutionist theory and its younger sibling, Darwinian theory.)

7. This pessimistic view has since been thoroughly rejected. See Sahlins 1974; Chase and Sutton 1981.

8. Mathews 1895:468.

9. Grey 1841:263. Substantial conjecture was generated by Grey's publication of the Wandjina paintings. It was suggested, for example, that the headdress design of one of the figures contained an inscription in Sumatran or Malay, an alphabet of the Red Sea, or Chaldaeo-Phoenician. (See Black 1964:23–24; Smyth 1878, vol. 1:290; Worsnop 1897:21–25; Carter 1987:116–17. Governor Phillip's descriptions of the rock engravings of the Sydney and Hawkesbury area provide a further paradoxical example of Western reluctance to credit Aborigines with the capacity to produce art that approached Western notions of "idealized nature."

10. Tylor 1892:301.

11. See Mathews 1894 for a discussion of early recorded examples.

12. Angas 1847:224. Angas returned to South Australia during the following year (1845) with his New Zealand watercolors and completed his South Australian series. The bulk of Angas's original watercolors of Australian, New Zealand, and South African subjects are in the collections of the South Australian Museum and the Art Gallery of South Australia. See Tregenza 1980.

13. An account of the history of the first bark painting collections made by Europeans in Australia is contained in Groger-Wurm 1973:1–5.

14. Ratzel 1896, vol.1:350. See e.g. Angas's painting of Aboriginal warriors, Cat. 75.

15. Spencer and Gillen 1899; Smyth 1878; Howitt 1904.

16. Another trader, Captain F. Carrington, obtained four bark paintings from the Field Island people in the 1880s, among the earliest surviving examples of this genre (see Fig. 53/Cat. 8).

17. Donald Thomson's Cape York and Arnhem Land collections provide one of the best examples of this methodical style. An early graduate of Radcliffe Brown's Department of Anthropology at the University of Sydney, Thomson spent nine months in Cape York Peninsula from April 1928 to January 1929 gathering anthropological data and more than two hundred glass-plate negatives as well as a small zoological collection. In this and later expeditions to Cape York, Arnhem Land, and Central Australia, Thomson's work was characterized by a precise attention to detail and, from his background in the natural sciences, a thorough grasp of environmental issues.

18. Reynolds 1981.

19. Gillen 1968:168. Spencer and Gillen observed in 1912 that a stick of tobacco or a single-blade knife readily purchased a shield, spear, or pitchi (wooden container). Half a stick was quite enough for a boomerang or a bunch of neck or arm ringlets. (Spencer and Gillen 1912, vol. 2:318.)

20. See e.g. Mulvaney and Calaby 1985:174–75. The regard with which men like Carl and Theodor Strehlow, Spencer, and Gillen were held as "law men" by Aborigines was a major factor contributing to their collections of ceremonial material.

21. Quoted in Jones 1987a:82.

22. Bolton and Specht 1984–85.

23. Gathercole 1978:277.

24. See Bean 1987 for a discussion of the literature relating to this subject.

25. Peltier 1984:100; Catalano 1977:572.

26. Scott 1884.

27. Hale 1956:63.

28. See South Australian Public Record Office GRG19/4 for letters documenting such acquisitions by the South Australian Museum.

29. See for example, Oldman 1903–1914 catalogue nos. 29,58,67,73,76,110,112 and Webster 1895–1901 catalogue nos. 1–6, 12–15; see Oldman catalogue nos. 73 and 110 for example of ornaments, baskets, and woven bags. See Oldman catalogue no. 58 for price differences between Australian and New Caledonian clubs.

30. One notable exception is the well-documented collection of R.E. Johns. See Cooper 1981:30–31. The general lack of early collections of southeastern Australian ethnography was increased by the disastrous Garden Palace fire of Sydney in September 1882, which destroyed the Australian Museum's entire ethnographic collection. See Strahan 1979:39.

31. Hale 1956; Strahan 1979.

32. The "scientific racism" which came to characterize the pursuit of museum ethnology in the last decades of the nineteenth century was developed within this overall framework. Although long discredited by social anthropologists, scientific racism has lingered on in museums, partly due to the taxonomic interests of their staff but mainly because of the persistence of nineteenth-century exhibition and collection arrangements. The "primitive peoples" have remained the main object of anthropological interest in museums, primarily because of the orientation of these institutions toward evolutionary theory, which singled out non-Western, nonliterate peoples as representative of those living when human culture began.

With the notable exceptions of Norman Tindale in Adelaide and Frederick McCarthy in Sydney, it has only been with the recent involvement of social anthropologists and the consequent withering of ethnology as a museum discipline in Australia that museums have begun to interpret their collections of Aboriginal material with more insight.

33. See Impeg and McGregor 1985.

34. Rainey 1955:15. Modern social anthropology in the period after about 1920 destroyed the idea that race and material culture possessed anything but an arbitrary relationship. (See Bean 1987.) This also was part of a movement away from *things* as characterizers of cultures.

35. The story of anthropology in the second half of the nineteenth century is largely the story of these investigations, carried out in several fields by emerging specialists. For example, kinship studies were undertaken by Bachofen, McLennan, Lubbock, and Morgan; religion was investigated by Tylor, Frazer, and Lang; technology by Pitt-Rivers; economics by Hahn; art by Stolpe, Holmes, Semper, Mason, Haddon, and Balfour. See Frese 1960:47; Haddon 1934; Lowie 1937.

36. Published in *Der Stil*, 1860–63.

37. *Transactions of the Lancashire and Cheshire Antiquarian* March 1889.

38. Stolpe 1891.

39. Balfour 1893; also see Haddon 1895.

40. Boas 1896: 271–304; Boas 1927. Also see Harris 1969: 258–59.
41. Smyth 1878, vol. 1.:285.
42. Curr 1886–87; Howitt 1904.
43. Davidson 1937.
44. See Jones 1987a for a summary of these early expeditions and the results obtained.
45. Tindale 1932. Also see Tindale 1925, 1926, and 1928 for information on the collection of Groote Eylandt bark paintings.
46. Stanner 1972.
47. See Ucko and Rosenfeld 1967; Sieveking 1984.
48. Spencer 1928:794. See Figs. 55/Cat. 9, 56/Cat. 10. Spencer's modest remark that his "own non-expert opinion in regard to their relative merits coincided with their own" should be read in the light that by the time of the Arnhem Land exhibition he had accumulated the largest private collection of Australian art. Spencer had also undertaken a year of conventional art schooling in his youth and was an accomplished sketchbook artist. See Mulvaney and Calaby 1985:335–359.
49. Redfield 1971:55–56. José Ortega y Gasset described the process of understanding a work of exotic art as akin to looking at a window ("the aesthetic form") before becoming aware of the garden beyond ("the content of human experience to which the form refers us"). Quoted in Redfield 1971:47.
50. Berndt and Berndt 1957b:4.
51. Chipp 1960:153.
52. von Siebold 1843. See Frese 1960 for a discussion of von Siebold's significance.
53. The events surrounding the "discovery" of primitive art are discussed in Donne 1978 and Peltier 1984.
54. Fraser 1971:27.
55. Guillaume and Munro 1925. Quoted in Samaltanos 1984:43. The French poet and critic Apollinaire was also one of the first to regret the tendency of the new connoisseurs to overlook the religious and symbolic function of this art. See Samaltanos 1984:46.
56. Fraser 1971:27. See Donne 1978 for a discussion of the influences of specific artifacts upon these artists.
57. See Peltier 1984; Rubin 1984.
58. The enthusiasm of Western artists for primitive art in the first decades of this century should not obscure the fact that this art was still alien to most of the art-viewing public. As Muensterberger has noted: "Both forms of artistic creativity, the anaturalism of the European artists as well as the masks and figures of the primitive craftsmen did not find acceptance for a good while . . ." (Muensterberger 1971:196.)
59. Graburn 1976:3. There were notable exceptions to this lack of insight. The library of Paris artist Jacques Doucet (visited by Apollinaire) contained a number of ethnographic texts, including Haddon's works and Ernst Grosse's *Les Debuts de l'Art* (1897) 1902.
60. Otten 1971:xi. Rubin has suggested that the lack of appreciation shown by the Cubists for the cultural context of primitive art is explained by their preference for African, rather than Oceanic, art and in the fact that "Cubism, like African art, was rooted—despite varying degrees of abstraction—in the concrete reality of the visible world. Surrealism, like much Oceanic, art . . . opted primarily for the world of the imagined, for the depiction of the fantastic rather than for the visually derived." (Rubin 1984:42.)
Rubin goes further: ". . . we can understand why Cubism, which is an 'iconic' art, would lead its makers to Africa, while Surrealism, which is a symbolically 'storytelling' art, would lead its practitioners to Melanesia, Micronesia, and the Americas." (Rubin 1984:55.)
61. Goldwater (1938) 1967; Samaltanos 1984:27; Preston 1925.
62. Apollinaire 1917. See Samaltanos 1984:46–49 for a discussion of this work. In Germany, Carl Einstein's "Negerplastik" (1915) and in America, Marius de Zayas's "On African Negro Art and its Influence on Modern Art" (1915) were other monographs that approached primitive art from a purely aesthetic point of view.
63. Guillaume and Munro 1926.
64. Chipp 1960:153.
65. Goldwater (1938) 1967; Donne 1978; Peltier 1984. Rubin writes: ". . . the shift . . . became particularly emphatic in 1906, after the large Gauguin retrospective held at the Salon d'Automne. That year Vlaminck acquired the famous Fang mask, soon sold to his friend Derain, which has become the principal tribal icon of twentieth-century primitivism." (Rubin 1984:13.)
66. Haddon 1894.
67. Samaltanos 1984:3.
68. Tylor 1892:300.
69. Thomas in Amadio et al. 1986:24; Thomas pers. comm. "Today the doodles of the Australians and the North American Indians have begotten a new progeny in the mysterious signs and symbols that appear in the canvases of Miro, Paul Klee, and Adolph Gottlieb . . ." (Hays (1958) 1971:160.)
70. Clouzot and Level 1919.
71. Quoted in Peltier 1984:109.
72. Quoted in Peltier 1984:111.
73. Peltier 1984:112.
74. Worsnop 1897.
75. See Rubin 1984:5–7.
76. Mulvaney and Calaby 1985:241. Particular examples of these paintings have appeared in most of the major exhibitions of Aboriginal art held in Australia and overseas since 1929.
77. Horne and Aiston 1924.
78. "Aboriginal Art Show Opened." *The Herald* July 9, 1929.
79. *The Leader*, July 20 1929. In the exhibition catalogue Kenyon was nevertheless careful to stress the ethnographic importance of the material rather than its aesthetic merits. Kenyon's comments contain further evidence of the durability of the image of stone-age man in discussions about the Aborigines: "We possess some knowledge of our own mentality through the kind offices of psychology; but though we have some—many in certain cases—material relics of our primitive and prehistoric ancestor, the only evidence of evolution of thought and of the development of his powers of abstract conception must be derived from his art remains, his pictographs, sculptures, and adornments." (Barrett and Kenyon 1929:15.)
80. The exhibition was the last to be held in National Socialist Germany before this art "was consigned to the Hitlerian category of the degenerate arts." Peltier 1984:113.
81. Stevens 1935:13.
82. Preston 1925:34. Butler 1987 assesses Preston's initiatives in this area, together with those of other artists and commentators.
83. Quoted in Tuckson 1964:67.
84. Black 1964:121–65.
85. This critic, Elizabeth Butel, goes on to observe that Cubism's

aim to create a parallel to rather than a reflection of reality by establishing a coded equivalent for every object with a language of visual signs was already realized in Aboriginal art. The simultaneous multiplicity of meanings present make it among the most complex of art forms. Butel 1987:9.

86. *Art in Australia*: 1925, 1930, 1940, and 1941. Preston's friend, the anthropologist and Aboriginal art specialist Frederick McCarthy, contributed an article in 1939, and anthropologist Ursula McConnel published one in 1935.

87. Butler describes this exhibition as the first in which Aboriginal art had received "official sanction." Butler 1987:23.

88. This focus was also apparent in the catalogue accompanying the 1946 *Arts of the South Seas* exhibition at the Museum of Modern Art in New York. In it Linton and Wingert gave precedence to both the sacred art of the *tjurunga* and to the secret ground paintings of Central Australia. Linton and Wingert 1946:191. *Tjurunga* were openly displayed in many Australian and overseas museums at this time. Aboriginal people expressed their dismay at this practice, and Australian museums have since withdrawn secret and ceremonial material, including *tjurunga* and other ceremonial paraphernalia such as headdresses, from exhibition.

89. Adam 1943:1.

90. Linton and Wingert 1946:7–10. The New York exhibition included six Western Arnhem Land bark paintings collected by Matthews and loaned by the South Australian Museum. "Each of these 'discoveries' of foreign art styles called for a new method of approach. The solution of formal problems admired in African Negro art can be appreciated in terms of *pure esthetics*. Yet an understanding of the relationship between content and form in Melanesian sculpture calls for some knowledge of the *cultural background* of the native artist. The growing realization in our art world that a work of art can best be appreciated in the context of its own civilization, together with the increasing interest in art shown by many scientists, holds a great promise." (Linton and Wingert 1946:7–8, emphasis added.)

91. Gombrich 1962.

92. Adam wrote: ". . . the religious side is so important that a purely aesthetic approach, restricted to formal qualities, is inadequate . . ." (Adam 1948:61.) Using the Upper Palaeolithic statuette known as the Venus of Willendorf as an example, he argued further: ". . . would not a merely formal approach leave us completely helpless, and is not our sensation entirely different when we learn that this is not a caricature of a fat woman but a goddess of motherhood?" (Adam 1948:62.)

93. Adam 1943:2.

94. Adam 1948:61.

95. Berndt 1973:36.

96. Kupka 1965:264–67.

97. Mountford 1950:4.

98. Mountford 1960:49.

99. Mountford 1966:10.

100. These collections, made in the Warburton Range of Western Australia and the Granites in the Northern Territory, are held in the South Australian Museum. See Jones 1987.

101. Mountford 1938a. Also see Mountford 1937a,b, 1938b, and 1939a,b.

102. There were notable exceptions to this response. For example, the director of the National Museum of Victoria in Melbourne declined the opportunity to purchase any of Namatjira's works, regretting ". . . that an aborigine was producing a secondhand version of European art instead of developing his own native art . . ." (Batty 1963:41.)

103. Elkin's remarks provide a cogent insight into academic attitudes of the time. He cited the "poverty of local pictorial art in Central Australia" as ". . . a justification for the lines taken by the Aranda 'school' of water-colour artists. They have deserted nothing for there was almost nothing in their own tradition which could be developed. It was therefore most fortunate that Albert Namatjira, a product of Hermannsburg Mission, was attracted by the work of a visiting white artist, felt the urge to paint, and was given encouragement and help." (Elkin 1964b:268.)

104. Tuckson 1964:68.

105. Thomas 1986. Also see Chapter VI.

106. Mountford 1950.

107. Leonhard Adam wrote the catalogue foreword for this exhibition. See Adam 1951.

108. Mountford 1953. On display were fourteen bark paintings, three cave paintings, six carved figures and associated objects, two painted paddles, six *tjurunga*, two pearl-shell ornaments, one carved baobab nut, one painted skull, four painted shields, one engraved shield, one engraved spearthrower and two Namatjira watercolors. The exhibition was held at the York Theatre, Adelaide, on September 23, 1953.

109. Herbert Read in Mountford 1957b.

110. See Berndt and Berndt 1957b.

111. Margaret Preston, Arthur Murch, Douglas Annand, Thea Proctor, Gert Sellheim, and Fred Leist were among the artists involved in the exhibition. See Butler 1987:44.

112. The *Bulletin*, July 1, 1959. Quoted in Tuckson 1964: 63. Stewart's view was challenged by The *Sun* critic, James Gleeson: "Whatever their symbolic significance might be they represent an ensemble of abstract shapes of considerable aesthetic appeal . . . Even in the artificial atmosphere of an art gallery they are impressive, for the painted posts stand about the grave in a protective ring, forming, as it were, a barrier between the world of living reality and the shadowy world of the spirit." (The *Sun* July 18, 1959. Quoted in Tuckson 1964:63.)

113. Berndt (ed.) 1964. The Sydney artist and curator Hal Missingham designed the book. With contributions from Elkin, Berndt, Mountford, McCarthy, Strehlow, and Tuckson, the book's interpretation of Aboriginal art was well balanced between aesthetic appreciation and anthropological analysis.

114. The Anglican Church Missionary Society maintained an outlet for bark paintings from Angurugu, Numbulwar, Oenpelli, and Roper River at its head office in Sydney from the mid-1950s, but as demand improved the Society opened a separate shop in 1962. By 1968 the Oenpelli community had become the main supplier, consigning 876 bark paintings for sale (Carroll 1983:45–46). Another key supplier in these early years of the Aboriginal art market was the small gallery and shop established by Rex Battarbee and his wife in Alice Springs in the 1950s as an outlet for the work of the Aranda watercolorists. The Battarbees also received consignments of bark paintings from Arnhem Land; these were sent by Dorothy Bennett, who had established herself as a local entrepeneur and marketer of Aboriginal art from her base in Darwin.

115. For a history of this company, see Peterson 1981. Morphy 1987 gives a detailed analysis of the changes affecting Aboriginal art in Northern Australia since the 1960s.

116. Morphy 1987.

117. Loveday and Cooke 1983; Morphy 1987.

118. "The Art of Aboriginal Australia." 1976. *Art International* 20:4–24; Cooper et al. 1981. The first Aboriginal chairman of the Aboriginal Arts Board, Dick Roughsey, was also an accomplished artist. His successor, the elder son of Mauwalan (whose name is at present under a publicity ban imposed by his community following his death in 1987), also belonged to a prominent family of artists.

119. Howie 1981, in Peterson 1981:28. Note that this case began five years after Yirrkala people presented a petition to the House of Representatives attached to a bark painting. Butler 1986:7.

120. See e.g. Michaels 1986.

CHAPTER VI

1. This has been a worldwide phenomenon. For a discussion of the politics of culture as commodity in the Aboriginal renaissance see Sutton in press.

2. Munn 1973a; Morphy 1977a.

3. Schrire 1982.

4. See Chaloupka 1985.

5. Gallus 1968; Wright (ed.) 1971; Bednarik 1986.

6. Bowler et al. 1970.

7. Rosenfeld, Horton, and Winter 1981. Here and below, *engraving* refers in general to what in technical language are more accurately described as petroglyphs.

8. See Davidson 1936; Nobbs 1984; Morwood 1985; Edwards 1966; Maynard 1977.

9. Basedow 1914; Hale and Tindale 1925; Mountford and Edwards 1963; Nobbs 1984.

10. For the concentric-arc motif in rock painting of the Everard Range region see Helms 1896: pls. 9,12. For more recent examples see e.g. Bardon 1979; nine of the twenty-four early Papunya acrylics shown there contain concentric arcs, which variably denote windbreaks, caves, boomerangs, and ancestral men. In general, concentric arcs in Central Australia refer to ancestral actors or to curved objects.

11. Cooper 1981:38; Smyth 1878, vol. 1:283.

12. Long made two spear-shields for the South Australian Museum's collection (A17537, A17538).

13. The Lower Murray culture, and in particular the life of Clarence Long, is the subject of a forthcoming book by Norman B. Tindale.

14. Taplin 1879:64. The plate shows some early examples of Lower Murray basketry at Point McLeay Mission.

15. Hale 1956; Strahan 1979.

16. Worsnop 1897; also see discussion in Chapter V.

17. As Frederick Rose observed, somewhat reflectively, in 1965: "The adaptation and appropriation of new techniques is a process to which apparently Aboriginal society does not offer any resistance." (Rose 1965:98.)

18. The first exhibition devoted to the theme of Aboriginal technical and artistic innovation was mounted by the Macleay Museum, Sydney, in 1976. Entitled *The Moving Frontier*, the exhibition included bark paintings depicting subjects such as a cow and butterflies, Jesus, and the "Darwin Madonna," as well as a container fashioned from a car hubcap, a fishing spear with fencing-wire prongs, and glass knives. "Aboriginal Recyling," 1976 *Aboriginal News* 3(2):22. Also see Stanbury 1977.

19. Kubler 1971:213.

20. Groger-Wurm 1973 provides a partial chronology of Western attention to bark paintings across Australia. Spencer's and Cahill's collection, obtained at Oenpelli in Arnhem Land, is housed in the Museum of Victoria, Melbourne, and the Australian Museum, Sydney. Some of the Spencer barks were displayed in Australia's first major Aboriginal art exhibition, held in Melbourne in 1929, and were among the items in the first overseas exhibition of Aboriginal art, which toured North America in 1941–42.

Bark paintings were first observed by Peron in Tasmania in 1802, and an illustration by Petit of one of these was published in 1816. Peron 1807–16, vol. 1:273; Peron 1807–16, vol. 2:pl. 16. Also see Bunce 1857:49–50 for a description of Tasmanian bark drawings, probably executed during the late 1820s. In 1876 Smyth published a reproduction of a bark drawing from Victoria made on the wall of a bark shelter probably during the 1860s. Smyth 1878: 286–87, fig.40. The British Museum holds the only other example of a bark-shelter drawing from Victoria. See Massola 1958. Illustrations of Port Essington bark paintings were published in Cox 1878. The South Australian Museum acquired its Field Island bark paintings (collected in 1885) in 1886; these are among the earliest surviving examples. See Carrington 1890:73.

21. Berndt 1983:35. Regarding the origins of the Arnhem Land bark painting "industry" Berndt writes: ". . . in the 1940s Aboriginal communities in north-eastern and western Arnhem Land, including Groote Eylandt, and western Arnhem Land-influenced people living in the Katherine area, were the only ones who produced bark painting as a traditional mode of expression. Now a number of other communities are making such paintings, mainly for an external market . . . The external entrepreneurs of Aboriginal art—the settlement storeman, the Darwin agent or the down-south purveyor—were having their effect on what was being produced. In other words, a separation was taking place between, on one hand, items prepared for the Aborigines' own social usage—particularly in Aboriginal ritual and ceremony—and, on the other, items made for sale to non-Aborigines." (Berndt 1983:32–33.)

22. See Morphy 1983b; Williams 1975.

23. Elkin and Berndt 1950.

24. Berndt 1983:33.

25. See Jones and Sutton 1986.

26. Stirling 1908.

27. Jones and Sutton 1986.

28. Kenyon 1920.

29. Aiston 1938. In a 1924 publication, Horne and Aiston had stated: "The shaped sticks stuck into the ground on departure and spoken of as *toas* were not known by the old men of the Wonkonguru [Wangkangurru]." (Horne and Aiston 1924:26.)

30. Aiston 1938.

31. Bardon 1979. Also see discussion in Chapter IV.

32. "Reuther neither rejected nor questioned the ethnographic facts as they were presented to him by his informants. The toas were described to him as direction markers and as he admitted in

his manuscript, he did not feel competent to doubt such explanations: 'Since the natives maintain it, I am bound, (whether I like it or not) to give credence to it, simply because I cannot prove the contrary.'" (Quoted in Jones and Sutton 1986:60–61.)

33. Reuther 1981:vol.12,180; Reuther 1981:vol.13,156.

34. Reuther 1981.

35. See e.g. Siebert 1910; Howitt and Siebert 1904; Hercus 1987.

36. Morphy 1972, 1977c; Wilson 1981.

37. Analysis of the toas has shown that they are often complex constructions. See Jones and Sutton 1986:63–66.

38. Jones and Sutton 1986:133–35.

39. Vanderwal (ed.) 1982:4; Mulvaney and Calaby 1985:192, 207–208. For accounts of Kite's sculptural work see The *Register* 1913; Lindsay 1968; National Museum of Australia 1986.

40. Gillen 1968:75–76.

41. Adam also mentioned the clay figurines produced by two Aborigines from the Kimberley region of Western Australia. Adam 1948:185–86. See Black 1964:111–15 for a discussion of Youngi's work.

42. Rose 1965:95.

43. Rose 1965:96.

44. Batty 1963.

45. Thomas 1986:26.

46. Namatjira's early sketchbook drawings bear comparison with the work of Aboriginal artists of southeastern Australia of the nineteenth century, such as Yertabrida Solomon, Tommy Barnes, and William Burak, who were also enthusiastic practitioners of this technique.

47. Cf. Graburn (ed.) 1976.

48. Nairne 1987:62–68.

49. Gombrich 1963:24,27.

50. Read (1931) 1950:17. We have substituted "culture" here for "periods," extending Read's argument perhaps a little beyond what he intended.

51. Nairne 1987:32.

52. Nickolls has denied being a political painter, but this is difficult to reconcile with many of his themes (Beier 1985:pls. 1.2,1.4–1.5,1.7,2,4,7,8,11-13,15,20). Fiona Foley (Fig. 250) is one of the least political Aboriginal artists, as far as her images are concerned, and one of those least likely to be recognized as Aboriginal simply on the basis of her works themselves (see e.g. Lambert 1984; Johnson and Johnson 1984; Johnson (ed.) 1987; Urban Koories 1986), but she considers her work to have political content nonetheless (see Butler 1986).

53. Simon 1987.

54. Cf. Trilling 1971; Handler 1986.

55. Hilliard 1980.

56. Johnson and Johnson 1984; Lambert 1984.

57. Lambert 1984:24.

58. Johnson (ed.) 1987.

59. No one has yet offered a satisfactory factual description of what triggers the "slick" response in viewers of certain kinds of Aboriginal art, but it may have something to do with extreme regularity of thickness of line, heavy use of a contrast (e.g. white on dark, even black, colors), oversmooth finish, lack of tension between symmetry and asymmetry, and so on. Fig. 248 would be called slick by many people.

60. Mercifully, also, they have not consciously identified truth with sincerity. When sincerity is practiced as a social virtue, it may lead to insincerity: "[W]e play the role of being ourselves, we sincerely act the part of the sincere person, with the result that the judgement may be passed upon our sincerity that it is not authentic." (Trilling 1971:11.)

61. An Aboriginal person is one who is regarded as such by the Aboriginal community and who also claims this identity. This legal definition actually reflects the realities of contemporary Australia, where it is sometimes difficult to identify a person of Aboriginal descent purely on the basis of appearance and where some people of Aboriginal descent do not ascribe Aboriginal cultural and political identity to themselves.

62. Hilliard 1968.

63. E.g. Newstead 1983.

64. Hopkins 1987.

65. Thorne 1986.

66. Beier 1985.

67. Haynes 1971.

68. Quoted in Isaacs 1982:34–35. The artist's name is also occasionally spelled Thanacoupie.

69. Melbiyoek (Melbiyerk) took shots on Stanner's Graflex at Daly River as early as 1933.

70. Thomas 1982; see Preston 1925; McQueen 1979; North (ed.) 1980; Butler 1987.

71. Preston quoted in Stephen 1980.

72. See Black 1964 for further details.

73. See Haese 1981 for a brilliant account of the social and political forces, and the individual histories, that met in the urban Australian art scene of that period.

74. Philipp 1967; Abbott-Smith 1978; Bail 1981.

75. Cf. Thomas 1982.

76. Catalano 1977.

77. Tillers 1982,1983; and see, for example, Norrie's painting *Untitled* (oil on canvas) from the series *Tall Tales and Time* 1987.

78. This phrase has been gaining currency. See Zimmer 1986, Johnson and Johnson 1986. Some, like Tim Johnson's wife Vivien Johnson, regard this tendency as part of decolonization—"Even intellectual miscegenation can sometimes be redemptive." (Johnson [ed.] 1987.) In the late 1980s some Aboriginal spokespersons have begun to speak of their commencement of "the healing process," a process that is being sought as a form of reconciliation after two hundred years of colonization.

79. Davila 1987.

80. Interview with Ann Newmarch and David Kerr (Sutton, October 30, 1987). The South Australian Museum, curiously enough, holds a large ceremonial serpent apparently made from car tires and another large ritual object that was certainly made from car tires by desert Aborigines and collected by Daisy Bates at Ooldea in 1930. They were unknown to Kerr before he created his own tire snake.

REFERENCES

A

Abbie, A. A. 1969. *The original Australians.* London: Frederick Muller.

Abbott-Smith, N. 1978. *Ian Fairweather. Profile of a painter.* Brisbane: University of Queensland Press.

Aboriginal Law Bulletin No. 17, December 1985. Sydney: University of New South Wales.

Adam, L. 1943. Introduction. In *Primitive art exhibition*, 1–9. (Catalogue). Melbourne: National Gallery and National Museum of Victoria.

———. 1948. *Primitive art.* Melbourne: Penguin.

———. 1951. The bark paintings of Groote Eylandt (Gulf of Carpentaria) in Melbourne University Collection. In *Sudseestudien, Gedenkschrift zur Erinnerung an Felix Speiser*, 162–68. Basel: Museum fur Volkerkunde.

Adams, J. 1986. *Crafts from Aurukun. Design for a local environment.* Aurukun, Queensland: Aurukun Community Inc.

Aiston, G. 1938. Letter to W. H. Gill, dated December 4, Mulka, South Australia. Sydney: Mitchell Library ML A2535-2437.

Allen, L. A. 1975. *Time before morning. Art and myth of the Australian Aborigines.* New York: Thomas Y. Crowell.

Amadio, N., J. Jones, D. Thomas, and A. Blackwell. 1986. *Albert Namatjira. The life and work of an Australian artist.* Melbourne: Macmillan.

Anderson, R. L. 1979. *Art in primitive societies.* Englewood Cliffs, New Jersey: Prentice-Hall.

Angas, G. F. 1846a. *South Australia illustrated.* London: Thomas McLean.

———. 1846b. *New Zealanders illustrated.* London: Thomas McLean.

———. 1847. *Savage life and scenes in Australia and New Zealand. Being an artist's impression of countries and people at the antipodes.* London: Smith, Elder & Co.

———. 1849. *The Kafirs illustrated.* London: J. Hogarth.

Apollinaire, G. 1917. *Sculptures Nègres. 24 Photographies precede d'un avertissement de Guillaume Apollinaire et d'un expose de Paul Guillaume.* Paris: Paul Guillaume.

Arndt, W. 1962a. The interpretation of the Delemere Lightning painting and rock engravings. *Oceania* 32:163–77.

———. 1962b. The Nagorkun-Narlinji cult. *Oceania* 32:298–320.

Art Gallery of New South Wales. 1986. *Origins, originality + beyond.* Catalogue Biennale of Sydney.

Australian Government Information Service. 1986. Calendar. Canberra: Australian Government Publishing Service.

B

Baglin, D., and R. Robinson, 1968. *The Australian Aboriginal in colour.* Sydney: A.W. Reed.

Bail, M. 1981. *Ian Fairweather.* Sydney: Bay Books.

Baillie, P. J. 1978. *Port Lincoln and district. A pictorial history.* Adelaide: Lynton Publications.

Balfour, H. 1893. *The evolution of decorative art.* London: Percival and Co.

Bardon, G. 1979. *Aboriginal art of the Western Desert.* Adelaide: Rigby.

———. 1981. Notes on Anmatjera Aranda territorial Possum Spirit Dreaming. In *Australian Perspecta* 1981, 137. (Catalogue). Sydney: Art Gallery of New South Wales.

———. 1987. Interview with Annemarie Brody. Transcript in South Australian Museum archives.

Barnes, M., A. Brock, and A. Marrie. 1982. Art by metamorphosis, an exhibition of Australian Aboriginal art. Flinders University Library (South Australia). Photocopy.

Barnett, H. G. 1953. *Innovation: The basis of culture change.* New York: McGraw-Hill.

Barrett, C., and R. H. Croll. 1943. *Art of the Australian Aboriginal.* Melbourne: The Bread and Cheese Club.

Barrett, C., and A. S. Kenyon. 1929. *Australian Aboriginal art.* Catalogue for Australian Aboriginal Art Exhibition, National Museum of Victoria, Melbourne, July 1929.

Basedow, H. 1914. Aboriginal rock carvings of great antiquity in South Australia. *Journal of the Royal Anthropological Institute* 44:195–211.

———. 1925. *The Australian Aboriginal.* Adelaide: F. W. Preece and Sons.

Basler, A. 1929. *L'art chez le peuples primitifs.* Paris: Libraire de France.

Battarbee, R. 1951. *Modern Australian Aboriginal art.* Sydney: Angus and Robertson.

Batty, J. 1963. *Namatjira. Wanderer between two worlds.* Melbourne: Hodder and Stoughton.

Beaglehole, J. C. (ed.). 1955. *The journals of Captain James Cook on his voyages of discovery.* Vol.1, 1768–71. Cambridge: Cambridge University Press.

Bean, S. S. 1987. The objects of anthropology. *American Ethnologist* 14(3):552–59.

Bednarik, R. G. 1986. Parietal finger markings in Europe and Australia. *Rock Art Research* 3:30–61.

Beier, U. 1985. *Dream time-machine time. The art of Trevor Nickolls.* Bathurst, New South Wales: Robert Brown.

Bennett, D. 1980. Malangi. The man who was forgotten before he was remembered. *Aboriginal History* 4(1):43–48.

Bern, J. E. 1974. Blackfella business, whitefella law. Political struggles and competition in a South-east Arnhem Land Aboriginal community. Ph.D. dissertation, Macquarie University.

Berndt, R. M. 1952. *Djanggawul. An Aboriginal religious cult of North-Eastern Arnhem Land.* London: Routledge & Kegan Paul.

———. 1964. Preface. In Berndt (ed.), 1964, 1–10.

———. 1971. Some methodological considerations in the study of Australian Aboriginal art. *Oceania* 29:26–43.

———. 1972. The changing face of the Aboriginal arts. *Anthropological Forum* 3(2):146–56.

———. 1973. The arts of life: an introduction. In Berndt and Phillips (eds.), 1973.

———. 1974. *Australian Aboriginal religion.* Leiden: E. J. Brill.

———. 1976. *Three faces of love. Traditional Aboriginal song-poetry.* Melbourne: Nelson.

———. 1983. A living Aboriginal art, the changing inside and outside contexts. In Loveday and Cooke (eds.), 1983, 29–36.

———. (ed.). 1964. *Australian Aboriginal art.* Sydney: Ure Smith.

Berndt, R. M., and C. H. Berndt. 1951. *Sexual behaviour in Western Arnhem Land.* New York: Viking.

———. 1957a. *An exhibition of Australian Aboriginal art, Arnhem Land paintings on bark and carved human figures.* Perth: Western Australian Museum.

———. 1957b. *The art of Arnhem Land.* Exhibition catalogue, Festival of Perth, December 1957–January 1958.

———. 1970. *Man, land and myth in North Australia. The Gunwinggu People.* Sydney: Ure Smith.

Berndt, R. M., C. H. Berndt, with J. E. Stanton. 1982. *Aboriginal Australian art. A Visual Perspective.* Sydney: Methuen.

Berndt, R. M., and E. S. Phillips (eds.). 1973. *The Australian Aboriginal heritage. An introduction through the arts.* Sydney: Australian Society for Education through the Arts in association with Ure Smith.

Biskup, P. 1982. Aboriginal history. In A. Osborn and W. Mandle (eds.). *New history. Studying Australia today.* Sydney: Allen & Unwin.

Black, R. 1964. *Old and new in Australian Aboriginal art.* Sydney: Angus and Robertson.

Boas, F. 1896. *Race, language, and culture.* New York: Macmillan.

———. 1927. *Primitive art.* Cambridge, Massachusetts: Harvard University Press.

———. (1927) 1955. *Primitive art.* New York: Dover.

Bolton, L. M., and J. Specht. 1984–85. *Polynesian and Melanesian artefacts in Australia. An inventory of major public collections.* 3 vols. Sydney: Australian Museum.

Bowler, J. M., R. Jones, H. Allen, and A. G. Thorne. 1970. Pleistocene human remains from Australia. A living site and human cremation from Lake Mungo, western New South Wales. *World Archaeology* 2:39–60.
Bradley, J. 1987. Letter to P. Sutton, August 11, 1987, Darwin, 3 pp.
Brandl, E. 1973. *Australian Aboriginal paintings in Western and Central Arnhem Land. Temporal sequences and elements of style in Cadell River and Deaf Adder Creek art.* Canberra: Australian Institute of Aboriginal Studies.
British Museum. 1910. *Handbook to the ethnographical collection.* London: British Museum.
Brock, A. 1983. A partial history of the gradual acceptance by Europeans of visual art produced by Aboriginal people. Hons. Thesis, Flinders University.
Brody, A. 1985. *The face of the centre: Papunya Tula paintings, 1971–84.* Melbourne: National Gallery of Victoria.
Brook, D. 1986a. Without wishing to tread on anyone's toas. *Artlink* 6:4–5.
———. 1986b. Touching one's toas. *Adelaide Review* 33:38.
———. 1987. Blah (letter to editor). *Adelaide Review* 34:2.
Broome, R. 1982. *Aboriginal Australians: Black response to white domination, 1788–1980.* Sydney: Allen and Unwin.
Buhler, C. A. 1971. *Oceanic art. Myth, man and image in the South Seas.* New York: Abrams.
Buhler, C. A., T. Barrow, and C. P. Mountford. 1962. *Oceania and Australia. The art of the South Seas.* (Art of the World series) London: Methuen.
Bunce, D. 1857. *Twenty three years wandering in the Australias and Tasmania.* Geelong: Brown.
Burke, J. 1980. *Australian women artists 1840–1940.* Melbourne: Greenhouse Publications.
Burkitt, M. C. 1931. Most primitive art. In M. C. Burkitt. *Early Man.* London: E. Benn.
Butel, E. 1987. The prints of Margaret Preston. *The Age Monthly Review* 7(7):8–10
Butler, R. 1986. From Dreamtime to machinetime. *Imprint* 21(3–4):6–14.
———. 1987. *The prints of Margaret Preston. A catalogue raisonné.* Melbourne: Australian National Gallery and Oxford University Press.
Butlin, N. G. 1983. *Our original aggression. Aboriginal populations of Southeastern Australia 1788–1850.* Sydney: Allen & Unwin.

C

Cameron, A. L. P. 1885. Notes on some tribes of New South Wales. *Journal of the Royal Anthropological Institute* 14:357.
Carrington, F. 1890. The rivers of the Northern Territory of South Australia. *Royal Geographic Society of Australasia (South Australian Branch) Proceedings* 2:56–76.
Carroll, P. J. 1977. Mimi from Western Arnhem Land. In Ucko (ed.), 1977, 119–30.
———. 1983. Aboriginal art from Western Arnhem Land. In Loveday and Cooke (eds.), 1983, 44–49.
Carter, P. 1987. Invisibility. *Age Monthly Review*, April 1987:2.
Catalano, G. 1977. Changing responses to Aboriginal art. *Meanjin* 36:572–81.
Catalogue of an exhibition of the art of primitive peoples. 1935. London: Burlington Arts Club.
Cato, N. 1976. *Mister Maloga. Daniel Matthews and his mission, Murray River, 1864–1902.* Brisbane: University of Queensland Press.
Chaloupka, G. 1977. Aspects of the chronology and schematisation of two prehistoric sites on the Arnhem Land plateau. In Ucko (ed.), 1977, 243–59.
———. 1985. Chronological sequence of Arnhem Land plateau rock art. In R. Jones (ed.). *Archaeological Research in Kakadu National Park.* Canberra: Australian National Parks and Wildlife Service.
Chase, A., and J. von Sturmer. 1979. "Mental man" and social evolutionary theory. In G. E. Kearney, P. R. de Lacey, G. R. Davidson (eds.), 3–15. *The psychology of Aboriginal Australians.* Sydney: John Wiley & Sons.
Chase, A., and P. J. Sutton. 1981. Hunter-gatherers in a rich environment. Aboriginal coastal exploitation in Cape York Peninsula. In A. Keast (ed.), 1817–52. *Ecological biogeography of Australia*, vol.3. The Hague: Junk.
Chipp, H. B. 1960. Formal and symbolic factors in the art styles of primitive cultures. *The Journal of Aesthetics and Art Criticism* 19:153–66.
Clark, K. (1949) 1961. *Landscape into art.* Melbourne: Penguin Books.
———. (1956) 1976. *The nude: A study of ideal art.* Harmondsworth, Middlesex: Penguin Books.
Clodd, E. 1895. *Primitive man.* London: George Newnes Ltd.
Clouzot, H., and A. Level. 19_9. *L'art sauvage—Oceanie, Afrique. Catalogue de la premiere exposition d'art Nègre et d'art Oceanien organise par Paul Guillaume.* Paris: Devambez.
Conroy, D. 1978. Tiwi designs. An Aboriginal silk-screen workshop. In Edwards (ed.), 1978, 50–53.
Coombs, H. C. 1986. Introduction. In Amadio et al., 1986, vii.
Cooper, C. 1981. Art of temperate, south-east Australia. In Cooper, et al., 1981, 29–40.
Cooper, C., H. Morphy, J. Mulvaney, and N. Peterson. 1981. *Aboriginal Australia.* Sydney: Australian Gallery Directors Council.
Cooper, C., and J. Urry. 1981. Art, Aborigines and Chinese: a nineteenth-century drawing by the Kwatkwat artist Tommy McRae. *Aboriginal History* 5:81–88.
Cooper, M., and H. Chalfant. 1984. *Subway art.* London: Thames and Hudson.
Cox, J. C. 1878. Drawings by Australian Aborigines. *Proceedings of the Linnean Society of New South Wales* 3:155–61.
Crawford, I. M. 1968. *The art of the Wandjina: Aboriginal cave paintings in Kimberley, Western Australia.* Melbourne: Oxford University Press.
———. 1977. The relationship of Bradshaw and Wandjina art in north-west Kimberley. In Ucko (ed.), 1977, 357–69.
Crocker, A. 1987. *Charlie Tjaruru Tjungurrayi. A retrospective, 1970–1986.* Orange, New South Wales: Orange City Council.
———. (ed.). 1983. *Papunya: Aboriginal paintings from the Central Australian Desert.* Sydney: Aboriginal Artists Agency & Papunya Tula Artists.
Curr, E. M. (1883) 1965. *Recollections of squatting in Victoria, then called the Port Phillip District.* Melbourne: Melbourne University Press.
———. 1886–87. *The Australian race.* 4 vols. Melbourne: John Ferres.

D

Davidson, D. S. 1936. *Aboriginal Australian and Tasmanian rock carvings and paintings. Memoirs of the American Philosophical Society* 5:iii–xi,1–151. Philadelphia: The American Philosophical Society.
———. 1937. A preliminary consideration of Aboriginal Australian art. *Memoirs of the American Philosophical Society* 9.
Davidson, H. R. E. 1964. *Gods and myths of northern Europe.* Harmondsworth, Middlesex: Penguin Books.
Davila, J. 1987. Aboriginality: a lugubrious game? *Art & Text* 23(4):53–56.
Degerando, J. M. (1800) 1969. *The observation of savage peoples.* Transl. by F. C. T. Moore. London: Routledge and Kegan Paul.
Diggins, L. 1987. Contemporary art finds a new home in the National Gallery of Victoria. *Federalist* 15(1):14–19.
Docker, J. 1984. *In a critical condition. Reading Australian literature.* Melbourne: Penguin Books.
Donne, J. B. 1978. African art and Paris studios. In M. Greenhalgh and V. Megaw (eds.), 105–20. *Art in society. Studies in style, culture and aesthetics.* London: Duckworth.
Duigan, V. 1984. When the first Australians stormed Paris. *The National Times*, Jan. 27–Feb. 2: 29.
Durkheim, E. 1912. *The elementary forms of the religious life.* London: Allen & Unwin.
Dutton, G. 1974. *White on black: The Australian Aborigine portrayed in art.* Melbourne: Macmillan.

E

Edwards, R. 1966. Comparative study of rock engravings in South and Central Australia. *Transactions of the Royal Society of South Australia* 90:33–38.
———. 1972. *Aboriginal bark canvases of the Murray Valley.* Adelaide: Rigby.

———. 1979. *Australian Aboriginal art. The art of the Alligator Rivers Region, Northern Territory.* Canberra: Australian Institute of Aboriginal Studies.
——— (ed.). 1975. *The preservation of Australia's Aboriginal heritage. Report of national seminar on Aboriginal Antiquities in Australia May 1972.* Canberra: Australian Institute of Aboriginal Studies.
——— (ed.). 1978. *Aboriginal art in Australia.* Sydney: Ure Smith.
Edwards, R., and B. Guerin. 1969. *Aboriginal bark paintings.* Adelaide: Rigby.
Einstein, C. 1915. *Negerplastik.* Leipzig.
Elkin, A. P. 1943. Review of primitive art exhibition, Melbourne, 1943. *Oceania* 13(4):376.
———. 1948. Grey's northern Kimberley paintings re-found. *Oceania* 19:1–15.
———. 1950a. Art in Aboriginal life. In Elkin, Berndt, and Berndt, 1950, 1–19.
———. 1950b. *Art in Arnhem Land.* Chicago: University of Chicago Press.
———. 1964a. *The Australian Aborigines. How to understand them.* Sydney: Angus and Robertson.
———. 1964b. Art and life. In Berndt (ed.), 1964, 11–19.
———. 1972. *Two rituals in South and Central Arnhem Land.* Sydney: Oceania Monographs.
Elkin, A. P., R. M. Berndt, and C. H. Berndt. 1950. *Art in Arnhem Land.* Melbourne: F. W. Cheshire.
Ellis, R. W. 1978. *Aboriginal culture in South Australia.* Adelaide: Government Printer.
Elsasser, A. B., and V. Paul. 1969. *Australian Aboriginal art. The Louis A. Allen collection.* Exhibition catalogue, R. H. Lowie Museum of Anthropology, University of California, Berkeley.
Eyre, E. J. 1845. *Journals of expeditions of discovery into Central Australia.* 2 vols. London: T. & W. Boone.

F

Faure, E. 1912. *Histoire de l'art. L'art medieval.* Paris: Floury.
Forge, J. A. W. (ed.). 1973. *Primitive art and society.* London: Oxford University Press.
Foucault, M. 1972. *The archaeology of knowledge.* London: Tavistock.
Fox, S. 1982. Quality is not necessarily a smooth straight line. In P. Cooke and J. Altman (eds.), 10–11. *Aboriginal Art at the top.* Maningrida, Northern Territory: Maningrida Arts and Crafts.
Fraser, D. 1957. The discovery of primitive art. *Arts Yearbook* 1:119–32. New York: The Art Digest Inc.
———. 1962. *Primitive art.* London: Thames and Hudson.
———. 1971. The discovery of primitive art. In Otten (ed.), 1971, 20–36.
Frese, H. H. 1960. *Anthropology and the public. The role of museums.* Mededelingen van het Rijksmuseum voor Volkenkunde. Leiden: E. J. Brill.

G

Gallus, A. 1968. Parietal art in Koonalda Cave. *Helictite* 6:43–49.
Gathercole, P. 1978. Obstacles to the study of Maori carving. The collector, the connoisseur, and the faker. In Greenhalgh and Megaw (eds.), 1978, 275–87.
Gerbrands, A. A. 1957. *Art as an element of culture, especially in Negro Africa.* Mededelingen van het Rijksmuseum voor Volkenkunde 12. Leiden: E. J. Brill.
Gillen, F. J. 1968. *Gillen's diary. The camp jottings of F. J. Gillen on the Spencer and Gillen expedition across Australia 1901–1902.* Adelaide: South Australian Libraries Board.
Goddard, R. H. 1939. Aboriginal sculpture. Report of 24th Meeting, Australian and New Zealand Association for the Advancement of Science, Canberra, 160ff. Sydney. Publisher not known.
Goldwater, R. (1938) 1967. *Primitivism in modern art.* New York: Random House.
Gombrich, E. H. 1962. *Art and illusion.* London: Phaidon.
———. 1963. *Meditations on a hobby horse and other essays on the theory of art.* London: Phaidon.
———. 1972. Icones symbolicae. Philosophies of symbolism and their bearing on art. In E. H. Gombrich, 123–95. *Symbolic images. Studies in the art of the Renaissance II.* London: Phaidon.
———. 1984. *The sense of order: A study in the psychology of decorative art.* London: Phaidon.
Goodale, J. C. 1971. *Tiwi wives. A Study of the women of Melville Island, North Australia.* Seattle: University of Washington Press.
Graburn, N. H. H. 1976. Introduction. Arts of the Fourth World. In Graburn (ed.), 1976.
——— (ed.). 1976. *Ethnic and tourist arts. Cultural expressions from the Fourth World.* Berkeley: University of California Press.
Greenhalgh, C. M. B., and J. V. S. Megaw (eds.). 1978. *Art in society. Studies in style, culture and aesthetics.* London: Duckworth.
Grey, G. 1841. *Journals of two expeditions of discovery in North-West and Western Australia during the years 1837, 38 and 39.* 2 vols. London: Thomas W. Borges & Co.
Groger-Wurm, H. M. 1973. *Australian Aboriginal bark paintings and their mythological interpretation.* Volume 1: Eastern Arnhem Land. Canberra: Australian Institute of Aboriginal Studies.
Grosse, E. (1894) 1902. *Les debuts de l'art.* (Transl.) New York: Appleton.
Guillaume, P., and T. Munro. 1925. Comment s'est developpe le gout pour l'art Africain. *Les Arts a Paris,* Oct. 1925, 10–11.
———. 1926. *Primitive Negro sculpture.* New York: Harcourt Brace.
Gunn, G. 1973. *Groote Eylandt art. Leonhard Adam ethnological collection part one.* (Exhibition catalogue.) Melbourne: University of Melbourne.

H

Haddon, A. C. 1894. *The decorative art of New Guinea.* Cunningham Memoirs. Dublin: Irish Academy.
———. 1895. *Evolution in art.* London: Walter Scott Ltd.
———. 1934. *History of anthropology.* London: Watts & Co.
Haese, R. 1981. *Rebels and precursors. The Revolutionary years of Australian art.* Melbourne: Allen Lane.
Hale, H. M. 1956. The first hundred years of the South Australian Museum 1856–1956. *Records of the South Australian Museum* 12.
Hale, H. M., and N. B. Tindale. 1925. Observations on Aborigines of the Flinders Ranges, and records of rock carvings and paintings. *Records of the South Australian Museum* 3:45–60.
Halverson, J. 1987. Art for art's sake in the paleolithic. *Current Anthropology* 28:63–89.
Handler, R. 1986. Authenticity. *Anthropology Today* 2(1):2–4.
Harris, M. 1969. *The rise of anthropological theory. A history of theories of culture.* London: Routledge and Kegan Paul.
Haselburger, H. 1961. Methods of studying ethnological art. *Current Anthropology* 2:351–84.
Haynes, L. M. 1971. Artist potters goal of ceramic research unit. *Northern Territory Affairs,* 4 October 1971, 14–15.
Hays, H. R. (1958) 1971. *From ape to angel. An informal history of social anthropology.* New York: A. A. Knopf.
Helms, R. 1896. Anthropology (part of report of Elder Scientific Expedition of 1891). *Transactions of the Royal Society of South Australia* 16:237–332.
Henderson, K. R. (ed.). 1978. *From earlier fleets.* Canberra: Curriculum Development Centre.
Hercus, L. A. 1987. Just one toa. *Records of the South Australian Museum* 20:59–69.
Hiatt, L. R. 1975. Introduction. In L. R. Hiatt (ed.), 1–23. *Australian Aboriginal mythology. Essays in honour of W. E. H. Stanner.* Canberra: Australian Institute of Aboriginal Studies.
———. 1983. The relationship between Aboriginal religion and customary law. Unpublished paper, Australian Law Reform Commission and Australian Institute of Aboriginal Studies report on a working seminar of the Aboriginal Customary Law Reference, Sydney, May 7–8, 1983, 8–11.
———. 1986. Aboriginal political life. (The Wentworth Lecture 1984.) Canberra: Australian Institute of Aboriginal Studies.
Hill, M. 1981. Untrammelled art. Travelling exhibition of Aboriginal art. In Henderson (ed.), 1978, 82–96.
Hill, M., and N. McLeod. 1984. *From the ochres of Mungo. Aboriginal art today.* Melbourne: Dorr/McLeod.
Hilliard, W. M. 1968. *The people in between. The Pitjantjatjara people of Ernabella.* London: Hodder and Stoughton.

———. 1980. Tradition—the root—free and life-sustaining or pot-bound and atrophying? Unpublished paper presented at ANZAAS conference, Adelaide, May 1980.
Hogan, P. 1986. Notes and inventory for the early consignments of Pintupi paintings. In Maughan and Zimmer (eds.), 1986, 55–57.
Holmes, S. L. B. 1972. *Yirawala. Artist and man.* Brisbane: Jacaranda Press.
———. 1976. Death of Yirawala. *Aboriginal News* 3(2):6.
Hopkins, N. 1987. Better by design. *The Advertiser Magazine* (Adelaide), March 7, 1987, 12–13.
Horne, G., and G. Aiston. 1924. *Savage life in Central Australia.* London: Macmillan.
Horton, D. 1978. Prehistory. In M. Hill and A. Barlow (comps.), 19–23. *Black Australia: An annotated bibliography and teacher's guide to resources on Aborigines and Torres Strait Islanders.* Canberra: Australian Institute of Aboriginal Studies.
Howie, R. 1981. Northern Territory. In N. Peterson (ed.), 48–52, *Aboriginal land rights: a handbook.* Canberra: Australian Institute of Aboriginal Studies.
Howitt, A. W. 1904. *The native tribes of south-east Australia.* London: Macmillan.
Howitt, A. W., and O. Siebert. 1904. Legends of the Dieri and kindred tribes of Central Australia. *Journal of the Royal Anthropological Institute* 34:100–129.
von Humboldt, A. (1808) 1849. *Aspects of nature.* 2 vols. Transl. by Mrs. Sabine. London. Publisher not known.

I

Impeg, O., and A. McGregor. 1985. *The origin of museums.* Oxford: Clarendon Press.
Isaacs, J. (comp. and ed.). 1980. *Australian Dreaming: 40,000 years of Aboriginal history.* Sydney: Lansdowne Press.
———. 1982. *Thancoupie the potter.* Sydney: The Aboriginal Artists Agency.
———. 1984. *Arts of the Dreaming. Australia's living heritage.* Sydney: Lansdowne.

J

Japaljarri Stockman, Billy. 1976. Art of Western Desert. *Art in Australia* 13(3).
Jelinek, J. (ed.). 1979. *Anthropology of the Rembrranga people. A contribution of the Czechoslovak Anthropos Expedition to Arnhem Land N.T. Australia*, special issue of *Anthropologie* 17:107–323.
Johnson, T., and V. Johnson (comps.) 1984. *Koori art '84.* (Exhibition catalogue.) Sydney: Artspace.
———. (comps.) 1986. *Two worlds collide. Cultural convergence in Aboriginal and white Australian art.* (Exhibition catalogue.) Sydney: Artspace.
Johnson, V. 1987. Art & Aboriginality 1987. Introduction to V. Johnson (ed.),*Australia. Art & Aboriginality 1987.* (Exhibition catalogue.) Portsmouth (U.K.): Aspex Gallery.
Jones, O. 1856. *The grammar of ornament.* London. Publisher not known.
Jones, P. G. 1985. Red ochre expeditions. An ethnographic and historical analysis of Aboriginal trade in the Lake Eyre basin. Parts 1 and 2. *Journal of the Anthropological Society of South Australia* 22(7):3–10; 22(8):4–11.
———. 1987a. South Australian anthropological history. The early expeditions of the Board for Anthropological Research. *Records of the South Australian Museum* 20:71–92.
———. 1987b. The great toa hoax? (letter to editor). *Age Monthly Review*, July: 22.
Jones, P. G., and P. J. Sutton. 1986. *Art and land. Aboriginal sculptures of the Lake Eyre region.* Adelaide: South Australian Museum.

K

Kaeppler, A. 1978. *"Artificial curiosities." An exposition of native manufactures collected on the three Pacific voyages of Captain James Cook, R.N.* Honolulu: Bishop Museum Press.
Keen, I. 1978. One ceremony, one song. An economy of religious knowledge among the Yolngu of North-East Arnhem Land. Ph.D. dissertation, Australian National University.
Kenyon, A. S. 1920. Letter to General Secretary, Public Library, Museum and Art Gallery, dated June 9, Melbourne. Adelaide: South Australian Public Record Office (GRG19).
Kimber, R. G. 1978. Mosaics that you can move. In Henderson (ed.), 1978, 49–57.
———. 1981. Catalogue notes for Warlugulong, 1976, by Clifford Possum Tjapaltjarri and Tim Leura Tjapaltjarri, 136. Australian Perspecta 1981. Sydney: Art Gallery of New South Wales.
———. 1982. Papunya Tula: artists of the Central and Western Deserts of Australia. In L. Paroissien (ed.), 122–25. *Australian Art Review.* Sydney: Warner Associates Pty. Ltd.
Kroeber, A. L. 1935. Primitive art. In *Encyclaeopodia of the social sciences*, vol.2, 226 ff. New York: Macmillan.
Kubler, G. 1971. On the colonial extinction of the motifs of pre-Columbian art. In Otten (ed.), 1971, 212–26.
Kupka, K. 1965. *The Dawn of art. Painting and sculpture of Australian Aborigines.* Sydney: Angus and Robertson.
———. 1972. *Peintres Aborigines d'Australie.* Paris: Musée de l'Homme.

L

Lambert, A. 1984. Shattering the myth that Aboriginal art exists only in traditional forms. *Australian Artist* 1(4):24–25.
Langer, S. K. 1967. *Philosophy in a new key.* Cambridge, Massachusetts: Harvard University Press.
von Leonhardi, M. 1908. Uber einige Hundefiguren des Dieristammes in Zentralaustralien. *Globus* 94:378–80.
Levi-Strauss, C. 1966. *The savage mind.* Chicago: University of Chicago Press.
Lewis, D. 1984. Mimi on Bradshaw. *Australian Aboriginal Studies* 1984/2:58–61.
Linton, R., and P. S. Wingert, in collaboration with R. d'Harnoncourt. 1946. *Arts of the South Seas.* New York: The Museum of Modern Art.
Lindsay, H. A. 1968. An Aboriginal sculptor. *Aboriginal Quarterly* 1(2):18–19.
Loveday, P., and P. Cooke (eds.). 1983. *Aboriginal arts and crafts and the market.* Darwin: Australian National University North Australia Research Unit.
Lovejoy, A. O. (1936) 1960. *The great chain of being.* New York: Harper Torchbooks.
Lowie, R. H. 1937. *The history of ethnological theory.* New York: Holt, Rinehart and Winston.
Luquet, G. H. 1926. *L'art et la religion des hommes fossiles.* Paris. Publisher not known.
———. 1930. *L'art primitif.* Paris: Gaston Doin.

M

McCarthy, F. D. 1957. Theoretical considerations of Australian Aboriginal art. *Journal of the Royal Society of New South Wales* 91:3–22.
———. 1960. Australian Aboriginal art. Introduction. Exhibition catalogue, State Art Galleries of Australia, 1960–61.
———. 1964a. *Australian bark paintings, 1912–1964.* Catalogue, Commonwealth Arts Festival.
———. 1964b. The Dancers of Aurukun. *Australian Natural History* 14:296–300.
———. (1938) 1974. *Australian Aboriginal decorative art.* Sydney: The Australian Museum.
———. 1978. Aurukun dances. Unpublished typescript, Australian Institute of Aboriginal Studies Library, Canberra.
———. (1958) 1979. *Australian Aboriginal rock art.* Sydney: The Australian Museum.
McCarthy, F. D., and M. McArthur. 1960. The food quest and time factor in Aboriginal economic life. In C. P. Mountford (ed.). *Records of the American-Australian scientific expedition to Arnhem Land. Volume 2: anthropology and nutrition.* Melbourne: Melbourne University Press.
McConnel, U. H. 1935. Inspiration and design in Aboriginal art. *Art in Australia* 59:49–68.
———. 1953. Native arts and industries on the Archer, Kendall and Holroyd Rivers, Cape York Peninsula, North Queensland. *Records of the South Australian Museum* 11:1–42.

———. 1957. *Myths of the Mungkan.* Melbourne: Melbourne University Press.
McDonald, J. (comp.). 1986. *Australian Artists' index: A biographical index of Australian artists, craft workers, photographers and architects.* Sydney: Arts Libraries Society, Australia and New Zealand.
McQueen, H. 1979. *The black swan of trespass. The emergence of modernist painting in Australia to 1944.* Sydney: Alternative Publishing Cooperative.
Mack, M., L. Dean, and W. Frost. 1950. Introduction. In Mack, Dean, Frost (comps.) *Modern Poetry.* Englewood Cliffs, New Jersey: Prentice-Hall.
Maddock, K. 1969. The Jabuduruwa. A study of the structure of rite and myth in an Australian Aboriginal religious cult on the Beswick Reserve, Northern Territory. Ph.D. dissertation, University of Sydney.
———. (1974) 1982. *The Australian Aborigines: A portrait of their society.* Melbourne: Penguin Books.
Maquet, J. 1979. *Introduction to aesthetic anthropology.* Malibu, Calif.: Undena Publications.
Marabottini, A. 1969. Raphael's Collaborators. In L. Becherucci et al., 199–301. *The complete work of Raphael.* New York: Harrison House.
March, H. C. 1889. The meaning of ornament. *Transactions of the Lancashire and Cheshire Antiquarian Society.*
Marrie, A. (comp.). 1987. A topical bibliography of Australian Aboriginal visual arts, including a bibliography concerning Aboriginal heritage issues. 3rd edn. Adelaide.
Massola, A. 1958. A Victorian Aboriginal bark drawing in the British Museum. *Victorian Naturalist* 75:124–27.
Mathews, R. H. 1894. The Aboriginal rock pictures of Australia. *Proceedings and Transactions of the Royal Geographical Society of Australasia* 10:46–70.
———. 1895. Rock carvings and paintings of the Australian Aborigines. *Proceedings of the American Philosophical Society* 36:466–78.
Maughan, J. 1986. Introduction. In Maughan and Zimmer (eds.), 1986, 15–28.
Maughan, J., and J. V. S. Megaw. 1986. *The Dreamtime today. A survey of contemporary Aboriginal arts and crafts.* Adelaide: Visual Arts Discipline, Flinders University.
Maughan, J., and J. Zimmer (eds.). 1986. *Dot & circle. A retrospective survey of the Aboriginal acrylic paintings of Central Australia.* Melbourne: Royal Melbourne Institute of Technology.
Maynard, L. 1977. Classification and terminology in Australian rock art. In Ucko (ed.), 1977, 387–402.
Meeks, R. 1987. Raymond Meeks. In A. Newstead and C. Watson. *Dalkuna Mnunuwa Nhe Rom.* Sydney: Cooee Australian Emporium.
Megaw, J. V. S. 1972. More eighteenth-century trophies from Botany Bay? *Mankind* 8(3):225–26.
———. 1981. Artists-in-residence: subjects or objects? *Australian Institute of Aboriginal Studies Newsletter* 15:50–62.
———. 1982. Western Desert acrylic painting: artefact or art? *Art History* 5(2):205–18.
———. 1984. Dot and circle. Paradox, politics and "Papunya" paintings. *Art Network* 13:55–61.
———. 1986. Contemporary Aboriginal art. Dreamtime discipline or alien adulteration. In Maughan and Zimmer (eds.), 1986, 61–54.
Meredith, C. 1844. *Notes and sketches of New South Wales during a residence in that colony from 1839 to 1844.* London: Murray.
Merkert, J., and I. Krueger. 1980. *Dubuffet retrospektive.* Berlin: Akademie der Kuenste.
Michaels, E. 1986. *The Aboriginal invention of television in Central Australia 1982–1986.* Canberra: Australian Institute of Aboriginal Studies.
———. 1987. Western Desert sandpainting and post-modernism. In Warlukurlangu Artists, 1987, 135–43.
Morphy, H. 1972. A reanalysis of the toas of the Lake Eyre tribes of Central Australia. An examination of their form and function. M.Phil. thesis, London University.
———. 1977a. "Too many meanings." An analysis of the artistic system of the Yolngu of Northeast Arnhem Land. Ph.D. dissertation, Australian National University.
———. 1977b. Yingapungapu—ground sculpture as bark painting. In Ucko (ed.), 1977, 205–209.
———. 1977c. Schematisation, meaning and communication in toas. In Ucko (ed.), 1977, 77–89.
———. 1980. What circles look like. *Canberra Anthropology* 3:17–36.
———. 1981. The art of Northern Australia. In Cooper et al. 1981, 52–65.
———. 1983a. "Now you understand." An analysis of the way Yolngu have used sacred knowledge to retain their autonomy. In N. Peterson and M. Langton (eds.). *Aborigines, land and land rights.* Canberra: Australian Institute of Aboriginal Studies, 110–33.
———. 1983b. Aboriginal fine art, the creation of audiences and the marketing of art. In Loveday and Cooke (eds.), 1983, 37–43.
———. 1984. Yolngu ceremonies and bark painting. In M. Charlesworth et al. (eds.). *Religion in Aboriginal Australia. A reader.* Brisbane: University of Queensland Press.
———. 1986. From dull to brilliant—the aesthetics of spiritual power among the Yolngu. Typescript 37pp.
———. 1987. Audiences for art. In A. Curthoys, A. W. Martin, and T. Rowse (eds.), 167–75. *Australians: a historical library. From 1939.* Sydney: Fairfax, Syme & Weldon Associates.
———. n.d. Representing Ancestral Beings. Typescript 17pp.
Morwood, M. 1985. Facts and figures. Notes on rock art in the Mt. Isa area, northwestern Queensland. *Rock Art Research* 2:140–45.
Mountford, C. P. 1937a. Aboriginal crayon drawings from the Warburton Ranges in Western Australia relating to the wanderings of two ancestral beings, the Wati Kutjara. *Records of the South Australian Museum* 6:5–28.
———. 1937b. Aboriginal crayon drawings relating to totemic places belonging to the northern Aranda tribe of Central Australia. *Transactions of the Royal Society of South Australia* 61:81–95.
———. 1938a. A contrast in drawings made by Australian Aborigines before and after initiation. *Records of the South Australian Museum* 20:111–14.
———. 1938b. Aboriginal crayon drawings 3. The legend of Wati-Jula and the Kunkarunkara women. *Transactions of the Royal Society of South Australia* 62:241–54.
———. 1939a. Aboriginal crayon drawings 4. Relating to everyday incidents of the Ngada tribe of the Warburton Ranges of Western Australia. *Transactions of the Royal Society of South Australia* 63:1–13.
———. 1939b. Aboriginal crayon drawings, Warburton Ranges, Western Australia. *Oceania* 10:72–79.
———. 1939c. Aboriginal decorative art from Arnhem Land, Northern Territory of Australia. *Transactions of the Royal Society of South Australia* 63:365–71.
———. 1944. *The art of Albert Namatjira.* Melbourne: The Bread and Cheese Club.
———. 1950. Introduction. In *Australian Aboriginal art.* (Exhibition catalogue: cave paintings by James Cant and photographs by Charles Mountford). London: Berkely Galleries.
———. 1953. Introduction. In *Aboriginal art of Australia.* (Exhibition catalogue.) Adelaide: York Theatre.
———. 1954. *Aboriginal paintings from Australia.* London: Collins, UNESCO.
———. 1956a. *Records of the American-Australian scientific expedition to Arnhem Land. Volume 1: art, myth and symbolism.* Melbourne: Melbourne University Press.
———. 1956b. Expedition to the land of the Tiwi. *The National Geographic Magazine* 59:417–40.
———. 1957a. Introduction. In *Bark Paintings: Aboriginal art of Australia.* (Exhibition catalogue.) London: Institute of Contemporary Arts.
———. 1957b. Aboriginal bark paintings from Field Island, Northern Territory. *Records of the South Australian Museum* 13:87–89.
———. 1958. *The Tiwi. Their art, myth and ceremony.* London: Phoenix House.
———. 1960. Introduction. In *Festival souvenir programme.* Adelaide: Adelaide Festival of Arts.
———. 1961. The artist and his art in Australian Aboriginal society. In M. W. Smith (ed.). *The Artist in tribal society.* New York: Free Press of Glencoe.
———. 1966a. Introduction. In *Aboriginal art from Australia.* (Exhibition catalogue.) Worcester, Massachusetts: Worcester Art Museum.
———. 1966b. *Aboriginal art from Australia.* (Exhibition catalogue.) Worcester, Massachusetts: Worcester Art Museum.
———. 1967. *Australian Aboriginal portraits.* Melbourne: Melbourne University Press.
———. 1976. *Before time began.* Melbourne: Nelson.

Mountford, C. P., and R. Edwards. 1963. Rock engravings ofd Panaramitee Station, north eastern South Australia. *Transactions of the Royal Society of South Australia* 86:131–46.
Moyal, A. 1986. *"A bright and savage land." Scientists in colonial Australia.* Sydney: Collins.
Muensterberger, W. 1971. Roots of primitive art. In Otten (ed.), 1971, 106–28.
Mulvaney, D. J., and J. H. Calaby. 1985. *"So much that is new." Baldwin Spencer 1860–1929.* Melbourne: Melbourne University Press.
Mundkur, B. 1983. *The cult of the Serpent. An interdisciplinary survey of its manifestations and origins.* Albany: State University of New York Press.
Munn, N. D. 1970. The transformation of subjects into objects in Walbiri and Pitjantjatjara myth. In R. M. Berndt (ed.), 141–63. *Australian Aboriginal anthropology. Modern studies in the social anthropology of the Australian Aborigines.* Perth: University of Western Australia Press for the Australian Institute of Aboriginal Studies.
———. 1973a. *Walbiri iconography.* London: Cornelld University Press. (2nd edn. 1987.)
———. 1973b. The spatial presentation of cosmic order in Walbiri iconography. In A. Forge (ed.). *Primitive art and society*, London: Oxford University Press.
Murphy, B. 1983. *Catalogue XVII Bienal de Sao Paolo: Australia.* Sydney: Aboriginal Artists Agency.
Myers, F. 1986. *Pintupi country, Pintupi self.* Washington and Canberra: Smithsonian and Australian Institute of Aboriginal Studies.

N

Nairne, S. 1987. *State of the art. Ideas & images in the 1980s.* London: Chatto & Windus/Channel Four.
National Museum of Australia. 1986. *On the horizon. Opening exhibition catalogue.* Canberra: National Museum of Australia.
National Museum of Victoria. 1929. *Australian Aboriginal art.* (Exhibition catalogue.)
Newstead, A. 1983. Tiwi Aboriginal designs. *Craft Australia*, Spring 1983/3:92–95.
Nobbs, M. 1984. Rock art in Olary Province, South Australia. *Rock Art Research* 1:91–118.
North, I. (ed.). 1980. *The art of Margaret Preston.* Adelaide: Art Gallery Board of South Australia.

O

O'Donnell, G. 1980. Bark paintings that died a dog's death (summary). *Bulletin of the Conference of Museum Anthropologists* 5:24–25.
Oldman, W. O. 1903–14. *Illustrated catalogue of ethnographical specimans, Eastern arms etc.* London: Oldman.
Otten, C. M. (ed.). 1971. *Anthropology and art.* New York: The Natural History Press, American Museum of Natural History.

P

Parezo, N. 1985. Cushing as part of the team. The collecting activities of the Smithsonian Institution. *American Ethnologist* 12(4):763–74.
Peltier, P. 1984. From Oceania. In Rubin (ed.), 1984, 99–123.
Pitt-Rivers, A. H. 1875. Principles of classification. *Journal of the Anthropological Institute* 4:293–308.
Peron, M. F. 1807–16. *Voyage de Decouvertes aux terres Australes, execute par ordre de sa Majeste L'Empereur et Roi, sur les corvettes le geographe, le naturaliste, et la goelette le casuarina, pendant les annees 1800, 1801, 1802, 1803 et 1804.* (vol. 1 edited by Peron in 1807; vol. 2 edited by Freycinet in 1816.) Paris: de l'Imprimerie Imperiale.
Peterson, N. 1981. Art of the desert. In Cooper et al., 1981, 42–51.
Philipp, F. 1967. *Arthur Boyd.* London: Thames and Hudson.
Phillip, A. 1789. *The Voyage of Governor Phillip to Botany Bay.* London. Publisher not known.
Poignant, R. 1967. *Oceanic mythology. The myths of Polynesia, Micronesia, Melanesia, Australia.* London: Paul Hamlyn.
Preston, M. 1925. The indigenous art of Australia. *Art in Australia* 11(3rd series, March):32–45.
———. 1930. The application of Aboriginal designs. *Art in Australia* 31(3rd series, March):44–58.
———. 1940. Paintings in Arnhem Land. *Art in Australia* 81(3rd series, September):58–59; 61–63.

R

Racinet, A. 1869. *L'ornement polychrome. Art ancien et asiatique, Moyen-Age, Renaissance, XVII, XVIII, XIX siecle: Recueil historique et prehistorique avec des notes explicatives.* 2 vols. Paris: Firmin Didot.
Raggett, O. 1980. *Stories of Obed Raggett.* Sydney: Alternative Publishing Cooperative.
Rainey, F. 1955. The new museum. *Bulletin, University Museum, Philadelphia* 19(3).
Ratzel, F. 1896. *The history of mankind.* Introduction by E. B. Tylor. 3 vols. London: Macmillan.
Read, H. (1931) 1950. *The meaning of art.* London: Penguin Books.
———. 1937. *Art and society.* London: Faber and Faber.
Redfield, R. 1971. Art and icon. In Otten (ed.), 1971, 39–65.
The Register. 1913. A black genius. Beautiful specimens of native art. Adelaide, July 18, 1913:7.
Reser, J. 1978. Values in bark. In Henderson (ed.), 1978, 27–34.
Reuther, J. G. 1981. *The Diari* (vols. 1–13). Transl. by P. Scherer. vol. 5 transl. by T. Schwarzschild and L.A. Hercus. Australian Institute of Aboriginal Studies, Microfiche no. 2. Canberra: Australian Institute of Aboriginal Studies.
Reynolds, H. 1981. *The other side of the frontier. An interpretation of the Aboriginal response to the invasion and settlement of Australia.* Townsville: James Cook University.
Richter, H. (ca. 1965). Dada. *Art and anti-art.* New York: Abrams.
Roberts, J. 1978. *From massacres to mining. The colonization of Aboriginal Australia.* London: War on Want.
Rose, F. G. 1960. *Classification of kin, age structure and marriage amongst the Groote Eylandt Aborigines. A study in method and a theory of Australian kinship.* Berlin: Akademie-Verlag.
———. 1965. *The wind of change in Central Australia. The Aborigines at Angas Downs, 1962.* Berlin: Akadamie-Verlag.
Rosenfeld, A., D. Horton, and J. Winter. 1981. *Early man in North Queensland. Art and archaeology in the Laura area.* Canberra: Department of Prehistory, Research School of Pacific Studies, Australian National University.
Ross, B. (ed.). 1986. *Aboriginal and historic places around metropolitan Adelaide and the south coast.* Adelaide: Anthropological Society of South Australia.
Rubin, W. 1984. Modernist primitivism. An introduction. In Rubin (ed.), 1984, 1–81.
———. (ed.), 1984. *"Primitivism" in 20th century art. The affinity of the tribal and the modern.* New York: The Museum of Modern Art.

S

Sahlins, M. 1974. *Stone age economics.* London: Tavistock Publications.
Samaltanos, K. 1984. *Appollinaire. Catalyst for primitivism, Picabia, and Duchamp.* Ann Arbor, Michigan: UMI Research Press.
Satterthwait, L. 1978. Colour—to add or subtract. *Hemisphere* 22(11):2–7.
Schebeck, B. 1986. Introductory remarks to A. Coulthard, "Boning a white man." In L. Hercus and P. Sutton (eds.), 217–25. *This is what happened. Historical narratives by Aborigines.* Canberra: Australian Institute of Aboriginal Studies.
Schrire, C. 1982. *The Alligator Rivers. Prehistory and ecology in Western Arnhem Land.* Canberra: Department of Prehistory, Research School of Pacific Studies, Australian National University.
Schwartz, G. 1977. *Rembrandt.* London: Oresko Books.
Scott, H. J. 1884. *Report to the Calcutta exhibition committee.* Adelaide: Government Printer.
Semper, G. 1861–63. *Der stil in den technischen und tektonischen kuensten oder praktische aesthetik.* Frankfurt am Main: Verlag fur Kunst und Wissenschaft.
Severin, T. 1973. *Vanishing primitive man.* London: Thames and Hudson.
Sharp, R. L. 1958. People without politics. In V. F. Ray (ed.), 1–8. *Systems of political control and bureaucracy.* Seattle: University of Washington Press.

Siebert, O. 1910. Sagen und sitten der Dieri und nachbarstamme in Zentral-Australien. *Globus* 97:44–50; 53–59.
von Siebold, P. 1843. *Lettre sur l'utilite des musées ethnographiques et sur l'importance de leur creation.* In E. T. Hamy. 1890. *Les origines du musée d'ethnographie.* Paris. Publisher not known.
Sieveking, A. 1984. *The cave artists.* London: Thames and Hudson.
Simon, J. 1987. James Simon. In Johnson, 1987.
Smith, B. 1985. *European vision and the South Pacific 1768–1850.* Sydney: Harper and Row.
Smith, L. R. 1980. The Aboriginal population of Australia. Canberra: Australian National University Press.
Smith, M. W. (ed.). 1961. The artist in tribal society. London: Routledge and Kegan Paul.
Smith, R. 1987. Last word (letter to editor). *Adelaide Review* 37:9.
Smyth, R. B. 1878. *The Aborigines of Victoria and other parts of Australia and Tasmania.* Melbourne: John Currey O'Neil.
Spencer, W. B. 1913. Field notes, Oenpelli 1912. Museum of Victoria. Spencer papers (old series) Box 26.
———. 1914. *Native tribes of the Northern Territory of Australia.* London: Macmillan.
———. 1915. *Guide to the Australian ethnological collection exhibited in the National Museum of Victoria.* 2nd edition. Melbourne: Trustees of the Public Library, Museums and National Gallery of Victoria.
———. 1928. *Wanderings in wild Australia.* 2 vols. London: Macmillan.
Spencer, W. B., and F. J. Gillen. 1899. *The native tribes of Central Australia.* London: Macmillan.
———. 1912. *Across Australia.* 2 vols. London: Macmillan.
———. 1927. *The Arunta.* 2 vols. London: Macmillan.
Stanbury, P. (ed.). 1977. *The moving frontier. Aspects of Aboriginal-European interaction in Australia.* Sydney: A. H. & A. W. Reed.
———. (1974) 1978. Art on bark. In Henderson (ed.), 1978, 60–65.
Stanner, W. E. H. 1963. *On Aboriginal religion.* Sydney: Oceania Monographs.
———. 1972. Comment on opening of exhibition of Walbiri and Pintubi art by Hon. Ralph Hunt, Minister for the Interior, Canberra, June 26, 1972.
———. 1977. The history of indifference thus begins. *Aboriginal History* 1:2–26.
———. (1962) 1979. Religion, totemism and symbolism. In W. E. H. Stanner, 106–43. *White man got no Dreaming, essays 1938–1973.* Canberra: Australian National University Press.
Stephans, E. 1907. *Sudseekunst.* Leipzig.
Stephen, A. 1980. Margaret Preston's second coming. *Art network* 2 Spring 1980:14–15.
Stevens, G. A. 1935. Educational significance of indigeneous African art. In M. Sadler (ed.). *Arts and crafts of West Africa.* Oxford: Oxford University Press.
Stirling, E. C. 1896. Anthropology. In W. B. Spencer (ed.), 1–157. *Report of the Horn scientific expedition. Vol. 4.* London: Dulau.
———. 1908. Letter to J. G. Reuther dated October 14, Adelaide, South Australia. Adelaide: South Australian Public Record Office (GRG19).
Stirling, E. C., and E. R. Waite. 1919. Description of toas. *Records of the South Australian Museum* 1:105–55.
Stocking, G. W. (ed.). 1983. *Observers observed. Essays on ethnographic fieldwork.* Madison: University of Wisconsin Press.
Stolpe, H. 1891. *Evolution in the ornamental art of sauage peoples.* Rochdale: Transactions of the Rochdale Literary and Scientific Society.
Strahan, R. 1979. *Rare and curious specimens. An illustrated history of the Australian Museum 1827–1929.* Sydney: Australian Museum.
Strehlow, T. G. H. 1964. The art of circle, line and square. In Berndt (ed.), 1964, 44–59.
von Sturmer, J. R. 1978. The Wik region. Economy, territoriality and totemism in Western Cape York Peninsula, North Queensland. Ph.D. dissertation, University of Queensland.
Sutton, P. 1978. Wik. Aboriginal society, territory and language at Cape Keerweer, Cape York Peninsula, Australia. Ph.D. dissertation, University of Queensland.
———. 1986. The sculpted word: A reply to Donald Brook on toas. *Adelaide Review* 32:8–9,36–37.
———. 1987a. The really interesting suggestion . . . : yet another reply to Donald Brook on toas. *Adelaide Review* 34:5.
———. 1987b. From horizontal to perpendicular. Two recent books on Central Australian Aboriginal painting. *Records of the South Australian Museum* 21:161–65.
———. 1988. Myth as history, history as myth. In I. Keen (ed.). *A way of life. Aboriginal cultural continuity in settled Australia.* Canberra: Australian Institute of Aboriginal Studies (in press).
Sutton, P., and B. Rigsby. 1982. People with "politicks." Management of land and personnel on Australia's Cape York Peninsula. In N. M. Williams and E. S. Hunn (eds.), 155–71. *Resource managers: North American and Australian hunter-gatherers.* Boulder, Colorado: Westview Press for American Association for the Advancement of Science.

T

Taplin, G. 1879. *The folklore, manners, customs, and languages of the South Australian Aborigines.* Adelaide: Government Printer.
Taylor, L. 1979. Ancestors into art. An analysis of Pitjantjatjara Kulpidji designs and crayon drawings. B.A. Hons. thesis, Department of Prehistory and Anthropology, Australian National University.
———. 1984. Dreaming transformations in Kunwinjku bark paintings. Typescript 12pp. Paper presented at the 1984 Biennial Conference of the Australian Institute of Aboriginal Studies.
———. 1986. Seeing the inside. Kunwinjku paintings and the symbol of the divided body. Typescript 27pp. Paper presented to the 1986 World Archaeological Conference, Southampton.
———. 1987. The same but different. Social reproduction and innovation in the art of the Kunwinjku of Western Arnhem Land. Ph.D. dissertation, Australian National University.
Thomas, D. 1978. Aboriginal art as art. In Edwards (ed.), 1978, 29–31.
———. 1982. Australian art. In J. Mollison and L. Murray (eds.), 194–266. *Australian National Gallery. An introduction.* Canberra: Australian National Gallery.
———. 1986. Albert Namatjira and the worlds of art. A re-evaluation. In Amadio et al., 1986, 21–26.
Thomas, K. 1983. *Man and the natural world. Changing attitudes in England 1500–1800.* Harmondsworth: Penguin.
Thomson, D. 1983. *Donald Thomson in Arnhem Land.* Melbourne: John Currey O'Neil.
Thorne, P. 1986. Australiana textile printing. *Craft Australia* Summer 1986/4:18–23.
Tillers, I. 1982. Locality fails. *Art & Text*, Winter 1982:51–60.
———. 1983. Fear of texture. *Art & Text* 10:8–18.
Tindale, N. B. 1925. Natives of Groote Eylandt and of the west coast of the Gulf of Carpentaria. Part 1. *Records of the South Australian Museum* 3(1):61–102.
———. 1926. Natives of Groote Eylandt and of the west coast of the Gulf of Carpentaria. Part 2. *Records of the South Australian Museum* 3(2):103–34.
———. 1928. Native rock shelters at Oenpelli, Van Diemen Gulf, North Australia. *South Australian Naturalist* 9(2):35–36.
———. 1932. Primitive art of the Australian Aborigines. *Manuscripts: A Miscellany of Arts and Letters* 3:38–42.
———. 1940. Distribution of Australian Aboriginal tribes. *Transactions of the Royal Society of South Australia* 44:140–231.
———. 1972. *Aboriginal tribes of Australia.* Berkeley: University of California Press.
———. 1987. Letter to Peter Sutton, September 30, 1987, Palo Alto, California.
Tindale, N. B., and B. George. 1971. *The Australian Aborigines.* Sydney: Golden Press.
Tregenza, J. 1980. *George French Angas. Artist, traveller and naturalist 1822–1886.* Adelaide: Art Gallery Board of South Australia.
Trezise, P. 1971. *Rock art of South-east Cape York.* Canberra: Australian Institute of Aboriginal Studies.
Trilling, L. 1971. *Sincerity and authenticity.* Cambridge, Mass. Publisher not known.
Trustees of the Public Library, Museums and National Gallery of Victoria. 1943. *Primitive art exhibition.* (Exhibition catalogue prepared by L. Adam). Melbourne.
Tuckson, J. A. 1964. Aboriginal art and the Western world. In Berndt (ed.), 1964, 60–68.

Tylor, E. B. 1892. *Anthropology. An introduction to the study of man and civilization.* London: Macmillan.

U

Ucko, P. J. 1967. Australian rock art in world perspective. *Australian Institute of Aboriginal Studies Newsletter* 2:44–53.
——— (ed.). 1977. *Form in indigenous art. Schematisation in the art of Aboriginal Australia and prehistoric Europe.* Canberra: Australian Institute of Aboriginal Studies.
Ucko, P. J., and A. Rosenfeld. 1967. *Palaeolithic cave art.* London: Weidenfeld and Nicolson.
Urban Koories. 1986. Sydney: Workshop Arts Centre.

V

Vanderwal, R. (ed.). 1982. *The Aboriginal photographs of Baldwin Spencer.* Introduced by John Mulvaney. Melbourne: National Museum of Victoria, John Currey O'Neil.

W

Waddy, J. A. 1984. Classification of plants and animals from a Groote Eylandt Aboriginal point of view. Ph.D. dissertation, Macquarie University.
Ward, P. 1986. Dreamtime at Ramingining. *The Weekend Australian Magazine* August 16–17, 1986:3.
Warlukurlangu Artists. 1987. *Kuruwarri: Yuendumu doors.* Canberra: Australian Institute of Aboriginal Studies.
Warner, W. L. 1937. *A black civilization. A social study of an Australian tribe.* New York: Harper and Brothers.
Webster, W. D. 1895–1901. *Illustrated catalogue of ethnographical specimans, European and Eastern arms and armour, prehistoric art and other curiosities.* Bicester: Webster.
Williams, N. M. 1976. Australian Aboriginal art at Yirrkala. The introduction and development of marketing. In Graburn (ed.), 1976, 266–84.
———. 1987. *Two laws. Managing disputes in a contemporary Aboriginal community.* Canberra: Australian Institute of Aboriginal Studies.
Wilson, R. S. 1981. Geography and the totemic landscape—the Dieri Case. A study of Dieri social organisation including territorial organisation. B. A. Hons. thesis, University of Queensland.
Worsnop, T. 1897. *The prehistoric arts, manufactures, works, weapons etc. of the Aborigines of Australia.* Adelaide: Government Printer.
Wright, B. J. 1977. Schematisation in the rock engravings of north-western Australia. In Ucko (ed.), 1977, 110–16.
Wright, R. V. S. (ed.). 1971. *Archaeology of the Gallus Site, Koonalda cave.* Canberra: Australian Institute of Aboriginal Studies.

Z

Zervos, C. (ed.). 1929. *Cahiers d'art* Nos.2–3. Paris.
Zimmer, J. 1986. Preface. In Maughan and Zimmer (eds.), 1986, 11–13.

INDEX

The names of artists whose works appear in the exhibition are listed in the Biographies.

ACKNOWLEDGMENTS

Individuals and Australian Institutions

Dale Chesson, Jane Goodale, Judith Hamilton-Shephard, Mary Laughren, F.D. McCarthy, Adrian Marrie, David Martin, Howard Morphy, Frank Price, Gary Robinson, Patricia Stanner, Judith Stokes, Patricia Vinnicombe, Julie Waddy, Nancy Williams. Aboriginal Artists Agency, Art Gallery of South Australia, Art Gallery of Western Australia, Aurukun Arts and Crafts, Aurukun Shire Council, Australian Institute of Aboriginal Studies, Australian Museum, Australian National Gallery, Australian National University, Buku-Larrngay Arts (Yirrkala), Central Land Council, Department of Aboriginal Affairs, Gunbalanya Council, Macleay Museum, Museum of Victoria, National Museum of Australia, National Gallery of Victoria, Northern Land Council, Northern Territory Museum, Papunya Community Council, Papunya Tula, Queensland Art Gallery, Queensland Museum, Queen Victoria Museum and Art Gallery, Ramingining Arts, State Library of South Australia, Tiwi Land Council, University of Melbourne Gallery, University of Queensland Anthropology Museum, University of Western Australia, Warlukurlangu Artists, Yuendumu Community Council.

Aboriginal People

Adelaide (Southeast Australia): Kerry Giles, Bluey Roberts, Donald Smith, Doreen Kartinyeri

Angurugu (Groote Eylandt): Murabuda Wurramarrba, Tula Lalara, Alan Lalara, Nanjiwara Amakula, Mila Amakula, Henry Wurramara, Arthur Wurramara, Gerald Minyawin

Aurukun (Cape York Peninsula): members of the Chivirri, Winchanam, Apalach, Puch, and Wanam ceremonial groups, especially Frederick Kerindun, Arthur Pambegan, Geraldine Kawangka, Clive Yunkaporta, George Sydney Yunkaporta, Francis Yunkaporta, Peter Peemuggina, Dorothy Pootchemunka, Cecil Walmbeng, Jackson Woolla, Rodney Karyuka, Joe Ngallametta, MacNaught Ngallametta

Birdsville (Lake Eyre Region): Frank and Linda Crombie

Garttji (Gadji Springs, Central Arnhem Land): Ray Munyal

Kingston (Southeast Australia): Janet Watson, Ron Bonney, Lola Cameron-Bonney

Maree (Lake Eyre Region): Reg Dodd, Norman Woods

Meningie (Lower Murray): George Trevorrow, Ellen Trevorrow, Glenda Rigney, Daisy Rankine, Harvey Karpany

Milikapiti (Melville Island): Paddy Henry, Laurie Cook, Polly Miller, Ruby McDowell, Doris Adams, Happy Cook, Rosemary Wilson, Raphael Apuatimi, Robert Tipungwuti, Mark Mangatopi

Oenpelli (Western Arnhem Land): Joseph Bumarda, Moses Mangiru, Bilinyarra Nabegeyo, John Nawirridj, Bruce Nabegeyo, Mukguddu Nabegeyo, Thompson Yulidjirri

Papunya (Central Australia): Michael Nelson Tjakamarra, Dinny Nolan Tjampitjinpa

Ramingining (Central Arnhem Land): David Malangi

Raukkan (Point McLeay, Lower Murray): members of the Point McLeay Council, Henry Rankine, Jean Rankine, Jacob Stengle, and the late Lola Sumner and Dorothy Kartinyeri

The Riverland (Southeast Australia): John Lindsay, Colin Cook, Yvonne Koolmatrie, Paul Kropinyeri, Agnes Rigney

Umbakumba (Groote Eylandt): Claude Mamarika, Robert Amaula, Ron Wurrawilya, Trevor Maminyamanja

Yirrkala (North East Arnhem Land): Gambali, Djikundurru Burarrwanga, Banduk Marika, Liwukang Bukurlatjpi, Stephen

Yuendumu (Central Australia): Dolly Nampijinpa Granites, Judy Nampijinpa Granites, June Napanangka Granites, Darby Jampijinpa, Francis Jupurrurla Kelly, Lucy Napaljarri Kennedy, Bronson Jakamarra Nelson, Paddy Jupurrurla Nelson, Paddy Japaljarri Sims, Larry Jungurrayi Spencer, Cookie Japaljarri Stewart

COLLECTIONS

Most of the works of art illustrated in this book and selected for the exhibition are from the collection of the South Australian Museum. Works illustrated from other collections are listed below by figure number. Exhibited works from other collections are listed in the Catalogue.

Chapter I

Fig. 6 National Museum of Australia
Fig. 10 Australian Museum, Sydney
Fig. 14 National Gallery of Victoria
Fig. 20 National Museum of Australia
Fig. 33 State Library of South Australia
Fig. 39 Australian Museum, Sydney
Fig. 40 Mrs. Douglas Carnegie, O.A.M., and Sir Roderick Carnegie
Fig. 42 Australian Museum, Sydney
Fig. 43 Australian Museum, Sydney
Fig. 44 Macleay Museum, Sydney

Chapter II

Fig. 51 Flinders University Art Museum
Fig. 64 Australian Museum, Sydney
Fig. 69 Anthropology Research Museum, University of Western Australia
Fig. 84 State Library of South Australia

Chapter III

Fig. 87 Private Collection
Fig. 88 Art Gallery of New South Wales
Fig. 98 Australian Museum, Sydney
Fig. 100 Art Gallery of South Australia
Fig. 102 Australian Museum, Sydney
Fig. 114 Australian Museum, Sydney
Fig. 115 Anthropology Research Museum, University of Western Australia
Fig. 117 Tim and Vivien Johnson
Fig. 124 Australian Museum, Sydney
Fig. 125 State Library of South Australia
Fig. 126 Australian Museum, Sydney

Chapter IV

Fig. 139 Private Collection
Fig. 156 Private Collection
Fig. 159 Collection of the artist
Fig. 161 Tim and Vivien Johnson
Fig. 165 Flinders University Art Museum
Fig. 166 Mrs. Douglas Carnegie, O.A.M., and Sir Roderick Carnegie
Fig. 169 Private Collection
Fig. 174 Tim and Vivien Johnson
Fig. 175 Mrs. Douglas Carnegie, O.A.M., and Sir Roderick Carnegie

Chapter V

Fig. 182 British Museum of Natural History
Fig. 183 National Library of Australia
Fig. 186 Art Gallery of South Australia
Fig. 188 State Library of South Australia
Fig. 189 Dixson Galleries, State Library of New South Wales
Fig. 209 Mrs. H. Christensen
Fig. 212 Reserve Bank of Australia

Chapter VI

Fig. 214 Collection of the artist
Fig. 226 Mitchell Library, State Library of New South Wales
Fig. 227 Mitchell Library, State Library of New South Wales
Fig. 231 Ubersee-Museum, Bremen, West Germany
Fig. 248 Australian Museum, Sydney
Fig. 249 Flinders University Art Museum
Fig. 250 Flinders University Art Museum
Fig. 252 Flinders University Art Museum
Fig. 253 Australian National Gallery
Fig. 254 Australian National Gallery
Fig. 256 Collection of the artist
Fig. 257 Private Collection
Fig. 258 Collection of the artist
Fig. 259 Collection of the artist

PHOTOGRAPH CREDITS

Fig. 1, Alan Thorne; Figs. 2, 6, 7, 12, 15, 10–25, 32, 35–45, 49, 52–58, 61–62, 64, 70–72, 75–81, 83–87, 89–104, 107, 114, 116–117, 119–128, 130–131, 134, 138, 141, 143–144, 148–152, 159–161, 163–178, 191, 194, 200, 206, 218, 220–224, 226–227, 230, 232, 234–239, 242–244, 248, 251, 257–258, 260, Michal Kluvanek for South Australian Museum; Fig. 3, Lewuld, South Australian Museum Archives; Figs. 4, 192, 198, 201, 204, 228, 240–241, 247, South Australian Museum Archives; Fig. 5, Tracey Moffat; Figs. 8, 231, Steven Hemming; Fig. 9, N.B. Tindale, South Australian Museum; Figs. 10, 199, Australian Museum; Figs. 14, 153–157, National Gallery of Victoria; Figs. 16–17, E. Cranstone, Australian Institute of Aboriginal Studies; Fig. 26, Dale Chesson; Figs. 27, 135, 197, D.F. Thomson, Museum of Victoria, by courtesy of Mrs. D.M. Thomson; Fig. 28, This air photograph is Crown Copyright and has been reproduced by permission of the Manager, Surveying and Land Information Group, Department of Administrative Services, Canberra, Australia; Figs. 30–31, Peter Sutton, Australian Institute of Aboriginal Studies; Fig. 46, Polly Sumner; Fig. 48, Josephine Flood, Australian Institute of Aboriginal Studies Library; Fig. 50, R.M. Berndt, Anthropology Research Museum, University of Western Australia; Figs. 51, 213, 249–250, 252, Flinders University Art Museum; Fig. 59, Joseph Reser, Australian Institute of Aboriginal Studies Library; Figs. 60, 82, 139, Andrew Pekarik; Fig. 65, P. Albrecht and S.B. Rutschmann; Fig. 69, John Stanton, Anthropology Research Museum, University of Western Australia; Fig. 73, Robert Edwards; Fig. 74, Ulli Beier; Fig. 88, Art Gallery of New South Wales; Fig. 118, Michael Morwood, Australian Institute of Aboriginal Studies Library; Figs. 136–137, 146, 180, Françoise Dussart; Fig. 140, Gerry Orkin for Australian Institute of Aboriginal Studies; Fig. 142, Christopher Anderson; Figs. 145, 147, J.V.S. Megaw, Flinders University Art Museum; Fig. 158, Grant Hancock; Fig. 179, Aboriginal Arts Board, Australia Council; Fig. 181, Tim Johnson; Fig. 183, National Library of Australia; Fig. 184, Colin Tatz, Australian Institute of Aboriginal Studies Library; Fig. 186, Art Gallery of South Australia; Fig. 187, Otto Siebert, South Australian Museum Archives; Fig. 188, State Library of South Australia; Fig. 189, Dixson Galleries, State Library of New South Wales; Fig. 195, Jennifer Hoff; Fig. 196, Museum of Victoria; Figs. 207–208, *The Leader* (Melbourne); Fig. 210, Ian Mitchell, Australian Overseas Information Service; Fig. 211, Alexis Omond, Bureau of the Northern Land Council; Fig. 214, Lin Onus; Fig. 215, Rohan Vassallo; Figs. 217, 219, Margaret Nobbs; Figs. 229, 231, 233, Steven Hemming, South Australian Museum; Figs. 245–246, Michal Kluvanek for South Australian Museum, Albert Namatjira reproductions by kind permission of Legend Press; Figs. 253–254, Australian National Gallery; Fig. 255, Georges Australia; Figs. 256, 259, Jan Dalman and Michal Kluvanek for South Australian Museum. Cats. 13–14, 27–28, 35, 58, 67, 69–70, 72–73, 75, 96, Michal Kluvanek for South Australian Museum; Cat. 44, Alan Jones.

Maps by Joseph Ascherl

Composition by Trufont Typographers, Inc., Hicksville, New York